THE MILITARY BALANCE 1984-1985

THE INTERNATIONAL INSTITUTE FOR STRATEGIC STUDIES LONDON

c/o Publications Distributor
Marketing International, Inc.
Suite 940
1120 Connecticut Avenue, NW,
Washington, DC 20036

The International Institute for Strategic Studies
23 Tavistock Street London WC2E 7NQ

Published by
The International Institute for Strategic Studies
23 Tavistock Street, London WC2E 7NQ

This publication has been prepared by the Director of the Institute and his
Staff, who accept full responsibility for its contents. These do not, and indeed
cannot, represent a consensus of views among the world-wide membership of
the Institute as a whole

First published Autumn 1984

ISBN 0 86079 083 5
ISSN 0459-7222

Printed and bound in England by The Alden Press, Oxford

CONTENTS

PREFACE

The Military Balance is an annual, quantitative assessment of the military power and defence expenditure of countries throughout the world.

It examines the facts of military power as they existed on 1 July 1984, and no projections of force levels or weapons beyond this date have been included, except where specifically stated. It also does not reflect the facts of geography, doctrine or efficiency, except where these are explicitly touched upon. We make no attempt to compare one country's military capacity against others. Material is reviewed each year, and differences between years may be due as much to re-evaluation of evidence as to new information. We must warn, therefore, that *The Military Balance* may have limitations for those attempting to construct time series comparisons.

The book is organized in three sections. In the first of these, national entries are in general grouped geographically, beginning with the US, the USSR, the Warsaw Pact and NATO. Information about some smaller countries, whose military forces are of a size which has not seemed to warrant fuller description at this stage, has been set out in a tabular form. Inclusion of a particular political entity or of a military organization connected to it in no way implies legal recognition of, or Institute support for, such entities.

In the second section, tables give comparative information on nuclear delivery vehicles and some static measurements of the strategic nuclear balance, defence expenditure (including a detailed comparison of NATO and Warsaw Pact expenditure over a ten-year period), military manpower (active and reserve) and major identified arms-transfer agreements.

In the final section, separate items assess the European theatre conventional balance; show the deployment of the strategic systems of the US and the USSR; illustrate graphically trends in defence expenditure of the NATO countries and Japan from 1970 to 1982; and analyse global economic trends with particular emphasis on defence expenditure.

Notes, which follow this Preface, will help the reader to use the current edition of *The Military Balance*. **It is absolutely necessary to read them, since they amplify and give precision to the data in the national sections and tables.**

Readers may use items of information from *The Military Balance* as required, without reference to the Institute, on condition that the Institute is cited as the source in any published work. However, reproduction of all major portions of the work must be approved in writing by the Institute prior to publication.

The Director and the staff of the Institute assume full responsibility for the facts and judgments which this study contains. The co-operation of governments has been sought and, in many cases, received. Not all countries have been equally co-operative, and some figures have necessarily been estimated. Inevitably, these estimates change as new information becomes available. The Institute owes a considerable debt to a number of its own members and consultants, who have helped in compiling and checking material.

September 1984.

READER'S NOTES

Regions and Countries
The main geographical regions are shown in the Table of Contents on p.iii. An index to individual country entries is on p. 2. To the extent that national variations permit, country entry format is standard: population, military service, total military manpower strength, NMP, GDP or GNP, defence expenditure, GNP/GDP growth rates, inflation rates, foreign military aid, Gross External Debt, and exchange rates; separate sub-sections on the army, navy and air force give broad organization and equipment and, where relevant, significant foreign deployments. Where possible, reserves and para-military forces are included. Precise definitions as to what are or are not para-military forces are difficult, and some latitude must be allowed: para-military forces are those elements whose equipment and training goes beyond that required for civil police duties and whose constitution and control suggest they may be usable in support, or in lieu, of regular military forces.

Defence Pacts and Agreements
A short description of multilateral and bilateral pacts and military aid agreements introduces each of the main regional sections of the study. Defence assistance given under less formal arrangements is also noted. Agreements which cover only economic aid are not included.

Defence Expenditure
The latest available defence expenditure or budget data are quoted (in some cases estimated). In consequence inconsistencies arise in the comparative tables at the end of the volume. Where possible capital equipment budgets/expenditures have been added to recurrent/administrative cost. Figures may therefore be radically different from previous issues (e.g. Tunisia). In cases of great variance between sources (government data, central banks, IMF, etc) central bank data has been preferred. In many cases, internal/border security force budgets have been included. Revised budget and expenditure figures are the result of changes by the governments themselves. Table 4 shows current and past expenditures, expressed in current US dollars so as to afford international comparisons; however, since many countries update these each year, the figures will not necessarily correspond with those shown in previous editions of *The Military Balance*. Table 3 compares NATO and Warsaw Pact defence expenditures 1970–82 in 1975 constant prices; here, and for the NATO countries in Table 4, a standard NATO definition of defence expenditure is used, but in most other cases national definitions are used. 'NATO definition' includes all spending on regular military forces, military aid to other nations (including equipment and training), military pensions, expenses by host governments for NATO tenant forces, NATO infrastructure and civilian staff costs; paramilitary forces (e.g., gendarmerie) are excluded. For the USSR we cite a range of estimates illustrating the variation of opinion as to these expenditures. The problem of arriving at these and an exchange rate to afford comparability is also discussed.

National Income
GNP and GDP figures are both used (where possible, GDP has been preferred). GDP is equal to GNP minus net income from abroad. GDP figures are quoted at current market prices (factor cost for East European countries). Where figures are not currently available from published sources, estimates have been made, and Table 4 uses both published and estimated GDP/GNP figures. GDP/GNP growth rates refer to real growth in real terms. Inflation rates are based on available consumer price indices and refer to annual averages. Wherever possible the UN System of National Accounts, based on the latest available IMF *International Financial Statistics* (IFS), has been used. For Eastern Europe data from *Economic Survey of Europe in 1982* (New York: UN, 1983) and the *World Economic Outlook* (IMF, 1984) is used. For the USSR GNP estimates are given based on commercial banking estimates. East European GDP/GNP figures at factor cost are derived from NMP. For China estimates of GDP/GNP are given.

Currency Conversion Rates
To make comparisons easier, national currency figures have been converted into US dollars, using the rate averaged for the national financial year (for 1984–5 figures, the mid-year rate). Wherever possible exchange rates have been taken from IFS, though they may not always be applicable to commercial transactions. High inflation rates in some countries and recent dollar developments distort conversions. For the USSR no attempt has been made to convert roubles into dollars (see p. 15). In certain East European countries which are not members of the IMF and Hungary and Romania (which are), the conversion rates used are those described in T. P. Alton, 'Economic Growth and Resource Allocation in Eastern Europe', *Reorientation and Commercial Relations of the Economies of Eastern Europe*, Joint Economic Committee, 93rd Congress, 2nd Session (Washington DC: USGPO, 1974).

Manpower

Unless otherwise stated, the manpower figures given are those of active forces, regular and conscript. An indication of the size of militia, reserve and para-military forces is also included in the entry where appropriate. Reserve figures are generally estimates based on a five-year post-conscription period, though some national definitions are given. Manpower information is summarized in Table 4.

Equipment

The equipment figures in the entries show total holdings, with the exception of combat aircraft, where front-line squadron strengths are normally shown. The symbol (–) indicates that part of an establishment is detached; the symbol (+) means that a unit has been reinforced. Except where the symbol ⟨ is used, naval vessels of less than 100 tons structural displacement have been excluded. The term 'combat aircraft' comprises aircraft normally equipped and configured to deliver ordnance (bomber, fighter-bomber, strike, interceptor, counter-insurgency and armed trainers), reconnaissance aircraft and those in operational conversion units (OCU) and armed helicopters when clearly identified as such. Basic technical details of the nuclear delivery vehicles (missiles, artillery and aircraft) available to NATO and Warsaw Pact countries are given in Table 1.

Strength of Military Formations

The table below gives the approximate average establishment strength of the major military formations in the text. Military organization is flexible, and the manning and structure of formations may vary.

	Division					Brigade				Squadron
	Armoured		Mechanized		Airborne	Armoured		Mechanized		Fighter aircraft
	Men	Tanks	Men	Tanks	Men	Men	Tanks	Men	Tanks	
United States	18,300	324	18,500	216	16,800	4,500	108	4,800	54	18–24
Soviet Union	11,000	335[a]	14,000	266[a]	7,000	1,300[b]	95[b]	2,300[b]	40[b]	12–15
China	9,200	270	12,700[c]	30[c]	9,000	1,200[b]	90[b]	2,000	—	9–10
Britain[d]	8,500	148	—	—	—	—	—	—	—	8–15
Germany	17,000	300	17,500	250	8–9,000	4,500[e]	110	5,000[e]	54	15–21
India	15,000	200	17,500[c]	—	—	6,000	150	4,500	—	12–20
Israel	—	—	—	—	—	3,500	80–100	3,500	36–40	15–20
Egypt	11,000	300	12,000	190	—	3,500	96	3,500	36	10–12

[a] These tank strengths are for Soviet divisions in Eastern Europe; other Soviet divisions have fewer.
[b] Strength of a regiment, which is the equivalent formation in the Soviet and Chinese command structures. (The term 'regiment' may also describe a battalion-size unit, particularly in West European countries. The term 'group', often used in Latin American countries, is imprecise and may apply to a reinforced battalion or understrength brigade with AFV and/or artillery.)
[c] Infantry division.
[d] Britain has reintroduced the brigade organization, but combat formations are battle groups based on an armoured regiment or mechanized battalion. Armoured division strength will rise to 11,500 on mobilization.
[e] Manpower levels currently under review.

Divisional strengths cover organic units only and exclude support units or services outside the divisional structure. Warsaw Pact forces and those of other Soviet-supported countries have establishments similar to those of the Soviet Union. NATO formations and squadrons not included in the table above have similar totals to those of Germany unless otherwise mentioned in the text. Iran, Pakistan, the Philippines, Thailand, Japan, South Korea and Taiwan have tended to adopt American military organization, while Australia, New Zealand, Malaysia and Singapore have broadly followed British practice.

Arms Transfers

Major arms supply agreements identified as being made during the year which ended on 1 July 1984 are listed, under geographical regions, in Table 5. Because the actual transfer of arms may take place outside that year, an indication is also given there of expected delivery dates, where known. Licensing arrangements, widespread among industrialized countries, are not normally included.

Abbreviations and Terms

A list of the abbreviations used in the text is on p.viii, immediately following these notes. For convenience, certain important abbreviations are explained again when first used. Where a $ sign appears it refers to US dollars, unless otherwise stated. The term billion (bn) equals 1,000 million (m).

ABBREVIATIONS

(	under 100 tons	ftr	fighter (aircraft)	n.a.	not available
–	part of unit is detached	FY	fiscal year	Neth	Netherlands
+	unit reinforced			NMP	net material product
		GDP	gross domestic product	nuc	nuclear
AA	anti-aircraft	GDR	German Democratic Republic		
AAM	air-to-air missile(s)			OCU	operational conversion unit(s)
AB	airborne	GLCM	ground-launched cruise missile(s)	off.	official
ABM	anti-ballistic missile(s)	GNP	gross national product	org	organized/organization
ac	aircraft	GP	general-purpose		
AD	air defence	gp	group		
adj.	adjusted	GW	guided weapon(s)	para	parachute
AEW	airborne early warning			pdr	pounder
AFV	armoured fighting vehicle(s)			Pol	Polish
ALCM	air-launched cruise missiles(s)	hel	helicopter(s)	Port	Portuguese
amph	amphibious	how	howitzer(s)		
APC	armoured personnel carrier(s)	hy	heavy	RCL	recoilless launcher(s)
Arg	Argentinian			recce	reconnaissance
armd	armoured			regt	regiment
arty	artillery	ICBM	inter-continental ballistic missile(s)	RL	rocket launcher(s)
ASM	air-to-surface missile(s)	incl	includes/including	RV	re-entry vehicle(s)
ASW	anti-submarine warfare	indep	independent		
ATGW	anti-tank guided weapon(s)	inf	infantry	SAM	surface-to-air missile(s)
ATK	anti-tank	IRBM	intermediate-range ballistic missile(s)	SAR	search and rescue
Aus	Australian			sigs	signals
avn	aviation			SLBM	submarine-launched ballistic missile(s)
AWACS	airborne warning and control system	km	kilometres		
		KT	kiloton (1,000 tons TNT equivalent)	SLCM	sea-launched cruise missile(s)
bbr	bomber			Sov	Soviet
bde	brigade	LCA	landing craft, assault	SP	self-propelled
bn	battalion *or* billion(s)	LCG	landing craft, gun	spt	support
Br	British	LCM	landing craft, medium/mechanized	sqn	squadron
bty	battery			SRAM	short-range attack missile(s)
		LCT	landing craft, tank		
Cdn	Canadian	LCU	landing craft, utility	SRBM	short-range ballistic missile(s)
cav	cavalry	LCVP	landing craft, vehicles and personnel		
cdo	commando			SS	diesel submarine(s)
Ch	Chinese (PRC)	LHA	amphibious general assault ship(s)	SSBN	ballistic-missile nuclear submarine(s)
comd	command				
COIN	counter-insurgency	log	logistic	SSM	surface-to-surface missile(s)
comms	communications	LPD	landing platform(s), dock		
coy	company	LPH	landing platform(s), hel	SSN	submarine(s), nuclear
CW	chemical warfare	LSD	landing ship(s), dock	sub	submarine
CY	current year	LSM	landing ship(s), medium		
		LST	landing ship(s), tank	TA	Territorial Army
def	defence	lt	light	tac	tactical
defn	definition			tk	tank
det	detachment	m	million(s)	tp	troop
div	division	MBT	main battle tank	tpt	transport
		MCM	mine counter-measures	trg	training
ECM	electronic counter-measures	mech	mechanized		
ELINT	electronic intelligence	med	medium	UNDOF	United Nations Disengagement Observation Force
elm(s)	element(s)	MICV	mechanized infantry combat vehicle(s)		
engr	engineer			UNFICYP	United Nations Force in Cyprus
eqpt	equipment	MIRV	multiple independently-targetable re-entry vehicle(s)		
est	estimate(d)			UNIFIL	United Nations Interim Force in Lebanon
EW	early warning	misc	miscellaneous		
excl	excludes/excluding	Mk	mark (model number)	UNTSO	United Nations Truce Supervisory Organization
exp	expenditure	mod	modified/modification		
		mor	mortar(s)		
FAC	fast attack craft (gun)	mot	motorized		
FAC(G)	fast attack craft (missile)	MR	maritime reconnaissance	veh	vehicle(s)
FAC(P)	fast attack craft (patrol)	MRBM	medium-range ballistic missile(s)	VIP	very important person
FAC(T)	fast attack craft (torpedo)			V(/S)TOL	vertical (/short) take-off and landing
fd	field	MRL	multiple rocket launcher(s)		
FGA	fighter(s), ground-attack	MRV	multiple re-entry vehicle(s)		
flt	flight	msl	missile	WP	Warsaw Pact
FMA	foreign military assistance	MT	megaton (1 million tons TNT equivalent)	Yug	Yugoslav
Fr	French				
FRG	Federal Republic of Germany				

1

COUNTRIES AND PRINCIPAL PACTS

INDEX

The United States

Strategic Forces

The slow retirement of the *Titan* ICBM continues. On 1 July the inventory was 37, and the ICBM total 1,037. This withdrawal reduces the ICBM warhead total to 2,129, and the potential deliverable megatonnage by 27 (to between 1,292.4 and 1,315.5 MT, depending upon payload).

Four *Ohio*-class SSBN are now at sea, bringing the total of *Trident* C-4 missiles in the inventory to 288. This increases the SLBM total by 24 (to 592), the SLBM warhead total by 192 to 5,344, and raises the estimated potential seaborne megatonnage by 19.2 to between 352 and 382.4 MT.

Within the strategic bomber force the B-52D has been withdrawn. Of the 151 operational B-52G, 61 have a non-nuclear role, and there is one training squadron. Some 84 B-52G aircraft have been fitted with the AGM-86B Air-Launched Cruise Missile. The most recent data suggest that the 90 B-52H, 84 B-52G and 56 FB-111A, at nominal average loadings, could carry a total of 1,020 ALCM, 924 AGM-69A SRAM and 812 bombs. On the basis of these loadings, air-deliverable megatonnage would be 204 for ALCM, between 157.1 and 184.8 for SRAM, and 2,030 MT for bombs (bomb yields are likely to average 2 MT each). Total aircraft-delivered megatonnage would thus be perhaps of the order of 2,400 MT (see Table 1).

Replacement programmes for existing strategic equipment have been receiving mixed support from within the government. The *Ohio/Trident* programme continues, as does development of the D-5 SLBM, due to replace C-4 in 1988/9. The MX ICBM purchase has been both limited and controlled, although the MX test programme continues on schedule. Feasibility studies are proceeding on a single-warhead mobile ICBM. Only 18 of the 100 B-1B bombers planned are so far on order; the Advanced Technology Bomber (ATB) design – the so-called 'stealth' bomber – is still in its early stages. Deployment of ALCM to the B-52H fleet is beginning, but, although these stand-off weapons are assumed to be capable of penetrating defences, the carrier aircraft may be approaching the end of their useful life, and replacements are still a long way from being operational.

On 10 June 1984 one *Minuteman* ICBM RV was intercepted in a test over the North Pacific. This event, the product of an earlier R&D programme but now subsumed under the President's 'Strategic Defense Initiative (SDI)', has tended to obscure the continuing organizational and technical changes to the US strategic defensive programmes. The reorganization of NORAD, intended to rationalize peacetime civil/military airspace control functions, has reduced the North American air defence regions from eight to six (two of them in Canada). It has also placed control of the surveillance and warning system at a higher command level, more capable of exercising the necessary direction and co-ordination. The Defense Department is proposing to enhance its nuclear detection capability by adding nuclear detection systems to its existing *Navstar*/Global Positioning System (GPS) satellites. Tests of the Over-the-Horizon-Backscatter (OTH-B) radar systems continue to demonstrate weaknesses in the system; nevertheless, it is still the intention to develop and enlarge the facility. Finally, action has been taken to upgrade the detection and control capabilities of the DEW Line, the northernmost of the NORAD aircraft attack warning systems. Plans have been laid to close the CADIN/Pinetree Line to the south of it.

Theatre Forces

During 1983–4, the first new US long-range theatre nuclear forces (or 'intermediate-range' nuclear forces) were deployed to Europe, with 9 *Pershing* II missiles in West Germany and 16 Ground-Launched Cruise Missiles (GLCM) in both Britain and Italy. Further deliveries are anticipated to a possible total of 108 *Pershing* II and 464 GLCM, as agreed with NATO in December 1979.

General-Purpose Forces

There is still a good deal of evidence to demonstrate that the US desires to increase the over-all flexibility of her forces for global deployment. This is most clearly seen in the general enhancement of US Central Command (CENTCOM) and in the pool of forces on which CENTCOM can draw. Upgrading lift capabilities (C-5B and 'stretched' C-141 aircraft), together with a greater capacity for in-flight refuelling and more forward stocking, tends to suggest a considerable improvement in speed of deployment to distant areas. The reorganization of logistic support units for the RDJTF should give greater confidence that operations could be sustained. Apart from the use of US forces in the Lebanon and Grenada, the most visible signs of US commitment have tended to be US AWACS (airborne warning and control system) aircraft or naval deployments.

Modernization and some reorganization of the Army continues, especially of forces assigned or earmarked for CENTCOM (the Rapid Deployment Joint Task Force), following a serious re-examination of the organization and roles of the infantry divisions. Considerable variation also exists in the other major formation structures, and this tends to add to the administrative burdens of planning movement and re-supply for them. Numbers of *Abrams* MBT have modestly increased, as have those of the *Bradley* MICV and the AH-1 and UH-60 helicopters.

The US Navy has received five more *Los Angeles*-class SSN, while the one remaining *Darter* diesel boat has been retired. A second *Iowa*-class battleship has returned to service to join the *New Jersey*, and a third is being refitted. There are four more *Perry*-class guided weapons frigates. Deployment of the BGM-109 submarine-launched nuclear cruise missile (TLAM-N) has begun, with four SSN now so equipped. The Marines have received more M-60 tanks, LVT, F/A-18 fighters and the first of their AV-8B V/STOL attack aircraft.

The Air Force has replaced the F-106 with the F-15 in its Regular interceptor squadrons. Some F-106 remain in the Air National Guard interceptor squadrons, but these are being replaced by F-4. Introduction of the F-16 into the tactical wings and the ANG continues.

Efforts continue to bolster all components of the Reserves by increasing strengths and equipment holdings. While volume deliveries are difficult to quantify, reports continue to suggest that greater attention is being paid generally to the provision and distribution of spare parts, ancillary equipment and munitions, thereby achieving greater utilization of equipment and better combat capability.

Population: 236,700,000.
Military service: voluntary.
Total armed forces: 2,135,900 (198,000 women).
GDP 1982: $3,025.7 bn. 1983: 3,264.8 bn.
Def exp outlays FY 1982: $213.75; NATO definition $196.345 bn. Def budget authority FY 1983: $239.40 bn; FY 1984: 273.40 bn; FY 1985: 299.00 bn.*
GDP growth: –1.9% (1982), 3.3% (1983).
Inflation: 6.0% (1982), 3.2% (1983).
Debt: $252 bn (1982).

Strategic Nuclear Forces:†
OFFENSIVE:
(a) *Navy*: 592 SLBM in 35 SSBN.
  4 *Ohio* SSBN × 24 *Trident* I/C-4 (96 msls).
  31 SSBN: 19 *Lafayette*, 12 *Franklin*: 12 × 16 *Trident* I/C-4 (192 msls); 19 × 16 UGM-73A *Poseidon* C-3 (304 msls).
  (On order: 7 *Ohio* SSBN; 168 *Trident* I/C-4 msls.)

(b) *Strategic Air Command* (SAC): 2 Air Forces. 12 divs (1 trg/spt).
  ICBM: 1,037. 9 strategic msl wings, 24 sqns:
    3 wings (9 sqns) with 450 LGM-30F *Minuteman* II.
    3 wings (11 sqns) with 550 LGM-30G *Minuteman* III (3 MIRV).
    3 wings (4 sqns) with 37 *Titan* II (phasing out by October 1987).
  Aircraft: some 356 combat ac: 18 bomb wings (1 trg).
    Long-range bombers: 241.
      5 wings (5 sqns) with 90 B-52H; 1 trg sqn with 6 B-52G/H.
      7 wings: (8 sqns) with 151 B-52G; 5 sqns (84 ac) with ALCM; 3 sqns (61 ac) in non-nuc role.

---

* Excl $4.95 bn (1982), $6.05 bn (1983), $7.1 bn (1984) and $7.9 bn (1985) for atomic energy defence and other defence-related activities. The 1985 figure is as revised in May 1984.
† Manpower incl in Army, Navy, Air Force totals.

Medium-range bombers: 56.
  2 wings (5 sqns incl 1 trg) with 56 FB-111A.
Active reserve: a further 6 FB-111A, 23 B-52 (17 G, 6 H).
ASM: perhaps 1,140 AGM-69A SRAM; AGM-86A, AGM-86B ALCM.
Recce:
  3 wings:
  1 sqn with 9 SR-71A/B, T-38A.
  1 sqn with 7 U-2CT/R.
  2 sqns with 9 TR-1A (mainly tac role), 2 TR-1B trg.
Comd:
  1 sqn with 1 E-4A (converting to B), 3 E-4B.
  5 sqns: 16 RC-135, 21 EC-135A/C/G/L.
Tankers: 5 wings, 2 gps: (34 sqns (1 trg)): 32 with 615 KC-135A/Q (incl 13 Air National Guard with 104 ac, 3 Air Force Reserve with 24 ac), 2 with 24 KC-10A.
(On order: MX ICBM, 18 B-1B bbrs (100 planned), 1 E-4B comd, 5 E-3A AWACS, 5 TR-1A recce ac (2 -1B trg), 36 KC-10A tankers, 240 AGM-86B ALCM.)

DEFENSIVE:
Space Command: HQ, Colorado Springs; comds incl North American Aerospace Defense Command (NORAD), a joint US– Cdn organization (HQ: Cheyenne Mountain, USA).
Warning Systems
1. ICBM, SLBM, Satellites:
  (a) *Space Detection and Tracking System* (SPADATS):
    (i) *Space Defense Operations Center* (SPADOC). NORAD Combat Operation HQ, Cheyenne Mountain. Tracking, identification and cataloguing of all space objects; command, control and communications to all space-associated commands and agencies. Surveillance, protection and countering of satellites.
    (ii) *Satellites*: Satellite Early Warning System (Defense Support Program), Defense Meteorological Satellites. TRW Block 647: 1 over Indian Ocean (eastern hemisphere); 2 in western hemisphere: infra-red surveillance and warning system. Control and tracking stations at Guam, Pine Gap and Nurrungar (Australia).
    (iii) *Ballistic Missile Early Warning System* (BMEWS). USAF 474N system: 3 stations: Clear, Alaska (AN/FPS-50, AN/FPS-92); Thule, Greenland (AN/FPS-50, FPS-49); Fylingdales Moor, England (AN/FPS-49 + other). 12 radars detect and track satellites, ICBM and IRBM. 4,800-km range.
    (iv) *Spacetrack*: USAF 496L system. FPS-17 detection, FPS-79 tracking radars at Pirinclik (Turkey); *Cobra Dane*, Shemya; FPS-85, BMEWS at Clear, Thule and Fylingdales; optical tracking systems in New Mexico, California, at St Margarets (NB, Canada), Pulmosan (S. Korea), San Vito (Italy), Maui (Hawaii), Mount John (New Zealand).
    (v) *Cobra Dane* phased-array radar system at Shemya, Aleutians: 120° arc, range to 46,000 km, augments BMEWS in Alaska. (*Cobra-Judy*, a Pacific-based, shipborne phased-array radar (AN/SPQ-11), supplements Shemya and research programmes, but is not part of SPADATS and has no early-warning function. *Cobra-Ball*, a RC-135 airborne system, supports both.)
    (vi) Pacific Radar Barrier (PACBAR). Detection and tracking radars. 1 site at San Miguel, Philippines, 1 at Kwajalein Atoll, third to be determined.
    (vii) 1 FPS-85 and 1 AN/FSS-7 station in Florida. Alternate Space Defense Center. Linked to *Spacetrack* and NAVSPASUR through NORAD HQ. Also to identify and track fractional-orbit bombardment systems (FOBS) (to be retired when *Pave Paws* completed).
  (b) *USN Space Surveillance System* (NAVSPASUR). 9 field stations in south-east US (3 transmitting, 6 receiving sites and civilian agencies).
  (c) *Perimeter Acquisition Radar Attack Characterization System* (PARCS). 1 north-facing phased-array, 130° arc, 2,800-km range system at Grand Forks ND. Identifies and tracks individual re-entry vehicles, incl SLBM, in Central US, Arctic Ocean areas. (Was Army *Safeguard* system support; to be enhanced.)
  (d) *Miscellanous radars*. US Army: Kwajalein Atoll (Pacific). USAF: Ascension Island (Atlantic), Antigua (Caribbean), Kaena Point (Hawaii); MIT Lincoln Laboratory, Westford, Mass.
  (e) Under development: Ground-based Electro-Optical Deep Space Surveillance system (GEODSS): White Sands NM, Taegu (S. Korea) and Maui (Hawaii); 2 more planned, 1 in Portugal, one in Indian Ocean (Diego Garcia).
2. SLBM:
  (a) *Pave Paws* system: 1 phased-array radar (AN/FPS-115) each in Massachusetts and California; 5,500-km range. 1 building in Georgia and 1 more planned in Texas.
  (b) *Sound Surveillance Underscan* (SOSUS): submarine detection systems deployed in the Atlantic, Arctic and Pacific oceans.
3. Intermittent programmed recce and ELINT satellites, incl:

(a) USAF: KH-8, KH-9 low-altitude, film return.

(b) Big Bird, Hitch Hiker med-altitude.

(c) USN: Ocean Surveillence (OSUS). 4 satellites to detect ships by infra-red and radar.

(d) CIA: KH-11 digital imagery.

(e) Rhyolite/Chalet.

4. Anti-air (aircraft, cruise missile):

(a) Over-the-Horizon-Backscatter (OTH-B). 414L system, 3,900-km+ range. 2 sites in Maine (2 transmitters, 5 receivers), arcs and range still under development; 1 in Oregon/N. California planned; another in southern US under consideration.

(b) Distant Early Warning (DEW) Line (under comd TAC). 31 AN/FPS-19/-30 radars (21 in Canada, 4 in Greenland, 1 in Scotland; 2 in Iceland being reopened), roughly along the 70°N parallel from Point Lay, Alaska to Greenland, Iceland and Scotland; range to 12,000 m at 320 km. (*Seek Igloo* FPS-117 automated system (minimally attended radar (MAR)) replacing 13 older radars; 7 to be operational by Oct 1984.)

(c) CADIN/Pinetree Line:
24 stations in southern Canada.

(d) Tactical Air Command:

(i) US–Cdn Joint Surveillance System (JSS). 7 Region Operations Control Centers (ROCC): 5 in US (1 in Alaska), 2 in Canada; 3 completing in 1984. 5 E-3A AWACS ac assigned (1 to each US ROCC).

(ii) Back-up Interceptor Control (BUIC). All stations but 1 semi-active (AD comd and tac control of interceptor forces): 84 radars (60 in US (14 in Alaska), 24 in Canada) for co-ordination/control of military and civil air traffic, surveillance and tracking of objects in high- and medium-altitude trans-polar flight.

(iii) Aircraft: (Tactical Air Comd: air defence): 42 air divs. Interceptors: 252 (does not incl 54 Cdn CF-101).

(a) Regular: Alaskan Air Command (30 alert locations): 5 sqns with 90 F-15 (8 AAM), T-33 (trg).

(b) Air National Guard (ANG): 10 sqns (to be 11); 7 with 126 F-4C/D (8 AAM), 3 with 36 F-106, T-33 (trg) (to get 144 F-15).

(c) Tactical Air Force augmentation: ac on call from naval, marine and air forces.

(d) Iceland: 1 sqn: See *Forces Abroad*.

AAM: *Genie, Falcon, Super Falcon, Sidewinder, Sparrow.*

Army: 780,800 (75,500 women).
4 Army HQ: 6 Corps HQ (1 AB).
4 armd divs (5–6 tk, 4–5 mech inf bns).
6 mech divs (4 tk, 5–6 mech inf, 3–4 arty, 1 hel, 1 SAM bns, 1 armd cav sqn, spt units).*
3 inf divs (1 trials).*
1 lt inf div (10,220 men).
1 air assault div (9 bns with integral hel).
1 AB div: 3 bdes (each 3 para bns, 1 arty bn), 1 armed hel bn, 1 armd cav sqn.
9 arty bdes.
5 AA arty bdes.
1 indep armd bde.
4 indep inf bdes.
1 indep air cav combat bde (hel-borne ATK).
3 armd cav regts.
4 *Pershing* (I/II) SSM bns (1 trg); 8 *Lance* SSM bns (in corps arty).
1 *Patriot* SAM bn forming (5 launchers, 60 msls); planned total 13½ bns.
1 Special Operations Comd: (7,000): 4 Special Forces Groups, 2 Ranger bns, misc units.
Army Avn: 1 air assault bde, indep bns and dets, mixed types of eqpt, assigned to HQ for tac, tpt and medical duties.

Tanks: 12,023, incl 1,703 M-48A5, 1,535 M-60, 4,207 M-60A1 (to be mod to A3), some 550 M-60A2, 2,695 M-60A3, 1,483 M-1 *Abrams* MBT; 400 M-551 *Sheridan* lt tks with *Shillelagh* (330 trg).

AFV: some 19,000, incl 1,100 M-2/-3 *Bradley* MICV; 3,100 M-577, 2,100 M-901 with *TOW*, 12,300 M-113 (some with *TOW*), 134 Lt AFV (*LAV*) APC.

Arty and Msls: about 2,000 105mm and 155mm towed guns/how; 3,140 155mm and 203mm SP how; 63 MLRS 227mm MRL; 3,200 81mm, 4,200 107mm mor; 1,000 90mm and 106mm RCL; some 600 *Hellfire* ATGW, 6,000 *TOW/TOW*-2, 10,400 *Dragon* ATGW launchers; 140 *Pershing* I, 48 -II, 72 *Lance* SSM launchers.

AD: 220 *Vulcan* towed, 380 M-163 20mm, 80 *Sgt York* DIVAD 40mm SP AA guns; *Redeye*, FIM-92A *Stinger*, 400 *Chaparral*, 27 *Roland*, *Nike Hercules, Improved HAWK* SAM (some being replaced by *Patriot* (9 launchers, 280 msls)).

Avn: some 625 ac, incl 98 OV-1D, 9 RU-21, 19 C-7, 92 C-12D, 37 U-3, 50 U-8, 10 UV-18A (DHC-6), 129 U-21A; 2 T-41, 54 T-42. Some 9,000 hel, incl some 900 AH-1G/Q, 900 AH-1S, 9 AH-64A *Apache*, 3,600 UH-1 (being replaced), 500 UH-60A, 453 CH-47A/B/C/D, 63 CH-54, 369 OH-6A, 1,784 OH-58A.

AAM: MIM-92A *Stinger*.

Trainers incl about 50 T-42 ac; 250 TH-55A hel.

(On order: 2,695 M-60A3, 840 M-1 MBT; 350 M-901 *Improved TOW/TOW*-2 AFV; 600 M-2, 2,200 M-3 *Bradley* MICV; 340 M-198 155mm towed, 232 M-109A2/A3 155mm,

---

* National Guard bde is incorporated in each of 2 mech and 2 inf divs.

M-110A2 203mm SP how; 2,500 81mm mor; 77 MLRS MRL; 95 *Pershing* II SSM; 66 *Sgt York* DIVAD 40mm SP AA guns; 3,000 *Stinger*, 32 *Rapier*, 17 *Roland* (595 msls), 300 *Chaparral*, 795 *Improved HAWK*, 129 *Patriot* SAM launchers (440 msls); 6 RC-12D ac; 11 AH-1S, 11 CH/MH-53, 50 AH-64A, 56 UH-60A, 43 CH-47D, 11 EH-60D *Quickfix* hel; 3,971 *Hellfire* ATGW (ASM).

DEPLOYMENT: *Continental United States* (incl Alaska, Hawaii and Canal Zone):
Strategic Reserve:
  (i) US Readiness Command: 2 corps HQ, 1 mech, 1 AB, 1 air assault divs, 1 air cav bde.
  (ii) Initial reinforcement, Europe: 2 armd, 3 mech, 2 inf divs, 1 inf bde, 1 armd cav regt.*
  (iii) US Central Command (USCENTCOM): (1,100): forces, incl naval and air, apportioned for planning purposes. Full deployment could involve 290,600 (assigned from existing units and spt elms on mobilization).
    HQ: 1 Army; 1 Army Corps (131,000): 1 mech (–), 1 lt inf, 1 AB, 1 air assault divs, 1 air cav bde, special forces, Rangers.
    1 Naval Force (112,300 incl 70,000 Marines): 3 carrier battle gps; 1 surface action gp; 5 ASW patrol sqns; 17 pre-positioned spt ships; 1⅓ Marine Amph Forces (MAF) (1 div (+), 1 air wing, 1 Force service spt gp), 1 Marine Amph Bde (MAB: 1 regt landing team, 1 air gp, 1 bde service spt gp).
    1 Air Force (33,000): 1 wing (2 sqns) B-52H, 7 tac fighter wings (11 sqns), 4 tac fighter gps, 1 airborne warning and control wing, tac airlift, recce, electronic combat sqns, 1 refuelling sqn (KC-135A/KC-10A).
  (iv) Alaska: (7,700): 1 inf bde (plus 1 res bde).
  (v) Panama: (9,170): 1 inf bde (6,560); Naval sqn (490): patrol boats; Marines (150); 1 air div (1,970): A-7, C-130 ac.
  (vi) Hawaii: (19,200): 1 inf div less 1 bde.
(See also *Forces Abroad*, below.)

RESERVES: 929,766 (99,500 women).
  (i) Army National Guard: 417,178 (21,500 women); 3,285 units; capable after mobilization of manning 2 armd, 2 mech, 5 inf divs, 19 indep bdes (3 armd, 6 mech, 10 inf), 4 bdes to complete regular army divs; 1 lt div to form 1985; 4 armd cav regts, 1 inf gp (Arctic recce, 5 bns); 2 Special Forces gps (6 bns). Indep bns: 5 tk, 2 mech, 50 arty, 4 ATK (*TOW*), 9 AD (1 *Roland* SAM, 8 40mm SP AA arty), 62 engr, 23 sigs, 115 other spt bns, 768 minor units. HQ to fill regular formations. 105 air units, 150 sections; 2,580 ac.
  (ii) Army Reserve: 266,188 (42,500 women); 3,410 units; 12 trg divs, 2 trg bdes; 1 mech, 2

inf indep combat bdes; 67 indep bns, incl 1 tk, 2 inf, 15 arty, 33 engr. 2 Special Forces gps (6 bns); 3,225 coys and dets; 130 indep air units and sections with 566 ac.
  (iii) Individual Ready Reserve: 246,400 (35,500 women); 49,000 a year do short active duty.

Navy: 564,800 (40,500 women): 4 cruise-missile, 95 attack subs, 206 principal surface combatants. A further 35 major surface combat ships are in active reserve and storage. Four Fleets.
Subs, cruise-missile (SSGN): 4.
    3 *Los Angeles* with *Harpoon* SSM, 1 *Sturgeon*. All have *Tomahawk* SSM.
Subs, Attack: 95:
    91 nuclear (SSN), 77 with *SUBROC*, to be fitted with *Harpoon* and *Tomahawk*: 26 *Los Angeles* with *Harpoon*; 1 *Lipscomb*, 1 *Narwhal*, 36 *Sturgeon*, 13 *Thresher*; 3 *Allen*, 2 *Washington* (converted SSBN); 5 *Skipjack*, 3 *Skate*, 1 *Tullibee*.
    4 diesel (SS): 3 *Barbel*, 1 *Tang*.
Aircraft carriers: 14 (1 trg).
    4 nuclear (CVN): 3 *Nimitz* (91,400 tons) (1 on refit), 1 *Enterprise* (89,600 tons).
    10 conventional (CV): 2 *Kitty Hawk* (78/80,800 tons), 1 *America* (79,000 tons), 1 *Kennedy* (82,000 tons), 3 *Forrestal* (76/79,000 tons) (1 on refit), 2 *Midway* (51/62,000 tons), 1 (*Lexington*) trg, no ac assigned.
    12 normally carry 1 air wing (70–95 ac) of 2 fighter sqns (with 24 F-14A (incl 3 RF-14 recce) or 24 F-4N/S), 3 attack (2 lt with 24 A-7E or F/A-18, 1 med with 10 A-6E), 2 ASW (1 with 10 S-3A ac, 1 with 6 SH-3/D/H hel), 1 ECM with 4 EA-6B, 1 AEW with 4 E-2B/C; 4 KA-6D tankers, 1 lt tpt ac. (New wing will have 2 more sqns, each 18 ac.)
Other surface ships:
192 principal surface combatants.
    2 *Iowa* battleships (BBG) with 4 × 4 *Harpoon*, 8 × 4 *Tomahawk* SSM.
    9 nuclear-powered GW cruisers (CGN) with 2 × 4 *Harpoon* SSM; 4 *Virginia* with 2 × 2 *Standard/ASROC* SAM/ASW, 1 SH-2F hel (SA-60B *Seahawk* to replace); 2 *California* with 2 × 1 *Standard* SAM, 1 × 8 *ASROC* ASW; 1 *Truxtun* with 1 × 2 *Standard/ASROC*, 1 SH-2F hel; 1 *Long Beach* with 2 × 2 *Standard/Terrier* SAM, 1 × 8 *ASROC* 1 *Bainbridge* with 2 × 2 *Standard* 1 × 8 *ASROC*.
    19 GW cruisers (CG): 1 *Ticonderoga* (CG-47) with 2 × 8 *Harpoon* SSM (to get *Tomahawk* SSM), 2 × 2 *Standard/ASROC*, 2 SH-2F hel (second CG-47 July 1984); 18 with 2 × 4

---

* 1 armd, 1 mech divs, 1 armd cav regt have hy eqpt stockpiled in FRG. Storage facilities for 2 more divs being built.

Harpoon, 1 × 8 *ASROC*, 1 SH-2F hel; (9 *Leahy* also have 2 × 2 *Standard/Terrier*, 9 *Belknap* have 1 × 2 *Standard/Terrier*).

37 GW destroyers (DDG): 23 with 2 × 4 *Harpoon* (4 *Kidd* with 2 × 2 *Standard/Tartar/ASROC*, 2 SH-2F hel; 8 *Farragut*, 11 *Adams*); 2 *Farragut*, 12 *Adams*.

31 *Spruance* (DD-963) gun/ASW destroyers (DD): with 2 × 4 *Harpoon*, 1 × 8 *Sea Sparrow*, 1 × 8 *ASROC*, 1 SH-3 or 2 SH-2F hel; (to get *Tomahawk* SSM).

41 GW frigates (FFG): 35 *Perry* with 1 *Harpoon/Standard*, 2 SH-2/-60 hel; 6 *Brooke* with 1 *Tartar/Standard*, 1 × 8 *ASROC*, 1 SH-2F hel.

53 gun frigates (FF) with 1 × 8 *ASROC*: 40 *Knox* (FF-1052) with 2 × 4 *Harpoon* SSM (30 with *Sea Sparrow* Mk 5 BPDMS, 1 with *Sea Sparrow* Mk 29 SAM, 2 SH-2F hel), 10 *Garcia*, 1 *Glover*, 2 *Bronstein*.

Some 89 minor surface combatants:

6 *Pegasus* GW hydrofoils with 2 × 4 *Harpoon*.
Some 80 inshore and river patrol craft (most in reserve).

MCM: 3 *Aggressive* ocean minesweepers.

61 amph warfare ships: 2 *Blue Ridge* comd (LCC); 5 *Tarawa* LHA with 4 LCU and mix of AV-8A ac or 12 CH-46, 4 CH-53, 3 UH-1N, 4 AH-1T hel; 7 *Iwo Jima* LPH (mix of 6 AV-8A, 4 OV-10 ac or 2 CH-46, 10 CH-53, 1 UH-1N hel); 12 *Austin*, 2 *Raleigh* LPD: 5 *Anchorage*, 5 *Thomaston* LSD (retiring), 18 *Newport* LST; 5 *Charleston* amph cargo ships (LKA).

54 LCU: 51 Type 1610, 3 Type 1466; many smaller amph craft; others with US Army.

85 principal auxiliary ships: 12 ammunition, 7 stores, 4 fast sealift, 14 oilers, 9 destroyer tenders, 12 sub tenders, 4 repair, 9 salvage/rescue, 1 fleet flagship, 1 hospital, 1 spt, 2 tpt, 9 tugs.

Military Sealift Command ships: 1 ammunition, 13 stores, 30 oil, 3 gasoline, 2 ocean surveillance, 5 oceanographic, 5 missile instrumentation, 9 survey. Chartered: 17 cargo, 3 tanker, 4 research, 1 fleet service ships.

Anti-sub msls, nuclear: *ASROC, SUBROC*.
SSM: *Standard* (SM-1), *Harpoon*, BGM-109B SLCM, *Tomahawk* (trials).
SAM: *Standard* (SA-1), *Aegis* (SM-2) (some nuclear), *Talos, Sea Sparrow, Tartar, Terrier*.

Ships in active reserve and storage: 2 SSN, 5 CV, 2 battleships (1 being reactivated (1984), 1 being studied), 4 cruisers, 4 DDG, 10 DD, 2 FFG, 6 FF, 3 LST, 46 log spt, 41 tp ships. National Defense Reserve Fleet: Ready Reserve Force, 30 dry cargo ships, 164 other vessels (579 govt-owned cargo ships and tankers could be used for auxiliary sea-lift).

Ships on refit (incl Service Life Extension Program (SLEP)) incl 6 SSBN (5 more planned to 1987), 11 SSN (3 *Los Angeles*, 4 *Sturgeon*, 2 *Thresher*, 2 *Allen*), 3 CVN/CV, 3 CGN, 5 DDG, 5 DD, 1 FFG, 8 FF, 1 LPH, 1 LPD, 3 LST.

(Authorized and funded: 6 SSBN, 3 SSN, 3 CVN, 9 *Ticonderoga* CG-47, 11 FFG, 5 MCM, 1 landing helicopter dock ship (LHD), 3 LSD, 13 landing craft (3 standard, 10 air cushion (hovercraft)), 2 fleet oilers, 5 supply ships; 51 BGM-109 *Tomahawk*, 222 *Harpoon* SSM, 1,100 *Standard* SAM, 37 *Phalanx* AD systems.)

Aircraft: 12 attack carrier air wings (1 more to form); some 1,450 combat ac, some 160 combat hel.

24 ftr sqns: 20 with 240 F-14A (30 ac configured for photo/infra-red recce); 4 with 48 F-4A/N/S.

38 attack sqns: 12 med with 120 A-6E, 48 KA-6D tankers; 24 lt with 288 A-7E; 2 with 25 F-18A.

1 trg sqn with 15 TF-18A.

2 ELINT sqns with 12 EA-3, 12 EP-3.

26 land-based MR sqns with 45 P-3B, 173 P-3C/-3C III.

11 ASW sqns with 110 S-3A *Viking*.

9 EW sqns with 35 EA-6B *Prowler*.

12 AEW sqns with 48 E-2C *Hawkeye*.

2 comms sqns with 14 C-130 TACAMO (= Take Charge And Move Out).

17 LAMPS/ASW hel sqns:* 2 with 22 SH-60B *Seahawk* (LAMPS Mk 3), 6 lt with 63 SH-2F *Sea Sprite* (LAMPS Mk 1), 9 with 66 SH-3D/H *Sea King* (ASW).

2 MCM hel sqns with 14 RH-53D, some 3 MH-53E.

2 aggressor trg sqns with 28 F-5E/F, A-4, T-38.

22 OCU: 5 fighter/strike trg (2 with 60 F-14, 1 with 18 TA-4F/J; 1 with 25 F-18, 1 with 20 F-4); 6 attack with 103 TA-7C, A-7E, A-6; 2 EW with EA-3; 2 MR with 40 P-3B/C; 2 AEW with 34 E-2B/C; 1 ASW with S-3A; 4 hel with 30 SH-2/-3.

17 misc spt sqns with 13 C-130F/LC-130F/R, 14 EC-130G/Q, 34 C-1A, 10 C-2A, 9 CT-39, 11 C-131, 4 C-117, 39 UC-12B ac; SH-3, CH/HH-46 hel.

16 trg sqns with T-2B/C/-28/-39D/-44, 210 T-34C ac; 112 TH-57A, TH/UH-1E hel.

(Other ac incl 35 F/A-18.)

AAM: *Sparrow*, AIM-54A/C *Phoenix*, *Sidewinder*.

ASM: *Standard ARM*, *Shrike*, AGM-88A *HARM* (anti-radiation); *Walleye*, *Harpoon*.

(On order: 24 F-14C ftrs, 38 A-6E attack, 6 E-2C AEW, 6 P-3C MR, 8 EA-6B ECM, 39 C-2A tpt, 15 *Citation* T-47A, 12 *Hawk* trg, 8 KA-6D tanker conversion ac; 44 SH-2F, some 8 MH-53 MCM, some 20 SH-60B, 108 TH-57C trg hel; 108 AIM-54C AAM, 190 AGM-65F *Maverick*, 230 *HARM*, 108 *Harpoon* SSM.)

---

* LAMPS = Light Airborne Multi-purpose System.

DEPLOYMENT AND BASES (average strengths of major combat ships):

Atlantic (Second Fleet): 31 SSBN, 53 attack subs, 7 carriers, 104 surface combatants, 27 amph. Norfolk (HQ), Mayport, Roosevelt Roads (Puerto Rico), Charleston, Jacksonville, Brunswick, New London, Newport, New York (Staten Island), Boston, New Orleans, Bangor, Kings Bay.

Eastern Pacific (Third Fleet): 3 SSBN, some 31 SSN, 9 carriers (5 hel), 71 other major surface combatants, 26 amph, 32 spt. Pearl Harbor (HQ), San Francisco, Whidbey Island, San Diego, Long Beach, Adak (Alaska), Everett (planned).

(See also *Forces Abroad*, below.)

RESERVES: 115,000.

35 ships: 1 DD, 2 *Perry* FFG, 6 *Knox* FF, 18 ocean minesweepers, 2 LST, 4 fleet tugs, 2 salvage ships. (13 more FFG, 2 FF authorized.)

2 carrier wings: 18 sqns: 5 attack with 60 A-7B; 1 with 12 F/A-18; 4 fighter with 48 F-4N/S; 2 recce with 18 RF-8G; 2 AEW with 8 E-2C; 2 ECM with EA-6A; 2 tanker with KA-3B).

2 MR wings: 13 sqns with 110 P-3A/B.

1 tac spt wing: 13 sqns (2 composite with TA-4J); 11 spt with C-9, C-118, C-130H.

1 hel wing: 7 sqns (4 ASW with 23 SH-3F/D, 2 lt attack with 16 HH-1K, 1 SAR with HH-3).

Naval Construction Bde: 9 regts, 17 bns.

2 Special Warfare Gps; 18 units.

2,100 specialist and spt units incl 16 undersea warfare units; 62 boats/patrol craft.

Marine Corps: 196,600 (8,900 women).

3 divs, each of 9 inf, 1 recce, 1 tk, 1 engr, 1 amph bns, 1 arty regt.

550 M-60A1 MBT; 984 LVT-7/-7A1 APC; 175mm SP guns; 84 105mm (being replaced), 126 M-198/M-14 155mm towed, 100 155mm, 203mm SP how; 216 81mm mor; *TOW, Dragon* ATGW; *Redeye, Stinger* SAM.

3 air wings: (27,000); some 436 combat ac, some 102 combat hel.

12 ftr sqns: 8 with 96 F-4N/S (being replaced), 4 with 48 F-18.

12 FGA sqns: 3 lt with 45 AV-8A/C *Harrier* V/STOL; 4 lt with 95 A-4M; 5 med with 50 A-6E.

1 recce sqn with 21 RF-4B.

1 ECM sqn with 15 EA-6B.

2 observation sqns with 36 OV-10A.

2 command sqns with 30 OA-4M/TA-4F.

3 tanker sqns with 36 KC-130F/R.

28 hel sqns: 3 attack with 72 AH-1J/T (*TOW*); 3 lt with 72 UH-1E/N; 14 med with 180 CH-46F; 8 hy with 96 CH-53A/D; 68 CH-53E.

Other ac incl 8 AV-8B trg, 20 F/A-18; 167

CH-53D/E, 30 AH-1T/J hel.

7 trg sqns.

2 SAM bns with *Improved HAWK*.

AAM: *Sparrow, Sidewinder*.

ASM: *Maverick*.

(On order: 329 LVT-7A1, 289 LAV-25 *Piranha* APC, 180 Mk-19 40mm grenade launchers, *SMAW* 83mm RL; *Stinger* SAM, 3 hovercraft (LCAC), 80 F/A-18, 33 AV-8B ftrs, 3 KC-130T tanker ac, 11 CH-53E hel; 263 AGM-65E ASM.)

RESERVES: 43,900 (1,265 women).

1 Marine div: 3 inf, 1 arty regts; 21 combat and spt bns.

1 Fleet Marine Force Gp; 1 Fleet Service regt (7 bns).

1 air wing: 106 combat ac, 8 combat hel.

4 aviation, 1 service, 1 air control gps, 19 sqns.

11 ac sqns (2 ftr with 24 F-4N, 6 attack with 60 A-4E/M, 1 EW with 4 EA-6A, 1 observation with 18 OV-10A, 1 tpt/tanker with 11 KC-130).

8 hel sqns (1 attack with 8 AH-1J, 4 lt with 40 UH-1N, 2 med with 24 CH-46C/D, 1 hy with 16 CH-53).

1 SAM bn with *HAWK*.

32 spt units.

DEPLOYMENT:

Continental United States: 2 Marine Amphibious Forces (MAF), (1 East, 1 West coast) each with 1 div, 1 air wing, 1 spt gp, 1 amph bde (MAB) (12,000).

Hawaii: 1 bde (from MAF in Japan (Okinawa).

(See also *Forces Abroad*, below.)

Air Force: 594,500 (65,500 women); some 3,700 combat ac.*

26 combat wings, comprising 78 sqns: 16 with 440 F-4 (8 being replaced with F-16); 16 with 384 F-15; 19 with 456 F-16; 10 with 230 F-111A/D/E/F; 12 with 288 A-10A; 5 *Wild Weasel* (1 trg) with F-4G.

8 tac recce sqns with 126 RF-4C.

1 Airborne Warning and Control div:

4 AWACS sqns (1 trg) with 34 E-3A/B *Sentry*.

3 electronic warfare sqns: 7 EC-130E/H; 11 EC-135K; 16 EF-111.

9 tac air control sqns: 6 with 96 OV-10/O-2A ac; 3 with 27 CH-3 hel.

6 special operations sqns: 3 with 14 MC-130E ac; 1 with 10 AC-130H ac; 1 with 6 CH-3E; 1 with 8 HH-53H, 5 UH-1N; 1 det with 4 UH-1H hel.

4 aggressor trg sqns with 77 F-5E, T-38.

OCU: 1 with 20 F-111A; 1 with 29 F-16; 7 with 130 F-4; 1 with 20 F-5; 2 with 40 F-15; 2 with

* Excl SAC, NORAD ac; incl ANG, Air Force Reserve ac and some 900 in active service storage.

40 F-106; 3 with 60 A-10; 1 with 16 RF-4C.

14 tac airlift sqns with 218 C-130.

17 hy (strategic) tpt sqns: 4 with 70 C-5A, 13 with 252 C-141B.

Other tpts: 8 C-135, 5 C-137, 11 C-140A/B, 1 C-6A, 5 C-12, 3 C-20A, 9 CT-39; 80 C-35A *Learjet* (leased).

8 SAR sqns (incl SAC msl spt): 23 HC-130H/N/P ac, 32 C/HH-3, 13 C/HH-53, 76 H/T/UH-1, 9 UH-60A hel.

3 medical tpt sqns with 23 C-9A/C.

3 weather recce sqns with 13 WC-130E/H, 5 WC-135B.

Trials/weapon trg units: 65 F-16, 4 C-141A.

30 trg sqns: 8 F-16B, 118 T-33A, 619 T-37B, 620 T-38, 112 T-39, 40 C-12F *Super King Air* (leased), 50 T-41A/C, 15 T-43A, 7 C-5A, 27 C-130, 12 C-141B, 5 HC-130, 2 UV-18A (DHC-6), 8 Schweizer Z-37 ac; 8 UH-60A, 8 C/HH-3, 8 HH-53, 19 U/TH-1F/N/P hel.

AAM: *Sidewinder, Sparrow*.

ASM: *Maverick*; *Standard ARM, Shrike, HARM*, GBU-15 glide bomb.

GLCM: 4 sqns, 1 trg unit.

(On order: 120 F-16, 392 F-15 ftrs, 5 F-5 FGA, 7 E-3C, 26 EF-111A, 13 C-5B, 3 C-17 hy tpt, 8 C-130H, EC-130H, 8 C-20A *Gulfstream*, 18 C-23 *Sherpa* lt tpt; 8–10 Ch F-7 (MiG-21), 16 C-12F *Super King Air* trg ac; 22 Bell AH-1T *Super Cobra*, 243 UH-60A/D, 69 HH-60D *Night Hawk*, 86 HH-60E hel; 108 launchers, 400 BGM-109 GLCM; 40 ALCM, *HARM*, 200 AGM-65D *Maverick* ASM, *Stinger*, 12 *Rapier* SAM.)

DEPLOYMENT:
(i) *Continental United States*:
  (a) *Tactical Air Command* (TAC; incl NORAD-, Iceland-assigned AD ac); (104,412); 2 Air Forces; 12 air divs; 28 wings: 36 combat sqns (30 fighter, 3 tac recce (converting to ftr/recce), 3 tac air control); 6 tac trg sqns.
  (b) *Alaskan Air Command*: (7,650): incl 1 ftr wing (1 sqn with F-15, 1 with T-33), 1 composite wing (1 sqn with A-10, 1 with O-2A), 1 control (warning) gp, 13 radars (being modernized), 2 combat spt gps, 1 strategic recce wing; air base: 1 gp, 2 sqns.
  (c) *Military Airlift Command* (MAC): (78,055): 2 Air Forces; 3 airlift divs, 24 wings (7 tac, 7 strategic, 1 special operations, 1 trg); 18 gps (2 tac, 1 strategic, 9 air base, 6 combat/airlift/trg spt). Ac deployed as required, world-wide.
  (d) Spt elm comds: (171,500). Comms, Log, Systems Trg, Electronic Security.
(ii) *Pacific Air Forces* (26,926): 2 Air Force HQ: 3 air divs; 4 tac ftr wings and 2 indep ftr sqns; 1 tac control gp; 3 Air Base wings and 1 indep sqn. 1 weather wing (attached from MAC).

Hawaii Air National Guard: 1 div: 2 AD sqns F-4 (8 AAM).
(See also *Forces Abroad*, below.)

RESERVES: 182,700, 41 wing equivalents.
(i) Air National Guard (ANG): (107,900); 24 wings (12 tactical), 67 gps, 91 sqns; some 1,090 combat ac.
  10 interceptor sqns; 162 ac (NORAD-assigned).
  34 fighter/FGA sqns (1 with 15 F-16, 1 with 20 F-4D, 12 (1 OCU) with 208 F-4C, 1 *Wild Weasel* with 12 F-4G, 14 (1 OCU) with 360 A-7D/K (11 getting F-16), 5 with 107 A-10A).
  8 recce sqns with 107 RF-4C.
  4 tac air control sqns (3 with 75 OA-37B, 1 with 20 O-2A).
  19 tac tpt sqns with 174 C-130A/B/E, 3 C-19A (Boeing 747 freight).
  13 tanker sqns (SAC) with 103 KC-135A/Q.
  1 electronic combat sqn with 8 EC-130.
  2 SAR sqns with 8 HC-130 ac, 11 HH-3E hel.
  Trg ac incl 43 T-33, 4 T-43A, 4 T-39 ac.
(ii) Air Force Reserve: (74,800); 17 wings, 56 sqns: some 233 combat ac, 5 combat hel.
  11 ftr sqns (TAC; 1 with 10 F-16, 5 with 113 F-4C/D, 5 with 100 A-10, more forming).
  15 tac tpt sqns (MAC; (1 trg) with 140 C-130A/B/E/H, 4 C-123K).
  3 tanker sqns (SAC) with 24 KC-135.
  2 special operations sqns (MAC; 1 with 10 AC-130 ac, 1 with 5 CH-3 hel).
  1 weather recce sqn with 7 WC-130H.
  4 SAR sqns with 15 HC-130H/N ac, 8 HH-3E, 10 UH-1N hel.
  20 Reserve Associate sqns (personnel only).
    MAC: 4 for C-5A, 13 for C-141, 1 aero medical for C-9A.
    SAC: 2 for KC-10A.
  137 non-flying spt units.
(iii) Civil Reserve Air Fleet: 321 long-range commercial ac (numbers fluctuate): 200 passenger (Boeing 747, L-1011, DC-8/-10), 121 cargo (80 Boeing 707, 30 747 (C-19A), DC-8/-10); 16 short-range commercial (Boeing 727, DC-9).

Forces Abroad (510,300):
GENERAL:
  Caribbean/Latin America: 20,200 (incl Bermuda (1,500), Guantánamo (2,500), Honduras garrison (1,700), Puerto Rico (3,500), Panama (9,170)); Europe: 349,200; Pacific/Far East: 138,900; other areas 2,000.

ARMY: (256,600).
Europe: 216,700.
  (i) Germany: (204,200). 1 Army, 2 corps HQ; 2 armd, 2 mech divs; 1 armd, 1 mech, 1 cav bdes; 2 armd cav regts; 30 AD btys with *HAWK*; 5,000 MBT.*

(ii) West Berlin: (4,300). HQ elms, 1 inf bde.

(iii) Greece: (480).

(iv) Italy: (3,800).

(v) Netherlands: (880).

(vi) Turkey: (1,200).

(vii) Other: (1,840).

Pacific (31,500):

(i) South Korea: 29,200. 1 inf div (13,900).

(ii) Japan: 2,100; base and spt personnel.

Caribbean/Latin America: 8,800.

NAVY: (89,900).

Atlantic (Second Fleet): Guantánamo Bay (Cuba 2,100), Bermuda, Keflavik (Iceland, 1,900), Holy Loch and other (Britain, 2,200). NATO-assigned (14,800).

Mediterranean (26,600). Sixth Fleet: 41 vessels, typically incl 1–2 SSN, 1–2 carriers and carrier gps of surface combatants, spt ships; Mid-Term Prepositioning Force: 3 stores ships. Italy (5,200): Gaeta (HQ), Naples, Sigonella, La Maddalena. Spain (3,700): Rota.

Western Pacific (40,700), Seventh Fleet: some 20 SSN and SS: 3 carriers (1 hel), 22 surface combatants, 6 amph, 8 spt ships. Japan (7,200): Yokosuka (HQ). Philippines (5,300): Subic Bay. Guam (4,900 incl Marine det): Midway.

Indian Ocean Dets (from 7th Fleet): 1 carrier battle gp (some 6 surface combatants). Near Term Prepositioning Force: (Diego Garcia) (1,600): 3 ammunition, 7 cargo ships, 3 barges, 3 oilers, 1 water tanker. Middle East Force (Persian Gulf-Bahrain): 1 comd ship, 4 destroyers/frigates.

MARINES: (36,500).

Caribbean: Cuba (Guantánamo) 455; 1 reinforced marine coy.

Europe/Middle East: 3,000; Mediterranean 1 MAU (1,900).†

Pacific: (Japan/Okinawa, 25,100); 1 MAF (1 div (–), 1 air wing, 1 log spt gp), MAU, 1 bn landing team.† (Philippines, 700).

Indian Ocean: (1,800); 1 MAU deployed intermittently.

AIR FORCE: (127,300).

Europe: (89,800): US Air Force, Europe (USAFE); some 729 combat ac; 32 GLCM.

(i) *Britain* (27,000): 1 Air Force HQ: 4 combat air wings: 306 combat ac; 16 GLCM. 16 sqns (7 with 150 F-111E/F, 6 with 108 A-10; 1 recce wing with 2 sqns: 1 with 18 RF-4C, 1 with 5 EF-111 *Raven*, 2 TR-1; 1 combat trg sqn with 18 F-5E); 1 tpt wing with 16 C-130 (MAC); 29 KC-135, 4 EC-135H (SAC); 1 tactical missile wing, 16 GLCM.

(ii) *Germany* (40,200): 1 Air Force HQ: 6 combat air wings: 327 combat ac, 7 armed hel. 12 sqns (3 with 72 F-16A/B, 4 with 96 F-4E, 1 with 24 F-4G; 3 with 72 F-15C/D;

1 recce sqn with 18 RF-4C); 1 air control wing of 3 sqns (2 with 42 OV-10A ac, 1 with 7 CH-53C hel); 1 tpt wing (MAC) of 4 sqns (1 with 18 C-130E); 1 special operations sqn with 3 MC-130E.

(iii) *Netherlands* (1,900): 1 sqn with 24 F-15C/D.

(iv) *Spain* (5,400): 1 Air Force HQ: 1 tac wing of 3 sqns with 72 F-16A/B, 1 ftr trg wing (no ac assigned), 1 strategic recce unit (SAC). (1 TAC fighter wing (F-4E) in US; on call as reinforcements.)

Italy, (5,100): 1 tac, 1 air base gps, 1 tac msl wing (16 GLCM).

Greece (2,600): 2 air base gps.

Turkey (3,800): HQ, 1 tac, 2 air base gps.

(v) *Other areas*: (3,800).

Iceland: (TAC, 1,100); 1 AD sqn with 24 F-4E, 4 T-33, 1–3 E-3A AWACS.

Pacific: Pacific Air Forces (PACAF): (38,950).

(i) *Guam* (3,900): Dets from SAC: 1 strategic bbr wing with 1 B-52 sqn; 1 refuelling wing with KC-135.

(ii) *Japan* (15,100): 1 Air Force HQ: 1 div: 1 wing (3 sqns) with 72 F-15C/D, 18 RF-4C, T-39A ac, UH-1E/F hel; det (TAC) with 3 E-3A AWACS. See *Korea*, below.

(iii) *Korea* (10,400): 1 div: 2 wings: 5 sqns (2 with 36 F-4E, 2 with 48 F-16, 1 with 18 A-10), 1 tac control gp with 18 OA-37).

(iv) *Philippines* (9,100): 1 Air Force HQ: 1 wing, 2 ftr sqns (1 with F-4E, 1 with F-4E/G); 1 special operations sqn with 4 MC-130E; 1 tac airlift wing (MAC) with 32 C-130 ac, 8 HH-3 hel; 1 trg gp with 15 F-5E, T-33, T-39A).

(v) *Australia* (450).

Middle East (all services): Sinai (MFO) 1,100; Egypt 1,500; Saudi Arabia 540.

RESERVES (individuals, all services): Standby 49,000; Retired 384,000 of which 120,000 are still eligible for active duty.

Para-Military Forces:

Coast Guard (by law a branch of the Armed Forces; in peacetime under the Department of

---

* Incl those stockpiled for the Strategic Reserve formations. The armd and mech bdes are from the divs in the US earmarked to reinforce 7th Army.

† Marine Amphibious Units (MAU) are embarked in Amphibious Ready Gps (ARG) comprising 4–7 amph ships with a reinforced inf bn gp, incl tks, arty, composite air sqn (incl hel) and log gp (1,800). Only 1 in Mediterranean and 1 in Pacific are regularly constituted. 1 Bn Landing Team (MAU less hel) also deployed in Pacific; 1 occasionally formed for the Atlantic. A Marine Amphibious Force may have up to 50,000 men with air support.

Transportation): 38,791 (2,342 women); 45 cutters (17 high-endurance (2,600–3,000 tons), 28 med-endurance (1,000 tons)), 6 icebreakers, 76 patrol craft, 2 hovercraft, 28 tugs, 88 other vessels; some 2,250 small craft; 611 shore installations; 64 ac (41 HU-25A, 21 HC-130B/E/H, 1 VC-4A, 1 VC-11A); 108 hel (37 HH-3F, 71 HH-52A (to be replaced by 90 HH-65A (AS-365G *Dauphin* 2)). (In reserve/storage: 4 C-130, 3 HU-25.)

Coast Guard Reserve: 11,800; 6,500 selected 2nd ready reserves; 167 port security units in 40 ports, 59 general spt units, 63 reserve gps, 1 cutter, 150 small vessels.

Coast Guard Auxiliary: 36,000 civilian volunteer force; augment regular force in emergencies.

Civil Air Patrol (CAP): 68,021 (26,215 cadets); HQ, 8 geographical regions, 52 wings, 1,936 units, 553 CAP ac plus 8,890 private ac. Roles: (a) emergency services, SAR, disaster relief, civil defence and comms (b) aerospace education, (c) cadet training and motivation.

The Soviet Union

Strategic Forces

The Soviet strategic inventory continues to be modernized. The SS-11 total has been reduced by 30; the SS-19 total shows a corresponding increase. We can assume that the earlier SS-19 single warhead has been replaced by the 6 MIRV of its Modification 3. Because the silos are outwardly similar, figures must be used with caution. Modification 4 to the SS-18 ICBM, introduced in 1982, may now affect some 170 launchers. The SLBM inventory shows one less *Y-I* submarine and one less *H-II* (with its SALT-accountable SS-N-5 SLBM), but one more *Typhoon*-class submarine (20 tubes) is now in service. Three or four more *Typhoon* boats are reported under construction. SS-20 IRBM deployment has continued; the total is now some 378 launchers. The SS-5 IRBM has been withdrawn; the SS-4 IRBM total remains at 224.

The ICBM launcher total remains at 1,398. With the introduction of smaller (and more accurate) warheads, total potential deliverable megatonnage is somewhat lower.

At sea, the retirement of more SS-N-5 and some SS-N-6 missiles and the introduction of the SS-N-20 missile, which last year at this time was not believed to be operational, has resulted in a net increase of launchers by one to 981. The total of SALT-accountable submarines remains the same. Newer SLBM warheads are almost all MIRV, and are believed to have greater accuracy than their predecessors. SLBM megatonnage has increased significantly.

IRBM changes increase the total number of IRBM launchers by 2, to 578. The number of warheads also increases by 38, to some 1,358, while the megatonnage decreases by 7.9, to 394.1. The overall missile total (long- and intermediate-range) is therefore 2,757 (excluding possible reloads). We have not here attempted to segregate missiles with a European role from the total but would observe that the 880 remaining SS-11 and the SS-19 ICBM have a variable-range capability, enabling them to target Europe and its approaches.

In the long-range bomber force the only change noted has been the modest increase of 20 in the Tu-26 *Backfire* inventory. The new *Blackjack* A bomber has not yet entered service. Some ten of the Tu-16 withdrawn last year may have been modified for the ECM role.

The strategic defensive forces also show some changes. Although the ABM launcher force still remains at 32, reports suggest that new missiles are being deployed. A little more information on radar deployments has become available; it is not clear whether this represents new deployments or merely new data.

General-Purpose Forces

Details of organizational changes within the Soviet defence structure remain scanty. The forces have been grouped into three main 'Theatres' – Western, Southern and Far Eastern – with a Central Strategic Reserve area comprising the Moscow, Volga and Ural Military Districts (MD). The Western Theatre, which includes the non-Soviet Warsaw Pact nations, is further subdivided into three Theatres of Military Operations (TVD) which provide strategic planning and operational control for continental, oceanic and intercontinental forces (missile forces, SSBN and bombers) assigned to them. The Western Theatre is the strongest, with the most modern equipment. The Far Eastern Theatre is not known to be divided into TVD, but, given its importance and the size and operational diversity of the area, some measure of local control would appear to be necessary.

In wartime, the East European Warsaw Pact divisions would be incorporated within the Soviet Army structure, thus providing integrated commands for the North-Western, Western and South-Western TVD. The basic operational command is the Front. A typical Front comprises a tank army and two all-arms armies plus supporting elements, a total of six tank and eight motor rifle divisions. Variations in this 'typical' organization are governed by operational conditions.

On the basis of present East European and Soviet army deployments, the Western TVD could have four Fronts: two in East Germany, one in Czechoslovakia, and one in Poland. The two Fronts in East Germany total 12 tank and 13 motor rifle divisions; three motor rifle divisions less than two typical Fronts. In Czechoslovakia and Poland the total would be 14 tank and 16 motor rifle divisions; two tank divisions above the 'normal' level. Reinforcements could be quickly available from the Byelorussian MD, which contains 10 tank and 4 motor rifle divisions.

The North-Western TVD would comprise the Baltic MD, which, by incorporating the Polish marine division, could operate as an independent (i.e., Moscow-controlled) Front against the Baltic Coast including Denmark. The Leningrad MD can field a Front of two all-arms armies against the northern Scandinavian regions. It, too, might come directly under Moscow. In the South (the South-Western TVD), though no Soviet troops are deployed in the countries concerned, national forces in Bulgaria and Romania can mobilize two all-arms armies, each 4 tank and 16 motor rifle divisions. Hungary can mobilize 1 tank and 5 motor rifle divisions or one all-arms army and 3 extra motor rifle divisions. Soviet forces in the Carpathian and Odessa MD would add 4 tank and 15 motor rifle divisions. The Kiev MD, with its 6 tank and 4 motor rifle divisions, could reinforce either the Western or South-Western TVD.

The Southern Theatre, opposite Turkey's eastern frontier, would comprise forces from the Trans-Caucasus MD, 12 motor rifle divisions, supported by forces from the North Caucasus MD (1 tank, 7 motor rifle divisions), plus perhaps a proportion of the 7 motor rifle divisions in the Odessa MD, or the 3 motor rifle divisions in the Volga MD.

The Soviet Air Force has also been reorganized and now comprises twenty Regional Commands and five Air Armies. This reorganization has had the effect of changing considerably the categorization of Soviet fighter aircraft, and a number of questions still remain. Three of these Armies have taken over the strategic and strategic/tactical roles of the Long-range Air Force. The *Voyska-PVO* (National Air Defence Troops) has taken over some of the former Frontal Aviation interceptor inventory, as well as that of the Air Defence Forces of the former *PVO-Strany* and the Army air defence troops. The ten air defence districts have now been reduced to five. The *Voyska-PVO* and the Air Armies are now co-ordinated at the Theatre HQ. In wartime, the control of air and ground forces and air defence would be integrated at the TVD level, which should give greater operational flexibility.

Tank regiments now have an integral artillery battalion. Some artillery regiments at the Army level are being equipped with the (nuclear-capable) 240mm SP mortar. The towed 122mm gun/howitzer is in many cases being replaced by an amphibious SP version. Two new versions of the BM-27 240mm MRL are in service. The divisional reconnaissance battalion is now a formidable and highly mobile force with a platoon of medium tanks and a mix of light combat vehicles, many with light guns or anti-tank missiles. Air support, in East Germany at least, includes a helicopter brigade integral to each Army, giving a total deployment of some 400 helicopters, about half of which are armed Mi-24 *Hind*, some with AS-14 ATGW. Battlefield support SSM – *Frog*, *Scud* and *Scaleboard* – are being replaced by SS-21, SS-23 and SS-22 respectively. The SS-22, which some sources suggest is an up-rated SS-12, has a range of about 950 km – somewhat less than that of the *Pershing* II – but its 500-KT warhead has about twice the yield of its US counterpart.

The Navy continues to develop its submarine fleet, and modernization of the surface fleet also continues. A second *O*-class cruise missile submarine and two more *V-III* attack submarines are in service. Some older *C-I*, *W*, and *E* boats have been withdrawn, and new *M* and *S* boats are on trials. Doubt remains over the new role for the 10 *Y-I* SSN whose SLBM were removed under SALT contraints. More *O, M, S, K* and *T* boats appear to be under construction.

A 75,000-ton nuclear aircraft carrier is under construction; a third *Kiev*-class carrier is now in service, and a fourth is on trials. Two more *Slava*-class cruisers are under construction. A third *Sovremennyy* and two more *Udaloy* GW destroyers have also joined the fleet. Five more of each are reported to be building, as are a number of smaller combat vessels.

New Equipment

There has been little new information regarding the two Soviet ICBM reported last year as being under development. One was reported as the PL-4 (believed to be a development of the SS-17), first test-launched in October 1982. The other was the PL-5 (originally reported as a modified SS-13 mobile ICBM), first launched in December 1982. (The PL designator stands for the test area, Plesetsk, where these missiles were first observed.) Both are reported to use solid fuel. They have been assigned the numbers SS-X-24 and -25 respectively. Controversy continues to surround the question of which is a 'new type' ICBM as defined in SALT II (or whether both are). A new SLBM – SS-NX-23 – is reported in development and may be a replacement for the SS-N-18.

Three new long-range cruise missiles are reported to be in development. Designated SS-NX-21, AS-X-15 and SSC-X-4 (sea-, air- and ground-launched respectively), their ranges are estimated at 3,000 km. The AS-X-15 is said to be capable of being launched from *Bear*, *Backfire* and the new *Blackjack* A bombers. *Bear* H bombers are reported back in production to carry ALCM. The SSC-X-4 is believed to be carried in a four-tube mobile launcher.

Finally two new anti-ballistic missile systems – the SH-04 (exo-atmospheric) and the SH-08 (endo-atmospheric) – have been reported. New aircraft types in service include the MiG-29 *Fulcrum*, equipped with a new air-to-air missile (the AA-X-10), and the Su-25 *Frogfoot*. The MiG-25 *Foxhound* has been redesignated the MiG-31. The Su-27 *Flanker* air superiority aircraft is being evaluated. Airborne command and control is being upgraded, and the Il-76 *Mainstay*, which is to replace the present *Moss*, is reported to be in production. A modest increase in the aircraft inventory is reported compared with 1983.

Defence Expenditure

No single figure for Soviet expenditure can be given, since precision is not possible on the basis of present knowledge. The declared Soviet defence budget excludes a number of elements such as military R&D, stockpiling and civil defence – indeed some contend that it covers only the operating and military construction costs of the armed forces. The problem of arriving at a current budgetary figure was discussed in previous editions of *The Military Balance*. The official defence budget of 17.05 bn roubles each for 1983 and 1984 equals about 4.8% of total government expenditure for 1983 and 4.66% of that for 1984, or about 3.2% of 1983 NMP, according to Soviet data of the latter. Some western estimates of the burden of military expenditures on the GNP range from 10–20%. Moreover, Western experts and defence agencies are not agreed on the real change in Soviet defence spending. For instance, whereas the US Central Intelligence Agency had been maintaining that such expenditure was increasing by 2% annually, in the summer of 1984 the US Defense Department argued that the increase had risen to 3–4% for 1982 and 1983. The British Ministry of Defence has concurred with the former view.

Soviet pricing practices are quite different from those in the West. Objectives are set in real terms with no strict requirement for money prices to coincide with the real costs of goods and services. The rouble costs of the defence effort may thus not reflect the real cost of alternative production forgone; and, in turn, a rouble value of defence, expressed as a percentage of NMP measured in roubles, does not reflect the true burden.

If rouble costs are converted into dollars to facilitate international comparisons, the difficulties are compounded. Ideally, the exchange rate should relate the purchasing power of a rouble in the USSR to that of a dollar in the USA. The official exchange rate – $1 = 0.7410 (1983), 0.8000 (1984) – is considered inadequate for this purpose, and there is no consensus on an alternative methodology.

One alternative approach (estimating how much it would cost to produce and man the equivalent of the Soviet defence effort in the USA, and by so doing to establish a common price base on which to make total cost comparisons) is also not entirely satisfactory. Incomplete and inaccurate data make such indexes unreliable. In practice this particular method is considered to overstate the USSR defence effort relative to that of the USA.

That the USSR, like other countries, faces mounting economic problems (e.g. falling NMP/GDP growth rates, inflation and ever-increasing military establishment costs) is indicated in an article by Prof. Maj.-Gen. Gurov (*Krasnaya Zvezda*, 9 December 1982) which is worth quoting at length:

Under present-day conditions the interrelationship between military matters and the economy has become unusually close, and demands on material provision for troops and naval forces have increased sharply. First, there has been an unprecedented increase in the volume and a substantial alteration in the structure of the military consumption of material facilities and resources. Second, armies and navies are now equipped with the most complex systems of weapons and military hardware, which, furthermore, are virtually renewed every 10–12 years, which requires a highly developed and dynamic economy and advanced scientific and technical potential. Third, there has been an increase in manpower costs and the cost of means of armed struggle. Fourth, substantially greater demands have been made on the moral-political qualities and general educational, technical and professional training both of workers engaged in the military production sphere and of Armed Forces' personnel.

Source	Price base	Soviet Defence Expenditure				% Annual growth rate	
		1970	1979	1981	1982	1970–80	1982–3
Billions of Roubles							
USSR[a]	Current	17.90	17.20	17.054	17.05	–0.4%	—
CIA[b]	1970	44–53	59–75	70.75	—	3.7%	—
Britain[c]	Current	—	76–81	84–92	—	4.0%	2.0%
Rosefielde[d]	1970	43.5	91	—	—	8.5%	—
DoD	—	—	—	—	—	—	3–4%
Billions of Dollars							
USSR[e]	Current	—	—	—	23	—	—
Joint Chiefs of Staff[f]	1983	188	241	267	—	2.8%	—
Rosefielde[g]	1978	104.5	160.9	—	—	4.9%	—

[a] Official declared budget.
[b] For 1970–1980: Joint Economic Committee, Congress of the USA: *USSR: Measures of Economic Growth and Development, 1950–1980* (Washington DC: USGPO, 1982) p. 123; for 1981: Joint Economic Committee, *Allocation of Resources in the Soviet Union and China – 1982* (Washington DC: USGPO, 1983) p. 79.
[c] *Statement of Defence Estimates 1984* (London: HMSO, Cmnd. 9227–I).
[d] Steven Rosefielde: *False Science, Under-estimating the Soviet Arms Build-up* (New Brunswick NJ: Transnational Books, 1982) pp. 186–8.
[e] British Broadcasting Corporation, *Summary of World Broadcasts* (SU/7156/A1/4), 14 Oct. 1982.
[f] Organization of the Joint Chiefs of Staff, *Military Posture for FY 1983* (Washington DC: USGPO, 1982) p. 16 (figures taken from diagram).
[g] Rosefielde, *op. cit.*, pp. 184–5, note 3.

A sample of different estimates of Soviet defence expenditure, both in roubles and dollars, is given in the table, together with official figures for the defence budget published by the USSR. For a critique of the CIA estimates of Soviet defence expenditure, see Franklyn D. Holzmann, 'Soviet Military Spending: Assessing the Numbers Game', *International Security*, Spring 1982, pp. 78–101. For a critique of Steven Rosefielde, see D. F. Burton, 'Estimating Soviet Defense Spending', *Problems of Communism*, March–April 1983, pp. 85–93. A convenient overview of the problems and the debate can be found in Subcommittee on International Trade, Finance and Security Economics, Joint Economic Committee, *Soviet Military Economic Relations*, proceedings of a workshop, July 7 and 8, 1982 (Washington DC: USGPO, 1983).

Population: 274,300,000.
Military service: Army and Air Force 2 years, Navy and Border Guards 2–3 years.
Total armed forces: 5,115,000.*
NMP 1982: r 523.4 bn. Est 1983: 544.0 bn.
Est GNP range 1983: $1,378.5–1,752.0 bn.
NMP growth: 4% (1982), 4% (1983).
Inflation: 1.0% (1982).
Debt: $20.1 bn (1982).
Est def exp and exchange rate: see text above.

Strategic Nuclear Forces:
OFFENSIVE:
(a) *Navy*: 981 SLBM in 79 subs (942 SLBM and 62 subs within SALT Agreement, plus 39 SLBM and 17 subs outside it).

2 *Typhoon* SSBN × 20 SS-N-20	(40 msls).
14 *D-III* SSBN × 16 SS-N-18	(224 msls).
4 *D-II* SSBN × 16 SS-N-8	(64 msls).
18 *D-I* SSBN × 12 SS-N-8	(216 msls).
1 *Y-II* SSBN × 12 SS-N-17	(12 msls).
23 *Y-I* SSBN × 16 SS-N-6	(368 msls).

1 *H-III* SSBN × 6 SS-N-8 (6 msls) ⎤ [msls (18)
2 *H-II* SSBN × 3 SS-N-5 (6 msls) ⎬ but not subs
1 *G-III* SSB × 6 SS-N-8 (6 msls) ⎦ within SALT]
13 *G-II* SSB × 3 SS-N-5 (39 msls non-SALT).

(b) *Strategic Rocket Forces* (SRF): 415,000.† 6 operational rocket armies, org in divs, regts, bns and btys; 1 msl launcher per bty; 300 launch control HQ, 3 msl test centres.
ICBM: 1,398.‡
520 SS-11 *Sego* (at 9 fields, some in SS-19 silos; may be converted to SS-19).§
60 SS-13 *Savage* (at 1 field).
150 SS-17 (at 2 fields; mod 1, 4 MIRV; mod 3, 4 MRV, being deployed; in mod SS-11 silos.)
308 SS-18 (at 6 fields, upgrading to mod 4, 10 MIRV, in progress).
360 SS-19 (at 4 fields; mostly mod 3, 6 MIRV; replacing some SS-11).
IRBM/MRBM: some 596 deployed (371 in western rest in central and eastern USSR).
378 SS-20 mobile IRBM; (6 fields: 135 launchers in Far East (being increased), 81 in Central Asia, 162 west of Urals (being increased)). 2 more sites, 18 launchers may be operational shortly.‖
224 SS-4 *Sandal* MRBM in western USSR (being retired).
(c) Strategic elms, *Air Armies of the Soviet Union* (Naval, tactical elms see below): 100,000. Some 752 combat ac; some 500 to 550 in western USSR.
5 Armies.

Long-range bombers: 143.
100 Tu-95 *Bear* B/C, 43 Mya-4 *Bison* (some 70 *Bear* B have AS-3 or AS-4 ASM). (*Bear* H for ALCM reported in production.)
Medium-range bombers: 475.¶
220 Tu-16 *Badger* G, 125 Tu-22 *Blinder* A/B, 130 Tu-26 *Backfire* B (AS-4 ASM).
Recce: 34.
4 Tu-95 *Bear* E, 15 Tu-16 *Badger* F, 15 Tu-22 *Blinder* C. (A long-range high-altitude ac, 'Ram-M', reported under development.)
ECM: 100 Tu-16 *Badger* H/J/K.
Tankers: 30 Mya-4 *Bison* A, 20 Tu-16 *Badger*.
ASM: AS-3 *Kangaroo*, AS-4 *Kitchen*, AS-5 *Kelt*, AS-6 *Kingfish*.

DEFENSIVE:
National Air Defence Troops (*Voyska-PVO*) (incl Air Defence Troops of the Ground Forces (AA arty), but not their SAM and radar tps): 370,00:**
5 Air Defence District Commands, numerous AD regts; 14 specialist schools.
ABM: 32 ABM-1B *Galosh*; range over 320 km, warheads nuclear, presumably MT range. 8 sites in 4 complexes around Moscow. New ABM being emplaced.
Aircraft: Some 4,000; in regts and indep sqns.
Interceptors (some will be assigned as air superiority fighters in spt of ground tps): 480 MiG-21 *Fishbed* J/K/L; some 2,100 MiG-23 *Flogger* B/G (6 AAM); 380 MiG-25 *Foxbat* A/E (A uprating to E) (4 AAM); some 12 MiG-29 *Fulcrum* (6 AA-X-10); 50+ MiG-31 *Foxhound* A (8 AA-9 AAM); 680 Su-15 *Flagon* E/F (2 AAM); 120 Tu-28P *Fiddler* B (4 AAM); 160 Yak-28P *Firebar* (2 AAM).

---

* Excl Border Guard, internal security, railroad and construction troops, totalling some 1,135,000, but incl some 1,500,000 comd and general spt tps not otherwise listed.
† The SRF and *Voyska-PVO*, separate services, have their own manpower.
‡ Figures may fluctuate slightly during conversion.
§ There are 360 SS-19 silos. SS-11, SS-19 have variable range capability, enabling them to be used for theatre support.
‖ Usually in some 42 complexes with an average of 9 launchers. A reload capacity has been reported.
¶ Staging and dispersal points in the Arctic could significantly increase aircraft ranges.
** The SRF and *Voyska-PVO*, seperate services, have their own manpower.

Airborne Warning and Control Aircraft: 10 modified Tu-126 *Moss*. (4 Il-76 *Mainstay* reported in production to replace *Moss*.)

AAM: AA-2 *Atoll*, AA-3 *Anab*, AA-5 *Ash*, AA-6 *Acrid*, AA-7 *Apex*, AA-8 *Aphid*, AA-9, AA-X-10.

AA artillery: 9,000 23mm, 57mm, 85mm, 100mm, 130mm towed, ZSU-23-4, ZSU-30-6 (trials) and ZSU-57-2 SP guns.

SAM: Some 9,600 launchers (some 13,000 launcher rails) in some 1,000 fixed sites: 3,000 SA-1 *Guild* (in reserve, replaced by SA-10); SA-2 *Guideline* (some 350 sites, SA-10 may be replacing); SA-3 *Goa* (2 or 4 launcher rails, over 300 sites, low- to med-altitude intercept); SA-5 *Gammon* (2,000 launchers, over 100 complexes, long-range intercept); some 35 quad SA-10 in strategic role. Field mobile systems 4,100: 1,400 SA-4 *Ganef* (twin), 900 SA-6 *Gainful* (triple), SA-7 *Grail* (man-portable), 600 SA-8 *Gecko* (2 × twin/2 × triple), 650 SA-9 *Gaskin* (2 × twin), SA-11, SA-X-12, 550 SA-13 (2 × twin replacing SA-9). (Two ABM types – 'SH-04' exo-atmospheric, 'SH-08' supersonic endoatmospheric – reported.)

Warning Systems: Over 7,000, incl satellites and EW and ground control intercept radars.
(a) *Satellites*: 9 with highly elliptical semi-synchronous orbits (anti-ICBM/SLBM launch detection capability); 9 EW, 6 ELINT, 2–4 recce, 1 launch detection.
(b) *Over-The-Horizon (Backscatter) radars*: 3: 2 near Minsk and Nikolayev (Caucasus), targeted on the US and polar areas; 1 near Nikolayev-na-Amur, on China.
(c) *Long-range early-warning radars*:
 (i) ABM-associated:
  (1) 5 phased-array systems located at Lyaki (Europe); Abalakova, Saryshagan, Pechora (Central Asia); Mishelevka (Far East). 2 other sites reported.
  (2) 11 radars, mostly *House* (Hen)-series; range 6,000 km, 6 locations covering approaches from the west and south-west, north-east and south-east and, partially, south. Linked to intermediate-range *Dog House* (range 2,800 km) and *Cat House* and *Try Add* missile control radar.
 (ii) AD-associated:
  Flat Twin/Pawn Shop (ABM-3/SH-04/-08); *Tall King*, range 600 km (SA-5); *P-12 Spoon Rest*, 275 km (SA-2).
(d) *Search, surveillance/target-acquisition radars*: (7,000; 1,200 sites):
  Long Track (SA-4, SA-6); P-15 *Flat Face/Squat Eye*, 200 km (SA-3); P-50 *Back Net*, 320 km (SA-5).
(e) *Height finder radars*:
  Thin Skin (SA-4, SA-6); *Cake*-series (e.g., *Rock Cake*), 200 km; *Side Net*, 180 km (SA-5).
(f) *Missile control radars*:
  Yo-Yo (SA-1); *Fan Song* A to E (SA-2); *Low Blow* (SA-3); *Pat Hand* (SA-4); *Square Pair* (SA-5); *Straight Flush* (SA-6); *Land Roll* (SA-8).
(g) *AA artillery fire control radars*:
  Gun Dish (ZSU-23-4); *Fire Can* (57mm, 85mm); *Whiff*; *Fire Wheel*; *Flap Wheel* (57mm, 130mm).
Plus civilian air control equipment.

Civil Defence: (150,000; 16,000,000 on mobilization). Nationwide programme under Defence Ministry down to city/rural/industrial level includes some 75 comd posts within 120 km of Moscow: 1,500 hardened deep shelters, accommodation for at least 175,000 officials, and local urban hardened shelters for essential workforce and some of the general population.

Army: 1,840,000 (perhaps 1,400,000 conscripts).
Five Theatre HQ.
50 tk divs (Type: 3 tk, 1 motor rifle, 1 arty, 1 SAM AA regts, 1 SSM, 1 MRL bns, spt units).
136 motor rifle divs (Type: 3 motor rifle, 1 tk, 1 arty, 1 SAM regts, 1 SSM, 1 ATK, 1 MRL bns, spt units).
7 AB divs (each 3 para, 1 arty regts, 1 AA bn).
Some 8 air assault bdes (each 3 rifle bns, mor, SAM, ATK, spt tps).
Front and Army tps:
 15 arty divs (Type (Army): 4 bdes of 4 bns of 18 guns).
 Tk, arty, SSM, ATK, AD (SAM and arty), engr bdes, sigs, electronic warfare, hy tk tpt, NBC defence, CW regts, bns, spt services.
 Special forces (*Spetsnaz*): 16 bdes, 3 regts.
Tanks: Some 51,000: some 35,000 T-54/-55/ -62, some 8,000 T-64, 7,700 T-72/-80 MBT (most fitted for deep fording); PT-76 lt.
AFV: 70,000: 7,500 recce, incl BRDM-2, GT-S, BMP variants, many with ATGW; ACRV -1/-2/-3 comd/recce; 23,000 BMP-1/-2, some 2,800 BMD (AB) MICV; BTR-50P/-60P/-70/ -152 (-70, BMP-2 replacing -50/-60), GT-T, MT-LB (with SA-13, -19 SAM) APC.
Arty: some 34,000 guns and how, incl M-1966 76mm, D-74 122mm, M-46 130mm, M-1976 152mm, S-23 180mm towed, M-1981 (2-S5) 152mm, M-1975 203mm SP guns; M-1937/ D-20 towed, M-1973 (2-S3) 152mm SP gun/how; M-1938/D-30 122mm, M-1938/D-1 152mm towed, M-1974 (2-S1) 122mm, M-1981 152mm and M-1975 203mm SP how; 14,000 82mm, 120mm, 160mm and 240mm (incl M-1975 SP) mor; 6,000 M-1944 (BM-21)/M-1972 (RM-70) 40-tube, M-1975 12-tube, M-1976 36-tube 122mm, BM-14

-16/-17 16/17-tube, RPU-14 16-tube 140mm, M-1977 (BM-27) 16-tube 220mm, BM-24 12-tube and BM-27 16-tube 240mm MRL.

ATK: 40mm RPG-7, 73mm RPG-16/-18 RL; 73mm SPG-9 RCL; 7,000 76mm, D-44/SD-44 85mm, T-12/-12A/M-55 100mm towed and ASU-57/-85 SP ATK guns; AT-2 *Swatter*, AT-3 *Sagger*, AT-4 *Spigot*, AT-5 *Spandrel*, AT-6 *Spiral* ATGW.

AD: 11,500 ZU-23 23mm, 37mm, S-60 57mm, KS-19 100mm towed, ZSU-23-4 23mm, 30mm, ZSU-57-2 57mm SP AA, some 28,000 SA-4/-6/-7/-8/-9/-11/-13 (*Gopher*)/-14 SAM.

SSM (nuclear-capable): about 1,400 launchers (units organic to formations), incl some 700 *FROG*/SS-21, 570 *Scud*/SS-23, 120 SS-12/SS-22

Hel: some 4,100: 800 Mi-1/-2 *Hare/Hoplite* (lt recce, ATGW, utility), 440 Mi-6 *Hook* (hy tpt), 1,500 Mi-8 *Hip* C, 300 Mi-17 *Hip* H (assault tpt), D, G (comms), E (armed/ATGW), J and K (ECM), 1,100 Mi-24 *Hind* (armed), 15 Mi-26 *Halo* A (hy tpt), 10 Mi-28 *Havoc* (armed). Being org as indep of Tac Air.

DEPLOYMENT:

Western Theatre: 3 main operational sub-theatres (TVD); North-western, Western, Southwestern. (See also Arctic and Atlantic Maritime Commands.)

Central and Eastern Europe (565,000): 30 divs (16 tk, 14 motor rifle), plus 1 arty, 10,500 MBT.* East Germany (380,000): 1 Gp, 5 Army HQ; 10 tk; 9 motor rifle, plus 1 arty divs; 1 air assault, *Scud*/SS-23 bdes; 19 *FROG*/SS-21 bns; 5 hel regts. Poland (40,000): 1 Gp, 1 Army HQ; 2 tk divs. Hungary (65,000): 1 Gp, 1 Army HQ; 2 tk, 2 motor rifle divs. Czechoslovakia (80,000): 1 Gp, 2 Army HQ; 2 tk, 3 motor rifle divs; 1 air assault bn; 1 SS-12/-22, 2 *Scud*/SS-23, 1 arty bdes. 1 hel regt in each ground army.

European USSR Military Districts (MD): 65 divs (23 tk, 37 motor rifle, 5 AB), plus 8 arty. Baltic: 3 tk, 6 motor rifle, 2 AB, plus 2 arty. Belorussian: 10 tk, 4 motor rifle, 1 AB, plus 1 arty. Carpathian: 4 tk, 8 motor rifle, plus 2 arty. Kiev: 6 tk, 4 motor rifle, plus 1 arty. Leningrad: 8 motor rifle, 1 AB, plus 1 arty. Odessa: 7 motor rifle, 1 AB, plus 1 arty.

Central Strategic Reserve: 16 divs (3 tk, 12 motor rifle, 1 AB). Moscow: 2 tk, 5 motor rifle, 1 AB. Ural: 1 tk, 4 motor rifle. Volga: 3 motor rifle.

Southern Theatre: 30 divs (1 tk, 28 motor rifle, 1 AB), plus 2 arty. N. Caucasus: 1 tk, 7 motor rifle, plus 1 arty. Trans-Caucasus: 12 motor rifle, plus 1 arty. Turkestan: 6 motor rifle. Afghanistan: 3 motor rifle, 1 AB divs (see *Forces Abroad*, below). Some hel regts.

Far Eastern Theatre (see also Pacific Fleet): 52 divs (7 tk, 45 motor rifle), plus 4 arty. Central Asian: 1 tk, 6 motor rifle, plus 1 arty. Under High Command Far East (HQ Irkutsk): Siberian, 6 motor rifle, plus 1 arty; Transbaykal, 2 tk, 8 motor rifle, plus 1 arty; Far Eastern, 2 tk, 22 motor rifle, plus 1 arty; Mongolia, 2 tk, 3 motor rifle (see *Forces Abroad* below).

Soviet divs have 3 categories of combat readiness: Cat. 1, combat ready, 75–100% strength, with complete eqpt; Cat. 2, 50–75% combat strength, complete with fighting vehicles; Cat. 3, below 50% strength, fighting vehicles possibly complete, but older models. The system may now be changing, with some units in a formation being at full strength, others at cadre only.

The 30 divs and 1 arty div in Eastern Europe and all AB divs are Cat. 1. About 35% of divs in European USSR and the Far East are in Cat. 1 or 2. Most in Central and Southern USSR are likely to be Cat. 3. Tk divs in Eastern Europe have up to 335 MBT, motor rifle divs up to 266, but elsewhere holdings may be lower.

Navy: 490,000 (some 70% conscripts), incl Naval Air Force, Naval Infantry, and Coastal Artillery and Rocket Troops; 278 cruise-missile and attack subs, (some 123 nuclear (incl 9 mod *Y-I*), 154 diesel), 293 principal, 797 minor surface combatants. There are 15 auxiliary subs, 331 auxiliary ships and AGI. A further 96 attack subs and 30 principal surface combatants are in reserve.

Subs, cruise-missile: 67:

49 nuclear (SSGN): 2 *O*-class (× 24 SS-N-19 SLCM); 1 *P* (10 msls; ?SS-N-9 *Siren*); 11 *C-I* (× 8 SS-N-7), 6 *C-II* (× 8 SS-N-9); 29 *E-II* (× 8 SS-N-3a; some 7 may carry 8 SS-N-12). (SS-NX-21 nuclear SLCM under development.)

18 diesel (SSG): 16 *J*-class (× 4 SS-N-3a), 2 *W-Long Bin* (× 4 SS-N-3).

Subs, attack: 201 (211 if *all* mod *Y-I* were SSN):

Some 65 nuclear (SSN); 6 *A*, 12 *N*, 16 *V-I*, 7 *V-II*, 17 *V-III*, 5 *E-I*; 1 *M* and 1 *S* on trials. (10 *Y-I* SSBN have been/are being/may be converted to other roles incl SSN). Apart from the older *N* and *E*, most SSN probably carry SS-N-16 and/or SS-N-15 nuclear ASW weapons.

136 diesel (SS): 4 *K*, 18 *T*, 50 *F*, 10 *R*, 4 *Z*, 50 *W*.

Subs, other roles: 3 *G-I* comms conversion, 4 *B* trg, 2 *I* rescue; 1 *U* and one other SSN research; 4 *H* (ex-SSBN) role unknown.

---

* Excl tks in reserve (replaced by new ones but not withdrawn).

Surface Ships:

293 principal surface combatants:

3 *Kiev* carriers (37,000 tons) (1 more trials) with 4 × 2 SS-N-12 *Sandbox* SSM, 2 × 2 SA-N-3 and 2 × 2 SA-N-4 SAM, 1 × 2 SUW-N-1 ASW, 14 Yak-36 *Forger* A/B VTOL ac, 19 Ka-25 *Hormone* A/B hel.

2 *Moskva* ASW hel carriers (17,000 tons) with 2 × 2 SA-N-3 SAM, 1 × 2 SUW-N-1 or FRAS-1 ASW; 18 *Hormone* A hel.

2 *Kirov* nuclear-powered GW cruisers (CGN) with 20 SS-N-19 SSM, 12 SA-N-6, 1 × 2 SA-N-4 SAM, 1 × 2 SS-N-14 *Silex* ASW, 2–4 Ka-25 *Hormone* B or Ka-27 *Helix* B hel.

1 *Slava* (ex-'Black-Com 1', ex-'*Krasina*') GW SSM/ASW cruiser with 8 × 2 SS-N-12 *Sandbox* SSM, 8 SA-N-6 SAM, 1 Ka-27 hel.

17 GW ASW cruisers with Ka-25 hel: 7 *Kara* with 2 × 4 SS-N-14 ASW, 2 × 2 SA-N-3, 2 × 2 SA-N-4 SAM (1 trials with 1 × 6 SA-N-6 replacing twin SA-N-3, trials); 10 *Kresta*-II with 2 × 4 SS-N-14, 2 × 2 SA-N-3.

8 GW cruisers: 4 *Kresta*-I with 2 × 2 SS-N-3b SSM, 2 × 2 SA-N-1 SAM, 1 *Hormone* B hel; 4 *Kynda* with 2 × 4 SS-N-3b, 1 × 2 SA-N-1.

8 *Sverdlov* cruisers (2 command with 1 × 2 SA-N-4, 1 Ka-25 hel).

45 GW destroyers (DDG): 9 SSM/SAM (3 *Sovremennyy* with 4 × 4 SS-N-22 SSM, 2 SA-N-7 SAM, 1 *Helix* B hel; 6 mod *Kashin* with 4 SS-N-2C, 2 × 2 SA-N-1); 4 ASW/SAM *Udaloy* with 2 × 4 SS-N-14, 2 Ka-27 *Helix* A hel; 3 mod *Kildin* SSM with 4 SS-N-2C; 29 SAM (13 *Kashin*; 12 with 4 × 2 SA-N-1, 1 with SA-N-7 (trials); 8 *Kanin* with 2 × 2 SA-N-1; 8 SAM *Kotlin* with 1 × 2 SA-N-1).

23 gun destroyers (DD): 12 *Kotlin*, 10 *Skory*, 1 *Kildin*.

32 *Krivak*-I/-II GW frigates (FFG): with 1 × 4 SS-N-14, 2 × 2 SA-N-4.

152 gun frigates (FF): 1 *Koni*, 48 *Grisha*-I/-III, (also with 1 × 2 SA-N-4 SAM), 8 *Grisha*-II (KGB), 18 *Mirka* I/II, 42 *Petya*, 35 *Riga*.

797 minor surface combatants:

30 GW corvettes: 1 *Tarantul* II with 2 × 2 SS-N-22 (trials); 6 *Tarantul* I/II with 2 × 2 SS-N-2c; 23 *Nanuchka* I/III with 2 × 3 SS-N-9 (*Siren*), 1 × 2 SA-N-4.

117 FAC(G): 17 hydrofoil (1 *Sarancha* with 2 × 2 SS-N-9, 1 × 2 SA-N-4; 16 *Matka* with 2 SS-N-2c); 65 *Osa*-I, 35 *Osa*-II with 4 SS-N-2.

220 FAC(T): 12 *Pauk* also with 1 × 4 SA-N-5, 58 *Poti*, 12 *Shershen*, 32 *Turya*, 4 *Muravey* hydrofoils. 100 *Stenka* (KGB); Trials: 1 *Slepen*, 1 *Babochka*.

73 patrol craft: 8 *Susanin* icebreakers (KGB; 6 armed), 25 SO-1 (some KGB), 14 T-43 (some KGB), 18 T-58 (some KGB); 2 T-58, 6

T-43/PFR radar pickets.

3 *Alesha* minelayers.

115 ocean minesweepers: 35 *Natya* I/II, 45 *Yurka*, 35 T-43.

175 coastal minesweepers: 2 *Andryusha*, 48 *Sonya*, 3 *Zhenya*, 5 *Sasha*, 72 *Vanya*, 45 *Evgenya*⟨.

64 minesweeping boats⟨: 10 *Ilyusha*, 4 *Olya*, 20 TR-40, 30 K-8.

78 amph ships:

2 *Ivan Rogov* LPD with 1 × 2 SA-N-4, 4 × 4 SA-N-5, 2–3 *Helix* A hel; 14 *Alligator* (some with 3 × 2, 1 with 2 × 2 SA-N-5), 17 *Ropucha* LST (some with 4 × 4 SA-N-5); 45 *Polnocny* LSM (some with 2 × or 4 × 4 SA-N-5).

109 amph craft:

45 LCU: 20 *Vydra*, 15 SMB-1, 10 *Ondatra*. 64 hovercraft: 15 *Aist*, 2 *Utenok*, 17 *Lebed*⟨, 30 *Gus*⟨.

269 principal auxiliary ships:

28 replenishment/tankers, 31 spt tankers, 12 msl spt, 10 supply, 80 cargo, 20 submarine tender, 36 repair, 2 hospital, 20 submarine rescue, 20 salvage/rescue, 10 trg ships. Merchant fleet – 1,700 ocean-going, 700 river ships, incl 61 ramp-fitted roll-on/roll-off (RoRo) – could augment these.

62 intelligence collection vessels (AGI). 134 naval, 350 civilian oceanographic, fishery, space-associated and hydrographic research vessels.

Additional ships in reserve:

10 *F*, 6 *Z*, 80 *W* subs; 4 *Sverdlov* cruisers (1 with 1 × 2 SA-N-2 SAM); 6 *Kotlin*, 10 *Skory* destroyers; 10 *Riga* frigates; 10 T-43 MCM; 1 *G-V* SSB in SLBM research role.

(On order: 3–4 *Typhoon*, *D-III* SSBN; *O* SSGN; *M*, *S* SSN; *K*, *T* SS; 1 75,000-ton nuclear, 1 *Kiev* carriers; 2 *Kirov* CGN; 2 *Slava* CG; 5 *Sovremennyy*, 5 *Udaloy* DDG; *Krivak*, *Grisha* III frigates; *Tarantul*, *Nanuchka* GW corvettes; *Muravey*, *Stenka* FAC(T); *Pauk* FAC; *Sonya* coastal MCM; *Ropucha* LST; *Aist*, *Lebed*, *Utenok* hovercraft).

NAVAL AIR FORCE: (70,000); some 839 combat ac, some 265 combat hel.

Four Fleet Air Forces; org in air divs, each with 2–3 regts, each with HQ elms and 2 sqns of some 10 ac each; recce, ASW, tpt/utility org in indep regts or sqns.

Strike bbrs: some 105 Tu-26 *Backfire* B with AS-4 ASM.

Med bbrs: some 290: 190 Tu-16 *Badger* C, 64 G/G-mod with AS-5 ASM, some 35 Tu-22 *Blinder* B.

FGA: 120: 55 Yak-36 *Forger* A/B VTOL, 65 Su-17 *Fitter* C.

ASW: some 190 ac: some 50 Tu-142 *Bear* F, 50

Il-38 *May*, 90 Be-12 *Mail*. Some 230 hel: 90
Mi-14 *Haze*, 120 Ka-25 *Hormone* A, 20
Ka-27 *Helix* A, Ka-32 *Helix* B.
MR/ECM: some 135 ac: some 80 Tu-16 *Badger*
D/E/F/H/J/K, 45 Tu-95 *Bear* D, 10 An-12
Cub B ac; 25 Ka-25 *Hormone* B hel.
MCM: some 10 Mi-14 *Haze* B hel.
Tankers: 75 Tu-16 *Badger*.
Tpt/trg ac: 350 ac and hel, incl An-12 *Cub* A,
An-26 *Curl*, Il-14 *Crate*, Il-18 *Coot*, An-24
Coke, Il-76 *Classic* ac; Mi-6/-8 *Hook/Hip* hel.
ASM: AS-2 *Kipper*, AS-4 *Kitchen*, AS-5 *Kelt*,
AS-6 *Kingfish*, AS-7 *Kerry*.

NAVAL INFANTRY (Marines): (16,000).
1 div HQ.
5 naval inf bdes/regts (each 2,500; 4 inf, 1 tk bn,
SP arty).
4 naval Special Forces (*Spetsnaz*) bdes (one in
each Fleet), 20 indep units.
T-54/-55 MBT; PT-76 lt tks; BRDM-2 recce;
BTR-60P/PA/PB APC; M-1974 122mm SP
how; 82mm, 120mm mor; BM-14 17-tube
140mm MRL; AT-3/-5 ATGW; ZSU-23-4 SP AA
guns; SA-7/-9/-13 SAM.

COASTAL ARTILLERY AND ROCKET TROOPS:
(14,000).
1 coastal arty div.
Hy coastal guns incl SM-4-1 130mm, perhaps
100 SS-C-1b *Sepal* SSM (similar to SS-N-3) to
protect approaches to naval bases and major
ports.

DEPLOYMENT AND BASES (average strengths,
excluding units in reserve):
Arctic Command:
Northern Fleet: 42 SSB/BN incl 2 *Typhoon*, 21
D, 15 Y-class. 138 other subs, 80 principal
(incl 1 carrier), 120 minor surface combatants, 15 amph, 85 principal auxiliary
ships, some 310 combat ac/hel incl 100 bbrs
and ftrs. 1 naval inf bde. Severomorsk (HQ),
Motovskij Gulf, Gremikha, Polyarny, Arch-
angelsk. Some 10 subs are normally
deployed in the Mediterranean (see below).
Atlantic Command:
Baltic Fleet: 32 subs (incl 6 *G-II* SSB), 45
principal, 260 minor surface combatants, 22
amph, 35 principal auxiliaries, some 210
combat ac/hel incl some 130 bbrs and ftrs, 6
SSM bns. 1 naval inf bde. Baltiysk (HQ),
Kronshtadt, Paldiski, Liepaja, Klaipeda,
Riga.
Black Sea Fleet (incl Caspian Flotilla): 24 subs,
80 principal (incl 2 ASW hel carriers), some
210 minor surface combatants, 23 amph, 55
principal auxiliaries, some 250 combat ac/hel
incl 80 bombers, 1 naval inf bde. Sevastopol
(HQ), Balaclava, Poti, Odessa.

Mediterranean sqn: with 8–10 subs, 12–14
surface combatants incl 2 amph, 10–12
auxiliaries, 4–6 AGI. All assigned from other
fleets).
Pacific Fleet: 31 SSB/BN (incl 15 D, 9 Y, 6
G-II), 102 other subs, 88 principal (incl
2 carriers), 220 minor combatants, 18 amph
incl 2 *Rogov*, 84 principal auxiliaries, 340
combat ac/hel incl 120 bombers. 1 naval
inf div (2 regts). Vladivostok (HQ), Petro-
pavlovsk, Sovyetskaya Gavan. Detachments
from this fleet (average 2–3 subs, 8 surface
combatants, 2 amph, 12 spt ships) are
normally deployed in the Indian Ocean and
South China Sea; facilities also in Vietnam
(Cam Ranh Bay), South Yemen (Aden,
Socotra) and Ethiopia (Dahlak Is).

Air Force: 400,000.
Air Armies of the Soviet Union: Strategic, AD,
see above. 16 MD Air Forces, 4 Air Armies.
Continuing reorganization makes eqpt estimates tentative.
Tactical: (315,000); some 3,260 combat ac.
20 air commands of varying strengths, mostly
org in divs of 3 sqns, totalling 45 ac; the
regts' roles may differ within the div.
FGA: some 2,600: some 160 MiG-21 *Fishbed*
L, 730 MiG-27 *Flogger* D/J, 130 Su-7 *Fitter*
A, 850 Su-17 *Fitter* D/H, 630 Su-24 *Fencer*,
75 Su-25 *Frogfoot*.
Fighters: A proportion of the 4,000 inter-
ceptors listed in Strategic AD will have a
battlefield air superiority role.
Recce: 620: 170 MiG-25 *Foxbat* B/D, 70
MiG-21 *Fishbed* H, 200 Yak-28 *Brewer* D,
180 Su-17 *Fitter* H.
ECM: 40 Yak-28 *Brewer* E.
Trainers: Some 1,000 ac; 700 hel.
AAM: AA-2 *Atoll*, AA-7 *Apex*, AA-8 *Aphid*,
AA-9.
ASM: AS-7 *Kerry*, AS-10; hel-borne: AT-2
Swatter, AT-6 *Spiral*.
Military Transport Aviation (VTA): (45,000);
some 750 ac. Org in regts. Incl An-2 *Colt*,
An-8 *Camp*, 320 An-12 *Cub*, An-24 *Coke*,
An-26 *Curl*, Il-14 *Crate*, 225 Il-76 *Candid*
M/MD (replacing *Cub*), 55 An-22 *Cock* hy.
(An-400 *Condor* under development).
Some 200 *Cub* and *Candid*, and 1,300 med- and
long-range passenger ac of the civilian *Aeroflot*
fleet and the 1,250 tpts of the other Services
could augment VTA airlift.

DEPLOYMENT:
1 HQ, 4 Tactical Forces (2,000 ac) in Eastern
Europe, 1 in each of 16 MD in USSR; total Far
East perhaps 2,700 ac incl 440 bombers, 1,500
fighters/attack ac.

RESERVES:
Soviet male citizens have a Reserve obligation to
50. Total Reserves could be 25,000,000, of
which some 5,300,000 will have served within
the last five years: Strategic Rocket Forces,
520,000; Army, 3,500,000; Navy, 840,000;
Air Force, 400,000. Reports suggest that the
remaining 19,700,000 would provide sufficient
forces to mobilize an equivalent to the peacetime force structure which, though equipped
with stored obselete equipment, would at least
double the size of the ground forces.

Forces Abroad:
Afghanistan: 115,000 (some 10,000 MVD, KGB.)
　Army: 1 HQ, 3 motor rifle, 1 AB divs, 1 air
　　assault bde.
　Air: equivalent possibly 2 air divs: (4 ac, 6 hel
　　regts: 180 ac, 270 hel); VTA and *Aeroflot* tpt
　　ac from USSR in spt.
Mongolia: 75,000: 2 tank, 3 motor rifle divs.
Vietnam: (7,000) averages: 4 subs, 2–4 combat
　vessels, 10 auxiliaries, 10 MR or ASW ac, AA
　SAM, electronic monitoring station.
Other: Algeria 1,000; Angola 500; Congo 100;

Cuba 4,600 (1 bde, advisers, technicians, plus
3,000 civilians); Ethiopia 1,700; India 200;
Iraq 600; Laos 500; Libya 1,800; Mali
200; Mozambique 300; Nicaragua 100; Peru
100; Syria 7,000; Vietnam 2,500; N. Yemen
500; S. Yemen 1,500; Africa (rest) 900.

Para-Military Forces: 675,000.
KGB 225,000: border tps, with tks, SP guns, AFV,
　ac and ships (1 *Purga* frigate, 90 *Stenka* FAC(P),
　12 *Pchela* hydrofoils, 30 *Zhuk*, some SO-1,
　T-58, T-43 patrol craft); Kremlin Guard;
　Special Guard; Special Sigs unit (40,000 tps).
MVD 300,000: security tps; some 30 divs with
　tks and AFV. By law part of armed forces of
　USSR.
Civil Defence 150,000 (permanent staff only).
Part-time   military   training   organization
　(DOSAAF); claimed active membership 80
　million (of which 5 million are instructors and
　activists) in 330,000+ units; flight training,
　shooting, parachuting and pre-military train-
　ing of those aged 15 and over in schools,
　colleges and workers' centres. Para-military
　training also in Young Pioneers (ages 8–15).

The Alliances and Europe

THE WARSAW PACT

We have seen no major changes in the organization, equipment or roles of the East European Warsaw Pact nations' ground forces over the past twelve months. Some small changes in military manpower are reported: in Bulgaria a decrease of 15,000; in Czechoslovakia and East Germany increases of 2,750 and 5,000 respectively; in Poland a decrease of 16,750. These changes have had the effect of increasing, very slightly, the ground force strength of East Germany and that of the air components of both East Germany and Czechoslovakia, while the Polish force reductions appear to have applied to the Army. There is no indication why these changes have come about.

The most significant Baltic naval delivery was the *Tarantul*-class missile corvette *Gornik*, reported commissioned in the Polish Navy in March. This vessel carries four SS-N-2 surface-to-surface missiles. A second is expected. Romania received the first of three *Tetal*-class frigates; no details have been received. These countries' naval forces need modernization, but the new arrivals do not make any significant change in their capabilities.

Bulgaria has increased her air reconnaissance element to a full regiment, adding 50% to her earlier capabilities, and Czechoslovakia has phased out some of her elderly MiG-15 and Su-7 FGA, replacing them with MiG-23 – a significant advance in both cases. There has been no reported major change in any of the other national forces.

Economic growth in Eastern Europe slowed in the late 1970s and early 1980s. Although regional NMP grew by 3% in 1983, after declining in 1981 and 1982, economic growth was not uniform throughout the Eastern Bloc. At the height of the Solidarity upheaval Poland experienced a sharp reduction in NMP (1981: –12.1%, 1982: –5.5%) and industrial production (1981: –10.5%, 1982: –2.1%) which began to rebound in 1983 (NMP 4 to 5%, Industrial Production 6.7%). NMP output growth was 0.5% in Hungary and 2.2% in Czechoslovakia in 1983. East Germany (4.4%), Bulgaria (3.0%), and Romania (3.4%), meanwhile, managed relatively stronger NMP growth through 1983. Another factor – inflation – seriously affected the economies of Poland (1982: 100.2%), Hungary (1982: 7%; 1983: 7.3%) and Romania (1982: 17%; 1983: 5.2%). Many East European economies during this period began adjusting their internal pricing, distribution, investment and planning structures to meet external trade and debt repayment requirements.

Reconciling foreign indebtedness with the resumption of economic growth is a major economic issue facing Eastern Europe. The levels of exports and debt repayments limit imports – and hence domestic expenditures and investment – particularly in Poland, Hungary and East Germany. The Eastern bloc has recently managed to lower its collective external debt from some $80 bn in 1981 to some $70 bn in 1983. Total imports from the West have declined from $50 bn in 1981 to $43 bn in 1982, although trade within COMECON increased by 9% in 1983 (largely due to changed oil pricing arrangements within COMECON). The Soviet Union continues to be the dominant trading partner. In addition, the Eastern Bloc accumulated a large rouble debt and saw its terms of trade deteriorate with all trading partners. The effect on the internal economies, particularly in Poland, was that investment was 20% less in 1983 than in 1979. Decreased productivity and output followed. Output and investment, as forecast by the IMF, are not expected to achieve their previously high rates in the near term.

BULGARIA

Population: 9,000,000.
Military service: Army and Air Force 2 years, Navy 3 years.
Total regular forces: 147,300 (94,000 conscripts).
NMP 1982: lev 22.80 bn. Est 1983: 23.50 bn.
Est GNP range 1983: $26.0–36.0 bn.
Est def budget 1982: lev 901 m ($1.287 bn). 1983: 932 m ($1.313 bn).
NMP growth: 4.2% (1982), 3.0% (1983).
Debt: $2.8 bn (1982).
  $1 = 1982: 0.95 (official), 0.70 (adjusted); 1983: 0.97 (off.), 0.71 (adj.).

Army: 105,000 (73,000 conscripts).
3 Military Districts:
  8 motor rifle divs (3 at Cat. 3 = cadre).
  5 tk bdes.
  3 SSM bdes with *Scud*.
  4 arty regts.
  3 AA arty regts.
  2 SAM regts.
  1 para regt.
  Special commando coys.
AFV: 400 T-34, 1,400 T-54/-55, some 60 T-72 MBT; some 60 BMP MICV; 250 BRDM-1/-2 scout cars; 1,000 BTR-50/-60, 35 OT-62, MT-LB APC.
Arty: 25 M-1942 76mm, 25 D/DS-44 85mm, M-1944 100mm, 700 M-1931 122mm, M-46 130mm towed guns; 100 M-1938 (M-30), D-30 122mm, M-1937 152mm towed gun/how; 100 BM-21 122mm, some M-51 130mm MRL; 82mm, 350 120mm and 160mm mor; 39 *FROG*-7, 27 *Scud* SSM.
ATK: 90 M-1942 76mm ATK guns; 150 SPG-9 73mm RCL; AT-1 *Snapper*, AT-3 *Sagger* ATGW.
AD: 500 ZU-23 23mm, M-1939 37mm, S-60 57mm, KS-12 85mm and KS-19 100mm towed, ZSU-23-4 SP AA guns; SA-4/-6/-7 SAM.

RESERVES: 150,000; 3 motor rifle divs on mobilization. 600,000 more have a Reserve liability.

Navy: 8,500 (3,000 conscripts); 3 combat hel.
2 *R*-class subs.
2 *Riga* frigates.
3 *Poti* corvettes.
6 FAC(G) with *Styx* SSM: 3 *Osa*-I, 3 *Osa*-II.
14 FAC(T): 6 *Shershen*, 8 P-4⟨.
13 patrol craft: 6 SO-1, 7 *Zhuk* coastal⟨.
30 MCM vessels: 2 T-43 ocean; 2 *Sonya*, 4 *Vanya* coastal; 18 PO-2, 4 *Yevgenya*⟨ inshore.
22 *Vydra* LCU, 5 MFP D-3 landing craft.
1 underway replenishment ship.
2 hel sqns: 1 ASW with 3 Mi-14 *Haze*; 1 SAR with 2 Mi-2, 6 Mi-4.
2 coastal arty regts (1,500): 20 btys; 100mm, 150mm guns.

3 Naval Guard coys.

Bases: Varna, Burgas, Sozopol, Atiya.

RESERVES: 25,000.

Air Force: 33,800 (18,000 conscripts); some 188 combat ac, some 12 armed hel.
1 air division: 3 combat regts:
  6 FGA sqns with 60 MiG-17, 12 MiG-23.
  6 interceptor/ftr sqns: 1 with some 20 MiG-23BM *Flogger* B; 5 with 60 MiG-21PFM.
  1 recce regt with 36 MiG-17/-21.
  1 tpt regt: 10 Il-14, 4 An-24, 2 Tu-134, 9 An-2.
  1 hel regt with 10 Mi-2, 40 Mi-4/-8, 12 Mi-24, 12 Ka-26 *Hoodlum*.
Trg ac incl 80 L-29, Yak-11/-18, L-39, 30 MiG-15UTI.
AAM: AA-1 *Alkali*, AA-2 *Atoll*, AA-7 *Apex*.
1 para regt.
1 AD div: 3 zones: 30 SAM sites; 280 SA-2/-3.

RESERVES: 20,000.

Para-Military Forces: Ministry of Interior border guards: 15,000; 16 regts. Security police: 7,500. People's Territorial Militia: 150,000. 'Voluntary Organization for Co-operation in National Defence'.

CZECHOSLOVAKIA

Population: 15,500,000.
Military service: Army 2 years, Air Force 3 years.
Total regular forces: 207,250 (118,000 conscripts).
NMP 1982: Kcs 497.2 bn. Est 1983: 508.1 bn.
Est GNP range 1983: $73.0–150.0 bn.
Def budget: 1982: Kcs 24.156 bn ($3.774 bn). 1983: 23.830 bn ($3.454 bn).*
NMP growth: 0.2% (1982), 2.2% (1983).
Inflation: 4.0% (1982), 8% (1983).
Debt: $4.1 bn (1982).
  $1 = koruny (1982): 6.03 (off.), 6.40 (adj.). 1983: 6.45 (off.), 6.90 (adj.).

Army: 148,000 (100,000 conscripts).
2 Military Districts:
  5 armd divs (1 at Cat. 2, 2 at 3).
  5 motor rifle divs.
  1 arty div: 2 arty, 3 *Scud* SSM bdes, 2 ATK regts (6 bns).
  1 AB bde.
  6 engr bdes.
  Civil Defence Troops (10,000): 5 regts.
AFV: 3,500 T-54/-55/-72 MBT; 1,100 BMP MICV, 1,250 OT-65 and BRDM scout cars; 2,700 OT-62/-64/-810 APC.

---

* Incl police and security budget.

Arty: 250 M-53 100mm, 100 M-1931/-37 122mm, 75 M-46 130mm guns; 90 M-1937 152mm gun/how; 250 D-30/M-30 122mm, M-1974 122mm SP, 250 M-18/46 and DANA (Tatra 813 truck-mounted) SP 152mm how; 200 RM-70 122mm, 120 M-51 130mm MRL; 40 *FROG*, 27 *Scud* SSM.
ATK: 100 82mm RCL; 112mm P-27 RL; 400 AT-3 *Sagger* and AT-4 *Spigot* ATGW.
AD: 600 S-60 57mm towed, M-53/59 30mm SP AA guns; SA-4/-6/-7/-9 SAM.

RESERVES: 200,000; 295,000 more with liability to age 50 (men) or 60 (officers).

Air Force: 59,250 (18,000 conscripts); 439 combat ac, some 24 armed hel.
2 air armies: 3 air divs: 15 combat regts:
  10 FGA sqns: 3 with 60 Su-7BM/U; 3 with 36 MiG-23; 3 with 42 MiG-21/-21U; 1 with 12 MiG-15.
  18 interceptor sqns with 252 MiG-21/-21U/-23 (about half AD, half battlefield spt).
  3 recce sqns: 2 with 25 MiG-21RF; 1 with 12 L-29.
  2 tpt regts with 2 An-12, 6 An-24, 40 Il-14, 1 Tu-134, 2 LET L-410M.
  1 hel regt, 3 indep hel sqns with 40 Mi-1, 20 Mi-2, 100 Mi-4, 10 Mi-8, 24 Mi-24.
Trg ac incl L-29.50, 24 L-39, Zlin 526.
Liaison ac incl Zlin Z-43.
AAM: AA-2 *Atoll*.
3 AD divs: 6 SAM regts: some 40 sites; 250 SA-2/-3.

RESERVES: 30,000.

Para-Military Forces: Border Troops 11,000: 7 bdes, AFV, ATK weapons. People's Militia 120,000. 'Association for Co-operation with the Army'.

GERMAN DEMOCRATIC REPUBLIC

Population: 16,860,000.
Military service: Army and Air Force 18 months, Navy (sea-going) 36 months.
Total regular forces: 172,000 (94,500 conscripts).
Est NMP 1982: DMO 201.0 bn. 1983: 210.0 bn.*
Est GNP range 1983: $85.2–172.0 bn.
Def budget 1983: DMO 15.850 bn ($7.709 bn). 1984: 16.961 bn ($7.538 bn).†
NMP growth: 2.5% (1982), 4.4% (1983).
Debt: $13.0 bn (1982).
  $1 = 1983: ostmarks 2.555 (off.), 2.056 (adj.). Mid-1984: 2.750 (off.), 2.250 (adj.)

Army: 120,000 (71,500 conscripts).
2 Military Districts, 2 Army HQ:
  2 tk divs (each 3 tk, 1 motor rifle regt).‡

4 motor rifle divs (each 1 tk, 3 motor rifle regts).‡
2 SSM bdes with *Scud*.
2 arty, 1 AA arty regts.
2 AD regts with SA-4 SAM.
3 sigs regts.
3 engr regts.
1 railway construction regt.
2 ATK bns.
1 AB bn.
AFV: About 1,500 T-54/-55/-72 MBT (1,600 more in storage); 1,000 BMP MICV; 1,000 BRDM-1/-2 scout cars; 1,500 BTR-50P/-60P/-152/-70 (M-1978), MT-LB APC.
Arty: 400 M-/D-30 towed and M-1974 122mm SP, 72 M-46 130mm guns; 108 M-1937/D-20 152mm towed, 54 M-1973 152mm SP gun/how; 108 RM-70 122mm MRL; 24 *FROG*-7, 18 *Scud* B SSM; 250 120mm mor.
ATK: 120 T-12 100mm towed ATK guns; AT-3 *Sagger*, AT-4 *Spigot* ATGW.
AD: 96 ZSU-23-4 SP AA guns; SA-4/-6/-7/-9 SAM.

RESERVES: 330,000; up to 3 months call-up per year to total 24 months; 250,000 more have a Reserve commitment to 50 (other ranks) or 60 (officers).

Navy: 14,000 incl Frontier Bde (8,000 conscripts); 15 combat hel.
2 *Rostock* (*Koni*) frigates with 1 × 2 SA-N-4 SAM.
10 *Parchim* corvettes with 2 SA-N-5 SAM.
15 *Osa*-I FAC(G) with 4 *Styx* SSM.
49 FAC(T): 18 *Shershen*, 31 *Libelle*.
6 *Hai* large patrol craft.
27 *Kondor*-II coastal minesweepers.
12 *Frosch* LST.
2 *Kondor*-I intelligence collection vessels.
4 supply ships 4 tankers, 2 mod *Frosch* lt tpts.
1 hel sqn with 13 Mi-8 (3 SAR), 5 Mi-14 ASW.
Coastal Frontier Bde (GBK; 2,750): 5 beach patrol bns, 3 afloat 'divs', 1 boat gp (recce); 37 vessels incl 3 *Parchim*, 10 *Bremse*, 19 *Kondor*-I; 152mm guns; *Samlet* SSM.

Bases: Peenemünde, Warnemünde, Dransk-Bug, Sassnitz, Wolgast, Tarnewitz, Barhöft.

RESERVES: 25,000.

Air Force: 38,000 (15,000 conscripts); 359 combat ac, 30 armed hel.
1 air div
  2 FGA regts:

---

* 1980 prices.
† Incl DMO 4.400 bn (1983), 4.739 bn (1984) for internal security.
‡ All divs Category 1.

4 FGA sqns: 2 with 35 MiG-17; 2 with some 12 MiG-23.
1 recce sqn with 12 MiG-21.
1 tpt regt: 3 sqns: 18 Il-14 (An-26 to replace), 15 Tu-134, An-2/-14/-26B.
3 hel regts: 9 sqns: 6 with 80 Mi-8 (about half armd); 3 with 30 Mi-24.
AD Command: 2 AD districts:
6 air regts: 18 sqns with 300 MiG-21F/MF/PF/U/-23.
7 SAM regts, some 30 sites with 200 SA-2/-3.
2 radar regts.
Trg ac incl Yak-11, L-39, Zlin 226, MiG-15UTI.
Liaison ac incl Zlin Z-43.
AAM: AA-2 *Atoll*.
ASM: AT-3 *Sagger* ATGW.

RESERVES: 30,000.

Forces Abroad: Algeria, 250; Angola, 500; Ethiopia, 550; Guinea, 125; Iraq, 160; Libya, 400; Mozambique, 100; S. Yemen, 75; Syria, 210.

Para-Military Forces: 82,500.
Ministry of Defence: Frontier Troops (50,000): 18 border, 2 indep, 1 special, 6 trg regts (?66 bns), 1 boat section; 24 patrol craft.
Ministry for State Security: 1 Guard regt (Berlin) (7,000): 6 motor rifle, 1 arty, 1 trg bns; PSZH-IV APC, 120mm mor, 85mm, 100mm ATK, ZU-23 AA guns, hel.
Ministry of Interior: People's Police Alert Units (10,500): 21 bns; BTR-40/-152 APC, 82mm mor. Transport Police (8,500): 16 coys; small arms, RPG-7 RL.
Workers' Militia: 15,000 combat groups; AFV incl SK-1 APC, 82mm mor, 76mm ATK, 23mm, 37mm AA guns.
Society for Sport and Technology (450,000, 75% active): 1 central, 14 regional subordinate district gps, some 15,000 units; small arms.
Thälmann Pioneers: School children, paramilitary trg.

HUNGARY

Population: 10,740,000.
Military service (incl Border Guard): 18 months; Air Force 24 months.
Total regular forces: 105,000 (58,000 conscripts).
NMP 1982: forints 696.4 bn. 1983: 730.0 bn.
Est GDP range 1983: $21.0–65.2 bn.
Def budget 1982: forints 20.260 bn ($1.318 bn). 1983: 21.070 bn ($1.22 bn).
NMP growth: 2.3% (1982), 0.5% (1983).
Inflation: 7.0% (1982), 7.3% (1983).
Debt: $7.7 bn (1982).
$1 = 1982: forints 36.631 (off.), 15.37 (adj.). 1983: 42.666 (off.), 17.26 (adj.).

Army: 84,000 (50,000 conscripts) incl Danube Flotilla.
1 tk div (at Cat. 2).
5 motor rifle divs (2 at Cat. 2, 3 at 3).
1 arty bde, 1 SSM bde with *Scud*.
1 AA arty, 4 SAM regts (1 indep with SA-4, 3 div with SA-6).
1 AB bn.
AFV: About 1,200 T-54/-55, 30 T-72 MBT; 100 PT-76 lt tks; 200 BMP-1 MICV; some 750 BRDM-2/FUG(OT-65) scout cars; 1,000 PSZH-IV, MT-LB APC.
Arty: 225 M-1938 towed, 50 M-1974 SP 122mm how; 40 D-20, 100 M-1943 towed, 20 M-1973 SP 152mm gun/how; 50 BM-21 122mm MRL; 24 *FROG*-7, 9 *Scud* SSM; 300 82mm, 100 M-43 120mm mor.
ATK: 125 SPG-9 73mm RCL; 125 85mm and T-12 100mm ATK guns; 100 AT-3 *Sagger*, 100 AT-4 *Spigot* ATGW.
AD: 100 S-60 57mm towed, 75 ZSU-23-4 SP AA guns; 30 SA-4, 60 SA-6, 500 SA-7, 50 SA-9 SAM.
Danube Flotilla (700); 10 100-ton patrol craft, river MCM, 5 small LCU, small tp tpts.

Air Force: 21,000 (8,000 conscripts); 145 combat ac, some 24 armed hel.
1 air div:
3 AD fighter regts: 9 interceptor sqns with 120 MiG-21F/PF/bis/U, 25 MiG-23BM.
1 tpt regt: 2 tpt sqns with 24 An-2/-24/-26, 2 Il-14.
1 hel regt: 3 hel sqns with 30 Mi-8, 24 Mi-24, 25 Ka-26 *Hoodlum*.
Trg ac incl L-29, MiG-15UTI.
AAM: AA-2 *Atoll*.
1 AD div: 3 SAM regts, some 20 sites; 120 SA-2/-3.

RESERVES (all services): 143,000.

Para-Military Forces: Border guards 15,000 (11,000 conscripts); 11 districts. Part-time Worker's Militia 60,000. 'Sport Association for National Defence'.

POLAND

Population: 36,900,000.
Military service: Army, internal security forces, Air Force 2 years; Navy, special services 3 years.
Total regular forces: 323,250 (185,000 conscripts).
Est NMP 1981: zloty 2,160.4 bn. 1982: 4,753.0 bn.
Est GNP range 1983: $92.2–178.0 bn.
Def budget 1983: zloty 193.0 bn ($6.433 bn). 1984: 218.0 bn ($6.229 bn).

NMP growth: −5.5% (1982), 4–5% (1983).
Inflation: 100.2% (1982).
Debt: $27.4 bn (1982).
$1 = 1983: 90.0 (off.), 30.0 (adj.). Mid-1984: 110.4 (off.), 35.0 (adj.).

Army: 210,000 (153,000 conscripts).
3 Military Districts:
5 armd divs (all at Cat. 1).
8 mech divs (3 at Cat. 1, 2 at 2, 3 at 3).
1 AB div (Cat. 1).
1 amph assault div (Cat. 1).
3 arty bdes, 1 arty regt.
3 ATK regts.
4 SSM bdes with *Scud*.
1 AD bde with SA-4; 9 AD regts: 7 with SA-6, 2 with SA-8 SAM.
AFV: 3,400 T-54/-55, 50 T-72 MBT; 110 PT-76 lt tks; 800 FUG/BRDM-2 scout cars; 800 BMP-1, 2,500 SKOT/SKOT-2AP and TOPAS/TOPAS-2AP APC.
Arty: 120 M-1931 (A-19) 122mm guns; 150 M-1937 (ML-20) 152mm gun/how; 520 M-1938 (M-30) towed and M-1974 (2S1) SP 122mm, 120 M-1943 (D-1) 152mm how; 250 BM-21 122mm, BM-14 140mm MRL; 51 FROG-3/-5/-7, 36 *Scud* B SSM; 750 82mm, 120mm mor.
ATK: 650 D-44 85mm and T-12 100mm towed ATK guns; 73mm RCL; AT-1 *Snapper*, AT-3 *Sagger*, AT-4 *Spigot* ATGW.
AD: 750 ZU-23 23mm and S-60 57mm towed, 130 ZSU-23-4 SP AA guns; SA-4/-6/-7/-8/-9 SAM.

Navy: 22,000 (5,000 conscripts).
3 *W*-class subs.
1 SAM *Kotlin* destroyer with 1 × 2 SA-N-1 *Goa*.
13 *Osa*-I FAC(G) with 4 *Styx* SSM.
18 FAC(T): 12 *Pilica*, 6 *Wisla*.
8 mod *Obluze* large patrol craft.
50 MCM: 12 *Krogulec*, 11 T-43 ocean, 2 *Notec* coastal minesweepers; 25 K-8 boats.
23 *Polnocny* LCT, 4 *Marabut* LCM, 15 *Eichstaden* LCA.
2 mod *Moma* intelligence vessels (AGI); 1 T-43 radar picket.
1 Naval Aviation Div (2,000); 44 combat ac:
1 attack regt: 3 sqns with 34 MiG-17.
1 recce sqn with 5 Il-28, 5 MiG-17.
1 hel regt: 2 sqns with 10 Mi-2, 20 Mi-4, 5 Mi-8.
(On order: 1 *Notec* coastal minesweeper.)

Bases: Gdynia, Hel, Swinoujscie, Kolobrzeg, Ustka.

Air Force: 91,250 (30,000 conscripts); 675 combat ac, 12 armed hel.
4 air divs:

6 FGA regts: 18 sqns: 3 with 35 Su-7/-7U; 3 with 35 Su-20; 12 with 150 MiG-17.
11 AD regts: 33 sqns with some 400 MiG-21/U/-23.
6 recce sqns: 35 MiG-21RF, 5 Il-28, 15 LIM-6.
2 tpt regts: 9 An-2, An-12, 12 An-26, 12 Il-14.
1 comms/liaison sqn with 2 Tu-134A, 6 Yak-40, Il-18 ac.
3 hel regts with 100 Mi-2, 12 Mi-4, 25 Mi-8, 12 Mi-24.
300 trg ac: TS-8/-11, MiG-15/-21UTI, Su-7U.
AAM: AA-1 *Alkali*, AA-2 *Atoll*.
3 AD divs: 9 SAM regts: some 50 sites; 400 SA-2/-3.

RESERVES (all services): 500,000.

Forces Abroad: Syria (UNDOF): 131.

Para-Military Forces: 218,000. Ministry of Interior border troops (160,000): 8 bdes, some 42 patrol craft incl 5 *Obluze*, 5 *Pilica*, 3 KP-131, 1 *Oksywie*, 12 *Wisloka*, 21 K-8, 9 *Gdansk*. Internal defence troops (58,000): tks, AFV, ATK guns. Citizen's Militia 350,000. 'League for National Defence' (some 200,000 active).

ROMANIA

Population: 23,000,000.
Military Service: Army, Air Force 16 months; Navy 30 months.
Total regular forces: 189,500 (109,000 conscripts).
NMP 1982: lei 628.8 bn. 1983: 654.5 bn.
Est GNP range 1982: $77.3–108.0 bn.
Est def budget 1983: lei 11.725 bn ($1.413 bn).
NMP growth: 2.6% (1982), 3.4% (1983).
Inflation: 17% (1982), 5.2% (1983).
Debt: $9.8 bn (1982).
$1 = (1982/3) lei 4.47 (off.), 8.3 (adj.).

Army: 150,000 (95,000 conscripts).
4 Army Areas:
2 tk divs (1 at Cat. 1, 1 at 2).
8 motor rifle divs (1 at Cat. 1, 3 at 2, 4 at 3).
3 mountain bdes/regts.
2 arty, 2 AA bdes, 4 arty, 2 AA arty, 5 ATK regts.
2 *Scud* SSM bdes.
2 AB regts.
AFV: 200 T-34, 1,000 T-54/-55, some M-77, 30 T-72 MBT; 400 BRDM-1/-2 scout cars; 2,600 BTR-50/-60, TAB-72 (BTR-60) APC.
Arty: 50 76mm, 50 D-44 85mm, M-1944 100mm towed, 250 SU-76/-100 SP guns; 600 M-1938/D-30 122mm, 150 M-1937/D-20

152mm guns/how; 175 BM-21/RO 122mm, 150 M-51 (ZIL) 130mm MRL; 30 *FROG*, 15 *Scud* SSM; 700 82mm, 200 120mm mor.
ATK: 57mm ATK guns; 73mm, 260 76mm and 82mm RCL; 120 AT-1 *Snapper* and AT-3 *Sagger* ATGW.
AD: 300 30mm, 37mm, 250 57mm, 85mm, 100mm towed AA guns; SA-6/-7 SAM.

RESERVES: 500,000+ (300,000 with service in last 5 years).

Navy: 7,500 (3,500 conscripts).
Black Sea Fleet, Danube Sqn, Coastal Defence.
1 *Tetal* frigate.
3 *Poti* corvettes.
6 *Osa*-I FAC(G) with 4 *Styx* SSM.
3 *Kronshtadt* large patrol craft.
19 Ch *Shanghai* FAC(P/ASW).
39 FAC(T): 21 Ch *Huchwan* hydrofoils⟨, 6 Sov P-4⟨, 12 *Epitrop*.
46 river patrol craft incl 18 VB-76 monitors.
16 minesweepers (4 GDR M-40 coastal, 12 Sov T-301 inshore); 8 Pol TR-40, 20 VD-141 minesweeping boats⟨; 2 MCM spt ships.
4 Mi-4 SAR hel.
Coastal Defence (2,000): HQ Constanta, 4 sectors; 18 arty btys with some 110 130mm, 150mm and 152mm guns, observer post tps, naval engineers. Would get 2 regts of naval inf on mobilization.
(On order: 2 *Tetal* frigates.)

RESERVES: 20,000.

Bases: Mangalia, Constanta; Danube: Braila, Giurgiu, Sulina, Tulcea.

Air Force: 32,000 (10,000 conscripts); 318 combat ac.
2 air divs: 4 combat regts:
  6 FGA sqns with 70 MiG-17.
  12 interceptor sqns: 11 with 200 MiG-21F/PF/U, 1 with 30 MiG-23.
  1 recce sqn with 18 Il-28.
  1 tpt regt with 4 Il-14, 3 Il-18, 2 Il-62, 11 An-24, 8 An-26, 4 Li-2, 1 Boeing 707.
  1 hel regt: 10 Mi-4, 25 Mi-8, 45 IAR-316B (*Alouette* III), 30 IAR-330 (*Puma*).
Trg ac: 40 L-29, 20 MiG-15UTI, 10 IAR-28MA; IAR-93 being introduced.
AAM: AA-2 *Atoll*.
1 AD div: 18 SAM sites with 108 SA-2.
(On order: some 45 IAR-93A, 165 IAR-93B FGA/trg ac.)

RESERVES: 45,000.

Para-Military Forces: 37,000. Border guards (17,000); 12 bdes. Ministry of Defence security troops (20,000); AFV, ATK guns. Local Defence: some 900,000 Patriotic Guard (perhaps 12,000 full time). Youth Homeland Defence: 650,000. 'Voluntary Sports Association'.

THE NORTH ATLANTIC TREATY

Although the year saw the first deployment of US *Pershing* II missiles in West Germany and GLCM (ground-launched cruise missiles) in Britain and Italy, much of the debate in NATO over the past twelve months has centred on the need to strengthen conventional forces. The basic principle – that only through reinforcement of conventional forces can NATO counter a Soviet advance in superior strength without early recourse to nuclear weapons – is generally accepted as valid. Any conventional force improvement that can raise the nuclear threshold is likely to be generally welcomed, but the precise direction of improvement is as yet by no means universally accepted throughout the Alliance.

Part of the disagreement stems from the fact that many of the so-called 'force multipliers' (systems to enhance the capability of the NATO defence by early and accurate identification of enemy activity, secure and durable communications to speed decision-making, command and control, weapons of precision to guarantee successful engagement of targets, penetration aids to by-pass enemy defences, etc.) depend for their effectiveness upon the detailed application of so-called high technology. Many of the weapons and systems now in the research and development phase are the products of American designers and manufacturers. There is naturally concern in Europe that many of the concepts of the high-technology battlefield may turn out to be extremely costly and may make European forces unduly dependent on the United States to the detriment of present and future European industrial development.

There is disagreement also over the most effective way to stop a Warsaw Pact conventional attack. Much of current thinking is focused on 'deep' strikes on the follow-on elements – the Pact second-echelon forces intended to give weight to deep penetrations and to subsequent exploitation of any breakthrough. Reservations are being expressed that forward defence may thus be weakened in favour of the deep-strike mission.

The facts of European geography play a significant part in the development of deep-strike doctrine. War on West German soil, for example, would produce enormous damage to the fabric of German society. Moving the area of destruction eastwards might therefore be regarded as desirable in principle, but the costs of new deep-strike weapons are likely to be high, and it seems highly doubtful whether it will prove possible to maintain forward defence at the same time. In addition, one would have to anticipate that the Soviet Union may also develop her own 'deep-strike' weapons, which would tend to shift the area of destruction back into West Germany.

Many in the United States have long criticized the West European partners for failing to assume an adequate share of the burden of defence against the Warsaw Pact. Comparisons between West European and US defence expenditures form the basis for much of this criticism. In 1978 NATO Ministers agreed to increase defence spending on conventional forces by 3% in real terms annually. Official NATO and IMF data suggest that the 3% goal has been met only by the US, Britain, Canada and France, whose defence spending has increased in percentage terms as follows:

	United States	Britain	Canada	France
1980	7.8%	4.9%	3.0%	4.0%
1981	7.8%	1.6%	4.0%	3.5%
1982	9.3%	5.2%	8.2%	1.0%
1983	11.1%	5.5%	4.5%	3.0%

Canada is certainly attempting to rebuild her conventional forces, but the others (especially France and the US) devote a significant proportion of their defence budgets to their nuclear forces. If spending on these nuclear forces is excluded, the national average growth rates are lower: some 6.5% for the US, about 4.0% for Britain and perhaps 2.0% for France. In Belgium, Denmark and the Netherlands, real defence spending actually decreased in 1983. Data from other official sources, such as Central Banks, which use different accounting procedures, suggest that in almost all NATO countries actual defence expenditures may indeed be lower than Defence Ministries have claimed.

The relative positions of the US and her European allies must be viewed, in part, in the light of their respective economic climates. In 1983 the US economy was characterized by strong growth, low inflation, declining unemployment and a rising dollar. This growth continued in early 1984, albeit at a slower rate. There was in the US a greater sense of optimism, of willingness to budget for growth. Political attitudes in the US towards defence have for some years now reflected a sense of perceived lack of security, and thus a desire to spend money on defence in order to achieve that security. Social and economic claims have been accorded lower priority, and the increased defence outlays which have marked the period since 1980 have demonstrated the US Government's commitment to enhanced defence. A comparable commitment from the European nations has been seen as fundamental to the health of the Alliance, and 1984 saw moves in the US Congress (the 'Nunn Amendment') to make US force levels in Europe contingent upon greater defence efforts on the part of Western Europe.

The economic recovery of the NATO Allies has undoubtedly lagged behind that of the United States. Throughout the period 1981–3 economic performance has been characterized by rising unemployment, mixed economic growth, declining exchange rates – which have a significant effect upon a country's ability to buy military equipment from the United States – severe capital flight to the higher interest rates paid in North America, mixed success against domestic inflation, and social pressures on the budget. Most severely hit were countries of the southern tier, especially Greece, Portugal and Turkey. Virtually all West European states have, with varying degrees of success, introduced measures to control inflation and to cut their respective budget deficits, but all are faced with rather ambitious social welfare programmes, and the high unemployment levels found throughout have placed heavy demands on welfare budgets. Nor is there the same perception of imminent threat as in the US, although there is no intention of compromising freedom. In the light of these circumstances, most West European governments believe that they are spending all they can afford on their defence establishments.

West Europeans are also sceptical of what they tend to regard as simplistic comparisons based on 'standard' criteria for defence expenditures. European nations argue that they bear other defence burdens, less clearly identified. These include indirect economic and social costs, such as those stemming from conscription (applicable to most European armed forces), while military use of public facilities and land, especially in West Germany, have no equivalent in the US. Because of their nature it is difficult to assess the true costs of these additional burdens, but they are politically relevant.

Nor is it easy to forecast when this situation is likely to ease. Operation, maintenance and capital costs are demonstrably higher in the military sector and are therefore subject to different inflationary pressure, usually higher than in the general economy. The OECD predicts that the US recovery will encourage economic growth in Europe and Canada through 1984 but 'with tight policies – dictated by concerns over budget deficits and inflation fears – the recovery outside North America seems likely to be weak and hesitant by past standards'.

The 3% real growth target was intended to upgrade conventional defences, to develop NATO infrastructure, to re-distribute NATO's costs more broadly across the Alliance, to facilitate US reinforcement of Europe and, overall, to reduce NATO's reliance on nuclear weapons. If past performance is an indicator, that figure is unlikely to be met, although some progress is being made. Moreover, most West European countries managed to increase their outlays and improve their military posture during the 1970s, when real defence spending in the US was decreasing. Some of the cushion from that investment still remains, although replacement of existing equipment with the more sophisticated wment still remains, although replacement of existing equipment with the more sophisticated weapons of the next generation will be costly. If it is true that little additional real investment can be achieved, there may be an increasingly strong initiatives to ensure more effective political and fiscal control of defence expenditure and military resources.

Economic pressures continue to have a significant impact on all national defence procurement. There is some evidence of closer attention to priorities, although budgetary constraints often impose delays in production schedules which result in overall increases in the unit costs of individual items. Co-operation in arms procurement, long a goal of NATO planners, continues to take place, but at a rather desultory pace. However, agreement was reached to begin a programme for the procurement of a NATO Standard Frigate. Initial US hesitation was overcome, but how many will be ordered remains to be seen. There has been co-operation between Germany and France over a new attack helicopter, and discussions have taken place between Germany, Britain, Italy, France and Spain over the joint procurement of the next generation of fighter aircraft.

There seems little doubt that the incorporation of advanced technology is going to add yet more inflationary pressure to defence procurement. In 1982 this was estimated by the US Congressional Budget Office to be 4.4% annually in real terms. Others suggest that real annual increases of the order of 8% are not unlikely. At the same time, the cost of munitions, spare parts and support facilities are likely to rise, as NATO attempts to raise stock levels to sustain a longer period of conventional conflict.

Joint NATO agreements include the following: artillery location systems; precision-guided 155mm munitions; battlefield target acquisition systems; Identification Friend or Foe (IFF) equipment standardization; passive electronic countermeasures (ECM) equipment for aircraft; electronic jamming systems for tactical aircraft; low-cost dispersal systems for sub-munitions; multiple-launcher rocket systems (MLRS); stand-off surveillance and target-acquisition systems; short-range anti-radiation missiles; and self-defence systems for battle-field helicopters. Other areas yet to be determined include agreement on runway attack munitions, very long-range target identification, the rapid and accurate transmission of data, improvement of command-and-control systems, and the development of better fighter air-craft, long-range remotely-piloted vehicles (RPV) and missiles for delivering conventional munitions and sub-munitions. It is possible, too, that some improvements can be achieved by greater use of existing assets, such as the rapid conversion of commercial aircraft in war for in-flight refuelling of combat aircraft – a practical and relatively inexpensive alternative to dedicated tankers, which are in markedly short supply in most West European air forces.

There has been a tentative move to revive the Western European Union (WEU), ostensibly to support and give political direction to the European contribution to NATO, and, in particular, to rationalize arms procurement. This is not without problems, as not all West European NATO nations are members of the WEU. At the same time, it is necessary to note a somewhat greater sense of urgency in the Franco-German staff talks, perhaps presaging a greater French interest in conventional co-operation with NATO, and increased emphasis on the work of the Independent European Programme Group (IEPG). Thus the West European members of NATO appear to be regarding the need to co-operate with rather greater seriousness – not least because of growing concern over the need to retain the goodwill of the US and to ensure that their interests are preserved within the Alliance – but it remains to be seen in which direction this somewhat vague impulse will lead.

BELGIUM

Population: 9,900,000.
Military service: 8 or 10 months.*
Total armed forces: 93,607 (3,559 women; 31,908 conscripts).
GDP 1982: B fr 3,940 bn. ($86.231 bn). Est GDP 1983: 4,149 bn. ($81.143 bn).
Def exp 1983: B fr 94.440 bn ($1.847 bn); NATO defn $2.682 bn. Def budget 1984: 99.000 bn ($1.769 bn); NATO defn $2.575 bn.
GDP growth: –2% (1981), –1.3% (1982).
Inflation: 8.7% (1982). 7.7% (1983).

Debt 1982: $31.0 bn.
$1 = francs 45.691 (1982), 51.132 (1983), 55.975 (mid-1984).

Army: 65,102 (incl Medical Service; 26,163 conscripts).
1 Corps HQ, 2 Div HQ.
1 armd bde (2 tk, 2 mech inf, 1 SP arty bns, spt units).
3 mech inf bdes each with 1 tk, 2 mech inf, 1 SP

* Conscripts serve 8 months if posted to Germany, 10 months if serving in Belgium.

arty bns, spt units.
1 para-cdo regt.
3 recce bns.
1 tk bn.
2 mot inf bns.
3 arty bns.
1 SSM bn with 4 *Lance*.
4 AD bns: 2 SAM with 39 *Improved HAWK*; 2 AA with *Gepard*.
5 engr bns (3 fd, 1 bridge, 1 eqpt).
4 lt aviation sqns.
AFV: 330 *Leopard* MBT, 119 *Scorpion* lt tks; 138 *Scimitar* AFV, 1,355 APC incl 130 FMC, 130 M-113, 262 *Spartan*, AMX-VCI (phasing out), M-75 (with reserves).
Arty: 15 203mm how; 90 M-108 105mm (to be retired), 25 M-44 (to be retired), 39 M-109 155mm (being upgraded), 10 M-110 203mm SP how; 5 *Lance* SSM.
ATK: 80 JPz C-90mm SP ATK guns; *Milan* ATGW; 40 *Striker* AFV with *Swingfire* ATGW.
AD: 36 20mm, 54 *Gepard* 35mm SP AA guns; 39 *Improved HAWK* SAM.
Avn: 5 *Islander* ac; 62 *Alouette* II hel.
(On order: 514 MICV, 475 M-113A2 APC; 124 M-109A2 155mm SP how.)

RESERVES: 160,000 (incl 40,000 Medical Service), some on immediate recall status; 1 mech, 1 mot inf bdes; combat, combat spt, log spt tps. Territorial defence: 11 mot inf regts, 4 mot inf bns.

Navy: 4,557 (1,227 conscripts).
4 E-71 frigates with 4 *Exocet* MM-38 SSM, 1 × 8 *Sea Sparrow* SAM.
7 US Type 498 ocean minehunters/mine-sweepers.
6 US Type 60 coastal MCM (4 in reserve).
14 *Herstal* inshore minesweepers.
2 log spt and comd ships (MCM).
6 river patrol boats.
3 *Alouette* III hel.
(On order: 10 *Flower* (tripartite) MCM ships.)

Bases: Kallo, Ostend, Zeebrugge.

RESERVES: 4,500 (on immediate recall status).

Air Force: 20,948 (4,518 conscripts); 147 combat ac.
5 FGA sqns: 3 with 54 *Mirage* 5BA/5BD; 2 with 22 F-16A, 14 F-16B.
2 AD sqns with 34 F-16A, 5 F-16B.
1 recce sqn with 18 *Mirage* 5BR (to get F-16).
2 tpt sqns with 12 C-130H, 2 Boeing 727QC, 3 HS-748, 5 *Merlin* IIIA, 2 *Falcon* 20.
1 SAR hel sqn with 3 HSS-1, 5 *Sea King*.
2 liaison sqns with 23 Fouga CM-170.
4 trg sqns: 2 with 28 SF-260MB, 2 with 32 *Alpha Jet*.
AAM: *Sidewinder*.

4 SAM sqns with 36 *Nike Hercules* (modernized).
1 NADGE command reporting centre, associated radar.
(On order: 34 F-16A ftr ac, 80 BDX (*Timoney*) APC.)

RESERVES: 14,000.

Joint Service: 3,000.

Forces Abroad: Germany: 24,794; 1 corps HQ, 1 div HQ, 1 armd, 1 mech inf bdes; 3 recce, 1 tk, 3 arty, 1 SSM, 2 AA, 3 engr bns; 3 aviation sqns, 6 *Nike* SAM sqns.
Para-Military Forces: Gendarmerie 16,200; 62 FN, 4 RM/62F armd cars, 5 *Alouette* II, 3 *Puma* hel.

BRITAIN

Population: 56,000,000.
Military service: voluntary.
Total armed forces: 325,909 (incl 16,246 women and some 9,732 enlisted outside Britain).
GDP 1982: $274.99 bn ($459.696 bn). 1983: 300.76 bn ($448.963 bn).
Def budget 1983/4: £15.973 bn* ($23.844 bn); NATO defn: $24.472 bn. 1984/5: 17.033 bn ($23.664 bn): NATO defn $24.216 bn.
GDP growth: 2% (1982). 3% (1983).
Inflation: 5.4% (1982). 5.3% (1983).
Debt 1983: $68.3 bn.
$1 = £ 0.5299 (1981/2), 0.5982 (1982/3), 0.6699 (1983/4), 0.7198 (mid-1984).

Strategic Forces: (2,300):
SLBM: 4 *Resolution* SSBN, each with 16 *Polaris* A3 msls with 3 MRV (being fitted with *Chevaline*).
Ballistic Missile Early Warning System (BMEWS) station at Fylingdales.

Army: 161,539 (incl 6,573 women and 9,357 enlisted outside Britain, of which 8,074 are Gurkhas).
1 corps, 3 armd, 1 inf, 1 arty divs, 25 bdes, 1 Field Force HQ.
13 armd regts (2 trg).
6 armd recce regts.
47 inf bns.
6 Gurkha inf bns.
3 para bns (1 in inf, 2 in para role).
1 special air service (SAS) regt.
1 msl regt with *Lance* SSM (4 btys, each 3 msls).
3 AD regts with *Rapier* and *Blowpipe* SAM: 2 of 3 btys with 36 launchers, 1 (in BAOR) of 4 btys, 48 launchers; 2 btys SP.

---

* Includes replacement costs for Falkland losses.

19 arty regts: 2 hy, 8 SP, 6 fd (1 cdo), 1 msl, 1 GW, 1 locating; 3 indep *Blowpipe* SAM btys.

12 engr regts: 3 armd div, 1 armd, 1 amph, 6 fd, 1 Gurkha.

4 army aviation regts; 16 sqns (1 cdo), 5 indep flts; 2 trg sqns, 6 flts.

AFV: some 70 *Challenger*, 900 *Chieftain* MBT (60 in reserve), 271 FV 101 *Scorpion* lt tks; 243 FV 601 *Saladin* armd cars; 290 FV 107 *Scimitar*, 1,429 *Ferret*, 200 *Fox* recce; 2,338 FV 432, 600 FV 603 *Saracen*, 60 FV 103 *Spartan*, 500 FV 1611, some *Saxon* APC.

Arty: 100 towed, 120 FV 433 *Abbot* 105mm SP, 4 5.5-in. (140mm) trg, 31 M-107 175mm SP guns; 95 FH-70 towed, 101 M-109/A2/A3 155mm SP, 16 M-110 203mm SP how; 12 *Lance* SSM.

ATK: *Carl Gustav* 84mm, 120mm RCL; *Milan*, *Swingfire* ATGW.

AD: *Blowpipe*, 108 *Rapier* (some 16 SP) SAM.

Avn: 9 *Beaver* AL-1, 22 *Chipmunk* ac; 41 *Scout*; 8 *Alouette* II, 155 *Gazelle* AH-1, 110 *Lynx* AH-1 hel, some with *TOW*.

14 landing craft (2 tk, 12 med); 3 patrol craft, 2 hovercraft; 3 log ships.

(On order: Some 62 *Challenger* MBT; 250 MCV-80 MICV; some 50 AT-105 *Saxon* APC; 10 227mm MLRS; *LAW*-80 RL, *Milan*, *TOW* ATGW; some 150 *Rapier* (100 SP), 48 *Blowpipe* SAM; 5 *Gazelle*, 24 *Lynx* AH-5 hel (6 with *TOW*), 3 patrol craft, 12 combat spt craft.)

DEPLOYMENT (see also Forces Abroad, below):

United Kingdom Land Forces (UKLF): Reinforcements for 1 Br Corps, Germany: 1 inf div HQ; 2 inf Regular, 2 inf TA bdes; *United Kingdom Mobile Force* (UKMF): 1 air portable inf bde and log spt gp; *Allied Command Europe Mobile Force (LAND)* (AML(L)): 1 inf bn, 1 armd recce, 1 sigs sqns, 1 arty bty, 1 log bn; 1 avn flt; Home Defence: 10 inf, 1 AB bdes.

HQ Northern Ireland: (some 9,400); 2 inf bde HQ, 8 major units in inf role (6 resident, 2 temporary inf bns), 1 SAS, 1 engr sqn, 1 army aviation regt of 2 sqns.

RESERVES: 219,642: Regular Reserves 141,769. Territorial Army (TA) 70,629 (to be 75,000 by 1986): 2 armd, 3 lt recce regts, 35 inf bns, 2 SAS, 2 fd, 3 AD, 7 engr regts. Ulster Defence Regiment 6,929 (4,200 part time): 10 bns (internal security role in Northern Ireland only in peacetime). Home Service Force: (315, to be increased to 5,000) 4 coys; 2-year pilot scheme.

Navy: 71,281 (incl Fleet Air Arm, Royal Marines, 3,929 women and 375 enlisted outside Britain); 56 major surface combat vessels (incl 2 LPD).

Submarines, attack: 28.

13 SSN (2 *Trafalgar*, 6 *Swiftsure*, 3 *Churchill*, 2 *Valiant*); 15 SS (13 *Oberon*, 2 *Porpoise*).

Surface Ships:

3 ASW carriers with 5 *Sea Harrier* V/STOL ac, 9 *Sea King* hel: 2 *Invincible* (1 more in late 1984) with 1 × 2 *Sea Dart* SAM, *Phalanx* AD system, 1 *Hermes* (future under review) 2 × 4 *Seacat* SAM.

12 GW destroyers: 2 *County* (1 to be sold 1984) with 1 × 2 *Seaslug*, 2 × 4 *Seacat* SAM, 4 *Exocet* SSM, 1 *Lynx* HAS-2 hel; 1 Type 82 with 1 × 2 *Sea Dart* SAM, 1 *Ikara* ASW; 9 Type 42 with 1 × 2 *Sea Dart*, 1 *Lynx* hel.

42 GP frigates: 6 Type 22 with 4 *Exocet* SSM, 2 × 6 *Sea Wolf* SAM, 2 *Lynx* hel; 6 Type 21 with 4 × 1 *Exocet* SSM, 1 × 4 *Seacat* SAM, 1 *Lynx* hel; 24 *Leander* (1 trg) with 1 *Wasp/Lynx* (7 with 4 *Exocet*, 3 × 4 *Seacat*; 8 with *Ikara* ASW, 2 × 4 *Seacat*; 5 with 1 × 4 *Exocet*, 1 × 6 *Sea Wolf*) (1 converting); 6 *Rothesay* (Type 12) with 1 × 4 *Seacat*, 1 *Wasp* hel.

1 *Whitby* (Type 12) ASW frigate (trg), to be replaced by *Leander* and retired end 1984.

37 minesweepers/minehunters: 6 *Hunt*, 28 *Ton* (9 reserves, 7 Fishery Patrol), 1 *River*, 2 auxiliaries (charter).

1 *Abdiel* MCM spt ship.

35 patrol craft: 3 *Peacock*, 7 *Island*, 2 *Castle*, 3 *Ton*, 4 *Bird* (2 trg), 2 *Loyal*, 3 *Falkland Islands* ex-tugs, 4 Fleet tenders (trg); 2 32-metre; 5 *Tracker* FAC (reserves).

2 assault ships (LPD) each with 4 LCM, 4 LCVP, 4 × 4 *Seacat* SAM.

Amph vessels: 6 landing ships incl 2 commercial (leased) (in Royal Fleet Auxiliary (RFA)), 2 large landing craft (Army), 13 LCM, 8 lt LCT, 29 LCVP.

1 ice patrol, 1 sub tender, 11 survey ships, 1 survey craft, 1 Royal Yacht (hospital ship).

2 hel spt ships, 1 forward repair ship.

1 BH-7 hovercraft.

ROYAL FLEET AUXILIARY (RFA): (2,600):
Naval vessels, civilian crews.
  15 tankers (1 chartered, being mod).
  4 fleet replenishment ships.

Included in above refitting or in reserve are: 1 SSBN, 3 SSN, 3 diesel subs, 3 frigates, 1 MCM, 1 LPD, 1 landing ship (RFA).

(On order: 1 ASW carrier, 3 *Trafalgar* SSN, 1 Type-2400 SS, 3 Type 42 destroyers, 6 Type 22 frigates, 5 *Hunt*, 11 Fleet MCM, 2 *Peacock*, 14 trg patrol craft, 3 LCT, 1 container ship (hel carrier auxiliary), 1 fleet tender; 72 *Trident* II SLBM, 2 *Phalanx* 20mm AD systems, *Sea Eagle*, 300 *Harpoon* SSM, *Javelin, Seawolf, Lightweight Seawolf* SAM.)

Bases: Devonport, Faslane, Portland, Portsmouth, Rosyth.

FLEET AIR ARM: 26 combat ac, 177 combat hel (incl some 53 in trg sqns).

3 ftr sqns (2 afloat, 1 trg) with 16 *Sea Harrier* FRS-1.

5 ASW hel sqns: 4 with 64 *Sea King* HAS-2/-5; 2 embarked); 1 with 5 HAS-5, 2 *Sea King* AEW (mod HAS-2); 1 with 2 *Sea King* HAS-2.

57 ASW hel flts (each 1 ac): 35 with *Lynx* HAS-2/-3; 22 with *Wasp* HAS-1.

2 cdo assault sqns: 1 with 9 *Sea King* HC-4 (to get 8 more; new sqn to form); 1 with 22 *Wessex* HU-5/HC-4.

1 ac trg sqn with 8 *Sea Harrier* FRS-1, 3 T-4N.

6 hel trg sqns: 1 with 10 *Wessex* HU-5; 2 with 22 *Sea King* HAS-2/-5; 1 with 11 *Lynx* HAS-2/-3; 1 with 10 *Wasp* HAS-1; 1 with 19 *Gazelle* HT-2.

5 hel flts with *Wasp* (hydrography/recce).

1 SAR sqn with 7 *Wessex* HU-5, 1 SAR/fleet requirements sqn with 3 *Wessex* HU-5 hel, 2 HS-125 (VIP) tpt ac.

1 observer trg sqn with 16 *Jetstream* T-2, 1 trg flt with 13 *Chipmunk* T-10.

Other ac incl 12 *Canberra* T-22/T-18, 27 *Hunter* T-7/-8/GA-1.

ASM: *Sea Skua*.

(On order: 14 *Sea Harrier* FRS-1, 4 *Jetstream* Mk-3 ac; 13 *Sea King* HAS-5, 15 *Sea King* HC-4, 3 *Lynx* HAS-3 hel.)

ROYAL MARINES: (7,571).

1 cdo bde with 3 cdo gps; 1 cdo arty regt, 2 cdo engr sqns (1 Regular, 1 Reserve) (with army); 1 lt hel sqn, 1 log regt, spt units.

1 Special Boat and 1 Assault sqns.

18 105mm lt guns; 18 81mm mor; *Milan* ATGW; *Blowpipe* SAM; 12 *Gazelle* AH-1, 4 *Lynx* AH-1 hel.

(On order: 2 *Lynx* hel.)

RESERVES: 34,928. Navy: Regular 23,611; Volunteer 5,320: 4 Regional Divisions. 11 MCM, 8 patrol vessels. Auxiliary Service: 2,800; 72 units, emergency assistance. Marines: Regular 2,217; Volunteer 980; 1 Assault sqn.

Air Force: 93,089 (incl 5,744 women); some 620 combat ac.

13 strike/attack sqns: 5 with 80 *Tornado* GR-1, 1 more converting; 2 with 25 *Buccaneer* S-2A/B (to retire); 4 with 48 *Jaguar* GR-1, 6 T-2.

5 close support sqns: 3 with 36 *Harrier* GR-3/T-4; 2 with 24 *Jaguar*.

8 interceptor sqns: 2 with 24 *Lightning* F-6/F-3/T-5; 6 with 72 *Phantom* (4 with FGR-2, 2 with FG-1); (36 more ac in reserve); (*Tornado* F-2 to come into service 1984).

2 recce sqns with 24 *Jaguar* GR-1, 1 flt with 3 *Canberra* PR-9.

4 MR sqns with 28 *Nimrod* MR-1/-1A/-2 (*Harpoon* ASM, *Sidewinder* AAM being fitted).

1 AEW sqn with 6 *Shackleton* AEW-2 (5 in reserve); (5 *Nimrod* AEW-3 to be phased in).

3 tanker sqns: 2 with 16 *Victor* K-2; 1 with 4 *Tristar* 500, 9 VC-10 (5 K-2, 4 K-3; being phased in).

1 strategic tpt sqn with 11 VC-10CI, 2 *Tristar* 500.

4 tac tpt sqns with 41 C-130H incl 6 C-130HC3.

3 comms sqns with 6 HS-125 CC1/2, 4 *Andover*, 6 *Pembroke*, 1 BAe-146-100 ac; 1 *Gazelle* hel.

Queen's Flt with 3 *Andover* ac, 2 *Wessex* hel.

3 ECM/target facilities/calibration sqns with 31 *Canberra*, 3 *Nimrod* MR-1, 5 *Andover* E-3/C-1.

12 OCU: 1 NATO Trilateral Trg Establishment with 21 Br, 22 FRG, 7 It *Tornado* GR-1; 11 others with: 22 *Tornado* GR-1, 9 *Buccaneer* Mk 2, 18 *Phantom* FGR-2, 20 *Jaguar* GR-1/T-2, 21 *Harrier* GR-3/T-4, 3 *Nimrod*, 4 *Canberra* B-2/T-4, 5 C-130, 7 *Victor* K-2 ac; 4 *Wessex* HC-2, 5 *Puma* HC-1, 2 *Sea King* HAR-3, 6 CH-47 *Chinook* hel.

2 tac weapons units with 6 *Hunter* F-6/GA-9/ T-7, 74 *Hawk* T-1, 2 *Jet Provost*.

7 hel sqns: 5 tac tpt (1 with 20 *Wessex*, 2 with 26 *Puma* HC-1, 2 with 25 CH-47 *Chinook* HC-1); 9 SAR flts (5 with 18 *Wessex* HAR-2, 4 with 14 *Sea King* HAR-3).

Trg units with 47 *Hawk* T-1, 145 *Jet Provost*, 11 *Jetstream* T-1, 112 *Bulldog* T-1, 60 *Chipmunk* T-10, 19 *Dominie* T-1, 1 *Husky* T-1 ac; 5 *Whirlwind*, 14 *Wessex* HC-2, 22 *Gazelle* HT-3 hel.

AAM: *Sidewinder, Sparrow, Red Top, Firestreak, Sky Flash*.

ASM: *Martel, Harpoon*.

2 SAM sqns with 64 *Bloodhound* 2.

(On order: 4 *Harrier* GR-3, some T-4, 15 *Phantom* F Mk 3 (F-4J), 123 *Tornado* (out of 220 GR-1 FGA, 165 F-2 AD planned), 11 *Nimrod* AEW-3, 4 HS-125-700, 1 BAe-146-100 (VIP); 9 VC-10K-2/-3 ac; 7 *Chinook*, 3 *Sea King* HAR hel; AIM-9L *Sidewinder*, 12 *Rapier* SAM, *Sky Flash* AAM; *Sea Eagle* ASM; 6 AR-3D AD radar.)

ROYAL AIR FORCE REGIMENT:

4 wing HQ.

6 SAM sqns (*Rapier*) and 5 lt armd sqns.

36 *Scorpion* lt tks; 90 *Spartan* APC; SAM.

DEPLOYMENT:

Strike Command: 3 Gps; operational home command responsible for the UK Air Defence Region and Near and Far East; overseas command (RAF Germany, Belize and the Falklands).

Support Command: training supply and maintenance support of other commands.

RESERVES: 29,893. Regular 28,962. Volunteer 931: 1 air movements sqn; 4 def, 6 fd def sqns RAF Regt. Auxiliary: 6 sqns.

Forces Abroad: Army: 72,176. Navy/Marines: 5,142. Air Force: 16,655.

Antarctica: Navy: 1 ice patrol ship.

Ascension Island: Navy: Det 3 *Wessex* HU-5 hel. RAF: *Victor*, *Hercules* C-1P tanker dets.

Belize: 1,500. Army: some 1,200; 1 inf bn, 1 armd recce tp, 1 fd arty bty, 1 lt AD (*Blowpipe*) tp, 1 engr sqn, 1 hel flt (4 *Gazelle* AH-1). Navy: 1 destroyer/frigate (guard ship), 1 spt ship. RAF: (200); 1 flt (4 *Harrier* GR-3 FGA, 4 *Puma* hel), 1 *Rapier* AD det (4 units) RAF Regt.

Brunei: Army: 1 Gurkha inf bn, det hel sqn. Royal Marines: 1 coy.

Canada: Army: training and liaison team.

Cyprus: Army: 3,367: UNFICYP (some 760); 1 inf bn less 2 coys, 1 armd recce sqn, 1 hel flt, engr sqn and log spt. Garrison: 1 inf bn plus 2 inf coys, 1 armd recce (8 tps), 1 engr spt sqns, 1 hel flt. RAF: 1,445; 1 hel sqn (incl 1 flt (4 ac) with UNFICYP), periodic dets of other ac, 1 fd sqn RAF Regt. Navy/Marines: 19.

Egypt (Sinai MFO): 35 technical and admin personnel.

Falkland Islands: 4,000. Army: 1 inf bn gp, armd recce sqn, 1 arty, 1 engr, (4 fd, 1 spt sqns) regts, 1 sqn army air. Navy: 1 SSN, 1 ASW carrier (*Harrier* and *Sea King* ASW hel sqns), 4 escorts, spt and auxiliary ships. RAF: 1 *Phantom* sqn, 1 *Harrier* flt, 2 *Buccaneer*, 1 *Hercules* K-1 ac dets, 3 *Sea King* HAR-3, 4 *Chinook* hel dets, 1 *Rapier* SAM sqn. (Details may vary through the year.)

Germany: British Army of the Rhine (BAOR): 56,761; 1 corps HQ, 3 armd divs, 1 arty div, 7 armed, 1 air mobile bdes; 3 army air regts (10 sqns, 2 indep flts), 3 AD regts. Berlin Inf Bde: 3,000; 3 inf bns, one armd sqn. RAF:10,200; 12 ac, 2 hel sqns: 2 *Phantom* FGR-2, 2 *Tornado*, 5 *Jaguar* (1 recce), (to be replaced by 6 sqns of *Tornado*), 2 *Harrier*, 1 *Pembroke* (comms); 1 *Puma*, 1 *Chinook* (tpt); (RAF regt) 3 *Rapier* SAM, 1 fd sqn.

Gibraltar: Army: 816; 1 inf bn, 1 engr team, 1 arty surveillance tp. Navy: 793; 1 frigate, 1 spt ship; Marine dets. RAF: 427; periodic *Jaguar* ac dets.

Hong Kong: Army: 7,840; (British 1,897, Gurkha 4,703, H.K. Regt 1,240); Gurkha Field Force with 1 Br, 4 Gurkha inf bns, 1 each Gurkha engr, sigs, tpt regts, 1 hel sqn (−) with 12 *Scout* AH-1, spt units. Navy: 656 (375 locally enlisted); 3 *Ton*, 2 *Peacock* patrol craft, 1 Marine Raiding sqn. RAF: 269; 1 *Wessex* sqn.

Indian Ocean (intermittent): 1–2 destroyers/frig-ates, 2 spt ships; Diego Garcia, 1 naval det.

Military Advisers: 700 in 30 countries incl Belize, Brunei, Kenya, Kuwait, Nigeria, Oman, Saudi Arabia, UAE, Uganda, Zimbabwe.

CANADA

Population: 25,000,000.
Military service: voluntary.
Total armed forces: 82,858 (6,667 women).*
GDP 1981: $C 350.65 bn ($US 291.528 bn), 1982: $C 369.720 bn ($US 298.571 bn).
Def budget 1983/4: $C 7.986 bn ($US 6.443 bn); NATO defn $US 7.061 bn. 1984/5: $C 8.767 bn ($US 6.771 bn); NATO defn $US 7.483 bn.
GDP growth: −4.4% (1982), 3% (1983).
Inflation: 9.7% (1982). 4.6% (1983).
Debt 1982: $99.5 bn.
   $US1 = $C 1.2028 (1981/2), 1.2383 (1982/3), 1.2394 (1983/4), 1.2948 (mid-1984).

Army (Land Forces): 13,000.*
Mobile Command (about 16,000 land and air).†
2 bde gps: each 1 armd regt, 3 inf bns, 1 arty (2 close spt, 1 AD btys), 1 engr regts, spt units.
1 special service force (4,000): 1 armd regt, 1 inf bn, 1 AB, 1 arty, 1 engr regts, 1 spt unit.
1 mech bde gp (under command Canadian Forces, Europe): 1 armd regt, 2 mech inf bns, 1 med SP arty, 1 mech engr regts, 1 spt unit, 1 lt hel sqn.
114 *Leopard* C-1 MBT; 100 *Lynx*, 195 *Cougar* AFV; 955 M-113, 269 *Grizzly* APC; 12 model 56 (L-5) pack, 159 towed 105mm, 50 M-109 155mm SP how; 633 *Carl Gustav* 84mm RCL; 108 *TOW* ATGW; 48 L-40/60 40mm AA guns; 122 *Blowpipe* SAM.

RESERVES: about 16,000 Militia; 131 combat arms units and spt units (all in Mobile Command), plus 1,560 in Communications Reserves. (Reserve strength (all components) to increase to 40,000 by end 1989.)

Navy (Maritime Forces): 5,500.*
Maritime Command (MARCOM; about 8,700).†
3 *Oberon* subs.

---

* The Canadian Armed Forces were unified in 1968. Of the total strength, some 49,000 are not identified by service.
† Mobile Command commands army combat forces, and Maritime Command all naval forces. Air Command commands all air forces, but Maritime Command has operational control of maritime air forces. Mobile Command has operational control of 10 TAG. HQ 4 ATAF in Europe has operational control of 1 CAG. There is also a Communications Command and a Canadian Forces Training System.

20 ASW destroyers: 4 DD-280, each with 2 *Sea King* hel, 2 × 4 *Sea Sparrow* SAM; 2 *Annapolis*, 6 *St Laurent* with 1 *Sea King* hel (to be retired from 1989); 4 *Improved Restigouche*, 4 *Mackenzie* with *ASROC*.
3 replenishment spt ships (one in refit), each with 3 *Sea King* hel.
6 coastal patrol ships (trg).
6 small patrol craft.
(On order: 6 ASW frigates.)

DEPLOYMENT AND BASES:
Atlantic: 3 subs, 13 destroyers (1 in reserve), 2 replenishment spt ships. Halifax.
Pacific: 10 destroyers (2 in reserve), 1 replenishment spt ship. Esquimalt.

RESERVES: about 3,250.

Air Force: 15,300;* some 160 combat ac, 32 combat hel.
Air Command (23,000).†
1 Air Group (1 CAG, Germany):
  3 fighter sqns with 42 CF-104/-104D (to get 54 CF-188 (F-18)).
Fighter Group:
  2 FGA sqns with 20 CF-116 (F-5A), 4 CF-116D (F-5D) (NATO assigned).
  1 trg sqn with 4 CF-116, 21 CF-116D.
  1 trg sqn 31 CF-188D (getting more).
  3 AD sqns with 38 CF-101 *Voodoo*, (2 to get CF-188; trg sqns to augment.)
  1 ECM trg sqn with 3 CC-117 (*Falcon* 20, to be 5); 17 CT-133, CF-101.
  4 main, 17 auxiliary sites of Distant Early Warning (DEW) Line; Semi-Automatic Ground Environment (SAGE).
  24 long-range radar sites (CADIN/Pine Tree Line).
  1 space tracking and identification site.
10 Tactical Air Group (10 TAG):
  6 hel sqns with 31 CH-135 (UH-1N), 36 CH-136, 7 CH-147 (*Chinook*).
Maritime Air Group:
  3 maritime patrol sqns: 18 CP-140 *Aurora*.
  1 MR, 1 reserve sqns: 15 CP-121 *Tracker* (4 in reserve).
  2 ASW, 1 trg hel sqns: 32 CH-124 (*Sea King*; afloat).
  2 utility sqns: 9 T-33, 3 CP-121 ac, 2 CH-135 hel.
Air Transport Group:
  5 tpt sqns: 3 with 26 CC-130E/H; 1 with 5 CC-137 (Boeing 707); 1 with 7 CC-109 *Cosmopolitan*, 5 CC-117 *Falcon*, 2 CC-132 (DHC-7R), 2 CC-144 *Challenger*.
  4 tpt/SAR sqns (2 MARCOM-assigned) with 11 CC-115 (DHC-5), 8 CC-138 (DHC-6) ac; 3 CH-113 *Labrador*, 7 CH-113A *Voyageur* (being uprated); 3 CH-135 (UH-1N) hel.
  1 SAR unit with 3 CH-113.

4 base hel flts with 9 CH-118 *Iroquois*, 2 CH-135.
Training Group:
  3 schools: 1 with 18 CT-134 *Musketeer* ac, 14 CH-139 hel; 1 with 83 CT-114 *Tutor*; 1 with 2 CT-134, 17 CT-114; 2 CC-129 (C-47).
  1 demonstration unit with 11 CT-114.
(On order: 138 CF-188 (113 F-18A, 25 -18B) *Hornet* ftrs; 1 CC-132 (DHC-7R *Ranger*).

RESERVES: 950. Air Reserve Group; 2 wings with 16 CH-136 hel, 1 sqn MARCOM-assigned. Other ac incl 18 CF-104 (2 D), 3 CC-129.

Forces Abroad: Europe: 6,700; HQ (1,440); 1 mech bde gp (3,200) with 59 *Leopard* 1 MBT, 375 M-113 APC/recce, 24 M-109 155mm SP how, 40 *TOW* ATGW, 50 40mm AA guns, 70 *Blowpipe* SAM, 11 CH-136 *Kiowa* hel. 2,500 reinforcements in Canada.
  1 Air Group: (760): 3 fighter sqns with 42 CF-104/-104D; (54 CF-188 to replace); 1 det with 2 CC-132 and 4 CT-133 liaison ac.
Cyprus (UNFICYP): 515.
Syria/Israel (UNDOF): 221.
Other Middle East (UNTSO): 20.

Para-Military Forces: Coast Guard: 6,561 (civilian-1manned): 25 icebreakers, 16 SAR patrol vessels, 2 DHC-7R ac, 37 hel, 3 SRN-5/-6 hovercraft. Cdn Rangers: 1,300.

DENMARK

Population: 5,150,000.
Military service: 9 months.
Total armed forces: 31,400 (9,500 conscripts).
GDP 1982: Kr 469.78 bn ($56.380 bn).
Est GDP 1983: Kr 515.60 bn ($56.380 bn).
Def exp 1983: Kr 10.314 bn‡ ($1.128 bn); NATO defn $1.221 bn. 1984 budget: 11.342 bn ($1.127 bn); NATO defn n.a.
GDP growth: 3.1% (1982). 2% (1983).
Inflation: 10% (1982). 6.9% (1983).
Debt 1982: $32.2 bn.
  $1 = kroner 8.3324 (1982), 9.145 (1983), 10.0643 (mid-1984).

---

* The Canadian Armed Forces were unified in 1968. Of the total strength, some 49,000 are not identified by service.
† Mobile Command commands army combat forces, and Maritime Command all naval forces. Air Command commands all air forces, but Maritime Command has operational control of maritime air forces. Mobile Command has operational control of 10 TAG. HQ 4 ATAF in Europe has operational control of 1 CAG. There is also a Communications Command and a Canadian Forces Training System.
‡ At January 1983 price level.

Army: 18,100 (6,800 conscripts).
2 div HQ.
5 mech inf bdes, each with 1 tk, 2 mech, 1 arty bns, 1 AD bty, 1 engr coy, spt units.
5 regimental combat teams, each with 2 inf, 1 arty bns, 1 ATK gp.
2 indep recce bns.
1 Army aviation unit, some 8 platoons.
AFV: 120 *Leopard* 1, 88 *Centurion* MBT; 48 M-41 lt tks; 650 M-113, 68 M-106 mor-armed APC.
Arty: 24 155mm guns; 144 105mm, 96 155mm, 12 M-115 203mm towed, 72 M-109 155mm SP how; 81mm, 120mm mor.
ATK: 400 *Carl Gustav* 84mm, 252 106mm RCL; *LAW* RL; 140 *TOW* ATGW.
AD: 36 L/60 40mm AA guns; *Hamlet* (*Redeye*) SAM.
Avn: 16 Saab T-17 lt ac; 12 Hughes 500M hel.

RESERVES: 125,400. Augmentation Force 6,000, subject to immediate recall; Field Army Reserve 45,000, comprising 15,000 Covering Force Reserve (to bring units to war strength and add 1 mech bn to each bde) and 30,000 to provide regimental combat teams, combat and log spt; Regional Defence Force 14,000 with 9 inf, 4 arty bns, ATK sqns, spt units; Army Home Guard 60,400 (8,400 women).

Navy: 5,900 (1,200 conscripts).
5 subs: 2 *Narhvalen*, 3 *Delfinen*.
5 frigates with 2 × 4 *Harpoon* SSM, *Sea Sparrow* SAM: 2 *Peder Skram*, 3 *Niels Juel*.
5 *Hvidbjørnen* fishery-protection frigates with 1 *Lynx* hel.
10 *Willemoes* FAC(G) with *Harpoon* SSM.
6 *Søløven* FAC(T) (2 in reserve).
22 large patrol craft: 8 *Daphne*, 3 *Agdlek*, 2 *Maagen*, 9 *Barsø*.
5 *Botved* coastal patrol craft.
7 minelayers: 4 *Falster*, 2 *Lindormen*, 1 *Langeland*.
6 US Type 60 coastal minesweepers.
Coastal defence unit: 2 coastal fortresses with 155mm guns.
Air: 8 *Lynx* hel (4 embarked).
(On order: *Harpoon* SSM, *Sea Sparrow* SAM.)

Bases: Copenhagen, Korsør, Frederikshavn.

RESERVES: 3,800; Navy Home Guard 5,200 (1,500 women): 37 coastal patrol craft.

Air Force: 7,400 (1,500 conscripts); 96 combat ac.
Tactical Air Command:
3 FGA sqns with 48 F-16A/B.
1 FGA/interceptor sqn with 16 F-35XD *Draken*.
1 FGA/recce sqn with 16 RF-35XD *Draken*.

1 interceptor sqn with 16 F-104G.
Air Materiel Command:
1 tpt sqn, 3 comms flts, with 3 C-130H, 3 *Gulfstream* III, 7 Saab T-17.
1 SAR sqn with 8 S-61A hel.
Flying School: 15 T-17.
AD gp: 1 SAM bn, 6 btys: with 36 *Improved HAWK* (2 more to be formed).
AAM: *Sidewinder*.
ASM: *Bullpup*.
(In reserve: 9 F-16.)
(On order: AIM-9L *Sidewinder* AAM.)

RESERVES: 9,400; Air Force Home Guard 12,400 (1,800 women).

Forces Abroad:
Cyprus (UNFICYP): 1 bn (341).

FRANCE

Population: 54,600,000.
Military service: 12 months and voluntary system 16–24 months.
Total armed forces: 471,350* (12,400 women; 244,900 conscripts).
GDP 1982: F fr 3,552.0 bn ($540.442 bn). Est GDP 1983: F fr 3,894.4 bn ($510.989 bn).
Est def exp 1983: F fr 133.22 bn ($17.480 bn); NATO defn $21.381 bn. 1984: 142.100 bn ($16.817 bn); NATO defn $20.237 bn.†
GDP growth: 0.4% (1981), 1.6% (1982), 5% (1983).
Inflation: 9.4% (1982), 9.9% (1983).
Debt 1982: $106.1 bn.
$1 = francs 6.5724 (1982), 7.6213 (1983), 8.4499 (mid-1984).

Strategic Nuclear Forces: (19,100; some 2,800 Army, 4,900 Navy, 10,600 Air Force, 800 *Gendarmerie*).
SLBM:
5 SSBN with 16 M-20 msls (1 more building, 1 on long refit) (M-4 msl replacing M-20 from 1985).
1 experimental/trials diesel sub with 2 SLBM tubes.
IRBM: 18 SSBS S-3 msls in 2 sqns.
Aircraft:
Bombers: 4 sqns with 28 *Mirage* IVA (AN-22 nuclear bombs); 7 being converted to IVP for ASMP nuclear ASM; total 18 by end 1986.
1 trg center with 4 *Mirage* IVR recce; 1 with 12 *Mirage* IIIB/BRV trg; 4 *Noratlas* N-2501/SNB.

---

* Incl inter-service central staff and *Service de Santé*, but not *Gendarmerie*.
† A 5-year military developement plan for 1983/8 totalling approx. F fr 830 bn has also been introduced.

1 tanker wing (3 sqns) with 11 KC-135F.
Reserve: 3 *Mirage* IVA (1 recce).
(On order: 1 SSBN, 16 M-4 SLBM, ASMP ASM; 4 *Transall ASTARTE* command post ac.)

Army: 304,500 incl Army Aviation, 5,700 women (190,000 conscripts); reorganizing and reducing.
1 army HQ, 3 corps HQ.
  6 armd divs.
  2 lt armd divs (mil schools).
  2 motor rifle (APC) divs.
Army corps regts: 3 recce, 2 drone, 1 motor rifle, 2 arty, 5 SSM with *Pluton*, 8 SAM (3 (11 btys) with 66 *HAWK*, 6 (each of 4 btys) with *Roland* I/II and twin 30mm AA guns), 5 engr, 6 sigs, 4 tpt.
3 log bdes.
Rapid Action Force (FAR): (47,000).
  1 para div (12,800): 6 para inf, 1 lt armd, 1 arty, 1 engr regts, 1 spt bn.
  1 air portable marine div (8,100): 4 inf, 1 lt armd, 1 arty, 1 engr, 1 comd/spt regts.
  1 lt armd div (summer 1984) (6,400): 2 lt armd, 2 APC inf, 1 arty, 1 engr, 1 comd/spt regts.
  1 alpine div (9,100): 1 mountain inf regt (6 bns), 1 lt armd, 1 arty, 1 comd/spt regts; 1 engr coy.
  (1 air mobile div to form (1985): 1 inf, 4 hel, 1 comd/spt regts.)
  1 log bde (spt units incl 1 tpt regt).
Foreign Legion: 8,000; 1 armd, 1 para, 4 inf (trg), 2 engr regts; 1 lt bde.
Indep regts: 1 EW, 2 para, 4 engr.
AFV: 1,102 AMX-30 (165 -30B2) MBT; 500 AMX-13 lt tks (158 with SS-11 ATGW); 189 AMX-10RC, 300 Panhard EBR-90 hy, 75 ERC-90S, 664 AML-60/90 lt armd cars; 835 AMX-10P/PC/VOA MICV; 1,100 AMX-13 VTT, 1,860 VAB, 42 VAB (*HOT*) APC.
Arty: 60 AU-F-1 155mm SP guns; 165 HM-2, 908 BF-50 155mm towed, 30 AU-50 105mm, 214 F-3 155mm SP how; 44 *Pluton* SSM; 596 120mm mor.
ATK: 135 AMX-13/SS-11, 1,400 *Milan*, 156 *ENTAC* ATGW, 12,000 89mm RL.
AD: 100 76T1, 280 53T2 20mm, 350 30mm and 40mm towed, 69 AMX-30 DCA twin 30mm SP AA guns; 69 *HAWK*, 128 *Roland* I/II SAM.
Air: 4 CL-89 recce drones.

ARMY AVIATION (ALAT): (6,600).
6 combat hel regts: 7 lt gps, 2 schools.
206 *Alouette* II, 68 *Alouette* III with AS-11 ATGW; 130 SA-330 *Puma*, 165 SA-341F and 90 SA-342M *Gazelle* hel with *HOT*; 70 *Broussard*, 30 L-19 lt ac.
(On order: 635 AMX-30B2 MBT conversion; 96 AMX-10RC, 162 ERC-90S armd cars; MICV; 122 AU-F1 155mm SP guns; 148 TR 155mm

how; 55 227mm MLRS; 23 120mm mor; 907 *HOT* (VAB and *Gazelle*), 407 20mm AA guns; SA-341, 15 SA-342 (*HOT*) hel.)

RESERVES: 305,000 (8 inf divs, 1 formed from military schools; 6 'Home' bdes: 2 mixed, 23 territorial defence regts; to be reorg 1985: some units to full strength).

Navy: 67,700 incl Naval Air, (1,100 women; 17,300 conscripts); 48 major surface combat vessels. 2 home (CECLANT, CECMED); 2 overseas comds.
17 attack subs: (2 *Rubis* SSN; 4 *Agosta*, 9 *Daphne*, 2 *Narval*).
2 *Clemenceau* carriers: 1 attack with 39 ac (2 flts with 20 *Super Etendard*, 1 with 7 F-8E, 1 with 6 *Alizé*; 1 det with 4 *Etendard* IVP), 4 hel; 1 ASW (LPH) with 40 hel (varies).
1 hel carrier (capacity 8 *Lynx* hel) with 6 *Exocet* SSM (trg).
1 command cruiser with 4 *Exocet* SSM, 1 × 2 *Masurca* SAM.
19 destroyers: 4 AA (2 *Suffren* with 4 *Exocet*, 1 *Malafon* ASW/SSM, 1 × 2 *Masurca* SAM; 2 T-47 with 1 *Tartar* SAM); 15 ASW (4 C-70 with 4 *Exocet*, 1 × 8 *Crotale* SAM, 2 *Lynx* hel; 3 F-67 with 6 *Exocet*, 1 × 8 *Crotale*, 1 *Malafon*, 2 *Lynx*; 1 T-56 with 1 *Malafon*, 1 hel; 1 T-53 with 4 *Exocet*, 1 *Lynx*; 5 T-47 with 1 *Malafon*; 1 C-65 with 4 *Exocet*, 1 *Malafon*).
25 frigates: 9 *Rivière*, (8 with 4 *Exocet*); 16 Type A-69 (4 with 2 *Exocet*; 5 with 4; 1 more in 1984).
1 D-400 FAC(G) with 2 *Exocet* MM-38 SSM.
5 FAC: 4 *Patra*, 1 *La Combattante* I.
4 large patrol craft: 1 *Sirius*, 2 Cdn *La Dunkerquoise*, 1 P-681 *Albatros*.
3 *Eridan*, 5 *Circe* minehunters, 5 US *Aggressive* ocean minehunters.
11 coastal minesweepers: 6 *Berlaimont*, 5 Type D.
6 assault ships: 2 *Ouragan* (with 4 *Super Frelon* or 6 *Gazelle/Alouette* hel, 9 LCM or 2 LCT), 4 *Batral*.
5 LST, 9 LCT, 30 LCM.
7 ocean-going tankers, 6 maintenance/log ships.
Msls: SSM: *Exocet* MM-38, MM-40; SM-39 sub-launched being introduced. ASW: *Malafon*. SAM: *Crotale*, *Masurca*, *Tartar*.

Bases: Cherbourg, Brest, Lorient, Toulon.

NAVAL AIR FORCE: (12,300); 121 combat ac, 37 combat hel.
3 strike sqns with 36 *Super Etendard* (AN-52 nuclear weapons; 5 to be mod for ASMP).
1 interceptor sqn with 14 F-8E (FN) *Crusader*.
2 ASW sqns with 16 *Alizé* (mod) (11 more to be modernized).
4 MR sqns with 27 *Atlantic*, 3 *Gardian*.
1 recce sqn with 8 *Etendard* IVP.

1 OCU: 12 *Etendard* IVM, 12 Fouga *Zephir*, 5 *Alizé*.

4 ASW hel sqns: 3 with 23 *Lynx*; 1 with 8 *Super Frelon*.

1 assault hel sqn with 6 *Super Frelon*.

14 comms/liaison/SAR units (1 VIP): with 14 *Navajo*, 8 Nord 262, 1 Nord N-25404, 4 *Xingu*, 2 mod *Alizé*, 3 *Rallye* 880, 5 *Gardian*, 8 MS-760, 5 *Falcon* 10MER ac; 28 *Alouette* II/III, 3 *Lynx*, 2 *Super Frelon* hel.

5 trg units with 13 Nord 262, 2 *Navajo* 9 EMB-121 *Xingu*, 13 *Rallye* 100S, 6 CAP-10 ac; 10 *Alouette* hel.

ASM: *Exocet* AM-39, AS-11/-12/-30, *Martel* AS-37.

AAM: R530, *Sidewinder*, R-550 *Magic*.

(On order: 6 SSN; 7 C-70 destroyers (3 ASW, 4 AA), 7 A-69 frigates, 70 P-400 FAC(G), 7 minehunters; 1 LSD, 2 LCT, 10 LCM; 1 ocean tanker, 33 *Exocet* SM-39 sub-launched SSM; 14 *Crotale* 8B SAM; 42 *Atlantic* II ASW ac.)

COMMANDOS (590): 4 assault units (1 reserve), 1 sub spt unit.

NAVAL BASE DEFENCE FORCE (2,400).

DEPLOYMENT: Atlantic Fleet: 5 SSBN, 9 other subs, 1 hel carrier, 20 escorts, 11 MCM, 8 amph. Channel Flotilla: 3 frigates, 7 MCM. Mediterranean Fleet: 2 SSN, 9 subs, 2 carriers, 14 escorts, 5 MCM, 5 amph.
See also *Forces Abroad*.

PUBLIC SERVICE FORCE (MHSP): Naval personnel, general coastguard duties; 1 *Sterne*, 1 *Mercure* patrol craft, 1 ex-trawler, 1 *Albatros* fishery protection vessel, 3 ac.

RESERVES: 30,000.

Air Force: 99,150 (5,600 women, 37,600 conscripts); some 492 combat ac.
Air Defence Command (CAFDA): (7,700).
12 interceptor sqns: 2 with 25 *Mirage* IIIC (1 (10 ac) in Djibouti), 1 with 15 *Mirage* IIIE, 8 with 120 *Mirage* F-1C, 1 with 14 *Mirage* 2000C (forming).
1 OCU with 15 *Mirage* F-1B.
4 trg flts with 30 *Magister* and *Broussard*.
Air-defence system: automatic *STRIDA* II, 10 radar stations.
12 SAM (1 trg) sqns with 24 *Crotale* btys (48 fire, 24 radar units).
200 AA btys (20mm guns).
AAM: R-530, Super 530F, R-550 *Magic* I/II, *Sidewinder*.
Tactical Air Force (FATAC): (19,600).
5 strike sqns: 3 with 45 *Jaguar*, 2 with 30 *Mirage* IIIE tactical (AN-52 nuclear weapons).
10 FGA sqns: 3 with 45 *Mirage* IIIE, 2 with 30 *Mirage* 5F, 5 with 75 *Jaguar* A.
3 recce sqns: 2 with 19 *Mirage* IIIR, 11 -IIIRD (F-1 replacing); 1 with 15 *Mirage* F-1CR.
2 OCU with 33 *Jaguar* A/E.
8 trg flts with *Magister*, *Broussard*.
AAM: *Sidewinder*, R-550 *Magic*, R-530.
ASM: AS-30/-30L, *Martel* AS-37.
Attached to COTAM:
2 AEW sqns: 1 with 5 *Noratlas*; 1 with 1 DC-8 (EE-51) ELINT.
3 liaison sqns with *Magister*, *Broussard*.
1 hel sqn with 9 *Alouette* II/III.
Air Transport Command (COTAM): (4,200).
1 hy tpt sqn with 5 DC-8F.
6 tac tpt sqns: 5 with 41 Transall C-160, 20 C-160NG, 1 with 10 *Noratlas*.
14 lt tpt/trg/SAR sqns with 140 ac, incl 19 Nord 262, 10 *Mystère* 20, 1 *Mystère* 50, 18 *Paris*, 23 *Broussard*, 8 DHC-6, 4 *Caravelle*, 6 EMB-121 *Xingu*.
1 OCU with 3 *Noratlas*, 7 Transall C-160.
5 hel sqns with 26 *Alouette* II, 28 *Alouette* III, 13 *Puma*, 15 *Dauphin*.
1 hel OCU with 9 *Alouette* II, 9 *Alouette* III, 2 *Puma*.
Training Command (CEAA): (6,600).
Some 400 ac, incl some 103 *Alpha Jet*, 157 *Magister*, 3 *Flamant*, 6 *Noratlas*, 16 EMB-121, *Xingu*-1, 12 *Epsilon*, 57 CAP-10B/-20.
Trials Units: 1 sqn with *Mirage* F-1, -2000, *Jaguar*; 1 sqn with 2 DHC-6, 1 N-262.
(On order: 60 *Mirage* 2000M, 31 -N, 45 F-1CR ftrs; 3 Transall C-160 tpts, 110 *Epsilon* trg ac; 20 AS-350D, 30 AS-335 *Ecureuil*-2 hel, 150 *Magic* I/II, 40 Super 530 AAM; 50 AS-30 laser ASM; 330 SATCP, 40 20mm AA guns, 100 *Crotale* SAM.)

RESERVES: 58,000.

Inter-service
Central Staff: 3,588.
Service de Santé: 8,712 (2,140 conscripts).

Forces Abroad:
Europe. *Germany*: 48,500; 3 armd divs. Berlin: 2,700; 1 armd regt, 1 inf regt.
Overseas Dependencies: 16,500; Army 9,800, Navy 2,000, Air 1,700, *Gendarmerie* 3,000. Four inter-service overseas commands: Antilles-Guyana (7,300; 1 marine inf regt, 1 marine inf bn, 2 ships, 1 *Atlantic* MR ac); South Indian Ocean (Mayotte, La Reunion) (3,350; 1 para, 1 inf, 1 marine regts, 1 inf coy); New Caledonia (2,800; 1 marine inf regt); Polynesia (5,000, incl ALPACI; 1 marine regt). Two naval commands: Indian Ocean (ALINDIEN): 3,500, 5 frigates, 3 minor combatants, 2 amph, 4 spt ships; Pacific (ALPACI:, 5 frigates, 5 minor combatants, 7 amph, 12 spt

ships, 2 *Gardian* MR ac).

Other Overseas: some 7,220 from all services (numbers vary according to local circumstances). Eqpt incl 120 AFV, spt vessels, 25 combat and 25 tpt ac, 43 hel.

Deployed:

Central African Republic (C.A.R.) (980). 1 bn gp incl 2 motor coys; 1 platoon AML armd cars (6); spt coy with L-19 lt ac, 120mm mor, *Milan* ATGW; 1 FGA det with *Jaguar*, 1 Army avn spt det with 3 SA-330 *Puma*, 2 C-160 tpt ac.

Chad (3,000). 1 Para, 1 marine regts; 1 armd coy with 3 sqns, 10 AMX-10RC; air elms with *Mirage, Jaguar,* 2 *Atlantic* MR, C-160 tpt ac; *Puma,* 12 *Gazelle* (*HOT*) hel. (Air may be based in the C.A.R.)

Djibouti (3,250). 1 mixed regt: 6 inf coys, 4 armd sqns, 2 arty (1 AA) btys; 1 sqn with 10 *Mirage* IIIC, 1 C-160 tpt ac, 3 *Alouette* II hel; naval elms incl 1 *Atlantic* MR ac.

Gabon (350). 1 marine inf bn; *Jaguar,* 1 C-160, *Atlantic* ac, 1 *Alouette* III hel.

Ivory Coast (480). 1 marine inf bn, 1 *Alouette* III hel.

Middle East. Lebanon (UNIFIL) (1,386): 1 inf bn, log bn. Sinai MFO (40): incl 2 *Twin Otter,* 1 C-160 tpt ac.

Saudi Arabia (80). Technical advisers.

Senegal (1,170). 1 marine inf regt, 1 *Atlantic* MR, 1 C-160 tpt ac, 2 *Alouette* II/III hel.

Africa, general: (956), trg teams.

Para-Military Forces: Gendarmerie 85,312 (incl 605 women, 8,700 conscripts, 950 civilians); 3,678 territorial squads, 130 intervention units; 93 general traffic units, 21 highway sqns, 4 platoons; 130 mobile sqns; 240 overseas units. 121 AML, 20 VBC-90 armd cars; 28 AMX-13 VTT, 155 VBRG-170 APC; 284 81mm mor; 11 patrol boats; 6 Cessna 206C ac; 31 *Alouette* II, 8 AS-350B *Ecureuil,* 11 *Alouette* III hel. Reserves: 125,000.

GERMANY: FEDERAL REPUBLIC

Population: 61,400,000 (incl West Berlin).
Military service: 15 months.
Total armed forces: 495,000* (100 women, 230,500 conscripts);† on mobilization about 1,250,000.
GDP 1982: DM 1,602.5 bn ($660.389 bn). 1983: 1,666.2 bn ($652.567 bn).
Est def exp 1983: DM 46.751 bn ($18.310 bn); NATO defn $22.127 bn. 1984: 47.846 bn ($17.396 bn); NATO defn $21.139 bn.
GDP growth: −1.1% (1982). 1.3% (1983).
Inflation: 4.8% (1982). 3.2% (1983).
Debt 1982: $120 bn.

$1 = DM 2.4266 (1982), 2.5533 (1983), 2.7504 (mid-1984).

Army: 335,600† (181,200 conscripts).
HQ Support Elements: 25,400: General Army Office subordinate echelon and spt tps.
Field Army: 266,000.
  3 corps: 12 divs (6 armd, 4 armd inf, 1 mountain, 1 AB):
    36 bdes: 17 armd (each with 3 tk, 1 armd inf, 1 armd arty bns), 15 armd inf (each with 1 tk, 3 armd inf, 1 armd arty bns), 1 mountain, 3 AB.
    Total: 66 tk, 62 armd inf, 33 armd arty, 4 mountain, 9 para bns.
  11 armd recce bns.
  11 div arty regts, 7 corps hy arty bns.
  4 SSM bns with *Lance.*
  3 AD regts, 1 AD bn with *Roland* II SAM.
  11 AA regts with *Gepard* 35mm SP guns.
  3 army aviation comds, each with 1 lt, 1 med tpt hel regt: 1 ATGW hel regt.
  1 mixed aviation regt.
Territorial Army: 44,200.
  3 Territorial Commands, 5 Military District Commands, 29 Military Region Commands, 80 Sub-region Commands (county/town level):
    6 Home Defence bdes (each with 2 tk, 2 inf, 1 arty bns): 1 at 85%, 3 at 65%, 2 at 52% manning levels.
    6 Home Defence bdes (each with 1 tk, 2 inf, 1 fd arty bns): weapons storage units only in peacetime.
  4 Territorial Service spt comds.
  Security tps: 15 Home Defence Regts (with 45 mot inf bns only), 150 coys, 324 security platoons; defensive, comms, military police and service units on mobilization.
AFV: 340 M-48A2/A2C, 650 M-48A2G/A2, 2,437 *Leopard* 1, 800 *Leopard* 2 MBT; 410 SPz-2 *Luchs,* 2,136 *Marder* MICV; 560 TPz-1, 3,095 M-113 APC.
Arty: 260 105mm, 216 FH-70, 586 M-109 155mm how, 230 M-110A2 203mm SP how; 987 120mm mor (500 SP); 209 *LARS* 110mm MRL; 26 *Lance* SSM.
ATK: 520 JPz-4-5 90mm SP ATK guns; 204 106mm RCL; 1,975 *Milan,* 346 *TOW* ATGW, 316 RJPz-(*HOT*) *Jaguar* 1, 2 RJPz-(*TOW*) SP ATGW.
AD: 1,748 20mm towed, 432 *Gepard* 35mm SP AA guns; 800 *Redeye,* 120 *Roland* SAM.
Air: 190 UH-1D, 150 *Alouette* III, 170 PAH-1 (BO-105P with *HOT*), 80 BO-105M, 107 CH-53G hel.
(On order: 1,000 *Leopard* 2 MBT; 430 TPz-1 APC; 200 227mm MLRS MRL; 160 RJPz-(*TOW*) *Jaguar* 2 ATGW veh (rebuilt JPz-4-5);

20 *Roland* II SAM; 40 PAH-1, 70 BO-105M hel.)

Navy: 36,200,† incl naval air (10,700 conscripts).
24 subs: 18 Type 206, 6 Type 205.
7 destroyers: 3 *Lütjens* (Type 103A) with 1 *Tartar* SSM and 8 *ASROC*; 4 *Hamburg* (Type 101A) with 2 × 2 *Exocet* MM-38 SSM.
8 frigates: 5 *Bremen* (Type 122) with 2 × 4 *Harpoon* SSM, 1 × 8 *Sea Sparrow*, 2 × 24 *Stinger*, 2 RAM-ASMD SAM, 2 *Lynx* hel; 3 *Köln* (Type 120).
5 *Thetis* corvettes.
38 FAC(G) with 4 *Exocet* MM-38 SSM: 10 Type 143, 8 Type 143A, 20 Type 148.
1 Type 142 FAC(T) (Type 143A FAC(G) replacing).
18 *Lindau* MCM: 12 Type 331 coastal minehunters (MHC), 6 Type 351 *Troika* drone control minesweepers (MSCD), 18 F-1 drone vessels (MCD).
21 *Schütze* coastal minesweepers.
18 inshore minesweepers: 4 Type 393/394B, 14 Type 393/394A.
10 *Rhein* depot, 4 *Lüneburg* (Type 701), 4 *Coburg* (Type 701C) spt ships, 4 tpts, 9 tankers.
22 Type 520 LCU, 26 Type 521 LCM.
(On order: 1 Type 122 frigates, 2 Type 143A FAC(G), 126 RIM-7M *Sea Sparrow* SAM.)

Bases: Flensburg-Murwik, Wilhelmshaven, Kiel, Olpenitz, Eckernförde.

NAVAL AIR ARM: 123 combat ac; 12 combat hel.
3 attack sqns: 1 with 30 F/TF-104G; 2 with 47 *Tornado*.
1 recce sqn with 27 RF-104G.
2 MR sqns with 14 *Atlantic*, 5 ELINT *Atlantic*.
1 ASW hel sqn with 12 *Sea Lynx* Mk 88.
1 SAR hel sqn with 22 *Sea King* Mk 41.
1 utility sqn with 19 Do-28-2 ac.
ASM: AS-30, AS-34 *Kormoran*.
(On order: 64 *Tornado* MRCA.)

Air Force: 106,000† (38,600 conscripts); 486 combat ac.
Tactical Command (GAFTAC): 456 combat ac.
4 divs: 2 tac, 2 AD.
20 FGA sqns: 5 with 90 F-104G; 4 with 53 F-4F; 4 with 60 *Tornado*; 7 with 126 *Alpha Jet*.
4 interceptor sqns with 60 F-4F.
4 recce sqns with 60 RF-4E.
ECM trg: 7 HFB-320 *Hansa Jet*.
8 SSM sqns with 72 *Pershing* 1A.
3 SAM regts (each 2 bns of 4 btys) with 216 *Nike Hercules* launchers.
3 SAM regts (each of 3 bns of 4 btys) with 216 *Improved HAWK* launchers.
4 aircraft control and warning regts; 13 sites.

AAM: *Sidewinder*.
Transport Command (GAFTC).
4 tpt sqns with 75 Transall C-160.
5 hel sqns with 92 UH-1D.
1 special air mission wing with 4 Boeing 707-320C, 3 C-140 *Jetstar*, 6 HFB-320 *Hansa Jet*, 3 VFW-614, 6 Do-28-2 *Skyservant* ac, 4 UH-1D hel.
Training Command: 30 combat ac.
Trinational *Tornado* trg det (Cottesmore, Britain); 22 *Tornado*.
OCU (George Air Force Base (AFB) USA): 8 F-4E.
Pilot trg wing (Sheppard AFB USA) 35 T-37B, 41 T-38A.
Primary trg unit: 34 P-149D.
Miscellaneous liaison, range and base flts with 65 Do-28D.
(On order: 129 *Tornado* FGA, 6 CL-600 *Challenger*.)

RESERVES: 750,000 (all services).

Para-Military Forces: Border Police (Ministry of Interior): 20,000; FV-601(D) (*Saladin*) armd cars, MOWAG SW-1/-2 APC; 2 P-149D, 1 Do-27A-3 ac, BO-105M, 21 *Alouette* II hel.

GREECE

Population: 10,200,000.
Military service: Army 22, Navy 26, Air Force 24 months.
Total armed forces: 178,000 (1,800 women; 137,000 conscripts).
GDP 1982: dr 2,518.0 bn ($37.693 bn). 1983: 3,064 bn ($34.793 bn).
Def exp 1983: dr 151.8 bn ($1.724 bn); NATO defn $2.416 bn. Est 1984: 247.722 bn ($2.287 bn); NATO defn n.a.
GDP growth: 0.5% (1982).
Inflation: 20.0% (1982). 20.0% (1983).
FMA 1983: $280 m.
Debt 1982: $10.6 bn.
$1 = drachmas 66.803 (1982), 88.064 (1983), 108.340 (mid-1984).

Army: 135,000 (99,500 conscripts incl 1,400 women).
3 Military Regions, 4 corps, 1 specialized comd HQ.
1 armd div.
1 mech div.
11 inf divs.

---

* Incl 11,200 military personnel in the Ministry of Defence, Central Military Agencies, Central Medical Agencies and 6,000 reserve duty training positions.
† *Not* incl inter-service personnel and part-time reservists.

1 para-cdo div (1 para, 1 cdo and 1 marine regts, 3 cdo bns).
3 armd bdes.
1 mech bde.
4 armd recce bdes.
13 fd arty bns.
7 AA arty bns.
2 SSM bns with 8 *Honest John.*
2 SAM bns with *Improved HAWK.*
3 army aviation bns.
1 indep aviation coy.
AFV: 350 M-47, 900 M-48 incl 212 M-48A3, 225 M-48A5, 200 AMX-30, 106 *Leopard* 1A3 MBT; 190 M-24, 54 *Kuerassier* (105mm) lt tks; 180 M-8 armd cars; 240 AMX-10P MICV; 100 *Leonidas*, 115 M-3 half-track, 430 M-59, 1,000 M-113 APC.
Arty: 36 M-107 175mm guns; 108 75mm pack, M-56, 300 M-101/-102 105mm, 270 M-114A1 155mm, 72 M-115 203mm towed, 126 M-52A1/M-108 105mm, 54 M-44, 72 M-109A2 155mm, 20 M-110 203mm SP how; 36 *Honest John* SSM; 81mm, 120mm mor.
ATK: M-18 57mm, 75mm, some 350 EM-67 90mm, 700 106mm RCL; 50 M-113A2 *Tow*; SS-11, *Cobra, TOW, Milan* ATGW.
AD: RH-202 twin 20mm, 40mm, incl M-42 Twin SP, M-51 75mm, M-117/118 90mm AA guns; 36 *Improved HAWK* (108 msls), 37 M-48 *Chaparral, Redeye* SAM.
Avn: 2 *Super King Air*, 2 *Aero Commander*, 1 DHC-2 Beaver, 50 U-17A ac; 8 AH-1 with *TOW*, 10 CH-47C, 5 Bell 47G, 22 UH-1D, 50 AB-204B/-205, 10 AB-206A hel.
(On order: 46 Kuerassier 'lt tks' (SP ATK); 50 M-113A2 *TOW* SP ATGW; 58 M-198 towed, 36 M-109A2 155mm SP how, 350 90mm RCL; *Artemis* 30 twin 30mm AA guns.)

RESERVES: about 350,000: Field Army 227,000; Territorial Army 123,000 (incl some 100,000 National Guard).
Territorial Army 23,000 incl 5,000 reservists on 4-week refresher trg. 3 Territorial (17 Sub-Commands: 12 indep inf bdes. National Guard: 100 bns (mainly coastal defence); lt tks; 120 M-20 armd cars; 120 M-2/-3 half-track APC; 36 75mm pack, 125 25-pdr (88mm), 105mm guns/how; M-18 57mm, 200 M-20 75mm, 106mm RCL; 40mm AA guns.

Navy: 19,500 (12,000 conscripts incl 200 women); 17 combat hel.
10 subs: 8 Type 209; 2 US *Guppy* IIA/III.
14 US destroyers: 7 *Gearing* (6 with 1 × 8 *ASROC*, 1 with 1 *Alouette* III hel), 1 *Sumner*, 6 *Fletcher*.
7 frigates: 2 *Kortenaer* (8 *Harpoon* SSM, *Sea Sparrow* SAM, 2 AB-212 hel), 4 US *Cannon*, 1 FRG *Rhein*.
18 FAC(G): 16 *La Combattante* II/III (8 with 4

Exocet, 6 with 6 *Penguin* SSM), 2 *L'Esterel* with 4 SS-12.
11 FAC(T): 6 *Jaguar*, 5 *Nasty*.
11 coastal patrol craft.
2 coastal minelayers, 14 coastal minesweepers (9 MSC-294, 5 US *Adjutant*).
1 LSD, 7 LST, 5 LSM, 2 LCT, 8 LCU, 13 LCM, 21 LCA, 34 LCVP.
2 ASW hel sqns: 1 with 5 AB-212, 3 AB-212 ECM; 1 with 4 *Alouette* III.

Bases: Salamis, Suda Bay.

RESERVES: about 24,000.

Air Force: 23,500 (15,000 conscripts incl 200 women); 303 combat ac.
Tactical Air Force: 7 combat wings: 1 tpt wing.
8 FGA sqns: 3 with 52 A-7H, 6 TA-7H; 3 with 53 F/TF-104G; 2 with 36 F-5A, 6 F-5B.
6 interceptor sqns: 3 with 53 F-4E; 1 with 24 F-5A/B; 2 with 36 *Mirage* F-1CG.
2 FGA/recce sqns: 1 with 15 RF-84F, 6 RF-4E; 1 with 8 RF-5A.
1 MR sqn with 8 HU-16B *Albatross* (with Navy).
3 tpt sqns with 12 C-130H, 6 YS-11, 6 C-47, 20 *Noratlas*, 1 *Gulfstream*, 9 CL-215.
9 base flts with 6 C-47, 48 T-33A ac, 8 AB-205A hel.
3 hel sqns with 14 AB-205A, 2 AB-206A, 5 Bell 47G, 8 UH-19D, 2 AB-212, 5 CH-47C.
Air Training Command:
4 sqns: 1 with 19 T-41A; 1 with 21 T-37B/C; 2 with 37 T-2E, 6 F-104 G.
AAM: *Sparrow, Sidewinder, Super Sidewinder, Falcon*, R-550 *Magic*.
ASM: *Maverick, Bullpup*.
1 SAM wing: 1 gp with 36 *Nike Ajax*.
(On order: some 14 F-104G ac, 6 CH-47C hel, 280 AIM-7M *Sparrow*, 300 *Super Sidewinder* AAM, 200 *Maverick* ASM, 40 *Skyguard* AD systems plus 4 extra twin 35mm AA guns.)

RESERVES: about 30,000.

Forces Abroad: Cyprus: 1,750; 1 inf bn (950), cdos (350); officers/NCOs seconded to Greek-Cypriot forces (450).

Para-Military Forces: Gendarmerie: 25,000; MOWAG *Roland*, 15 UR-416 APC. Coast-guard and Customs: 4,000; some 100 patrol craft, 2 Cessna *Cutlass* ac.

ITALY

Population: 58,000,000.
Military service: Army and Air Force 12, Navy 18 months.

Total armed forces: 375,100 (239,000 conscripts).

GDP 1982: L 469,797 bn ($347.355 bn). Est 1983: 535,904 bn ($352.847 bn).

Def exp 1983: L 11,649 ($7.670 bn); NATO defn $9.788 bn. 1983: 13.820 bn ($8.143 bn); NATO defn $10.279 bn.

GDP growth: –0.3% (1982). –0.9% (1983).

Inflation: 15% (1982). 15.9% (1983).

Debt 1982: $66.0 bn.

$1 = lire 1,352.5 (1982), 1,518.8 (1983), 1,697.2 (mid-1984).

Army: 260,000 (189,000 conscripts).
3 corps HQ.
1 armd div (2 armd, 1 mech bdes).
3 mech divs (each of 1 armd, 2 mech bdes).
2 indep mech bdes.
4 indep mot bdes.
5 alpine bdes.
1 AB bde.
2 amph bns.
1 msl bde (1 *Lance* SSM, 3 *Improved HAWK* SAM bns).
AFV: 550 M-47, 300 M-60A1, 920 *Leopard* 1 MBT; 4,410 M-106, M-113, M-548 and M-577, AMX-VC1 APC.
Arty: 1,116: 36 M-107 175mm SP guns; 320 105mm model 56 pack, 724 155mm (incl 150 FH-70 towed, 220 M-109E (SP), 36 203mm how; 81mm; 120mm mor; 6 *Lance* SSM.
ATK: 57mm, 106mm RCL; *Cobra*, SS-11, *TOW*, *Milan* ATGW.
AD: 20mm, 230 40mm AA guns; 40 *Improved HAWK* SAM.

ARMY AVIATION:
4 wings (10 sqns, 29 flts); 10 indep sqns (21 flts). (Flt usually has 6 ac/hel).
19 lt ac and hel sqns: 8 with SM-1019 ac, 9 with AB-206, 2 with AB-205A hel.
10 recce hel sqns with AB-206.
2 target acquisition sqns: 1 with SM-1019 ac, 1 with AB-206 hel.
17 multi-role hel sqns: 1 with AB-204B, 15 with AB-205A, 1 with AB-205B.
4 med tpt hel sqns with CH-47.
1 trg, 4 repair units.
75 SM-1019, 30 O-1E lt ac, 100 AB-205A, 140 AB-206A/A1, 24 CH-47C, 5 A-109 *Hirundo*, 18 AB-204B, 14 AB-212, 70 AB-47G/J hel.
(On order: 20 FIROS 6 × 51mm MRLS, 850 *TOW*, *Milan* ATGW; FIM-92A *Stinger* SAM + msls; 60 A-129 *Mangusta* hel.)

RESERVES: 550,000, immediate mobilization perhaps 250,000.

Navy: 44,500, incl 1,500 air arm, 750 marines (24,590 conscripts).
10 subs: 4 *Sauro*, 4 *Toti*, 2 US *Tang*.

1 *Vittorio Veneto* hel carrier with 9 AB-212 ASW hel, 4 *Teseo* (*Otomat* Mk 2) SSM, 1 × 2 *Terrier* SAM.
2 *Andrea Doria* cruisers each with 4 AB-212 ASW hel, 1 × 2 *Terrier* SAM.
4 GW destroyers: 2 *Audace* with 2 AB-212 ASW hel, 1 *Standard* SAM; 2 *Impavido* with 1 *Standard*.
15 frigates: 7 *Maestrale* with 4 *Teseo* SSM, 1 × 4 *Albatros/Aspide* SAM, 2 AB-212 hel; 4 *Lupo* with 8 *Teseo* SSM, 1 × 8 *Sea Sparrow* SAM, 1 AB-212 hel; 2 *Alpino* with 2 AB-212 hel; 2 *Bergamini* with 1 AB-212 hel.
8 corvettes: 4 *De Cristofaro*, 4 *Albatross*.
7 *Sparviero* hydrofoils with 2 *Teseo* SSM.
2 *Freccia* FAC (1 with 1 × 5 *Sea Killer* SSM).
4 US *Aggressive* ocean, 13 *Agave* coastal, 5 *Aragosta* inshore minesweepers; 1 *Lerici*, 1 *Agave* minehunters.
2 US *De Soto County* LST, 19 US LCM. 2 *Stromboli* replenishment tankers.
1 Marine inf gp with 30 VCC-1, 10 LVTP-7 APC, 16 81mm mor, 8 106mm RCL, 6 *Milan* ATGW.

Bases: La Spezia, Taranto, Ancona, Brindisi, Augusta, Messina, La Maddalena, Cagliari, Naples, Venice.

NAVAL AIR ARM: (1,500); 93 combat hel.
5 ASW hel sqns: 30 SH-3D, 10 AB-204AS, 55 AB-212.
ASM: *Marte* Mk 2.

(On order: 2 *Sauro* subs, 1 hel carrier, 2 *Audace* destroyers, 1 *Maestrale* frigate, 4 *Minerva* corvettes with *Albatros* multi-role weapon system, 3 *Lerici* minehunters, 2 LPD, 6 SH-3D, 7 AB-212 hel.)

RESERVES: 221,000.

Air Force: 70,600 (28,300 conscripts); 300 combat ac.
6 FGA/recce sqns: 2 with 36 *Tornado*, 2 with 36 F-104S, 2 with 36 G-91Y.
1 lt attack sqn with 15 MB-339.
3 lt attack/recce sqns with 36 G-91R/R1/R1A.
6 interceptor sqns with 72 F-104S.
2 recce sqns with 30 F/RF-104G.
2 MR sqns with 14 *Atlantic* (Navy assigned; being increased).
1 ECM/recce sqn with 2 G-222VS, 6 PD-808.
1 navigation aid calibration sqn: 4 G-222, PD-808, C-47, MB-339.
1 OCU with 18 TF-104G.
3 tpt sqns: 2 with 32 G-222, 1 with 10 C-130H.
Comms sqns with 16 P-166M, 32 SIAI-208M, 8 PD-808, MB-326, 2 DC-9 ac; 2 SH-3D hel.
SAR sqns with 15 AB-204, 6 AB-212, 20 HH-3F hel.
1 combat trg det (Cottesmore, Britain) with 7 *Tornado*.

6 trg sqns with 50 G-91T, 70 MB-326/-339A, 25
SF-260M ac; 35 AB-47G2, 3 AB-204B hel.
AAM: AIM-7E *Sparrow*, AIM-9B/-9L *Side-
winder*.
ASM: *Kormoran*.
8 SAM groups with 96 *Nike Hercules*.
(On order: 64 *Tornado* MRCA, 187 AM-X FGA
ac; 18 AB-212 hel; 4 *Spada* SAM systems,
Aspide AAM.)

RESERVES: 28,000 some additional ac (logistic
reserve).

Forces Abroad:
Egypt (Sinai MFO) (90); 3 minesweepers. Lebanon
(UNIFIL) (40).

Para-Military Forces: *Carabinieri* 90,000: 1
mech bde with 13 bns, 1 AB bn, 2 cav sqns; 37
M-47 MBT; Fiat 6616, 80 M-6, M-8 armd cars;
470 Fiat 242/18AD, 240 M-113 APC; 23
AB-47, 2 A-109, 5 AB-205, 23 AB-206 hel.
Ministry of Interior: Public Security Guard
67,927: 11 mobile units; 40 Fiat 6614 APC, 3
P-64B ac; 1 AB-47Y3B-1, 6 A-109A, 12
AB-206A1, 4 AB-212 hel. Treasury Depart-
ment: Finance Guards 48,691; 6 AB-47J, 69
NH-500M hel, 350 patrol craft⟨.
(On order: 3 AB-212, 1 A-109A hel.)

LUXEMBOURG

Population: 365,300.
Military service: voluntary, 3 years.
Total armed forces: 720.
GDP 1982: fr 154.250 bn ($3.376 bn). Est 1983:
163.995 bn ($3.207 bn).
Est def exp 1982: fr 1.44 bn ($31.516 m); NATO
defn $41.430 m. 1983: 1.596 bn ($31.213
m); NATO defn $42.577 m. Budget 1984:
2.295 bn ($41.0 m); NATO defn n.a.
GDP growth: –1.5% (1981), –3.5% (1982).
Inflation: 9.4% (1982), 9.5% (1983).
$1 = francs 45.691 (1982), 51.132 (1983),
55.975 (mid-1984).

Army: 720.
1 lt inf bn.
1 indep coy.
5 *Commando* APC; *LAW* RL; *TOW* ATGW.

(**Air**: Luxembourg has no air force of her own,
but for legal purposes all NATO's airborne early
warning ac will have Luxembourg registration.

1 sqn with 10 E-3A NATO standard.
(On order: 8 E-3A.)

Para-Military Forces: Gendarmerie 470.

NETHERLANDS

Population: 14,400,000.
Military service: Army 14–16, Navy and Air
Force 14–17 months.
Total armed forces: 103,267 (incl Royal Military
Constabulary; 1,450 women; 46,368 con-
scripts).
GDP 1982: gld 365.90 bn ($137.031 bn). 1983:
370.550 bn ($129.831 bn).
Est def exp 1983: gld 12.646 bn ($4.431 bn);
NATO defn $4.572 bn. Budget 1984: 13.071 bn
($4.227 bn); NATO defn $4.216 bn.
GDP growth: –1.7% (1982). –3% (1983).
Inflation: 5.5% (1982). 2.5% (1983).
Debt 1982: $16.8 bn.
$1 = guilders 2.6702 (1982), 2.8541 (1983),
3.0925 (mid-1984).

Army: 64,664 (40,785 conscripts), though see
Reserves.
1 Corps HQ, 3 mech div HQ.
2 armd bdes.
4 mech inf bdes.
3 armd recce bns.
3 SP AA bns.
1 SSM bn with *Lance*.
3 hel sqns (Air Force manned).
AFV: 468 *Leopard* 1 (10 mod to 1A4), 135
Leopard 2, 322 *Centurion* MBT; 79 AMX-13 lt
tks; 66 AMX-VC1, 698 M-113, 735 YP-408
(to retire), 1,307 YPR-765 APC.
Arty: 44 M-101 105mm, 134 M-114 155mm, 75
AMX 105mm (being retired), 222 M-109
155mm, 13 M-107 175mm (being replaced by
203mm), 61 M-110 203mm SP guns/how; 6
Lance SSM; 92 81mm, 194 107mm, 153
120mm mor.
ATK: *Carl Gustav* 84mm, 253 106mm RCL;
LAW RL; 350 *Dragon*, 320 *TOW* ATGW.
AA: 54 L-40/70 40mm towed, 95 *Gepard* 35mm
SP AA guns.
Avn: 67 *Alouette* III, 30 BO-105 hel (Air Force
crews).
(On order: 310 *Leopard* 2 MBT; 660 YPR-765
APC; 486 *Stinger* SAM.)

RESERVES: 145,000, many on short leave,
immediate recall. 1 armd, 2 mech inf bdes,
corps troops and 1 indep inf bde would be
completed by call-up of reservists; 2+ inf bdes
could be mobilized for territorial defence.
Home Guard: 4,300; 3 sectors; inf weapons.

Navy: 16,867, incl naval air arm and marines
(1,437 conscripts).
6 subs: 2 *Zwaardvis*, 2 *Potvis*, 2 *Dolfijn* (1 in
reserve).
2 *Tromp* GW destroyers (flagships) with 8
Harpoon SSM, 1 *Standard*, 8 *Sea Sparrow* SAM,
1 *Lynx* hel.

16 frigates with 8 *Harpoon* SSM: 10 *Kortenaer* with *Sea Sparrow* SAM, 1–2 *Lynx* hel; 6 *Van Speijk* with 2 × 4 *Seacat* SAM, 1 *Lynx* hel.
4 *Wolf* corvettes (2 in reserve).
3 *Balder* large patrol craft.
9 *Dokkum* coastal minesweepers (5 in reserve); 4 *Dokkum*, 6 *Alkmaar* minehunters.
2 *Poolster* fast combat spt ships.
3 survey ships (2 North Sea, 1 oceanographic).
10 LCA⟨.

Bases: Den Helder, Flushing, Curaçao.

NAVAL AIR ARM: (1,700); 13 combat ac, 17 combat hel.
3 MR/ASW sqns with 11 P-3C *Orion* II, 2 F-27MPA (Air Force manned). (6 *Atlantic* MR in reserve).
1 ASW hel sqn with 17 *Lynx* SH-14B/C.
1 SAR hel sqn with 5 *Lynx* UH-14A.

MARINES: (2,800).
2 amph combat gps.
1 mountain/arctic warfare coy.

(On order: 2 *Walrus* subs; 4 multi-role, 2 AD *Kortenaer* frigates; 9 *Alkmaar* minehunters; 4 LCVP; 2 P-3C MR ac; *Harpoon* SSM.)

RESERVES: about 20,000; 7,500 on immediate recall.

Air Force: 16,810 (3,565 conscripts); some 174 combat ac.
5 FGA sqns: 3 with 54 NF-5A, 1 with 18 F-104G (getting F-16), 1 with 18 F-16.
2 FGA/interceptor sqns with 36 F-16A/B.
1 recce sqn with 18 F-16 (RF-104G phasing out in 1984).
2 OCU: 1 with 18 NF-5B, 1 with 12 F-16B.
(Some 16 more F-16A/B have been delivered).
1 tpt sqn with 12 F-27.
1 SAR flt with 4 *Alouette* III.
AAM: AIM-9 *Sidewinder*.
12 SAM sqns with 36 *Improved HAWK* (8 in Germany).
2 SAM sqns with 23 *Nike Hercules*.
25 *Shorad/Flycatcher*, 40 L-70 AA systems.
(On order: 46 F-16A FGA, 10 F-16B ac; 20 *Patriot* SAM launchers, 160 msls.)

RESERVES: 6,000 on immediate recall.

Inter-Service Organization: 1,071 (271 conscripts).

Forces Abroad:
Germany: 5,500; 1 armd bde, 1 recce, 1 engr bns, spt elements.
Lebanon (UNIFIL): 165: 1 inf coy.
Egypt (Sinai MFO): 105: 1 det.
Netherlands Antilles: 1 frigate, 1 amph combat det, 1 MR det with 2 F-27MPA ac.

Para-Military Forces: Royal Military Constabulary (*Koninklijke Marechaussee*): 3,855 regulars, 310 conscripts; 3 divs comprising nine districts with 87 'bdes'. Civil Defence (*Corps Mobiele Colonnes*): 22,000 on mobilization under Army command.

NORWAY

Population: 4,146,000.
Military service: Army 12, Navy and Air Force 15 months.
Total armed forces: 36,785 (22,500 conscripts).
GDP 1982: N kr 362.560 bn ($56.176 bn). Est 1983: 401.277 bn ($54.997 bn).
Def exp 1983: N kr 12.696 bn ($1.740 bn); NATO defn: $1.706 bn. 1984: 12.948 bn ($1.657 bn); NATO defn $1.662 bn.*
GDP growth: 0.9% (1982), 3.3% (1983).
Inflation: 14% (1982), 12% (1983).
Debt: $31.7 bn (1982).
  $1 = kroner 6.4540 (1982), 7.2964 (1983), 7.8142 (mid-1984).

Army: 19,500 (12,000 conscripts).
1 lt bde gp of 3 inf bns, 1 tk coy, 1 SP fd bn, 1 AA bty (North Norway), 2 border garrison bns.
1 all-arms gp: 1 inf bn, 1 tk coy, 1 SP fd, 1 AA btys (South Norway).
Indep armd sqns, inf bns and arty regts.
70 *Leopard* 1, 30 M-48A5 MBT; 70 NM-116 (M-24/90) lt tks; NM-135 (20mm) MICV; M-113 APC; 250 105mm and 155mm towed; 130 M-109 155mm SP how; 107mm mor; *Carl Gustav* 84mm, 106mm RCL; M-72 66mm RL; *ENTAC* (being retired), *TOW* ATGW; FK20-2 20mm, 40mm AA guns; RBS-70 SAM; 23 O-1E, 8 L-18 lt ac.
(On order: M-113 APC, RBS-70 SAM).

RESERVES: 165,000: 12 bdes of about 5,000 men each (some being reorg), 2 armd sqns, spt units and territorial forces; 21 days refresher training each 3rd/4th year to age 44. Home Guard 72,100 (90 days initial service); 18 Districts, areas and sub-areas.

Navy: 7,500, incl 1,000 coast artillery (5,500 conscripts).
14 *Kobben* (Type 207) subs.
5 *Oslo* frigates with 6 *Penguin* SSM, 1 × 8 *Sea Sparrow* SAM.
2 *Sleipner* corvettes.
38 FAC(G) with *Penguin* SSM: 18 *Storm* (6 × 1), 14 *Hauk* (6 × 1), 6 *Snögg* (4 × 1).
1 *Vadsø* coastal patrol craft.
2 *Vidar* minelayers, 9 US MSC-60 minesweepers, 1 minehunter.

---

* Incl UNIFIL costs.

1 *Horten* depot/trg ship, 7 coastal tpts.
7 LCT: 2 *Kvalsund*, 5 *Reinøysund*.
15 coast def fortresses (to be rebuilt): 50 arty, mine and torpedo btys: 75mm, 105mm, 120mm, 127mm, 150mm guns.
1 SAR/recce hel sqn with 6 *Lynx* (coastguard).
8 *Tjeld* FAC(T) in reserve.
(On order: 6 *Ula* (Type 210) subs; 8 120mm guns.)

Bases: Horten, Bergen, Ramsund, Tromsø.

RESERVES: 25,000. Coastguard (352 incl 55 civilians): 6 patrol vessels incl 3 *Nordkapp* fitted for 6 × 1 *Penguin* II SSM, 6 *Lynx* hel (Air Force manned), 7 armed fishery protection vessels. Home Guard (5,400).

Air Force: 9,500 (5,000 conscripts); 114 combat ac.
5 FGA sqns: 4 with 72 F-16; 1 (OCU) with 35 F-5A.
1 MR sqn with 7 P-3B *Orion*.
2 tpt sqns: 1 with 6 C-130H, 3 *Falcon* 20S; 1 with 4 DHC-6 ac, 2 UH-1B hel.
1 SAR hel sqn with 10 *Sea King* Mk 43.
2 utility hel sqns with 26 UH-1B (10 in storage).
21 *Safari* trg ac.
AAM: *Sidewinder*.
ASM: *Bullpup*.
4 lt AA bns with 32 L-60/-70 40mm guns.
1 SAM bn (4 btys) with 128 *Nike Hercules*.
(On order: 54 *HAWK* launchers and 162 msls (lease), *Penguin* Mk 3 ASM.)

RESERVES: 25,000. 7 lt AA bns for airfield defence with 56 L-60 40mm guns. Home Guard 2,500: 2 bns, airfield def btys.

Joint Services Orgs: 285.

Civil Defence: 53 Districts, 14 mobile columns. 108 local units. Permanent staff some 400; total mobilization strength 62,500 (planned).

Forces Abroad: Lebanon (UNIFIL): 838; 1 bn, 1 service coy, plus HQ personnel.

PORTUGAL

Population: 10,200,000.
Military service: Army 16, Navy 24, Air Force 21–24 months.
Total armed forces: 63,500 (37,700 conscripts; see Army).
GDP 1982: esc 1,858.0 bn ($23.379 bn). 1983: 2,274.0 bn ($20.527 bn).
Est def exp 1982: esc 50.10 bn ($630.403 m); NATO defn 803.0 m. 1983: 60.60 bn ($547.030 m); NATO defn $713.315 m.
GDP growth: 3.5% (1982), −5% (1983).

Inflation: 26% (1982), 38% (1983).
Debt: $18.5 bn.
　$1 = escudos 79.473 (1982), 110.780 (1983).

Army: 39,000 (30,000 conscripts, 3 intakes a year, 4 months alternating service).
6 Territorial Commands (4 military regions, 2 island commands).
1 mixed bde.
3 cav regts.
11 inf regts, 3 indep inf bns.
1 cdo regt.
2 fd, 1 AA, 1 coast arty regts.
2 engr regts.
1 sigs regt.
1 military police regt.
1 Special Forces, 4 spt bns.
AFV: 25 M-47, 23 M-48A5 MBT; 11 M-24 lt tks; 43 Panhard EBR/ETT hy, 63 AML-60/-90 lt armd, 32 *Ferret* Mk 4 scout cars; 75 M-113 (incl -A2 *TOW*), 9 M-577A2 (81mm mor); 86 *Chaimite* APC.
Arty: 24 5.5-in. (140mm) guns; 36 M-101A1 105mm towed, 6 M-109A2 155mm SP how; 39 150mm, 152mm, 234mm coast arty; 54 107mm, 81 120mm mor.
ATK: 100 90mm, 127 106mm RCL; 45 *TOW* ATGW.
AD: 18 Rh-202 20mm, 20 Bofors L-60 40mm AA guns; 16 *Blowpipe* SAM.

Navy: 15,000 incl marines (4,200 conscripts).
3 *Albacora* (Fr *Daphne*) subs.
17 frigates: 4 *Andrade*, 6 *Coutinho*, 4 *Belo*, 3 *Silva*.
10 *Cacine* large patrol craft.
13 coastal patrol craft: 2 *Aleixo*, 6 *Albatroz*, 4 *Bonanca*, 1 river.
4 minesweepers.
2 LCT, 10 LCM, 1 LCA.

Base: Lisbon (Alfeite), Faro.

MARINES: (2,500; 1,000 conscripts).
3 bns (2 inf, 1 police), spt units.
Chaimite APC, mor, amph craft.

Air Force: 9,500, incl 1,800 para (3,500 conscripts); 74 combat ac.
1 combat command, 5 administrative wings:
　3 FGA sqns: 1 with 20 A-7P; 1 with 20 G-91R3, 8 T3; 1 with 20 G-91R4, 2 T3.
　1 recce sqn with 4 C-212B.
　1 OCU with 12 T-38.
　2 tpt sqns: 1 with 5 C-130H; 1 with 12 C-212.
　3 SAR sqns: 1 with 6 C-212 ac; 2 with 12 SA-330 *Puma* hel.
　2 hel/utility sqns with 37 *Alouette* III.
　2 liaison sqns with 32 Reims-Cessna FTB-337G.
　3 trg sqns: 1 with 2 C-212A ac, 3 *Alouette* III

hel; 1 with 24 T-37C; 1 with 30 *Chipmunk*.
1 para gp (1 bn, 2 coys).
(On order: 30 A-7 FGA (6 trg), 3 C-130 tpt ac; 12
 A-109A hel (4 with *TOW*).)

RESERVES (all services): 169,000.

Para-Military Forces: National Republican
Guard 14,600; *Commando* Mk III APC. Public
Security Police 15,291. Fiscal Guard: 7,385.

SPAIN

Population: 38,800,000.
Military service: 15 months. (Army to reduce to
 12 months).
Total armed forces: 330,000 (214,000 con-
 scripts); force reduction programme being
 introduced).
Est GDP 1982: pts 19,737 bn ($179.656 bn).
 1983: 22,703 bn ($158.286 bn).
Est def exp 1983: pts 480.00 bn ($3.347 bn);
 NATO defn: n.a.*
GDP growth: 1.2% (1982), 2.3% (1983).
Inflation: 16.5% (1982), 16.0% (1983).
FMA: $400 m (1983).
Debt: $37.4 bn (1982).
 $1 = pesetas 109.86 (1982), 143.43 (1983).

Army: 240,000 (170,000 conscripts); to reduce to
 195,000 by 1985.
Immediate Intervention Force:
 1 corps HQ.
 1 armd div ⎫
 1 mech div ⎬ each with 2 bdes.
 1 mot div ⎭
 1 armd cav bde.
 1 inf bde (Reserve).
 1 para bde (3 bns).
 1 airportable bde.
 1 arty bde.
 1 locating, 1 fd rocket, 1 lt AA regts.
 1 engr, 1 sigs regts.
 1 chemical/nuclear defence regts.
Territorial Defence Force:
 9 Military Regions (being reorg, incl Ceuta and
  Melilla), 2 overseas comds (see *Deployment*).
 2 mountain divs (each 1 bde and 1 cadre bde).
 Legion: HQ, 4 regts, spt units (overseas forces).
 9 inf bdes (8 may be disbanded).
 1 mountain bde.
 1 arty bde (incl 1 *HAWK* SAM gp, 1 *Nike
  Hercules* bty).
 2 hy arty regts.
 7 coast/AA arty regts.
General Reserve Force:
 1 ATK inf regt.
 1 engr, 2 railway engr regts.
 1 sigs regt.
Independent Units:

Army HQ inf gp.
Royal Guard Regt (incl inf, naval, air force
 coys and escort cav sqn).
Army Aviation (FAMET): 40 armed hel.
 HQ with 1 hel, 1 spt, 1 trg sqn.
 1 attack bn.
 1 tpt bn (1 med, 1 hy coys).
 3 hel units.
AFV: 300 AMX-30, 350 M-47E, 110 M-48
 (105mm) MBT; 180 M-41 lt tks; 60 AML-60,
 80 AML-90 armd cars; 200 BMR-600 MICV;
 BLR, 500 M-113 APC.
Arty: 168 122/46 122mm towed, 12 M-107
 175mm SP guns; 911 105mm M-26 and M-56
 pack, 84 M-114 155mm, 12 M-115 8-in.
 (203mm) towed, 48 M-108 105mm, 24 M-44,
 96 M-109A 155mm, 4 M-55 203mm SP how;
 200 88mm, 200 6-in. (152.4mm), 24 203mm,
 some 12 12-in. (305mm), some 12 15-in.
 (381mm) coast guns; 1,200 81mm, 107mm,
 400 120mm mor; R-2B 105mm, *Teruel*
 140mm, L-21 216mm, L-10 300mm, L-8
 381mm MLRS.
ATK: 350 106mm RCL; 42 M-65 88.9mm RL; 50
 Milan, 50 *Cobra*, 18 *Dragon*, *HOT*, 12 *TOW*
 ATGW.
AD: 20mm, 64 35/90, 280 40/90, 120 90mm AA
 guns, 14 *Nike Hercules*, 24 *Improved HAWK*
 SAM.
Avn: 59 HU-8/-10B (UH-1B/H), 3 HA-16
 (*Alouette* III), 60 HA-15 (BO-105; 12 with
 20mm guns, 28 with *HOT*), 5 AB-206A, 6
 AB-212, 12 HR-12B (OH-58A), 12 HT-17
 (CH-47C) hel.
(On order: VEC 3562 recce, 220 BMR-600 MICV,
 176 M-113 APC; 540 *TOW* msls; 12 CH-47C,
 28 AB-412, 18 OH-58A hel; 96 *Chaparral*
 SAM (1,760 msls); 18 *Roland* SAM launchers,
 500 msls); 28 *Skyguard* AD systems.

DEPLOYMENT:
Ceuta/Melilla: 19,000; 2 armd cav, 3 Foreign
 Legion, 2 coast/AA Arty, 2 engr regts, 4
 Regulares inf gps, 2 special sea coys.
2 Overseas Forces comds:
 Balearic Islands: 5,800; 3 inf, 2 coast/AA regts,
  1 engr bn, 1 lt cav gp, 1 cdo coy.
 Canary Islands: 16,000.
  3 inf regts (1 cadre).
  1 Foreign Legion (2 bns, 1 lt cav gp).
  2 coast/AA arty regts.
  1 engr gp (2 bns).
  1 lt cav gp.
  1 cdo coy.

Navy: 57,000, incl marines (44,000 conscripts).
9 Commands (Escort, Naval Air, Submarine,

---

* An additional budget of pts 3.1 bn, plus $400 m per
annum in US FMA for modernization of the armed
forces, runs concurrently as of 1983.

Mine Warfare, Marines, 4 Naval Region HQ).
8 subs: 2 *Agosta*, 4 Daphne, 2 *Guppy* IIA.
1 US *Independence* carrier (9 AV-8A, 24 hel).
11 destroyers: 6 with 1 hel (1 *de Lauria*, 5 US
   Gearing with 1 Hughes 369 hel, 4 with 1
   ASROC), 5 US *Fletcher*.
11 frigates: 5 *Baleares* (F-70) 1 with 2 × 4
   Harpoon SSM, 16 *Standard* SAM, 1 × 8
   ASROC; 6 *Descubierta* (F-30) with 1 × 8 *Sea
   Sparrow/Aspide* SAM.
4 *Atrevida* corvettes.
12 FAC(P): 6 *Lazaga*, 6 *Barcelo*.
18 large patrol craft (3 ex-minesweepers).
26 coastal and 38 inshore patrol craft(.
4 US *Aggressive* ocean, 8 *Jucar* coastal MCM.
2 attack tpts.
1 LSD, 3 LST, 7 LCT, 2 LCU, 20 LCM.

NAVAL AIR: 11 combat ac, 51 combat hel.
1 attack sqn with 9 AV-8A *Matador*, 2 TAV-8A.
1 comms sqn with 2 *Commanche*, 2 *Citation*.
5 hel sqns (3 ASW); 1 with 11 AB-212 (4 ECM), 1
   with 11 Hughes 369, 1 with 14 SH-3D *Sea
   King*; 1 with 4 AH-1G (armed), 11 Bell 47G.

MARINES: (11,925).
1 marine regt (2 inf, 1 spt, 1 log bns).
5 marine garrison regts.
18 M-48S MBT; LVTP-7 amph APC; 8 Oto
   Melara 105mm towed, 8 M-52A1 105mm SP
   how; 81mm mor; M-72 66mm RL; 72 106mm
   RCL; *TOW, Dragon* ATGW.

(On order: 2 *Agosta* subs, 1 carrier, 3 FFG-7
   frigates, 4 32.2-metre patrol craft, 20
   15.9-metre patrol vessels; 12 *Bravo* (AV-8B)
   ac, 6 SH-60B hel; 12 RGM-84A *Harpoon* SSM,
   SM-1 *Standard* SAM.)

Bases: Ferrol (Galicia), Cadiz (San Fernando)/
   Rota, Cartagena.

Air Force: 33,000; 215 combat ac.
Air Combat Command (MACOM):
   3 wings.
   6 interceptor sqns: 2 with 35 F-4C, 4 RF-4C; 2
      with 21 *Mirage* IIIEE, 6 IIIEB; 2 with 45
      Mirage F-1CE, 3 F-1CE/BE.
   1 liaison flt with 1 Do-27.
Tactical Command (MATAC):
   2 wings.
   2 FGA sqns with 14 F-5A, 13 RF-5A, 6
      F-5B.
   1 recce sqn with 9 AR-10C (HA-220).
   1 MR sqn with 6 P-3B *Orion*.
   1 liaison flt with 6 O-1E, 11 Do-27, Do-28.
   AAM: *Sparrow, Sidewinder*, R-550 *Magic*.
Air Command, Canary Islands (MACAN):
   1 FGA sqn with 24 *Mirage* F-1C.
   1 SAR sqn with 3 F-27-400 MR ac, 8 AB-205
      hel.
   1 tpt sqn with 7 C-212, 2 Do-27.

Transport Command (MATRA):
   3 wings:
   5 sqns with 5 C-130H, 6 KC-130H, 6 *Azor*, 25
      C-212 *Aviocar*, 12 DHC-4, 8 Do-27.
Training Command (MAPER):
   2 OCU with 23 F-5A/B, 2 Do-27.
   14 sqns with 6 *Aztec*, 29 F-33C *Bonanza*, 50
      C-101, 14 C-212E, 1 *Navajo*, 49 T-33A, 45
      T-6, 6 *King Air*, 3 *Baron*, BU-131A/CASA
      I-131.
   2 hel sqns with 28 HE-7A (AB-47), AB-205,
      Hughes 300C and UH-1H.
Air Force HQ Group (ACGA):
   2 tpt sqns with 2 DC-8-52, 4 *Mystère* 20, 1
      Navajo, 4 C-212.
   3 spt sqns with 14 CL-215, 2 Do-27, 5 C-212,
      2 DHC-4A, 8 C-7.
   1 utility hel sqn with 5 *Puma*.
   2 SAR sqns with 4 C-212, 4 Do-27 ac, 12 *Super
      Puma*, 9 AB-205, 4 AB-206, 3 AB-47, 3
      Alouette III hel.
   1 trg sqn with 4 C-101, 2 C-212.
(On order: 72 F-18 ftrs; 2 P-3C *Orion* MR; 4
   C-212 SAR, 13 C-101 trg ac; 17 Hughes 300C
   hel; *Super Sidewinder* AAM.)

RESERVES (all services): 1,085,000.

Para-Military Forces: *Guardia Civil* 63,500: 25
   inf *tercios* (regts), 3 reserve mobile comds, 1
   railway security, 1 traffic security gps, 1 anti-
   terrorist special gp (UAR); BLR APC, 1 B-11T
   (BK-117) hel. (On order: 20 BO-105, 3
   BK-117 hel). *Policía Nacional* 47,000: 26 inf
   bns, 2 cav sqn gps, 3 cav tps, 1 special ops cdo
   gp (GEO), civil security gps. Ministry of Transportation and Communications: *Maritime
   Surveillance Force*; some 54 patrol boats, (10
   320-ton, 4 32-metre, 16-metre), many armed.

TURKEY

Population: 48,600,000.
Military service: 20 months.
Total armed forces: 602,000 (544,000 con-
   scripts).
Est GDP 1982: TL 8,578.0 bn ($52.771 bn).
   1983: 12,250.0 bn ($54.333 bn).
Est def exp 1983: TL 444.0 bn ($1.952 bn); NATO
   defn: $2.469 bn. Budget 1984: 583.6 bn
   ($1.635 bn); NATO defn n.a.
GNP growth: 4.5% (1982), 3.0% (1983).
Inflation: 30% (1982), 41% (1983).
Est FMA: $460 m (1983).*
Debt: $22.3 bn (1982).
   $1 = liras 162.55 (1982), 225.46 (1983), 357.01
   (mid-1984).

---

* Calculated from US published information and
estimates for other contributors.

Army: 500,000 (475,000 conscripts).†
4 army HQ: 10 corps HQ.
1 armd div.
2 mech divs.
14 inf divs.
4 armd bdes.
4 mech bdes.
11 inf bdes.
1 para bde, 1 cdo bde.
4 SSM bns with *Honest John*.
1 SAM bty forming.
Corps units: 10 tk, 30 hy/med, 20 AA arty bns,
indep fortress defence regts.
AFV: 500 M-47, 2,775 M-48A1, 180 M-48A5,
77 *Leopard* 1A3 MBT; 2,000 M-113 APC.
Arty: 150 M-59 155mm towed, 36 M-107
175mm SP guns; 95 M-116A1 75mm pack,
some 600 M-101A1 105mm, 400 M-114A1
155mm, 116 M-115 203mm towed, 345
M-7/M-108 105mm, 108 M-44/M-109
155mm, 8 M-55 203mm SP how; 1,750 60mm,
81mm, M-2 4.2-in. (107mm), 120mm mor; 18
Honest John SSM.
ATK: 1,200 M-18 57mm, 390 M-20 75mm,
1,000+ M-40 106mm RCL; 85 *Cobra*, SS-11,
TOW, Milan ATGW.
AD: 300 twin 20mm, 900 M-1A1 40mm, M-51
75mm, M-117/-118 90mm guns, some *Rapier*
SAM.
Avn: 2 DHC-2, 20 U-17, 8 Cessna 206, 20
Cessna 421, 5 Do-27, 14 Do-28, 15 *Baron*, 5
T-42, 40 *Citabria* 150S trg ac; 156
AB-204/-205, 20 Bell 47G, 30 UH-1D, 30
TH-300C hel.
(Plus eqpt in store incl 200 M-47 MBT, 100 M-4
lt tks; M-8 recce, 350 M-59, 800 M-2/-3 APC;
M-7 towed, M-52 SP 105mm, M-44 SP 155mm
how.)
(On order: *TOW*, 1,500 *Milan* ATGW, 40 UH-1H
hel, some 12 *Rapier* SAM.)

RESERVES: 700,000.

Navy: 46,000, incl marines (36,000 conscripts);
18 combat ac, 13 combat hel.
16 subs (2 in reserve): 5 Type 1200, 10 US
Guppy, 2 *Tang* (on loan).
13 US destroyers: 8 *Gearing* (3 leased, 5 with 1 ×
8 ASROC), 1 *Sumner*, 1 *Carpenter*, 2 *Fletcher*,
1 *Smith*.
2 *Berk* frigates, each with 1 hel.
14 FAC(G): 5 *Dogan* (Lürssen FPB-57) with 2 × 4
Harpoon SSM; 9 *Kartal* (Type 141 *Jaguar*)
with 4 *Penguin* 2 SSM.
4 FRG *Jaguar* FAC(T).
25 large patrol craft (incl 1 *Girne*, 2 US
Asheville, 6 PC-1638, 4 PGM-71.)
4 83-ft coastal patrol craft⟨.
1 *Nusret*, 6 coastal minelayers.
26 minesweepers: 12 US *Adjutant*, 4 Cdn MCB,
6 FRG *Vegesack* coastal, 4 US *Cape* inshore.

7 LST (3 dual-purpose minelayers), 32 LCT, 16
LCU, 20 LCM.
56 auxiliary ships incl 1 US destroyer tender, 2
FRG depot ships (trg), 9 tankers (5 fleet).
Naval Aviation:
1 ASW sqn: 18 S-2E ac; 3 AB-204B, 6 AB-212
ASW, 4 UH-1H ECM, 10 UH-1H SAR hel; (2
S-2A in reserve).
1 marine bde (5,000): HQ, 3 bns, 1 arty bn (18
guns), spt units.
(On order: 1 Type 209 sub, 4 *Meko*-200 frigates,
7 *Zobel* FAC(G), 13 LCT, 1 tanker.)

Bases: Gölçük, Istanbul, Izmir, Ereğli, Isken-
derun.

RESERVES: 70,000.

Air Force: 56,000 (33,000 conscripts); some 458
combat ac.
2 tac, 1 tpt, 1 air trg commands.
17 FGA sqns: 2 with 42 F-5A, 10 F-5B; 2 with 40
F-100D; 5 with 80 F-4E; 8 (2 forming)
with 96 F-104G, 12 TF-104.
2 interceptor sqns with 32 F-104S, 4 TF-104G.
2 recce sqns: 1 with 27 RF-5A, 1 F-5B; 1 with 7
RF-4E.
6 tpt sqns: 1 with 7 C-130E; 1 with 20 C-160D; 3
with 60 C-47A, 2 Beech 18; 1 (VIP) with 3
Viscount 794 ac, 15 UH-1H hel.
1 VIP flt with 2 C-47A.
3 comms flts, 3 liaison flts with C-47, AT-11, 10
T-33A ac; UH-1H hel.
10 base flts with 24 T-33A, AT-11, 2 C-47A ac,
UH-1H, UH-19B hel.
5 OCU: 2 sqns with 36 F-5A/B, 17 F-104G; 2
with 20 T-33A/-38A; 1 with 25 T-37C.
3 trg sqns with 24 T-34A, 40 T-38A, 20 T-41D.
2 *Rapier* SAM sqns forming.
Schools with C-47 ac; UH-1H, UH-19B hel.
AAM: *Sidewinder*, 750 AIM-9P3 *Super Sidewinder*, *Sparrow*, *Falcon*, *Shafrir*.
ASM: AS-12, *Bullpup*, *Maverick*.
8 SAM sqns with 72 *Nike Hercules*.
(On order: 160 F-16 ftr, 52 G-222 tpt, 2 *Citation*
II trg ac; *Super Sidewinder*, *Sparrow* AAM; 24
Rapier SAM.)

RESERVES: 66,000.

Forces Abroad:
Cyprus: 1 corps of 2 inf divs (17,000); 150
M-47/-48 MBT; M-113 APC; 212 105mm,
155mm, 203mm guns/how; 40mm AA guns.

Para-Military Forces: Gendarmerie 125,000
(incl 3 mobile bdes with V-150, UR-416 APC).
Coastguard 1,100: 35 large, 10 coastal patrol
craft. (On order: 5 SAR-33 FAC.).

---

† About half the divs and bdes are below strength.

OTHER EUROPEAN COUNTRIES

Albania: Albania joined the Warsaw Pact in 1955 but left it in 1968, moving into a closer relationship with China. After Chairman Mao's death in 1976, Chinese aid was progressively reduced. Since 1978 little military aid has been received from any source. The Constitution precludes the establishment of foreign bases or the stationing of foreign troops in Albania.

Austria: Austria's constitution contains a declaration of permanent neutrality. A small indigenous arms industry supplies many of the needs of the armed forces and provides a few foreign sales.

Cyprus: In 1959 Britain, Greece and Turkey signed a Treaty of Guarantee assuring the independence, territorial integrity and security of the newly independent bi-national state. Under this Treaty Britain maintains a garrison in two Sovereign Base Areas at Akrotiri and Dhekelia. Under an associated Treaty of Alliance with the Republic of Cyprus, Greece and Turkey are each also entitled to maintain a contingent on the island. In 1963 a constitutional dispute led the Turkish-Cypriot community to withdraw from the central government and ultimately, on 15 November 1983, to form a 'Turkish Republic of Northern Cyprus'. Both Turkish-Cypriot and Greek-Cypriot communities maintain their own armed forces. The United States maintains a signals establishment on the island, and the United Nations has a peace-keeping force (UNFICYP) there.

Finland: A 1948 Treaty of Friendship, Co-operation and Mutual Assistance requires Finland to fight any aggression directed against the USSR across her territory. In case of need the Soviet Union will provide assistance or joint action. Finland has her own defence industry, but has tended to buy her major arms from the USSR and Sweden, together with some equipment from Britain, France and the United States.

Ireland: Independent since 1922, Ireland plays an active role in UN peace-keeping operations. With no significant arms industry, Ireland has bought arms from many sources, e.g. Britain, France, Sweden and the US.

Malta: After independence in 1964, Malta had a defence agreement with Britain. The island was a NATO base from 1972 to 1979. In September 1980 Malta undertook to remain neutral, outside any alliances, and banned foreign troops and bases, including Soviet warship docking facilities. Italy agreed to consultation if Malta were attacked and to guarantee her independence. In December 1981 France and Algeria also agreed to support and guarantee her neutrality.

Sweden: Neutral in both World Wars, Sweden has a permanent peace-keeping organization which has provided personnel for UN duties since 1964. Her self-defence organization is largely supported by a domestic defence industry but some external purchases have been made, mainly from the United States.

Switzerland: Permanently neutral since 1815, Switzerland belongs to no defence alliance. Her small armaments industry produces most of her equipment and plays a significant role in the Swiss export trade.

Yugoslavia: Expelled from the Cominform in 1948, she has since been a leading force in the Non-Aligned Movement, maintaining a balanced relationship with each Bloc. She has no defence alliances, though a limited naval repair agreement exists with the USSR. She has her own defence industry but has bought most of her major military equipment from the USSR.

ALBANIA

Population: 2,800,000.
Military service: Army 2 years; Air Force, Navy and special units 3 years.
Total armed forces: 40,400 (22,400 conscripts).
Est GNP 1981: lek 11.900 bn ($2.380 bn).
Def budget 1982: lek 935 m ($155.8 m). 1983: 910 m ($137.3 m).
GDP growth: 4% (1982), 4% (1983).
Debt 1983: $5.4 bn.*
$1 = lek 5.0 (1981), 6.0 (1982), 6.63 (1983).

Army: 30,000 (20,000 conscripts).
1 tk bde.
5 inf bdes.
4 arty regts.
8 lt coastal arty bns.
70 T-34, 15 T-54, 15 T-59 MBT; 20 BA-64 armd, BRDM-1 scout cars; BTR-40/-50/-152, K-63 APC; M-1942, SU-76 SP 76mm, D-44 Type-56 85mm, M-1931 122mm, Type-59 130mm guns; M-1938, Type-60 122mm, M-1937, Type-66 152mm gun/how; D-1 152mm how; 82mm, 120mm, 160mm mor; Type-63 107mm MRL; T-21 82mm RCL; M-1942 45mm, M-1943 57mm, D-44, Type-56 85mm ATK guns; M-1939 37mm, S-60 57mm, KS-12 85mm, KS-19 100mm AA guns.†

RESERVES: 150,000.

Navy: 3,200 (1,000 conscripts).†
3 Sov *W*-class subs (1 trg).
2 Sov *Kronshtadt* large patrol craft.
6 Ch *Shanghai*-II FAC.
32 Ch *Huchwan* hydrofoil.
12 Sov P-4 FAC(T).
9 Sov PO-2 patrol craft.
5 Sov minesweepers: 1 T-43 ocean, 4 T-301 inshore.
(Plus, in reserve: 1 *W*-class sub, 2 *Kronshtadt* patrol craft, 1 T-43, 2 T-301 minesweepers).
Bases: Durres, Valona, Sazan I., Pasha Liman

Air Force: 7,200 (1,400 conscripts); 100 combat ac.†
6 ftr sqns with 20 MiG-15/F-2, 30 MiG-17, 30 MiG-19/F-6, 20 Ch F-7.
1 tpt sqn with 3 Il-14M, 10 An-2.
2 hel sqns with 30 Mi-4.
1 trg sqn with MiG-15UTI.
SAM: Some 5 SA-2 sites.

RESERVES: 5,000.

Para-Military Forces: 12,500. Internal security force 5,000; frontier guard 7,500.

---

* Estimated total since 1949.
† Spares are short; some eqpt may be unserviceable.

AUSTRIA

Population: 7,500,000.
Military service: 6 months recruit trg; 60 days reservist refresher trg during 15 years, 30–90 days additional for specialists.
Total armed forces: 50,000 (32,000 conscripts); some 70,000 reservists on refresher trg.
Est GDP 1983: OS 1,208 bn ($67.249 bn).
Def exp 1983: OS 14.844 bn ($826.365 m). Def budget 1984: 14.823 bn ($767.038 m).
GDP growth: 1.1% (1982), 1.5% (1983).
Inflation 5.4% (1982), 3.3% (1983).
Debt 1982: $ 13.2 bn.
$1 = schilling 17.963 (1983), 19.325 (mid-1984).

Army: 45,300 (29,500 conscripts).
Army HQ.
Standing Alert Force (some 15,000):
1 mech div of 3 mech bdes (each 1 tk, 1 mech inf, 1 SP arty, 1 SP ATK bns), 1 comd, 1 AA, 1 engr, 1 sigs bns.
Standing Field Units:
Army: 1 HQ, 1 recce bns; 1 sigs, 1 log regts.
Corps: 2 HQ, 1 arty, 1 SP ATK, 2 AA, 3 engr, 2 sigs bns; 2 log regts.
Indep: 1 air-mobile, 2 mountain, 1 guards bns.
9 Regional (county) Commands.
28 *Landwehrstammregimente* (trg regts).
Peacetime: trg and maintenance.
Mobilization: active personnel for mobile and territorial forces.
Cadre Force (full strength on mobilization):
8 mobile bde HQ:
Bde tps (45,000): 24 inf, 8 arty, 8 engr/ATK, 8 comd/spt bns.
Territorial tps (82,000): 33 inf bns, 21 lt inf, 6 engr/ATK bns, 40 engr/ATK coys.
AFV: 50 M-60A3, 120 M-60A1 MBT; 464 Saurer 4K4F APC.
Arty: 108 IFH 105mm, 24 FHM-1 155mm, 56 M-109 155mm SP how; 22 SFKM2 155mm fortress guns; 18 M-51 130mm MRL; 351 81mm, 105 M-2/M-30 107mm, 82 120mm mor; 552 20mm, 56 35mm towed, 38 M-42 40mm SP AA guns.
ATK: 300 M-68 105mm turret-mounted guns; *LAW* RL; 74mm, 84mm, 397 M-40 106mm RCL; 240 M-52/M-55 85mm towed, 225 *Kuerassier* JPz SK 105mm SP ATK guns.
(On order: 42 155mm SP how.)

RESERVES: 158,000; 970,000 have a reserve commitment.

Air Force:‡ 4,700 (2,500 conscripts); 32 combat ac.
1 Air Div HQ; 3 Air Regts:

---

‡ Austrian air units, an integral part of the Army, are listed separately for purposes of comparison.

4 FGA sqns with 32 Saab 105OE.
6 hel sqns with 12 AB-206A, 23 AB-212, 23 *Alouette* III, 12 OH-58B *Kiowa*, 17 AB-204.
1 trg/liaison sqn with 2 *Skyvan*, 12 *Turbo-Porter*, 6 O-1E, 18 Saab 91D, 19 L-19.
6 PC-7 *Turbo-Trainer* ac.
3 AD bns with 36 20mm, 18 35mm AA guns; *Super-Bat* and *Skyguard* AD systems.

Forces Abroad: Cyprus (UNFICYP): 1 inf bn (299). Syria (UNDOF): 1 inf bn (530). Other Middle East (UNTSO): 13.

CYPRUS

Population: 664,000 (500,000 Greek-, 150,000 Turkish-Cypriots, 14,000 others).

REPUBLIC OF CYPRUS.
Military service: conscription, 26 months.
Total armed forces: 10,000.
GDP 1982: £C 1.006 bn ($2.120 bn). Est 1983: 1.092 bn ($2.076 bn).
Est def exp 1982: £C 21.5 m ($45.301 m). 1983: 30.395 ($57.796 m).
GDP growth: 4.8% (1982), 2.6% (1983).
Inflation: 6.4% (1982), 5.1% (1983).
   $1 = £C 0.4746 (1982), 0.5259 (1983).

National Guard:* 10,000.
1 armd bn.
2 recce/mech inf bns.
20+ inf bns (under strength).
7 arty gps.
8 spt units.
10 T-34 MBT; 100 EE-9 *Cascavel*, 20 Marmon-Harrington armd cars (in reserve); 17 BTR-50 APC; 130 M-1944 100mm, M-101 105mm and 25-pdr (88mm) guns and M-116 75mm how; Yug YMRL-32 128mm MRL; M-18 57mm, M-40 106mm RCL; M-55 20mm, 40mm, 3.7-in. (94mm) AA guns; 1 58-ft patrol craft; 2 AB-47J hel.
(On order: 84 VAB APC.)

RESERVES: 60,000 (have yearly refresher training): 30,000 immediate; 30,000 second-line.

Para-Military Forces: 3,000 armed police; 2 96-ft patrol boats, 1 *Islander* lt tpt ac.

NORTHERN CYPRUS
Military service: conscription, 24 months.
Est GDP 1982: TL 36.750 bn ($226.084 m).
Def exp 1982: TL 750 m ($4.61 m). Def budget 1983: 1.071 bn ($4.750 m).
   $1 = Turkish lira 162.55 (1982), 225.46 (1983).

Security Forces: some 4,500.
7 inf bns.
1 armd coy.
8 T-34 MBT (operability questionable).

RESERVES: 5,500 first-line, 10,000 second-line.

FINLAND

Population: 4,840,000.
Military service: 8–11 months (11 months for officers and NCOs); three entries per year.
Total armed forces: 36,500 (25,000 conscripts; total mobilizable strength about 700,000).
GDP 1982: m 236.770 bn ($49.104 bn). 1983: 265.38 bn ($47.644 bn).
Est def exp 1983: m 4.400 bn ($789.932 m). Def budget 1984: 4.180 bn ($718.090 m).†
GDP growth: 2.6% (1982), 2.0% (1983).
Inflation: 10.4% (1982), 9.3% (1983).
Debt 1982: $19.1 bn.
   $1 = markkaa, 4.8204 (1982), 5.5701 (1983), 5.8210 (mid-1984).

Army 30,900 (22,300 conscripts).
7 Military Areas; 25 Military Districts:
1 armd bde.
7 inf bdes (1 cdo).
2 fd arty regts.
2 coast arty regts.
7 indep inf bns.
2 indep fd arty bns.
3 coast arty bns (1 mobile).
1 AA arty regt (incl 1 SAM bn with SAM-79).
5 indep AA arty bns.
2 engr bns.
1 sigs regt, 1 bn.
T-54/-55 MBT; PT-76 lt tks; BMP-1 MICV; BTR-50P, BTR-60 (to retire) APC; M-41 105mm, M-60 122mm, M-54 130mm guns; M-37/-61 105mm, M-38/D-30 122mm, M-40 150mm, ML-20 152mm, M-68/-74 155mm how; 81mm, 120mm mor; M-55 55mm, *Miniman* 74mm, SM-58-61 95mm RCL; SS-11, M-82 (AT-4 *Spigot*) ATGW; 20mm, ZU-23 23mm, 30mm, GDF-002 35mm, L-60/L-70 40mm, S-60 57mm towed, ZSU-57-2 SP AA guns; SAM-79 (SA-3), SAM-78 (SA-7) SAM.
(On order: T-72 MBT, 59 A-180 *Sisu* APC, *TOW* ATGW.)

Navy: 2,700 (1,400 conscripts).
2 *Turunmaa* corvettes.
6 FAC(G): 1 *Helsinki* with RBS-15SF SSM; 4 *Tuima* (Sov *Osa*-II), 1 *Isku* (experimental) with MTO-66 (*Styx*) SSM.

---

* Mainly Greek-Cypriot conscripts, but some seconded Greek Army officers and NCOs.
† Defence budget likely to increase as Government spending plans are revised.

4 *Nuoli* FAC.
1 *Hurja* coastal patrol craft⟨ (experimental).
5 *R*-class large patrol craft.
3 minelayers (1 trg), 6 *Kuha*, 7 *Kiiski* inshore minesweepers.
1 HQ/log ship.
5 *Valas* tpts, 14 small LCU/tpts, 3 *Pukkio* spt ships; 6 *Hauki* tpts.
(On order: 3 *Helsinki* FAC(G), RBS-15SF SSM.)

Bases: Upinniemi (Helsinki), Turku.

Air Force: 2,900 (1,300 conscripts); 76 combat ac.
3 AD districts: 3 fighter wings.
3 ftr sqns with 27 MiG-21bis, 24 J-35S *Draken*.
1 OCU: 8 MiG-21U/UM, 3 J-35C, 8 *Hawk* trg ac.
1 recce flt with 6 MiG-21F.
1 tpt sqn: 2 C-47 (retiring), 3 F-27-100, 3 *Learjet* 35 ac; 1 hel flt with 6 Mi-8 (also SAR), 2 Hughes 500.
Trainers incl 15 *Magister*, 27 *Hawk*, 30 *Vinka* (Leko 70).
Liaison ac: 9 *Cherokee Arrow*, 6 *Chieftain*.
AAM: AA-2 *Atoll*, RB-27, RB-28 (*Falcon*).
(On order: 10 J-35 *Draken* AD, 15 *Hawk* trg ac, AD system.)

RESERVES (all services): some 700,000 (36,000 a year do conscript training; 42,000 reservists: total obligation 40–100 days refresher training (average 8 days annually) between service and age 50; officers to 60). Some 210,000 would, with the Regulars, form the 'fast deployment force' to cover full mobilization. Mobilization units supporting general, local or spt forces are org in bdes, bns etc., under Military Areas.

Forces Abroad: (UN only, not within Force totals): Cyprus (UNFICYP) 10. Syria (UNDOF) 1 bn (395). Lebanon (UNIFIL) 1 bn (495). Other Middle East (UNTSO) 21. Pakistan (UNMOGIP) 4.

Para-Military Forces: Ministry of Interior: Frontier Guards 3,500, four districts, 7 bns; Coastguard (600), 3 districts; 4 large, 9 coastal 34 patrol craft; ac and 3 Mi-8 hel (SAR). (On order: 2 large patrol boats.)

IRELAND

Population: 3,550,000.
Military service: voluntary.
Total armed forces: 13,943.
GDP 1982: £E 12.436 bn ($17.687 bn). Est 1983: 13.943 bn ($17.405 bn).
Def exp 1982: £E 247.7 m ($352.297 m), 1983: 261.3 m ($326.177 m). Def budget 1984: 230.0 m ($256.955 m).

GDP growth: –1.4% (1982), 0.5% (1983).
Inflation: 17% (1982), 10.3% (1983).
Debt: $18.3 bn (1982), $19.6 bn (1983).
$1 = £E 0.7031 (1982), 0.8011 (1983), 0.8951 (mid-1984).

Army: 12,205.
1 inf force (2 inf bns).
4 inf bdes: 2 with 2, 1 with 3 inf bns, 1 fd arty regt, 1 motor recce sqn, 1 engr coy; 1 with 2 inf bns, 1 armd recce sqn, 1 fd arty bty.
Army tps: 1 tk sqn, 1 AD regt, 1 Ranger coy.
Total units:
  11 inf bns (3 with MICV coy; UNIFIL bn *ad hoc* – dets from other bns).
  1 tk sqn.
  1 armd sqn.
  3 recce sqns.
  3 fd arty regts (each of 2 btys); 1 indep bty.
  1 AD regt (1 regular, 3 reserve btys).
  3 fd engr coys.
  1 Ranger coy.
12 *Scorpion* lt tks; 20 AML-90, 32 AML-60 armd cars; 60 Panhard VTT/M3, 8 *Timoney* APC; 35 25-pdr (88mm) gun/how; 12 105mm lt guns; 199 60mm, 250 81mm, 92 120mm mor; 447 *Carl Gustav* 84mm, 96 PV-1110 90mm RCL; 4 *Milan* ATGW; 24 L/60, 2 L/70 40mm AA guns; 4 RBS-70 SAM.

RESERVES: 954 first-line, 14,377 second-line. 4 second-line Reserve Army Gps (garrisons): 2 Gps have 6 inf bns (1 Gp has 4, 1 has 2); 6 fd arty regts (2 Gps have 2; 2 have 1); 3 Gps have 1 motor sqn, 1 engr, 1 supply/tpt coy, 1 sigs coy; 3 AA btys (1 Gp has 2, 1 has 1).

Navy: 896 (to be increased to about 1,500).
1 P-31 offshore patrol vessel with 1 hel.
4 patrol vessels.
2 Br *Ton* coastal MCM (fishery protection).

Base: Cork.

RESERVES: 5 coys (361).

Air Force: 842; 15 combat ac.
3 Wings (1 trg):
  1 COIN sqn with 6 CM-170-2 *Super Magister*.
  1 COIN/trg sqn: 9 SF-260WE ac; 2 SA-342L *Gazelle* trg hel.
  1 liaison sqn with 7 Cessna FR-172H, 1 FR-172K.
  1 hel sqn with 8 *Alouette* III.
  1 composite sqn with 3 *King Air* (2 MR, 1 trg), 1 HS-125-700 (VIP).
(On order: 5 AS-365F *Dauphin* II MR hel (2 for Navy).)

Forces Abroad: Cyprus (UNFICYP) 6. Lebanon (UNIFIL) 1 bn+ (722); 4 AML-90 armd cars, 13 VTT/M3 APC. Other Middle East (UNTSO) 21.

MALTA

Population: 355,000.
Military service: voluntary.
Total armed forces: 800.
GDP 1982: £M 461.80 m ($1.123 bn).
Est def exp 1982: £M 6.20 m ($15.078 m). 1983:
6.50 m ($15.038 m).
FMA 1982: $3.642 m.
$1 = £M 0.4112 (1982), 0.4322 (1983).

Army: 800.
1 inf bn (incl 1 arty coy (6 40mm AA guns),
RPG-7 RL; 50 ZPU-4 14.5mm quad machine
guns.
1 task force.
1 marine section with 15 patrol craft.
1 air flt with 1 AB-206 *Jet Ranger*, 3 *Alouette*
III, 3 AB-47G hel (serviceability questionable).

Para-Military Forces: Reserves (*Id Dejma*) some
800: Voluntary general duties (500), women's
service (280). Pioneers/labour corps, 3 bns;
1,000.

SWEDEN

Population: 8,380,000.
Military service: Army and Navy 7½–15 months,
Air Force 8–12 months.
Total armed forces: 65,650 (47,850 conscripts;*
mobilizable to about 800,000 in 72 hours, excl
500,000 auxiliary orgs). 25,000 civilians pro-
vide spt services.
GDP 1982: S kr 622.64 bn ($99.105 bn). 1983:
695.41 bn ($90.701 bn).
Def budget 1982/3: S kr 19.110 bn ($2.688 bn).
1983/4: 20.488 bn ($2.589 bn).†
GDP growth: 0.5% (1982), 2.3% (1983).
Inflation: 9.0% (1982), 8.9% (1983).
Debt: $36.8 bn (1981), $38.9 bn (1982).
CY: $1 = kronor 6.2826 (1982), 7.6671 (1983).
FY: $1 = kronor 7.1101 (1982/3), 7.9129
(1983/4).

Army: 47,000 (37,000 conscripts).*
6 Military commands; 26 Defence districts
(*Laens*).
Peace establishment:
50 armd, cav, inf, arty, AA, engr and sig regts
(local defence, cadre for mobilization, basic
conscript trg).
War establishment (700,000 on mobilization,
incl 100,000 Home Guard):
4 armd bdes.
1 mech bde.
19 inf, 5 *Norrland* bdes.
60 indep armd, inf, arty and AA arty bns.
1 army aviation bn (39 hel).
11 arty aviation platoons (66 ac).

Local Defence Districts: 100 indep bns,
400–500 indep coys and Home Guard units.
AFV: 340 Strv-101, Strv-102/-104 (*Centurion*),
330 Strv-103B MBT; 200 Ikv-91 lt tks; Pbv-302
APC.
Arty: Type-4140 105mm, M-39 150mm, 155mm
SP guns, FH-77 Model 50 155mm how;
Bkv-1A 81mm, 120mm mor.
ATK: *Miniman* 74mm, *Carl Gustav* 84mm,
PV-1110 90mm RCL; RB-53 *Bantam*, RB-55
TOW ATGW.
AD: 20mm, 40mm AA guns; RB-69 (*Redeye*),
RBS-70 (incl (late 1984) Lvrbv SP), RB-77
(*Improved HAWK*) SAM.
Avn: 66 SK-61C (*Bulldog*) ac; 15 HKP-3
(AB-204B) tpt, 10 HKP-5 (Hughes 300C) lt
trg, 24 HKP-6 (*Jet Ranger*) utility hel.
(On order: Pvrbv 551 *TOW* veh).

Navy: 9,650, incl coast arty (6,250 conscripts),*
10 combat hel.
12 subs: 3 *Näcken*, 5 *Sjöormen*, 4 *Draken*.
2 *Halland* destroyers.
28 FAC(G): 16 *Hugin* with 6 RB-12 (*Penguin*), 12
Spica II (R-131) with RBS-15 SSM.
6 *Spica* I (T-121) FAC(T).
6 *Hanö* large, 10 coastal patrol craft.
2 minelayers, 1 minelayer/trg ships.
9 *Arko* coastal, 18 inshore minesweepers.
13 LCM, 74 LCU, 54 LCA.
5 coast arty bdes; 12 mobile, 53 static btys with
75mm, 105mm, 120mm, 152mm guns; RB-08,
RB-52 SSM; 30 defence (arty/SSM/inf) bns and
coys; coast rangers (coys): 10 coastal, 16 minelayers; 18 60-/70-class coastal patrol craft; 8
LCM, 81 LCU, 54 LCA.
2 hel sqns with 10 HKP-4 (Vertol 107)
ASW/MCM, 3 HKP-2 (*Alouette* II) utility, 10
HKP-6 liaison.
(On order: 4 A-17 subs, 2 *Stockholm* (*Spica* III)
FAC(G), 1 LCU, 6 *Landsort* minehunters;
RBS-15 SSM.)

Bases: Muskö, Härnösand, Karlskrona, Göte-
borg (spt only).

Air Force: 9,000 (4,600 conscripts);* 410 combat
ac.
1 attack gp.
4 AD districts.
12 wings (liaison ac 48 SK-50 (Saab 91) *Safir*).

* There are normally some 95,000 more conscripts
(70,000 Army, 4,500 Navy, 6,000 Air Force) plus
15,000 officer and NCO reservists doing 11–40 days
refresher training at some time in the year. Obligation
is 5 times per reservist between ages 20 and 47.
† Plus a further budget of S kr 854.5 m for Civil
Defence and S kr 525.6 m for economic defence
(strategic material stockpiling, etc.,). Additional
funding for a defence development plan: S kr 2.2 bn for
1984–7.

6 FGA sqns: 5 with 95 AJ-37 *Viggen*, 1 with 20 SK-60B/C (Saab 105).

12 AD sqns: 6 with 110 J-35F *Draken*, 2 with 36 J-35D, 4 with 70 JA-37 *Viggen*.

6 recce sqns with 52 SH/SF-37 *Viggen*.

2 OCU: 1 with 15 SK-37 *Viggen*; 1 with 12 SK-35C *Draken*.

1 tpt sqn with 8 C130E/H, 2 *Caravelle*.

Comms units with SK-60A, 1 C-47, lt civil ac.

Trainers incl 124 SK-60A/B/C, 57 SK-61, 24 J-32B/D/E *Lansen* (drone).

1 SAR sqn with 10 HKP-4, 10 HKP-5 hel.

1 utility unit with 6 HKP-2, 7 HKP-3 hel.

AAM: Rb-24, AIM-9J/L *Sidewinder*, Rb-27 (*Falcon*), Rb-28 (*Improved Falcon*), Rb-71 (*Skyflash*).

ASM: Rb-04E, Rb-05A, Rb-75 (*Maverick*).

AD: Semi-automatic control and surveillance system, *Stril* 60, co-ordinates all AD components.

(On order: 76 JA-37 *Viggen*, 30 JAS-39 *Gripen* multi-role ac, RBS-15F ASM.)

RESERVES (all services): 735,500; voluntary auxiliary organizations 500,000.

Forces Abroad: Cyprus (UNIFICYP): 1 inf bn (400). Lebanon (UNIFIL): HQ/log/medical tps (140).

Para-Military Forces: Coast Guard (550): 2 TV-171 fishery protection vessels, 67 patrol craft; (Air Arm) 2 Cessna 337G, 1 402C. Civil Defence: shelters for some 5 million people outside military ages (16–65).

SWITZERLAND

Population: 6,500,000.

Military service: 17 weeks recruit training followed by reservist refresher training of 3 weeks for 8 out of 12 years for *Auszug* (20–32), 2 weeks for 3 years for *Landwehr* (33–42), 1 week for 2 years for *Landsturm* (43–50).

Total armed forces: about 1,500 regular and 18,500 recruits* (mobilizable to some 1,100,000 incl Civil Defence in 48 hours).

GDP 1982: fr 196.0 bn ($96.537 bn). 1983: 202.66 bn ($96.546 bn).

Def exp 1983: fr 4.313 bn ($2.055). Def budget 1984: 4.476 bn ($1.974 bn).†

GDP growth: 1.2% (1982), 6.4% (1983).

Inflation: 6.6% (1981), 5.7% (1982), 3.0% (1983).

Debt 1982: $28.6 bn.

$1 = francs 2.0303 (1982), 2.0991 (1983), 2.2676 (mid-1984).

Army: *War establishment*: 580,000 on mobilization.

3 fd corps, each of 1 mech, 2 inf divs, corps units.

1 mountain corps of 3 mountain inf divs, corps units.

Fd corps tps: 3 infantry, 3 cyclist, 3 engr regts (3 bns); 3 sigs, 3 traffic control bns; 3 hel sqns, 3 lt ac flts.

Mountain corps tps: 1 mountain inf, 1 engr, 1 sigs regts; 7 indep inf, 2 pack horse bns; 1 traffic, 1 hel sqn.

17 indep bdes (11 frontier, 3 fortress, 3 redoubt).

6 Territorial Zones: 13 medical, 12 log, 11 civil def regts.

Indep units: 3 hy arty, 3 engr, 2 sigs regts.

20 Fortress Guard companies.

AFV: 300 Pz-55/57 (*Centurion*), 160 Pz-61, 400 Pz-68 MBT; 1,350 M-113 APC.

Arty: 900 105mm Model-35 guns and Model-46 how; M-50 towed, 476 PzHb-66 (M-109U) 155mm SP how; RWK-014 30-tube 81mm MRL; 3,000 81mm, 120mm mor.

ATK: 1,340 Model-50/-57 and 90mm ATK guns; 106mm RCL; 20,000 83mm RL; 6 MOWAG *Piranha* with *TOW*; 800 *Bantam*, *Dragon* ATGW.

AD: 1,200 20mm, 600 GDF-002 35mm AA guns.

Marine: 11 *Aquarius* patrol craft⟨.

(On order: 210 *Leopard* 2 MBT, 125 M-113 APC, *Dragon* ATGW.)

Air Force:‡ 45,000 on mobilization (maintenance by civilians); some 310 combat ac.

3 air regts.

11 FGA sqns: 2 with 32 F-5E and some *Venom* (in service to December 1984); 9 with 145 *Hunter* F58/T-68.

4 fighter sqns with 72 F-5E/F.

2 interceptor sqns with 31 *Mirage* IIIS/BS.

1 recce sqn with 16 *Mirage* IIIRS, 7 *Venom* FB-54.

4 liaison/SAR sqns with 16 *Porter*, 24 *Turbo-Porter*, 6 Do-27, 3 *Twin Bonanza*.

4 hel sqns with 21 *Alouette* II, 76 *Alouette* III hel.

Trainers incl 10 PC-7, 37 *Vampire* T-55, 65 *Vampire* DM-100 Mk 6, 2 *Mirage* IIIBS, 68 Pilatus P-3.

AAM: *Sidewinder*, AIM-26B *Falcon*.

ASM: AS-30.

1 air force fd bde (3 fd regts, 1 para coy, 1 lt ac wing).

1 airbase bde with 3 AA arty regts, each with 4 batteries of 20mm and 35mm guns.

1 AD bde with 1 SAM regt (2 bns, each of 2 btys; 64 *Bloodhound*), 7 AA arty regts (each of 3 btys; 20mm and 35mm guns, *Skyguard* fire control).

---

* Two recruit intakes a year (Jan/Jun) each of 17,000. Some 400,000 reservists a year do refresher training.

† Including civil defence outlays.

‡ Aviation Corps, an integral part of the Army.

3 comd and comms, 1 log regts.
(On order: 4 F-5F ftrs; 30 PC-7 *Turbo-Trainer* ac; 60 *Rapier* SAM launchers (from end-1984); 500 AGM-65 *Maverick* ASM.)

RESERVES (all services): 625,000 (45,000 officers, 110,000 NCOs, 3,000 women auxiliaries).

Para-Military Forces: 480,000 (300,000 fully trained). Shelter programme for 5,108,000; emergency supplies and medical facilities.

YUGOSLAVIA

Population: 23,100,000.
Military service: 15 months.
Total armed forces: 239,700 (154,000 conscripts).
GMP* 1981: YD 2.208 bn ($63.147 bn). 1982: 2.903 bn ($57.741 bn).
Est def exp 1982: YD 119.0 bn ($2.367 bn). 1983: 150.58 bn ($1.622 bn).
GNP growth: 1.5% (1981), 0.0% (1982).
Inflation: 32% (1982), 39% (1983).
Debt 1982: $19.0 bn.
   $1 = dinar 34.966 (1981), 50.276 (1982), 92.839 (1983).

Army: 191,000 (140,000 conscripts).
7 Military Regions:
   10 inf divs.
   8 indep tk bdes.
   9 indep inf bdes (incl 3 mech, 3 lt).
   3 'mountain' bdes.
   1 AB bde (Air Force manned, Army control).
   12 fd, 11 AA arty regts.
   6 ATK regts.
   4 SAM regts (SA-6).
AFV: 1,500 T-34/-54/-55, some T-72, 60 M-47 MBT; PT-76 lt tks; M-3A1, M-8, BRDM-2 scout cars; some M-80 MICV; 200 BTR-40/-50/-152, M-60 APC.
Arty: 1,800 M-1955, M-1931/-37 122mm, M-46 130mm and ML-20 152mm guns; M-48 76mm, 105mm incl SP, M-1938, D-30 and M-1974 SP, 122mm 155mm how; 82mm, 120mm mor; M-73 and M-63 128mm MRL; 4 *FROG*-7 SSM.
ATK: M-1943, PAK-40 75mm, T-12 100mm, M-36B2 90mm towed and SP ATK guns; 57mm, M-60 82mm, M-65 105mm RCL; Bov-1 veh with ATGW; *Snapper, Sagger* ATGW.
AD: M-55/-75 20mm, M-53 30mm, M-1939 37mm, L/70 40mm, S-60 57mm, M-1944 85mm, M-127 90mm, 3.7-in. (94mm) towed, Bov-3 (20mm), M-53/59, ZSU-57-2 SP AA guns; SA-6/-7/-9 SAM.
(On order: some 500 M-80 MICV.)

RESERVES: 500,000; (mobilization troops to complete units to war establishment). (Some

500 T-34/85, M-4 MBT; 300 M-18 *Hellcat* 76mm, M-36B2 90mm SP ATK guns in store.)

Navy: 12,000 incl 1,500 marines (6,000 conscripts).
7 subs: 2 *Sava*, 3 *Heroj*, 2 *Sutjeska*.
2 *Koni* frigates with 4 *Styx* SSM, 1 × 2 SA-N-4 SAM.
3 corvettes: 2 *Mornar*, 1 *Le Fougueux* (reserve).
16 FAC(G) with *Styx* (6 *Rade Koncar*, 10 *Osa*-I).
15 Sov *Shershen* FAC(T).
24 large patrol craft: 10 *Kraljevica*, 7 Type 131, 7 *Mirna* (some in reserve).
31 minesweepers: 4 *Vukov Klanac* coastal, 10 inshore (4 *Ham*, 6 M-117), 17 river (10 M-301, 7 *Nestin*) (some in reserve).
13 DTM-211 LCU/minelayers, 22 601-type LCA.
1 ASW hel sqn with 10 Ka-25.
1 tpt hel sqn with 20 Mi-8, *Partizan* (*Gazelle*).
2 marine bdes (2 regts, each of 2 bns).
25 coast arty btys with M-44 85mm, M-36 88mm, M-37 122mm, M-54 130mm, D-20 152mm guns; *Styx* SSM.
(On order: some 6 *Mirna* patrol craft.)

Bases: Lora/Split, Pula, Sibenik, Kardeljevo, Kotor.

Air Force: 36,700 (8,000 conscripts); some 420 combat ac, 20 armed hel.
2 air divisions:
12 FGA sqns with 25 *Kraguj*, 150 *Galeb/Jastreb*, some 25 *Orao*, some G-4 *Super Galeb*.
9 interceptor sqns with 130 MiG-21F/PF/M/bis, 20 MiG-21U.
2 recce sqns: 35 *Galeb/Jastreb* RJ-1, some *Orao*.
1 OCU: 30 *Galeb/Jastreb* J-1/Ty-1, some *Orao*.
2 tpt sqns: 15 C-47, 6 Yak-40, 2 An-12, 15 An-26, 2 DC-6B, 12 Il-14M, 2 *Mystère*-50 (VIP), 4 CL-215, PC-6.
Trainers incl 80 *Galeb/Jastreb*, 100 UTVA-75, UTVA-66 ac, 15 *Partizan* hel.
4 hel tpt sqns: 20 Mi-4, 70 Mi-8, 45 *Partizan*, 2 A-109 *Hirundo*. (Some 20 hel are armed.)
AAM: AA-2 *Atoll*.
ASM: AGM-65 *Maverick*.
Air Defence Force: (Army personnel, eqpt, Air Force control):
   15 AA regts.
   8 SA-2, 6 SA-3 SAM bns.
(On order: *Super Galeb*, some 180 *Orao* FGA, *Turbo-Porter* tpt ac, some 94 SA-341H *Partizan* hel.)

Para-Military Forces (under Army): Frontier Guards 15,000. Territorial Defence Force 1–3 million; mobile bdes, bns with arty and AA guns. Civil Defence 2 million on mobilization. Militia with TAB-71/-72 APC.

---

* Gross Material Product.

The Middle East and North Africa

Bilateral Agreements with External Powers

The Soviet Union signed a fifteen-year Treaty of Friendship and Co-operation with Iraq in April 1972 and a further agreement in December 1978. A similar treaty was signed with Syria on 8 October 1980, and Soviet air defence units are deployed in Syria under this Treaty. A Treaty of Friendship and Co-operation, signed with South Yemen in October 1979, was ratified in February 1980, and an agreement of Joint Co-operation was signed in January 1983. Soviet units use Aden's naval and air facilities. All three countries have received significant Soviet arms deliveries. Despite this, Iraq has tried to broaden her contacts with the West, particularly with France and Italy. In November 1979 Iran unilaterally abrogated two paragraphs of a 1921 treaty under which Moscow reserves the right to intervene in Iran's internal affairs if a third country threatens to attack the USSR from Iranian territory. The USSR has refused to accept this abrogation. Egypt still has major stocks of Soviet-pattern equipment, and spares and supplies have been provided by other Warsaw Pact nations, the People's Republic of China, Western nations and domestic manufacture.

Bulgaria and the People's Democratic Republic of Yemen (South Yemen) signed a Protocol for Co-operation in April 1980 and a Treaty of Friendship and Co-operation on 14 November 1981. Similar agreements with Hungary were reported in April and November 1981. Libya signed treaties of Friendship and Co-operation with Bulgaria and Romania in January 1983. Sudan and Romania signed an agreement providing technical co-operation and training in November 1982.

The United States concluded a mutual defence agreement with Israel in July 1952. A strategic co-operation understanding, reported in early 1982, led in March 1984 to a series of agreements covering aid and support, details of which have not been published. A similar agreement with Egypt (April 1952) was probably in abeyance between 1971 and 1975. A 1981 agreement enables the US to use Egyptian bases, but with significant reservations on Egypt's part. The status of US funding is in doubt. A similar agreement was reached with Morocco in May 1982. A 1959 mutual security agreement with Iran, though only an executive agreement, not a formally ratified treaty, has not been specifically abrogated. An agreement has been concluded with Oman to provide economic and military aid in exchange for permission to use Salalah and Masirah as staging bases. An agreement with Bahrain permits the US Navy to use port facilities. In November 1981 a strategic co-operation agreement was signed with Tunisia.

Britain concluded treaties of friendship with Bahrain, Qatar and the United Arab Emirates (UAE) in August 1971. She has supplied arms to Bahrain, Egypt, Jordan, Kuwait, Oman, Qatar, Saudi Arabia, Sudan and the UAE. France has continuing arms-supply arrangements with Egypt, Iraq, Lebanon, Libya, Morocco, Sudan and Tunisia. West Germany has provided technical training assistance to Sudan under a 1982 agreement. Spain has reached a defence agreement with Morocco enabling her navy to use Moroccan ports. The benefits to Morocco have not been identified.

China signed a Treaty of Friendship with North Yemen in 1964, under which minor arms were provided. Arms and spare parts were sent to Egypt under agreements signed in 1978/9 and 1983. A military co-operation agreement was signed with Sudan in January 1982 and arms supplied. North Korea and Libya signed a Treaty of Alliance or Friendship and Co-operation in November 1982 which permits exchanges of military data, specialists and supplies.

Peace-Keeping Forces

The United Nations withdrew the 4,000-man United Nations Emergency Force (UNEF) from the Sinai on 24 July 1979; its duties were temporarily assumed by the United Nations Truce

Supervisory Organization (UNTSO), 298 officers, which has been active in the region since 1949. The Egyptian/Israeli border is now patrolled by the 2,200-man Multi-national Force and Observers (MFO) under the Israeli/Egyptian peace treaty; contingents come from the US (1,100), Australia (110), Britain (35), Colombia (500), Fiji (469), France (40), Italy (90), the Netherlands (105), New Zealand (35) and Uruguay (70).

The United Nations also deploys in the Golan Heights the 1,279-man Disengagement Observer Force (UNDOF), made up of contingents from Austria (529), Canada (221), Finland (383) and Poland (151).

The United Nations Interim Force in Lebanon (UNIFIL) consists of some 6,285 men from France (496), Fiji (623), Finland (1,386), Ghana (557), Ireland (732), Italy (40), Netherlands (807), Norway (839), Senegal (559) and Sweden (144).

A Multi-National Force, set up in Beirut, Lebanon, in September 1982 to monitor the cease-fire and composed of Italian (2,038), French (1,100), US (2,000) and British (87) troops, was withdrawn in March 1984.

Arrangements within the Region

Algeria, Bahrain, Djibouti, Iraq, Jordan, Kuwait, Lebanon, Libya, Mauritania, Morocco, Oman, the Palestine Liberation Organization (PLO), Qatar, Saudi Arabia, Somalia, Sudan, Syria, Tunisia and North and South Yemen are members of the League of Arab States (Egypt's membership was suspended in March 1979). Among its subsidiary bodies are the Arab Supreme Defence Council, comprising Foreign and Defence Ministers (set up in 1950), the Permanent Military Committee of army general staffs (1950), which is an advisory body, and the Unified Arab Command (1964).

Syrian and Palestine Liberation Army forces, comprising the Arab Deterrent Force, remain in northern Lebanon. Syria has reinforced her component and maintains a degree of control over the Arab guerrilla group elements in the Beqa'a Valley and northern Lebanon. Israeli forces, supported by a Lebanese militia, control the south.

Algeria and Libya signed a defence agreement in 1975; though a merger was discussed in 1982, this has not yet occurred. Egypt and Sudan came to a joint defence agreement in 1977. The Joint Defence Council's minutes of December 1981 were tantamount to another, and in October 1982 an 'Integration Charter' was signed, covering, amongst other activities, military policy. This Charter will be studied 'for 10 years', but Egyptian defence co-operation has been noted during successive crises between Sudan and Libya. Saudi Arabia has long supported Morocco against *Polisario* guerrillas; the two countries signed a security pact in February 1982. An understanding between Saudi Arabia and Iraq is believed to have been signed in 1979. Jordan and Iraq ratified a Defence agreement in March 1981. The Gulf Co-operative Council, created in May 1981 by Bahrain, Kuwait, Oman, Qatar, Saudi Arabia and the UAE, is developing a mutual defence structure to include a joint strike force, air defence, transport and procurement. It is being reinforced by internal security pacts between Saudi Arabia and Bahrain, Qatar, Oman (1982) and the UAE. A draft Gulf security agreement is being considered. Libya, South Yemen and Ethiopia formed an Aden Treaty Tripartite Alliance in 1981; it included a joint defence commitment but nothing more concrete has been reported. North and South Yemen have agreed to a merger (1981); the details remain obscure. Jordan, Morocco and North Yemen have announced the departure of unspecified numbers of volunteers to assist Iraq against Iran, but no formed units have been despatched. Iraq has stated that multi-national composite units have been formed; their roles are obscure. Sudan and Ethiopia agreed a regime of security, stability and non-interference in each other's internal affairs in July 1982.

Arms movements in the region are peculiarly complex. Egypt has supplied arms to Morocco, Sudan and Iraq. Algeria and Libya have supplied arms to *Polisario*, and most Arab countries have supplied Palestinian guerrillas with arms. In some cases a third nation funds the recipient's foreign arms purchases. Iran has reportedly received arms, supplies and spares from, *inter alia*, Israel, North Korea and Eastern Europe and is also buying material on the open market in Western Europe. Iraq has apparently recently received arms from Egypt, the USSR, China, North Korea, France, Portugal and Brazil.

In 1975 an Arab Organization for Industrialization (AOI) was set up in Egypt under the aegis of Saudi Arabia, Qatar, the UAE and Sudan to encourage indigenous Arab arms production. Arab involvement ended following Egypt's rapprochement with Israel. Egypt has been entering into co-production agreements with Britain, France, the US and Yugoslavia. To replace the AOI, Iraq, Kuwait, Qatar, Saudi Arabia and the UAE agreed in 1979 to set up an $8-billion arms industry in the UAE. This proposal is still being studied by the Gulf Co-operative Council.

ALGERIA

Population: 21,700,000.
Military service: 6 months.
Total armed forces: 130,000.
GDP 1981: DA 188.1 bn ($43.584 bn), 1982: 206.3 bn ($44.924 bn).
Est def operating budget 1982: DA 3.893 bn ($847.742 m).* 1983: 4.200 bn ($877.046 m).*
GDP growth: 4.2% (1982), 7.3% (1983).
Inflation: 6.7% (1982), 4.0% (1983).
Debt: $15.5 bn (1982).
$1 = dinar 4.3158 (1981), 4.5922 (1982), 4.7888 (1983).

Army: 110,000.
7 Military Regions.
2 armd bdes.
5 mech bdes.
6 mot inf bdes.
1 AB/special force bde.
28 indep inf bns.
2 para bns.
5 indep arty bns.
11 AD bns.
4 engr bns.
12 coys desert troops.
AFV: 300 T-54/-55, 300 T-62, 100 T-72 MBT; 100 BRDM-2 armd cars; 500 BMP-1 MICV; 350 BTR-50/-60, 300 BTR-152 APC.
Arty: 60 ZIS-3 (M-1942) 76mm, 100 D-44 85mm, 150 M-1931/37 122mm towed, 40 ISU-122, 30 M-1974 122mm, 30 ISU-152 152mm SP guns; 40 M-1938, 150 D-30 122mm, 20 M-1937 152mm towed how; 150 BM-21 122mm, 20 BM-24 240mm MRL; 180 120mm, and 160mm mor.
ATK: 90 215-2 57mm, 50 SU-100 SP guns; 20 AT-3 *Sagger, Milan* ATGW.
AD: 440 37mm, 57mm, 85mm, 100mm, 130mm towed, 100 ZSU-23-4 and ZSU-57-2 SP AA guns; 18 SA-6, SA-7/-9 SAM.
(On order: 44 Panhard M-3 APC.)

RESERVES: up to 100,000.

Navy: 8,000.
2 *R*-class subs.
2 *Koni* frigates with 2 × 2 SA-N-4 SAM.
3 *Nanuchka* corvettes with 4 SS-N-2b SSM, 2 × 2 SA-N-4 SAM.
12 FAC(G) with *Styx* SSM; 3 *Osa*-I, 9 *Osa*-II.

4 Brooke Marine FAC.
1 T-43 ocean minesweeper (in reserve).
1 *Polnocny* LCT, 1 *Brooke* LST.
(On order: 2 FAC(G), 1 LST.)

Bases: Algiers, Annaba, Mers el Kebir.

Air Force: 12,000; some 300 combat ac, 37 armed hel.
7 FGA sqns: 2 with 20 Su-7BM; 2 with 60 MiG-17; 3 with some 40 MiG-23BM, some 18 Su-20 (*Fitter* C).
4 interceptor sqns: 3 with 95 MiG-21MF/F; 1 with 18 MiG-25 *Foxbat* A.
1 recce sqn with 4 MiG-25R *Foxbat* B.
1 COIN sqn with 24 *Magister*.
1 MR sqn with 7 F-27 (Navy-assigned).
1 OCU with 4 MiG-15.
1 tpt sqn with 8 An-12, 8 C-130H, 6 C-130H-30, 1 Il-18, 1 *Mystère-Falcon*, 1 *Caravelle*.
6 hel sqns with 4 Mi-6, 28 Mi-4, 12 Mi-8, 37 Mi-24, 5 *Puma*, 6 Hughes 269A, 4 *Alouette* II.
Other ac incl 6 *King Air*, 2 *Super King Air* T-200T (MR), 3 *Queen Air*.
Trainers incl MiG-15/-17/-21UTI, Su-7U, 2 MiG-23U, 3 MiG-25U, 6 T-34C.
1 SAM regt: 24 SA-2 (96 msls), some 20 SA-3.
AAM: AA-2 *Atoll*.

Para-Military Forces: Gendarmerie 24,000: 44 Panhard M-3 APC. Coastguard 550: 2 P-6 FAC(T), 16 *Baglietto* FAC(G) (6 Gemini 36, 10 Type 20).

BAHRAIN

Est population: 400,000.
Military service: voluntary.
Total armed forces: 2,800.
GDP 1981: BD 1.698 bn ($4.516 bn). 1982: 1.736 bn ($4.617 bn).
Est def exp 1982: BD 84.1 m ($223.670 m).†
1983: 95.2 m ($253.191 m).†
GDP growth: 6.7% (1982), 5.0% (1983).
Inflation: 8.9% (1982), 3.0% (1983).
Debt: $410 m (1982).
$1 = dinar 0.3760 (1981/2/3).

---

* Excl eqpt expenditure.

† Excl BD 21.4 m (1982) and 9.7 m (1983) defence and security development budget.

Army: 2,300.
1 bde:
  1 inf bn.
  1 armd car sqn.
  1 arty, 2 mor btys.
8 *Saladin*, 20 AML-90 armd, 8 *Ferret* scout cars;
110 M-3 APC; 8 105mm lt guns; 6 81mm mor;
6 120mm RCL; *TOW* ATGW; 6 RBS-70 SAM.
(On order: 7 M-198 155mm how; *TOW* ATGW).

Navy: 300.
2 Lürssen 45-metre FAC(G) with 4 *Exocet* SSM.
2 Lürssen 38-metre FAC.

Air Force: 200.
1 hel sqn with 10 AB-212.

Para-Military Forces: Coastguard: 180; 16
coastal patrol craft, 2 landing craft (1
Loadmaster, 1 60-ft). Police: 2,500; 2 Bell 412,
2 *Scout*, 3 BO-105, 2 Hughes 500D hel.

EGYPT

Population: 47,200,000.
Military service: 3 years (selective).
Total armed forces: 460,000 (255,000 con-
scripts).
GNP 1982: £E 20.396 bn ($29.141 bn). 1983:
22.225 bn ($31.755 bn).
Def budget 1982/3: £E 1.746 bn ($2.495 bn).
1983/4: 2,130 bn ($3.043 bn). Est 1984/5:
2,600 bn ($3.715 bn).
GDP growth: 6.5% (1982), 7.3% (1983).
Inflation: 15% (1982), 16% (1983).
Est FMA: $1 bn (1982), $1.5 bn (1983).
Debt: $22.2 bn (1982).
  $1 = £E 0.6999 (1982/4).

Army: 315,000 (180,000 conscripts).*
3 Army HQ.
3 armd divs (each with 1 armd, 2 mech bdes).
5 mech inf divs (each with 2 mech, 1 armd bdes).
4 inf divs (each with 2 inf, 1 mech bdes).
1 Republican Guard Div (2 bdes).
2 indep armd bdes.
9 indep inf bdes.
2 airmobile, 1 para bdes.
12 arty bdes.
2 hy mor bdes.
6 ATGW bdes.
7 cdo gps.
2 SSM regts (1 with *FROG*-7, 1 with *Scud* B).
AFV: 800 T-54/-55, 600 T-62, some 350
AM-60 (M-60A3) MBT; 30 PT-76 lt tks; 300
BRDM-1/-2 scout cars; 200 BMP-1, 250
BMP-600P MICV; 2,500 OT-62, *Walid, Fahd*,
BTR-40/-50/-60/-152, 550 M-113A2 APC.
Arty: 1,500 85mm, M-1955, 200 SU-100 SP

100mm, D-30 122mm, M-46 130mm, SU-152
SP 152mm and S-23 180mm guns; M-1938
122mm, M-1943 152mm how; 400 120mm,
160mm and 240mm mor; about 300 122mm
(incl *Saqr* 30), 132mm, 140mm and 240mm
MRL; 12 *FROG*-7, 12 *Scud* B SSM.
ATK: 900 57mm (incl SP), 76mm and 100mm
guns; 900 82mm and B-11 107mm RCL; 1,000
*Sagger, Snapper, Swatter, Milan, Beeswing,
Swingfire* and *TOW* ATGW.
AD: 350 ZSU-23-4 and ZSU-57-2 SP AA guns;
75 SA-6, SA-7/*as-Saqr*, SA-9, 16 *Crotale* SAM.
(On order: some 300 M-60A3 MBT; 350
BMR-600P, some 500 M-113A2 APC;
M-109A2 155mm SP how; JPz SK-105 SP ATK
guns, 52 M-901 SP *TOW* AFV; 100 M-106A2
and M-125A2 mor carriers; 200 *TOW*
launchers, 4,000 msls (incl 2,500 *Improved
TOW*), 2,000 *Swingfire* ATGW; *as-Saqr* (SA-7),
Skyguard twin 35mm/*Sparrow* SAM AD sys-
tems, 4 *Crotale* SAM.)

RESERVES: about 300,000.

Navy: 33,000 (15,000 conscripts).*
12 subs: 8 *R*-class (4 Ch), 4 Sov *W*-class.
5 destroyers: 4 Sov *Skory* (1 with 1 x 2 *Styx* SSM),
1 Br *Z*-class.
5 frigates: 2 Spanish F-30 (*Descubierta*); 3 Br (1
Black Swan, 1 *Hunt*, 1 *River* (trg and sub
spt ship)).
24 FAC(G): 6 *Ramadan*⟨ with 4 *Otomat* SSM; 6
October-6 (P-6)⟨ with 2 *Otomat*; 8 Sov *Osa*-1
with 4 *Styx* SSM, SA-7 SAM; 4 *Komar* with 2
SS-N-2A SSM⟨.
22 large patrol craft: 12 Sov SO-1, 6 with 40
BM-21 122mm MRL, some with SA-7 SAM; 4
Ch *Hainan*, 6 *Timsah*.
14 Sov FAC(T): 2 *Shershen*, 8 P-6⟨, 4 P-4 with 1 ×
8 122mm MRL⟨.
14 Sov FAC with 1 BM-21 122mm MRL: 4
Shershen with SA-7 SAM; 12 P-6 with BM-21
or 1 × 12 BM-24 240mm MRL⟨.
12 Sov minesweepers: 10 ocean (6 T-43, 4
Yurka), 2 T-301 inshore.
3 SRN-6 hovercraft (may be minelayers).
3 Sov *Polnocny* LCT.
13 Sov LCU (9 *Vydra*, 4 SMB1).
1 ASW hel sqn with 6 *Sea King* Mk 47.
Coastal defence unit (Army manpower, Navy
control): SSM-4-1 130mm guns, 30 *Otomat*
and *Samlet* SSM.
(On order: 4 *Lüda* DDG; 6 *Cormoran* FAC(G); 6
Shanghai II FAC, 2 *Hainan*, 9 *Swift*, 12
Timsah patrol boats; 14 SRN-6 hovercraft; 16
Harpoon, Otomat SSM.)

---

* Most Soviet equipment now in reserve. Incl 1,200
MBT, 269 combat aircraft. Some shown as Soviet has
been refurbished with Western, Chinese and domestically produced components.

Bases: Alexandria, Port Said, Mersa Matruh, Port Tewfig, Hurghada, Safaqa.

RESERVES: about 15,000.

Air Force: 27,000 (10,000 conscripts); 504 combat ac, 36 armed hel (incl AD comd).*
5 FGA regts: 2 with 33 F-4E, 44 Ch F-6; 2 with 50 MiG-17F (replacing with *Alpha Jet* MS-2 (6)), 36 Su-7BM; 1 with 53 *Mirage* 5SDE2.
2 recce sqns with 6 *Mirage* 5SDR, 12 MiG-21R/RF, 20 Su-7.
1 MR sqn with 5 Il-28.
ELINT ac: 2 EC-130H, 2 E-2C *Hawkeye*.
4 hel sqns with some 64 *Gazelle* (some 36 with *HOT* ATGW).
1 tpt bde of 5 sqns with 21 C-130H, 18 Il-14, 10 An-12, 4 *Falcon* 20 (VIP), 10 DHC-5D *Buffalo*, 1 Boeing 707, 1 Boeing 737.
8 utility hel sqns with 20 Mi-4, 40 Mi-8, 52 SA-342H, 4 SA-342K *Gazelle*, 25 *Commando* (2 VIP), 15 CH-47C.
Trainers incl F-7, F-6, MiG-21U/US, 11 *Alpha Jet* MS-1, 59 L-29 (being replaced), 60 *Gomhouria*, 36 Yak-18, *Wilga* 35/80, 4 FT-6, 6 *Mirage* 5SDD, 6 F-16B.
AAM: AA-2 *Atoll*, R-530, *Sparrow*, AIM-9P3, -9L, *Sidewinder*.
ASM: AS-1 *Kennel*, AS-5 *Kelt*, *Maverick*, *HOT*.
(On order: Some 55 Ch F-7 (MiG-21-type), 40 F-16C/D, 40 *Mirage* 2000, 16 *Mirage* 5E2 ftrs; 42 Ch F-6, some 33 *Alpha Jet* (11 MS-2 FGA, 9 MS-1 trg); 2 E-2C AEW; 6 C-130H tpt, 120 EMB-312 *Tucano* trg ac; 12 *Sea King* ASW, *Super Puma*, 24 *Cobra* with *TOW*, 15 CH-47, 18 UH-12E, 24 *Gazelle* (some 12 with *HOT* ATGW), 4 AS-61 hel; *Sparrow*, 150 *Sidewinder* AAM; *Exocet* AM-39, *Maverick* ASM.)

RESERVES: about 20,000.

Air Defence Command: 85,000 (50,000 conscripts): (230 combat ac).*
12 centres under construction.
2 AD divs: regional bdes.
100 msl and AA bns, radar bns; some 60 SA-2 (360 launchers), 50 SA-3 (200 launchers) sites. 360 SA-2, 200 SA-3, 75 SA-6, 12 *Improved HAWK* (36 msls), 16 *Crotale* SAM; 2,500 20mm, 23mm, 37mm, 40mm, 57mm, 85mm and 100mm AA guns; AN/TPS 63, AN/TS9-73, *Fan Song*, *Flat Face* P-15, *Spoon Rest* P-12, *Low Blow*, *Straight Flush* missile/gun and *Squint Eye*, *Long Track* EW radars.
3 interceptor bdes: 235 combat ac.
5 sqns with 122 MiG-21F/PFS/FL/PFM/M/ MF, 2 with 25 F-7; 2 with 34 F-16A, 54 *Mirage* 5SDE1.
(On order: Ch CSA-1, *Spada*, LPD-20 search

radar; 8 btys totalling 96 launchers, 288 *Improved HAWK* SAM.)

Forces Abroad: Iraq, Oman, Sudan, Somalia, Zaire.

Para-Military Forces: 139,000: National Guard, 60,000; Frontier Corps, 12,000; Defence and Security, 60,000; Coast Guard, 7,000; 3 *Nisr*, 6 *Crestitalia*, 6 *Bertram* patrol boats, 34 rescue launches.

IRAN

Population: 42,500,000.
Military service: 24 months.
Total armed forces: 555,000 regular. Paramilitary forces recruited for specific offensives could add 200,000–250,000.
GDP 1981: rial 7,271 bn ($92.828 bn). 1982: 8,700.0 bn ($104.063 bn).
Est def exp 1982/3: rial 1,300 bn ($15.550 bn). 1983/4: 1,500 bn ($17.370 bn).
GDP growth: 5.6% (1981), 5.0% (1982).
Inflation: 23.0% (1982), 20% (1983).
Debt: $3.4 bn (1982).
$1 = rial 78.328 (1981), 83.603 (1982), 86.358 (1983).

Army: 250,000 (100,000 conscripts).
3 mech divs (each 3 bdes: 9 armd, 18 mech bns).
7 inf divs.
1 AB bde.
2 Special Forces divs.
Some indep armd, inf bdes.
12 SAM bns with *HAWK*.
Ground Forces Air Support units.
AFV: 100 T-54/-55, 50 T-62, 100 T-72, 300 *Chieftain* Mk 3/5, 200 M-47/-48, 250 M-60A1 MBT; 50 *Scorpion* lt tks; 130 EE-9 *Cascavel* armd cars, 180 BMP-1 MICV; about 280 M-113, 600 BTR-40/-50/-60/-152 APC.
Arty: some 1,000 M-116 75mm pack, M-1965 85mm, M-46 130mm towed, 30 M-107 175mm SP guns; M-101 105mm, M-109A1 SP 155mm, M-115 towed, 10 M-110 SP 203mm how; 65 BM-21 122mm MRL; 81mm, M-30 4.2-in. (107mm), 3,000 120mm mor.
ATK: 57mm, 75mm, M-40 106mm RCL; RPG-7 RL; some 120 ASU-85 SP guns; *ENTAC*, SS-11/-12, *Dragon*, *TOW* ATGW.
AD: 1,500 ZU-23 towed, ZSU-23-4 SP 23mm, 37mm towed, ZSU-57-2 SP 57mm, 85mm

---

* Most Soviet equipment now in reserve. Incl 1,200 MBT, 269 combat aircraft. Some shown as Soviet has been refurbished with Western, Chinese and domestically produced components.

towed AA guns; *HAWK/Improved HAWK*, SA-7 SAM.*

Ac incl 46 Cessna (40 185, 6 310), 10 O-2A, 2 F-27, 5 *Shrike Commander*, 2 *Falcon*.*

Hel: AH-1 *Cobra*, CH-47C, (270 Bell 214A, 35 AB-205A, 15 AB-206 were also held.)*

RESERVES: 350,000, ex-service volunteers. '*Quds*' bns.

Revolutionary Guard Corps (*Pasdaran*): 250,000; 8 div-sized formations, org in bns, serve indep or with Army; small arms, spt weapons from Army. Naval element; some Air.

Navy: 20,000, incl naval air and marines.*
3 destroyers with 4 *Standard* SSM; 1 Br *Battle* with 1 × 4 *Seacat* SAM; 2 US *Sumner* (in reserve).
4 *Saam* frigates with 1 × 5 *Seakiller* SSM, 1 × 3 *Seacat* SAM (1 probably non-operational).
2 US PF-103 corvettes.
10 *Kaman* (*La Combattante* II) FAC(G) with a total of 7 *Harpoon* SSM (?6 serviceable).
7 large patrol craft: 3 Improved PGM-71, 4 *Cape*; (5 lost?).
3 US coastal, 2 inshore minesweepers; (2 lost?).
10 SRN-6, BH-7 hovercraft.
2 landing ships, 1 US LCU.
2 fleet supply ships.
3 Marine bns.
(On order: 1 replenishment ship).

Bases: Bandar Lengeh, Bandar Abbas, Bushehr, Kharg, Bandar-e-Anzali, Bandar-e-Khomeini.

NAVAL AIR: 2 combat ac, 12 combat hel (may be under Air Force control).*
1 MR sqn with 2 P-3F *Orion* ⎫ may have
1 ASW hel sqn with 10 SH-3D ⎬ combined.
1 MCM hel sqn with 2 RH-53D. ⎭
1 tpt sqn with 4 *Shrike Commander*, 4 F-27, 1 *Mystère* 20, 7 AB-212.

Air Force: 35,000; perhaps 95 serviceable combat ac.*
4 FGA sqns with some 35 F-4D/E.
4 FGA sqns with some 50 F-5E/F.
1 recce sqn (dets) with some 10 F-14A, 3 RF-4E.
2 tanker/tpt sqns with 12 Boeing 707, 7 747.
5 tpt sqns with 28 C-130E/H, 10 F-27, 2 *Aero Commander* 690, 4 *Falcon* 20.
Hel: 10 HH-34F, 10 AB-206A, 5 AB-212, 39 Bell 214C, 10 CH-47 *Chinook*, 2 S-61A4.
Trainers incl F33A/C *Bonanza*, T-33, 6 PC-7.
5 SAM sqns with *Rapier*, 25 *Tigercat*.
AAM: *Phoenix, Sidewinder, Sparrow*.
ASM: AS-12, *Maverick*.

Forces Abroad: Lebanon: some 650 Revolutionary Guard.

Para-Military Forces: *Basidj* 'Popular Mobilization Army' volunteers, mostly youths, small arms, ancillary to main field forces. Gendarmerie (5,000 incl border guard element); *Mostazafin* (Guards); *Hezbollahi* (Home Guard) 2,500,000; Border Tribal Militia. Cessna 185/310 lt ac, AB-205/-206 hel, patrol boats.*

IRAQ

Population: 14,900,000.
Military service: basic 21–24 months, extended for war.
Total armed forces: 642,500 (mostly conscripts).
Est GDP 1981: ID 9.4 bn ($31.832 bn). 1982/3: 10.324 bn ($34.600 bn).
Est def exp 1982: ID 2.40 bn ($8.043 bn). 1983: 3.20 bn ($10.296 bn).
GDP growth: −5.0% (1982), −7.4% (1983).
Inflation: 16% (1982), 18% (1983).
Est FMA: $25–35 bn (1981/3).
Debt: $6.2 bn (1982).†
  $1 = dinar 0.2953 (1981), 0.2984 (1982), 0.3108 (1983).

Army: 600,000.*
4 corps HQ.
6 armd divs.
5 mech/mot inf divs.
5 inf divs.
4 mountain divs.
2 Republican Guard armd bdes.
3 special forces bdes.
9 Reserve bdes.
15 Peoples Army/Volunteer inf bdes.
AFV: 4,500 T-54/-55/-62/-72, 260 Ch T-69, 60 Romanian M-77 MBT; 100 PT-76 lt tks; about 3,200 AFV, incl BRDM, FUG-70, ERC-90, MOWAG *Roland*, 200 EE-9 *Cascavel*, EE-3 *Jararaca* armd cars, BMP MICV, BTR-50/-60/ -152, OT-62/-64, 100 VCRTH (with *HOT* ATGW), Panhard M-3, EE-11 *Urutu* APC.
Arty: some 3,500 guns incl 75mm pack, 1,000 85mm, 50 SU-100 100mm SP, D-30 and ISU 122mm SP and M-46 130mm; 150 GHN-45 155mm gun/how; M-56 pack, M-102 105mm, M-1938, SP-74 122mm, M-1943, M-1955 towed, M-1973 SP 152mm, M-114, M-109 SP 155mm how; FGT 108-R (SS-06) 108mm, BM-21 122mm, BM-14 140mm MRL; 19 *FROG*-7, 9 *Scud* B, 15 SS-12 SSM; 120mm, 160mm mor.
ATK: SPG-9 73mm, B-10 82mm, 107mm RCL; 85mm, 100mm towed, 100 JPz SK-105

---

* Losses and resupply system make estimates very tentative.
† Excl debt to Gulf states.

105mm SP guns; *Sagger*, SS-11, *Milan*, *HOT* ATGW.

AD: 4,000 23mm, ZSU-23-4 SP, M-1939 and twin 37mm, 57mm incl ZSU-57-2 SP, 85mm, 100mm and 130mm AA guns; SA-2/-3/-6/-7/-9, 30 *Roland* SAM.

(On order: 140 M-77, T-62 MBT; 100 EE-9 *Cascavel*, EE-3 *Jararaca* armd cars; 80 EE-11 *Urutu* APC; 85 155 GCT 155mm SP guns; SP-73 152mm SP how; 6 *Astros* MLRS; SS-11 ATGW; X-40, *Scud* B SSM; SAM).

(Some captured Iranian eqpt, incl tks, AFV, arty, ATGW, has been taken into service.)

RESERVES: 75,000.

Navy: 4,500.*
1 frigate (trg).
10 Sov *Osa* FAC(G) with 4 *Styx* SSM.
5 Sov large patrol craft: SO-1, *Poluchat*; (2 or 3 lost?).
12 Sov P-6 FAC(T)((7 lost ?).
10 Sov coastal patrol craft: *Nyryat* II, PO-2, *Zhuk*; (5 lost ?).
5 minesweepers: Sov T-43 ocean, *Yevgenya*(inshore.
4 Sov *Polnocny* LCT (1 lost ?).
1 spt ship.
(On order: 4 *Lupo* frigates, 6 Italian 650-ton corvettes.

Bases: Basra, Umm Qasr.

Air Force: 38,000 incl 10,000 AD personnel; some 580 combat ac, some 150 armed hel.*
2 bbr sqns: 1 with perhaps 7 Tu-22, 1 with 8 Tu-16 (ex-Egypt).
11 FGA sqns: 4 with some 100 MiG-23BM; 6 with some 95 Su-7 and 80 Su-20; 1 with 12 (2?) *Hunter* FB-59/FR-10; 5 *Super Etendard*.
5 interceptor sqns with some 25 MiG-25, some 40 MiG-19, some 150 MiG21, 45 *Mirage* F-1EQ, 4 F-1BQ.
1 recce sqn with 5 MiG-25.
2 tpt sqns with 10 An-2, 10 An-12, 8 An-24, 2 An-26, 9 Il-76, 2 Tu-124, 13 Il-14, 1 *Heron*.
11 hel sqns with 35 Mi-4, 15 Mi-6, 150 Mi-8, 40 Mi-24, 40 *Alouette* III (some with AS-12 ASM), 11 *Super Frelon* (some with *Exocet* AM-39 ASM), 50 (15?) *Gazelle* (some with *HOT*), 13 *Puma*, 30 BO-105 (some with SS-11), 7 *Wessex* Mk 52.
Trainers incl MiG-15/-21/-23U, Su-7U, *Hunter* T-69, 10 Yak-11, 50 L-29, 40 L-39, 48 AS-202/18A, 16 *Flamingo*, 50 PC-7 *Turbo-Trainer*.
AAM: *Magic* I, R-530, R-550, AA-1/-2/-6/-7/-8.
ASM: 360 *HOT*, AS-11/-12, *Swatter* ATGW, *Exocet* AM-39, AS-4 *Kitchen*, AS-5 *Kelt*.
(On order, status unclear: some 100 MiG-23/-25, 39 *Mirage* F-1 ftrs; 80 EMB-312 *Tucano* trg

ac; 3 *Super Frelon*, 10 *Gazelle*, *Lynx*, 26 *Puma*, Mi-24, 6 AS-61TS, 8 AB-212 (ASW) hel; MPS-1, 20 *Exocet* AM-39 ASM; Super 530 AAM.)

Para-Military Forces: Frontier Guards; security troops 4,800; People's Army 650,000; Perhaps 10,000 volunteers from Arab countries.

ISRAEL

Population: 4,200,000.
Military service: men 39 months, women 24 months (Jews and Druze only; Christians may volunteer). Annual training for reservists thereafter up to age 54 for men, 34 (or marriage) for women.
Total armed forces: 141,000 (98,300 conscripts); mobilization to 500,000, of which 100,000 can report in about 24 hours.
GDP 1982: IS 557.613 bn ($22.978 bn). Est 1983: 1,350 bn ($24.015 bn).
Est def exp 1982: IS 200.0 bn ($8.242 bn). 1983: 280.0 bn ($4.981 bn). 1984: $4-8 bn.†
GDP growth: 1.2% (1982), 1.1% (1983).
Inflation: 120.4% (1982), some 150% (1983).
FMA: some $1.5 bn (1982), some $1.7 bn (1983).
Debt: $28 bn (1982).
$1 = shekels 24.267 (1982), 56.214 (1983).

Army: 104,000 (88,000 conscripts, male and female), 600,000 on mobilization, incl civil defence units.
11 armd divs.
33 armd bdes (3 tk, 1 mech inf bns).
10 mech inf bdes (5 para-trained).
12 territorial/border inf bdes with *Nahal* militia.
15 arty bdes (each 5 bns of 3 btys).
AFV: 3,600 MBT, incl 1,100 *Centurion*, 600 M-48, 1,210 M-60, 250 T-54/-55, 150 T-62, 250 *Merkava* I/II; about 4,000 AFV/recce incl *Ramta* RBY, BRDM-1/-2, *Shoet* Mk 2, M-2/-3; 4,000 M-113, OT-62, BTR-50P APC.‡
Arty: M-46 130mm, 140 M-107 175mm SP guns; 70 M-101 105mm, 100 D-30 122mm, M-68/-71 155mm towed, 300 Soltam L-33, M-50, M-72, 300 M-109 155mm, 48 M-110 203mm SP how; 122mm, 160mm, BM-24 240mm, MAR-290 290mm MRL; *Lance* SSM; 900 81mm, 120mm and 160mm mor (some SP).‡

---

* Losses make eqpt estimates very tentative.
† Total war costs reported as an additional $1.5-2 bn. High inflation rates and continued occupation costs make defence expenditure estimates highly unreliable, and thus meaningless in shekel terms.
‡ Does not include captured PLO equipment reported as some 120 T-34, T-54 APC, 130mm guns, BM-21 MRL, 2 SU-23-4 AA guns, SA-9 SAM.

ATK: B-300 82mm RL; 106mm RCL; *TOW, Cobra, Dragon, Picket, Milan* ATGW.
AD: 2 btys with 24 *Vulcan/Chaparral* 20mm gun/msl systems, 900 20mm, ZSU-23-4 23mm SP, 30mm and 40mm AA guns; *Redeye* SAM.
(On order: 125 M-60 MBT; *Re'em* AFV; 800 M-113 APC; 200 M-109A1B SP 155mm how, M-107 175mm SP guns; *Lance* SSM; *TOW, Dragon* ATGW.)

Navy: 9,000 (3,300 conscripts), 10,000 on mobilization.
3 Type 206 subs.
4 *Aliya* (*Saar*-4.5) corvettes with 4 *Gabriel* and 4 *Harpoon* SSM, 1 Bell 206 ASW hel.
20 FAC(G): 8 *Reshef* (*Saar*-4) with 5 *Gabriel* III and 4 *Harpoon* SSM; 6 *Saar*-2 with 6 *Gabriel*; 6 *Saar*-3 with 5–8 *Gabriel*.
2 *Flagstaff* 2 hydrofoil FAC(G) with 2 *Gabriel* and 2 *Harpoon* SSM.
45 coastal patrol craft⟨: 37 *Dabur*, 2 *Dvora*, 6 *Hawk*.
3 LSM, 6 LCT, 3 LCU.
4 *Seascan* 1124N MR ac.
Naval cdo: (300).
(On order: 2 *Saar*-5 corvettes, 10 *Flagstaff* hydrofoils, 3 *Seascan* MR ac.)

Bases: Haifa, Ashdod, Eilat.

Air Force: 28,000 (2,000 conscripts, in AD), 37,000 on mobilization; some 555 combat ac (perhaps 90 stored), 60 armed hel.
15 FGA/interceptor sqns: 2 with 40 F/TF-15; 5 with 131 F-4E; 5 with 150 *Kfir* C1/C2/C7; 3 with 67 F-16A, 8 F-16B.
4 FGA sqns with 130 A-4N/J *Skyhawk*.
Recce: 13 RF-4E, 2 OV-1E; 4 E-2C AEW; 4 RU-21J, 2 C-130, 4 Boeing 707 ECM ac.
1 tpt wing: incl 7 Boeing 707 (2 tanker mods), 20 C-130E/H, 18 C-47, 2 KC-130H.
Liaison: 1 *Islander*, 5 Do-27, 14 Do-28D; 18 Cessna U-206C, 2 T-41D, 2 180; 12 *Queen Air* 80; 2 *Westwind*; 20 *Super Cub*.
Trainers incl 73 TA-4E/H, 50 *Kfir* (incl TC-2), 85 *Magister/Tzugit*.
Hel incl 30 AH-1S, 30 Hughes 500MD ATK, 8 *Super Frelon*, 33 CH-53A, 2 S-65E, 25 Bell 206, 60 Bell 212, 17 UH-1D hel.
Drones: *Mastiff* 2, *Scout*, Teledyne Ryan 124R.
15 SAM bns with *Improved HAWK*.
AAM: *Sidewinder*, AIM-7E/F *Sparrow*, *Shafrir*, *Python* III.
ASM: *Luz*, *Maverick*, *Shrike*, *Walleye*, *Bullpup*, *Gabriel* III (mod).
(On order: 11 F-15, 75 F-16 ftrs; 60 *Kfir*-C7 and TC-2 trg ac; 200 *Improved HAWK* SAM; 200 *Sidewinder* AAM.)

RESERVES (all services): 328,000.

Forces Abroad: Lebanon (10,000).

Para-Military Forces: Border Guards 4,500; BTR-152 APC. Arab Militia: small arms. Coastguard: 3 US PBR, 3 other patrol craft⟨.

JORDAN

Population: 2,555,000 (excluding West Bank).
Military service: voluntary; People's Army (militia): conscription, 2 years.
Total armed forces: 76,300.
GNP 1982: JD 1.343 bn ($3.813 bn). 1983: 1.487 bn ($4.098 bn).
Est def budget 1983: JD 196 m ($540.094 m). 1984: 205 m ($541.755 m).*
GDP growth: 6.0% (1982), 5.5% (1983).
Inflation: 7.4% (1982), 5.0% (1983).
Est FMA: some $800 m (1982).
Debt: $2.1 bn (1982).
   $1 = dinar 0.3523 (1982), 0.3629 (1983), 0.3784 (mid-1984).

Army: 68,000.
6 armd bdes.
4 mech bdes.
1 indep Royal Guards bde.
1 Special Forces bde.
16 arty bns.
2 AA bdes.
AFV: 150 M-47/-48, 200 M-60, some 200 *Khalid*, 200 *Centurion* MBT; 850 M-113, 32 *Saracen* APC.
Arty: 17 M-59 155mm guns; 30 M-102 105mm, 38 M-114 towed, 20 M-44, 190 M-109A2 SP 155mm, 40 M-115 towed, 40 M-110 SP 203mm guns/how; 350 81mm, 107mm and 120mm mor.
ATK: 240 106mm and 120mm RCL; 250 *TOW*, 310 *Dragon* ATGW.
AD: 80 M-163 *Vulcan* 20mm, 16 ZSU-23-4, 200 M-42 40mm SP AA guns; 200 *Redeye*, 20 SAM-8, *Improved HAWK* SAM.
(On order: some 248 *Khalid*, 40 M-60A3 MBT; 78 M-113 APC; 200 GHN-45 155mm how.)

Navy (Coast Guard): 300.
9 armed patrol craft⟨.

Base: Aqaba.

Air Force: 8,000; 103 combat ac.
3 FGA sqns with 46 F-5E/F.
2 interceptor sqns with 35 *Mirage* F-1C/E.
2 OCU with 17 F-5A, 5 F-5B.
1 tpt sqn: 3 C-130B/H, 2 *Sabreliner* 75A, 2 C-212A.

---

* Incl internal security.

1 VIP sqn: 1 Boeing 727, 3 *Falcon* 20, 1 T-39 ac, 4 S-76 hel.
1 hel sqn: 2 *Alouette* III, 7 S-76, 8 Hughes 500D hel.
Trainers: 12 T-37C, 15 Bulldog, 1 C-212 ac.
AAM: *Sidewinder*.
14 AD btys: 112 *Improved HAWK* SAM.
(On order: 24 AH-1Q *Cobra* hel with *TOW*; 6 *Maverick* ASM.)

RESERVES (all services): 35,000.

Para-Military Forces: 11,050; Civil Militia 7,500.

KUWAIT

Population: 1,750,000.
Military service: 18 months.
Total armed forces: 12,500.
GDP 1982: KD 5.728 bn ($19.903 bn).
Est def budget 1982/3: KD 330.0 m ($1.147 bn).* 1983/4: 399 m ($1.360 bn).*
GDP growth: −7.6% (1982), 4% (1983).
Inflation: 7.7% (1982), 4.7% (1983).
$1 = dinar 0.2878 (1982), 0.2915 (1983), 0.2934 (mid-1984).

Army: 10,000.
1 armd bde.
2 mech inf bdes.
1 SSM bn.
70 Vickers Mk 1, 10 *Centurion*, 160 *Chieftain* MBT; 100 *Saladin* armd, 60 *Ferret* scout cars; 175 M-113, 100 *Saracen* APC; 20 AMX Mk F-3 155mm SP how; *FROG*-7 SSM; 81mm mor; *HOT*, *TOW*, *Vigilant* ATGW; SA-7 SAM.
(On order: *Scorpion* lt tks, 188 M-113 APC, 56 M-113 SP *TOW* veh, 4,800 *Improved TOW* ATGW.)

Navy: 500 (coastguard).
6 Lürssen TNC-45 FAC(G) with 4 *Exocet* MM-40 SSM.
2 Lürssen FPB-57 FAC.
47 coastal patrol craft⟨ (15 armed).
6 landing craft.
(On order: 6 SRN-6 hovercraft; SA-365N *Dauphin* II hel; *Exocet* MM-40 SSM.)

Air Force: 2,000;† 49 combat ac.
2 FB sqns with 30 A-4KU.
1 interceptor sqn with 17 *Mirage* F-1C, 2 F-1B.
Tpts: 2 DC-9; 2 L-100-20, 4 L-100-30 (used also in civil role).
3 hel sqns with 23 SA-342K *Gazelle*, 12 SA-330 *Puma*.
Trainers incl 9 *Strikemaster*.
1 SAM bn with *Improved HAWK*.
AAM: R-550 *Magic*, Super 530, *Sidewinder*.

(In store: 12 *Lightning*, 9 *Hunter*.)
(On order: 24 *Mirage* F-1C ftrs; 12 *Hawk* COIN/trg ac; 6 SA-332F *Super Puma* hel; 12 *Exocet* AM-39 ASM; AD radar and command system.)

Para-Military Forces: National Guard: Palace, border guard.

LEBANON

Population: 2,700,000.
Military service: conscription, term unknown.
Total armed forces: 20,300.
Est GDP 1981: £L 17.0 bn ($3.941 bn). 1982: 12.30 bn ($2.593 bn).
Def budget 1982: £L 770 m ($162.327 m). Est exp 1983: 6.0 bn ($1.325 bn).‡ Budget 1984: 2.030 bn ($349.488 m).
GDP growth: −2.5% (1982), −6% (1983).
Inflation: 20% (1982), 17% (1983).
FMA: $150 m (1982).
Debt: $350 m (1982).
$1 = £L 4.3139 (1981), 4.7435 (1982), 4.5282 (1983), 5.8085 (mid-1984).

Army: 19,000 (all units below strength).§
1 mech inf bde (1 armd recce, 3 inf bns).
5 inf bdes.
1 armed recce bn
9 inf bns }below strength.
3 arty bns
AA bns.
142 M-48A5 MBT (storage); 13 AMX-13 lt tks; 100 *Saladin*, 30 *Ferret* armd cars; 480 M-113, *Saracen*, 35 VAB APC; 10 122mm, 36 155mm guns; 18 105mm how; 200 81mm, 83mm RPG-7 85mm, 88mm RL; 106mm RCL; *ENTAC*, 18 *Milan*, *TOW* ATGW; 20mm, ZU-23 23mm, 30mm towed, M-42 40mm SP AA guns.
(On order: 355 M-113A2 APC, 12 155mm how.)

Navy: 300.
4 patrol craft⟨: 1 37 metre, 3 *Byblos* coastal.

Air Force: 1,000; 3 combat ac, 4 armed hel.
1 sqn with 3 *Hunter* F-70.
1 hel sqn with 11 *Alouette* II/III, 11 AB-212, 6 *Puma*, 4 *Gazelle* with SS-11/-12 ASM.
Trainers: 6 *Bulldog*, 5 *Magister*.

---

* Incl National Guard.
† Excluding expatriate personnel.
‡ Plus £L 3 bn ($955 m) spread over 10 years to rebuild the armed forces (most already spent in 1983).
§ Army divided on sectarian lines: perhaps 10,000 pro-Gemayel Christian (3 bdes); 2+ bdes half pro-Sunni Muslim, half Christian; 1 bde pro-Shia.

Tpts: 1 *Dove*, 1 *Turbo-Commander* 690A.
(On order: 6 *Gazelle* hel.)

Para-Military Forces: Internal Security Force
7,500: 30 *Chaimite* APC. Border Guard
(forming, to be 20,000). Customs: 5 *Aztec*
patrol craft.

Private militias (strengths are estimates only):
Maronite Christian:
    Lebanese Forces Militia (*Phalange*) (6,000).
    21 M-4, T-54/-55 MBT, 50 155mm how, 3
    patrol boats.
    Marada Brigade (1,000).
    National Liberation Party (few hundred).
Christian (some Shia):
    South Lebanon Army (formerly under Haddad
    now under Maj.-Gen. Lahad) (2,500).
    'Partisans of the Army' (Tyre area).
    'Forces of Kerbala' village militia.
Druze:
    Militia: 5,000.
    Popular Socialist Party (Jumblatt) (1,500).
    T-34/-54 MBT.
Sunni:
    Islamic Coalition (few hundred).
    Mourabitoun Militia (underground; 1,500).
Shia:
    Amal (3,500).

LIBYA

Population: 3,490,000.
Military service: selective conscription; term
    varies.
Total armed forces: 73,000.
GDP 1981: LD 9.192 bn ($31.044 bn). Est 1982:
    8.445 bn ($28.520 bn). 1983: 7.728 bn
    ($26.100 bn).
Est def exp 1981: LD 165.0 m ($557.244 m).
    1982: 210.0 m ($709.22 m).*
GDP growth: −2.0% (1982), −2.0% (1983).
Inflation: 6% (1982), 9.0% (1983).
Debt: $1.7 bn (1982).
    $1 = dinar 0.2961 (1981/3).

Army: 58,000.
1 tk, 1 mech inf div HQ.
20 tk bns.
30 mech inf bns.
1 National Guard bn.
10 arty, 2 AA arty bns.
2 special forces gps.
3 AD regts.
2 SSM bns.
6 AD regts with SA-2, SA-3, SA-6; 9 div SAM bns
    with SA-6, SA-8, SA-9/-13.
AFV: 2,500 T-54/-55/-62, 300 T-72 MBT; 200
    BRDM-2, 300 EE-9 *Cascavel* armd cars; 700

BMP MICV; 900 BTR-50/-60, OT-62/-64, 100
    EE-11 *Urutu*, Fiat 6614, 160 M-113A1 APC.
Arty: 360 130mm guns; some 60 M-101
    105mm, 330 D-30, 60 D-74 122mm towed,
    78 M-1974 122mm SP, 48 M-1973 152mm SP,
    200 *Palmaria*, 18 M-109 155mm SP how; 450
    81mm, 120mm, 160mm and 240mm mor;
    some 600 BM-11 107mm, BM-21/RM-70
    122mm and M-51 130mm MRL; 48 *FROG*-7,
    70 *Scud* B SSM.
ATK: 200 106mm RCL; 3,000 *Vigilant, Milan*
    and *Sagger* ATGW.
AD: 450 23mm incl ZSU-23-4 SP, 30mm incl
    M-53/59 SP, 57mm AA guns; 72 SA-2, 144
    SA-3, 350 SA-6, SA-7/-8/-9/-13 SAM.†
(On order: Fiat 6616, EE-9 armd cars; 100 *Urutu*
    APC; *Astros* II SS-40 MRLS.)

Navy: 6,500.
6 Sov F-class subs.
1 Vosper Mk 7 frigate with 4 *Otomat* SSM, 4
    Albatros/Aspide SAM.
8 corvettes: 4 *Assad* with 4 *Otomat* SSM, 1 with 1
    × 4 *Aspide* SAM; 3 Sov *Nanuchka* II with 4
    SS-N-2C SSM, 1 × 2 SA-N-4 SAM; 1 Vosper
    440-ton.
25 FAC(G): 12 Sov *Osa*-II with 4 SS-N-2C SSM; 3
    Susa with 8 SS-12M SSM; 10 *Beir* (*La
    Combattante*) with 4 *Otomat* SSM.
8 patrol craft: 4 *Garian*, 3 *Benina*, 1 coastal.
6 Sov *Natya* minesweepers.
1 LSD (log spt/HQ ship); 2 PS-700 LST; 3
    Polnocny, 3 C-107 LCT.
1 tpt, 1 Thornycroft repair ship.
50 drone craft.
(On order: 4 *Assad* corvettes, 1 *Benina* patrol
    craft; 16 C-107 LCT.)

Bases: Tarabulus, Benghazi, Darnah, Tubruq,
    Bandiyah.

Air Force: 8,500; some 535 combat ac, 42 armed
    hel.†
1 bbr sqn with 7 Tu-22 *Blinder* A.
3 interceptor sqns and 1 OCU: some 26 *Mirage*
    F-1ED, 6 F-1BD, 143 MiG-23 *Flogger* E, 50
    MiG-25 *Foxbat* A, 55 MiG-21, 5 MiG-25U.
5 FGA sqns and 1 OCU: 45 *Mirage* 5D/DE, 13
    5DD, 14 *Mirage* F-1AD, 18 MiG-23BM
    Flogger F, 14 MiG-23U, some 100 Su-20/-22
    Fitter E/F/J.
1 COIN sqn with 30 J-1 *Jastreb*.
1 recce sqn with 7 *Mirage* 5DR.

---

* Costs of Libya's military involvement in Chad
unknown.
† Some eqpt, incl 1,400 MBT, 450 combat ac (Tu-22,
MiG-21/-23/-25, Su-22) in storage. Soviet, Syrian,
Pakistani, N. Korean and Palestinian pilots also
reportedly fly Libyan ac; expatriates form a large
proportion of the technical support staff.

2 tpt sqns: 18 An-26 *Curl*, 8 C-130H, 1 Boeing 707, 12 G-222, 2 *Mystère-Falcon*, 4 C-140 *Jetstar*, 2 CL-44, 17 Il-76, 1 *Corvette* 200, 2 *King Air*, 8 F-27-600, 3 LET-410.

7 hel sqns: 2 with 30 Mi-24 *Hind*, 2 Mi-8; 1 with 12 Mi-14 *Haze* (ASW); 1 with 8 *Super Frelon* (SAR); 1 with 10 *Alouette* III; 1 with 19 CH-47C; 1 with 5 AB-206, 2 AB212.

Other hel incl: 9 AB-47, 1 AS-61A.

4 trg sqns: 2 with 61 *Galeb* ac; 2 with 20 Mi-2 (*Hoplite*) hel.

Trainers incl 2 Tu-22 *Blinder* D, 100 L-39ZO, 12 *Magister*, 119 SF-260WL.

3 SAM bdes with 30 *Crotale* (60 systems).

AAM: AA-2 *Atoll*, R-550 *Magic*.

ASM: *Swatter* ATGW.

(On order: MiG-25, MiG-23, some 40 *Mirage* F-1 ftrs; 10 *Twin Otter* tpts; 25 EMB-121 *Xingu*, 70 SF-260 trg ac; *Gazelle*, 2 A-109 hel; Super 530 AAM.)

RESERVES: People's Militia, some 40,000.

Forces Abroad: Chad: up to 7,000, Lebanon: 'Volunteers' (800).

Para-Military Forces: Pan-African Legion some 10,000: 1 armd, 1 inf, 1 para/cdo bdes; some 75 T-54/-55, MBT; EE-9 MICV; BTR-50/-60 APC (army inventory). Customs/coastguard: 2 SAR-33 Lürssen-type FAC with SSM/SAM, 3 *Jihan* patrol craft. Muslim Youth. People's Cavalry Force parade unit.

MOROCCO

Population: 23,350,000.
Military service: 18 months.
Total armed forces: 144,000.
GDP 1982: MD 88.520 bn ($14.697 bn).
Est def exp 1982: MD 8.0 bn ($1.328 bn). 1983: 7.80 bn ($1.097 bn).
GDP growth: 5.6% (1982), 0.6% (1983).
Inflation: 10.6% (1982), 7.0% (1983).
Est FMA: $115.0 bn (1982).
Debt: $10.8 bn (1982).
$1 = dirham 6.0230 (1982), 7.1113 (1983), 8.7228 (mid-1984).

Army: 125,000.
4 mech inf bdes.
1 lt security bde.
1 para bde.
1 AA gp.
10 mech inf regts.
9 arty groups.
7 armd bns.
1 Royal Guard bn.
5 camel corps bns.
2 desert cav bns.

1 mountain bn.
3 cdo bns.
4 engr bns.
4 armd car sqns.

AFV: 120 M-48, 40 AMX-13 lt tks; 50 EBR-75, 15 AMX-10RC, 162 AML-90, 250 *Eland* 90mm, 150 AML-245, 40 M-8, 364 M-113, 200 VAB, 70 UR-416, 80 *Ratel*, 56 M-3, Steyr 4K-7FA APC.

Arty: 20 M-101 105mm, 36 105mm lt, 12 M-46 130mm, 152mm, 52 AMX-F-3 SP 155mm guns; 20 M-114 155mm towed, 42 M-1950, 22 105mm SP, 56 M-109 155mm SP how; 300 60mm, 600 81mm, 70 82mm, 320 120mm mor; BM-21 122mm MRL.

ATK: 20 M-56 90mm, 121 *Kuerassier* 105mm SP ATK guns; 75mm, 106mm RCL; STRIM-89 RL, *Dragon*, *Milan*, *TOW* ATGW.

AD: 100 20mm, 37mm, 57mm and 100mm towed, 40 M-163 *Vulcan* 20mm SP AA guns; SA-7, 30 *Chaparral* SAM.

(On order: 108 M-60 MBT; AML-90, 76 AMX-10RC armd cars; 126 VAB APC.)

Navy: 6,000 incl naval infantry.
1 *Descubierta* frigate with 4 *Exocet* MM-38 SSM, 1 × 8 *Aspide* SAM.
4 *Lazaga* FAC(G) with 4 *Exocet* MM-38.
2 PR-72 FAC.
4 *Murene* large patrol craft.
9 coastal patrol craft.
1 minesweeper.
4 landing ships (3 *Batral*).
1 naval inf bn (600).
(On order: 2 PR-72 FAC.)

Bases: Casablanca, Safi, Agadir, Kenitra, Tangier.

Air Force: 13,000; 106 combat ac.
5 FGA sqns: 3 with 22 *Mirage* F-1E, 18 F-1C; 2 with F-5 (5 A, 14 E, 3 B, 4 F, 12 RF-5A).
1 COIN/recce sqn with 22 *Magister*, 6 OV-10 *Bronco*.
1 tpt sqn with 12 C-130H, 3 KC-130H, 1 *Gulfstream*, 1 *Falcon* 50, 8 *King Air*, 3 Do-28D.
33 AB-205A, 5 AB-206, 13 Hel incl AB-212, 27 *Puma*, 4 HH-43B SAR, 8 CH-47C.
Trainers: 11 T-34C, 11 AS-201/18 *Bravo*, 28 SF-260M, 24 *Alpha Jet*.
AAM: *Sidewinder*, R-550 *Magic*.
(On order: 7 Do-28D tpt; 25 *Gepal* Mk IV trg ac; 24 *Gazelle*, 19 AB-206 hel; 381 *Maverick* ASM.)

Forces Abroad: Equatorial Guinea: 300.

Para-Military Forces: 30,000 incl 11,000 *Sureté Nationale*: 2 *Rallye* ac; 5 *Alouette* II/III, 3 6 *Lama*, 6 *Gazelle*, 6 *Puma*, 6 A-109 hel.

OMAN

Est population: 1,000,000–1,600,000.
Military service: voluntary.
Total armed forces: 21,500.*
GDP 1981: RO 2.148 bn ($6.219 bn). 1982: 2.488 bn ($7.203 bn). 1983: 2.625 ($7.600 bn).
Def budget 1983: RO 612 m ($1.772 bn). 1984: 677 m ($1.960 bn).
GDP growth: 4.9% (1982), 5.5% (1983).
Inflation: 2.8% (1982), –2.0% (1983).
Debt: $800m (1982).
$1 = rial 0.3454 (1981–4).

Army: 16,500.
2 bde HQ.
1 Royal Guard bde.
1 armd regt (3 armd car, 2 tk sqns).
2 fd arty regts, 2 med arty btys, 1 lt AA bty.
1 recce bn.
8 inf 'regts' (bns).
1 special force.
1 sigs regt.
1 fd engr regt (2 sqns).
1 para regt.
6 M-60A1, some *Quayid Al Ardh* (*Chieftain*) MBT; 30 *Scorpion* recce; 24 25-pdr (88mm), 39 105mm, 12 M-1946, 12 59-1 130mm guns; 60mm, 81mm mor; *Milan* ATGW; *Blowpipe* SAM.
(On order: some 15 *Chieftain* MBT being delivered).

RESERVES: National Volunteer Reserve Force.

Navy: 2,000.
1 Royal Yacht.
4 FAC(G) with *Exocet* SSM: 3 *Province* (2 with 8, 1 with 6 MM-40), 1 Brooke Marine with 2 MM-38.
4 Brooke Marine FAC.
4 inshore patrol craft⟨.
1 log spt ship (amph).
4 LCM.
1 trg ship.
(On order: 1 log spt amph ship).

Bases: Muscat, Raysut, Ghanam (Goat) Island; (Wadam Alwi, under construction).

Air Force: 3,000; 52 combat ac.
2 FGA sqns with 20 *Jaguar* S(O) Mk 1, 4 T-2.
1 FGA/recce sqn with 12 *Hunter* FGA-6, 4 T-7.
1 COIN/trg sqn with 12 BAC-167.
3 tpt sqns: 1 with 3 BAC-111, 1 *Falcon* 20; 2 with 7 *Defender*, 15 *Skyvan*, 3 C-130H.
Royal flt with 1 *Gulfstream*, 1 DC-8, 1 VC-10 tpts; 2 AS-202 *Bravo* trainers; 4 AB-212, 2 *Super Puma* hel.
2 hel sqns with 20 AB-205, 3 AB-206, 5 AB-214B.

2 AD sqns with 28 *Rapier* SAM.
(On order: 1 C-130H, 2 DHC-5D tpts; 6 Bell 214ST hel; *Exocet* AM-39 ASM; 28 *Blindfire* radars.)

Para-Military Forces: tribal Home Guard (*Firqats*) 3,500. Police Coastguard: 19 coastal patrol craft⟨; 7 landing craft⟨. Air Wing: 1 *Learjet*, 2 Dornier 228-100, 2 *Merlin* IVA, 2 *Buffalo* ac; 5 AB-205, 3 AB-206 hel.

QATAR

Population: 270,000.
Military service: voluntary.
Total armed forces: 6,000.
Est GDP 1981: QR 24.888 bn ($6.839 bn). 1982: 28.758 bn ($7.903 bn).
Est def exp 1981/3: QR 3.260 bn ($896 m).†
1983/4: 604 m ($165.98 m).‡
GDP growth: –9.4% (1982), –16% (1983).
Inflation: 11.5% (1982), 4% (1983).
$1 = rial 3.639 (1981/3).

Army: 5,000.
1 Royal Guard regt.
1 tk bn.
5 inf bns.
1 arty bty.
1 SAM bty with *Rapier*.
24 AMX-30 MBT; 10 *Ferret* scout cars; 30 AMX-10P MICV; 25 *Saracen*, 136 VAB APC; 8 25-pdr guns (88mm), 6 Mk F-3 155mm SP how; 81mm mor; *Rapier* SAM.
(On order: 8 *Commando* Mk 3 APC; *Blowpipe* SAM.)

Navy: 700 incl Marine Police.
3 *La Combattante* FAC(G) with 8 *Exocet* MM-40 SSM.
6 Vosper Thornycroft large patrol craft.
36 coastal patrol craft⟨ (2 75-ft, 2 45-ft, 7 P-1200 type, 25 *Spear*).
2 *Interceptor* fast assault/SAR craft.
3 *Exocet* MM-40 coast defence systems.

Base: Doha.

Air Force: 300; 11 combat ac; 2 armed hel.
3 *Hunter* FGA-6, 1 T-79, 8 *Alpha Jet* FGA/trg ac.
1 *Islander*, 1 Boeing 727, 2 707 tpt ac.
2 SA-342 *Gazelle*, 2 *Whirlwind*, 4 *Commando*, 3 *Lynx* hel.
SAM: 5 *Tigercat*.

---

* Including some 3,700 foreign personnel.
† 18-month transition budget about half for military aid to Iraq.
‡ Excl capital exp, est at QR 600 m, and military aid to Iraq.

(On order: 14 *Mirage* F-1C ftrs, SA-330 *Puma* hel.)

Para-Military Forces: Police: 3 *Lynx*, 2 *Gazelle* hel.

SAUDI ARABIA

Est population: 8–12,000,000.
Military service: conscription, males aged 18–35.
Total armed forces: 51,500.
GDP 1982: SR 524.73 bn ($153.099 bn). 1983: 414.45 bn ($119.967 bn).
Def budget* 1983/4: SR 75.733 bn ($21.952 bn). 1984/5: 79.900 bn ($22.731 bn).
GDP growth: 1.7% (1982), –10.8% (1983).
Inflation: 1.0% (1982), 0.1% (1983).
$1 = rial 3.4274 (1982), 3.4547 (1983), 3.5150 (mid-1984).

Army: 35,000.
3 armd bdes (1 more to form).
2 mech bdes.
2 inf bdes (1 to be mech).
1 AB bde (2 para bns, 3 special forces coys).
1 Royal Guard regt (3 bns).
5 arty bns.
18 AA arty btys.
14 SAM btys: 12 with *Improved HAWK* (216 msls); 2 with 12 *Shahine* (48 msls) and AMX-30SA 30mm SP AA guns.
AFV: 300 AMX-30, 150 M-60A1 MBT; 200 AML-60/-90 armd cars; 350 AMX-10P (some with *HOT*), some 20 VCC-1 (with *TOW*) MICV; 800 M-113, Panhard M-3 APC.
Arty: Model 56 105mm pack, 100 M-101/-102 105mm, 29 FH-70, 18 M-198 towed, M-109 and GCT 155mm SP how; 81mm, M-30 107mm mor.
ATK: 75mm, 90mm, 106mm RCL; *TOW*, *Dragon*, *HOT* ATGW.
AD: M-163 *Vulcan* 20mm, AMX-30SA 30mm, 200 35mm, M-42 40mm SP AA guns; *Redeye*, *Shahine*, *Improved HAWK* SAM.
(On order: 100 M-60A3 MBT; 150 M-60A3 conversion kits; 60 AMX-10P, 140 BMR-600 some 180 VCC-1 *TOW* MICV (1984); *Urutu* APC; 43 FH-70 155mm how; some 400 JPz SK-105 SP ATK guns; *TOW* ATGW; 100 *Shahine*, 200 *Stinger* SAM.)

Navy: 2,500.
2 Fleet HQ.
1 F-2000 frigate with 8 *Otomat* SSM, 1 × 26 *Crotale* SAM, 1 SA-365 hel.
4 PCG-1 corvettes with 2 × 4 *Harpoon* SSM.
9 PGG-1 FAC(G) with 2 × 2 *Harpoon* SSM.
1 large patrol craft (US coastguard cutter).
3 *Jaguar* (Lürssen) FAC(T).

4 MSC-322 coastal minesweepers.
4 US LCU, 8 US LCM-6 LCM, 4 LCVP.
24 AS-365N *Dauphine* 2 hel (4 SAR, 20 with AS-15TT ASM).
(On order: 3 F-2000 frigates; 2 log spt ships; 2 *Atlantic* II MR ac; 8 BH-7 hovercraft, *Otomat* coast defence SSM, 200 AS-15TT ASM.)

Bases: Jiddah (Western Fleet), Al Qatif/Jubail (Eastern Fleet), Ras Tanura, Damman, Yanbu, Ras al Mishab.

Air Force: 14,000; 203 combat ac.
3 FGA sqns with 65 F-5E.
4 interceptor sqns: 1 with 15 *Lightning* F-53, 2 T-55; 3 (1 forming) with 62 F-15.
4 E-3A airborne warning and control ac.
2 OCU with 24 F-5F, 16 F-5B, 15 TF-15D.
3 tpt sqns with 50 C-130E and C-130H, 8 KC-130H, 2 *Jetstar*.
2 hel sqns with 12 AB-206B, 14 AB-205, 10 AB-212.
Trainers: 40 BAC-167.
AAM: *Red Top*, *Firestreak*, *Sidewinder*, AIM-7F *Sparrow*.
ASM: *Maverick*.
(In reserve: 17 *Lightning* F-53/T-55.)
(On order: 5 F-5E ftrs; 1 F-5F trainer; 10 RF-5E recce; 1 E-3A *Sentry* AWACS; 1 Boeing 747, 4 CN-235, 40 C-212-200 tpts; 8 Boeing KE-3 (KC-707) tankers; 2 ECM ac; 22 AB-212, 8 KV-107 hel; 1,000 AIM-7F *Sparrow*, 1,177 *Sidewinder* AAM; 1,600 *Maverick* ASM.)

Para-Military Forces:
National Guard (25,000): Bde HQ; 4 all-arms, 16 regular inf, 24 irregular inf bns, 1 ceremonial cav sqn, spt units; 240 V-150 *Commando* APC, M-102 105mm how, 81mm mor; 106mm RCL, *TOW* ATGW, 20mm *Vulcan*, 90mm AA guns. (On order: 489 *Commando* incl V-300 APC, V-150 SP 20mm AA, SP *TOW*, 90mm armed AFV.)
Foreign contract military personnel: 10,000.
Ministry of Interior:
Counter-terrorist unit with hel.
Frontier Force and Coastguard 8,500: 184 coastal, incl 16 SRN-6 hovercraft, 300 small patrol craft. (On order: 8 BH-7 hovercraft).
General Civil Defence Administration units. 10 Kawasaki hel.

SUDAN

Population: 23,250,000.
Military service: voluntary; conscription legislated but not yet implemented.

---

* Includes budget for National Guard.

Total armed forces: 58,000.

Est GDP 1982: £S 5.909 bn ($6.300 bn). 1983: 9.230 bn ($7.100 bn).

Est def exp 1982: £S 220 m ($234.54 m). 1983: 300 m ($230.77 m).

GDP growth: 4.6% (1982), −2.7% (1982).

Inflation: 26% (1982), 31% (1983).

FMA: $100 m (1982).

Debt: $4.5 bn (1982).

$1 = £E 0.5349 (1981), 0.9380 (1982), 1.300 (1983).

Army: 53,000 (incl AD).

6 Regional Commands.

4 div HQ.

2 armd bdes.

7 inf bdes.

1 para bde.

3 arty regts.

1 engr regt.

Air Defence (3,000):

2 AA arty bdes.

1 SAM bde with 3 btys of SA-2.

AFV: 53 T-55, 20 M-60A3 MBT; 55 M-41, 78 Ch Type-62 lt tks; 6 AML-90, 48 *Saladin* armd, 55 *Ferret*, BRDM-1/-2 scout cars; 20 Panhard M-3, 50 BTR-50/-152, 30 OT-62/-64, 35 V-100 *Commando*, 30 M-113, 40 *Walid* APC.

Arty: 30 D-44 85mm, 55 25-pdr (88mm), 25 100mm, 20 Ch 130mm guns; 18 105mm pack, 64 D-30 122mm, 6 F-3 SP 155mm how; 30 120mm mor.

ATK: 20 D-48 85mm ATK guns; *Swingfire* ATGW.

AD: ZU-23-2 23mm, 100 37mm, 80 40mm, 100mm towed guns; 20 SA-2, SA-7 SAM.

(On order: 24 M-163 *Vulcan* 20mm SP AA guns.)

Navy: 2,000.

1 Yug *Kraljevica*, 4 Yug PBR large, 3 70-ton coastal patrol craft.

2 Yug DTK-221 LCT, 1 DTM-231 LCU◁.

Base: Port Sudan.

Air Force: 3,000; 34 combat ac.

1 FGA/interceptor sqn: 2 F-5EF, 8 MiG-21.

1 FGA sqn with 8 Ch F-5, 6 Ch F-6, 10 MiG-17.

1 COIN sqn with 3 *Strikemaster* (forming).

1 tpt sqn with 6 C-130H, 1 *Mystère-Falcon*, 4 DHC-5D, 8 *Turbo-Porter*, 6 EMB-110P2.

1 hel sqn with 9 *Puma*, 10 BO-105, 5 Bell 212.

Trainers incl 3 *Jet Provost* Mk 55, 3 MiG-15UTI, 2 MiG-21U, 2 Ch FT-5, 2 Ch FT-6.

AAM: AA-2 *Atoll*.

(On order: 10 F-5E, 6 Ch F-6 ftr, 7 *Strikemaster* Mk 90 (*Jet Provost*) COIN, 6 C-212, 2 C-130 tpt ac; 6 Bell 212 hel.)

Para-Military Forces: 3,500: National Guard (500); Republican Guard (500); Border Guard (2,500).

Opposition: Southern People's Liberation Movement: est 3,000.

SYRIA

Population: 10,400,000.

Military service: 30 months.

Total armed forces: 362,500 (some 140,000 conscripts).

GDP 1981: £S 66.492 bn ($16.941 bn), 1982: 72.484 bn ($18.467 bn).

Def budget* 1983: £S 11.073 bn ($2.821 bn). 1984: 12.600 bn ($3.210 bn).

GDP growth: 6.9% (1982), 7.3% (1983).

Inflation: 14.3% (1982), 7.5% (1983).

Est FMA: $3.1 bn (1982).

Debt: $3.2 bn (1982).

$1 = £S 3.9250 (1981/4).

Army: 240,000 (120,000 conscripts, 50,000 reservists).

4 armd divs (each 2 armd, 1 mech bdes; 1 is Presidential Guard unit).

4 mech divs (each 1 armd, 2 mech bdes).

3 indep armd bdes.

4 indep mech bdes.

5 arty bdes.

9 para/cdo regts.

3 SSM regts: 1 × Scud, 1 × *Frog*, 1 × SS-21.

102 SAM btys with SA-2/-3/-6/-8.

AFV: 1,800 T-54/-55, 1,200 T-62, 1,100 T-72 MBT; 200 BRDM recce/ATK vehs; 400 BMP MICV; 1,600 BTR-40/-50/-60/-152, OT-64 APC.

Arty: 2,700 122mm (incl ISU-122 and M-1974 SP), M-46 130mm, M-1976 152mm and S-23 180mm guns; M-38, D-30 122mm, 152mm how incl M-1943 and M-1973 SP; BM-21 122mm, 140mm, 240mm MRL; 18 *FROG*-7, 12 SS-21, 18 *Scud* SSM; 120mm, 160mm, 240mm mor.

ATK: 57mm, 85mm, 100mm guns; 1,300 *Sagger*, *Spigot* and *Milan* ATGW.

AD: 23mm, 37mm, 57mm towed, ZSU-23-4, ZSU-57-2 SP AA guns; SA-2/-3/-6/-7/-8/-9 SAM.

AIR DEFENCE COMMAND: 50,000 (Army comd, Army and Air Force manning).

63 SAM btys with SA-2/-3; 31 with SA-6; 8 with some 48 SA-5 (2 Soviet-manned sites); AA arty, and radar.

---

* Incl internal security budget of $S 613 m (1983), $S 635 m (1984). Additional def exp financed through supplementary support.

RESERVES: 460,000: 175,000 active (being reorganized); 9 mech and inf bdes.

Navy: 2,500.
2 Sov *Petya* I frigates.
20 Sov FAC(G) with *Styx* SSM: 6 *Osa*-I, 8 *Osa*-II; 6 *Komar*⟨.
8 Sov P-4 FAC(T)⟨.
1 Fr CH large patrol craft.
4 Sov minesweepers: 1 T-43 ocean, 2 *Vanya* coastal, 1 *Yevgenya* inshore.
3 Sov *Zhuk* coastal patrol craft.
(On order 1981: 4 *Nanuchka* II corvettes.)

Bases: Latakia, Tartus, Minet el-Baida.

RESERVES: 2,500.

Air Force: 70,000; some 503 combat ac; some 90 armed hel.*
11 FGA sqns: 4 with 85 MiG-17; 1 with 18 Su-7; 2 with 40 Su-20; 4 with 70 MiG-23BM *Flogger* F.
12 interceptor sqns: 2 with 50 MiG-25 *Foxbat* A; 10 with 200 MiG-21PF/MF, 40 MiG-23 *Flogger* E.
2 tpt sqns with 3 An-24, 4 An-26, 4 Il-76, 8 Il-14, 4 Il-18, 2 *Mystère* 20F.
Trainers incl 40 L-39, 60 L-29, 10 MiG-15UTI, 50 MBB-223 *Flamingo*.
Hel incl 10 Mi-2, 95 Mi-8, 30 Mi-24, 4 Ka-25 (ASW), 45 *Gazelle* (35 with ATGW).
AAM: AA-2 *Atoll*.
ASM: AT-2 *Swatter* ATGW.
(On order: 12 *Gazelle*, 18 AB-212, 21 *Super Frelon* hel; AAM.)

Forces Abroad: Lebanon: 57,000, (3 divs); 800 MBT.

Para-Military Forces: 38,800: Defence Companies: 25,000: 4 armd bdes. Gendarmerie 8,000, Desert Guard (Frontier Force) 1,800. 2 Palestine Liberation Army bdes of 6,000 with some Syrian officers (nominally under PLO); 90 T-54/-55 MBT; 105mm, 122mm, 152mm how; MRL; AT-3 *Sagger* ATGW; SA-7 SAM. Workers Militia (People's Army).

TUNISIA

Population: 7,000,000.
Military service: 12 months selective.
Total armed forces: 35,100 (13,000 conscripts).
GDP 1982: TD 4.670 bn ($7.906 bn). 1983: 5.263 bn ($7.757 bn).
Def budget† 1983: TD 764.18 m ($1.126 m). 1984: 339.64 m ($454.307 m).
GDP growth: 0.3% (1982), 4.5% (1983).
Inflation: 13.7% (1982), 9.0% (1983).

FMA: $250 m (1982).
Debt: $3.7 bn (1982).
$1 = dinar 0.4938 (1981), 0.5907 (1982).

Army: 30,000 (12,000 conscripts).
2 combined arms bdes (each with 1 armd, 2 mech inf bns).
1 Sahara bde.
1 para-cdo bde.
1 armd recce regt.
3 fd, 2 AA arty regts.
1 engr regt.
AFV: 14 M-48 MBT; 40 AMX-13, 10 M-41 lt tks; 20 *Saladin*, 30 EBR-75, 10 AML-60 armd cars; 50 M-113A1, 18 EE-11 *Urutu* APC.
Arty: 6 25-pdr (88mm), 48 M-101A1 105mm towed, 12 M-114A1 155mm how; 60mm, 81mm, 82mm, 107mm mor.
ATK: 54 JPz SK-105 105mm SP ATK guns; STRIM-89 RL; *TOW, Milan*, SS-11 ATGW.
AD: 45 37mm and 40mm AA guns; RBS-70, 62 MIM-72 *Chaparral* SAM.
(On order: 54 M-60A3 MBT; 12 M-106A2, (with 4.2-in. (107mm) mor), 20 M-113A2 (with *TOW*) APC; 19 M-109 155mm SP how; 800 *TOW* ATGW.)

Navy: 2,600 (500 conscripts).
1 US *Savage* frigate.
2 FAC(G): 5 *La Combattante* III with 8 *Exocet* MM-40 SSM; 3 P-48 with 8 SS-12 SSM.
4 Fr large patrol craft: 1 *Le Fougeux*, 3 P-48.
2 Vosper Thornycroft 103-ft FAC(P).
2 Ch *Shanghai*-II FAC.
2 US *Adjutant* coastal minesweepers.
12 coastal patrol boats⟨.
(On order: 1 *La Combattante* FAC(G), 2 23-metre FAC.)

Bases: Tunis, Susa.

Air Force: 2,500 (500 conscripts); 8 combat ac.
1 COIN sqn with 5 MB-326K, 3 MB-326L.
Trainers: 17 SF-260, 7 MB-326B, 12 T-6, 12 *Safir*.
Liaison: 4 S-208M ac.
1 hel wing: 7 *Alouette* II, 5 *Alouette* III, 4 UH-1H, 1 *Puma*, 18 AB-205, 6 Bell 205-A1, 6 AS-350B *Ecureuil*.
(On order: 8 F-5E FGA, 6 F-5F trg, 1 C-130H tpt ac.)

Para-Military Forces: Gendarmerie 5,000: 3 bns; 110 Fiat 6614 APC. National Guard 3,500.

---

* Some aircraft believed to be in storage. Casualties and reinforcements of Lebanon during June 1982 are difficult to estimate.

* Incl equipment budgets.

UNITED ARAB EMIRATES (UAE)

Population: 1,300,000.
Military service: voluntary.
Total armed forces: 43,000.*
GNP 1982: Dh 128.403 bn ($34.978 bn).
Def budget† 1983: Dh 8.892 bn ($2.422 bn).
   1984: 6.855 bn ($1.867 bn).
GDP growth: −5% (1982), −7% (1983).
Inflation: 10% (1982), 0% (1983).
   $1 = dirham 3.6710 (1982/4).

Army: 40,000.
3 regional commands: Western (Abu Dhabi),
   Central (Dubai), Northern (Ras al Khaimah).
1 Royal Guard 'bde'.
1 armd/armd car bde.
2 inf bdes.
1 arty, 1 AD bde (each 3 bns).
100 AMX-30, 18 OF-40 Mk 1 (*Lion*) MBT; 60
   Scorpion lt tks; 90 AML-90, VBC-40 armd
   cars; AMX-10P MICV; 30 AMX VCI, VCRTT,
   300 Panhard M-3, VAB APC; 50 105mm guns;
   M-56 105mm pack, 20 AMX 155mm SP how;
   81mm mor; 84mm RCL; *Vigilant* ATGW;
   Rapier, Crotale, RBS-70 SAM.
(In store: 70 *Saladin* armd, 60 *Ferret* scout cars;
   12 *Saracen* APC.)
(On order: 18 OF-40 Mk 2 MBT; 20 *Scorpion* lt
   tks; 66 *Urutu* APC with *TOW*; 54 *TOW* ATGW;
   42 *Improved HAWK* SAM; 343 msls.)

Navy: 1,500.
6 Lürssen TNC-45 FAC(G) with 2 × 2 *Exocet*
   MM-40 SSM.
6 Vosper Thornycroft large patrol craft.
3 Keith Nelson coastal patrol craft⟨.
2 Cheverton spt tenders⟨.

Base: Abu Dhabi.

Air Force (Police Air Wing & Central Air Force):
   1,500; 43 combat ac, 7 armed hel.
2 interceptor sqns with 25 *Mirage* 5AD, 3
   5RAD, 2 5DAD.
1 FGA sqn with 3 *Alpha Jet.*
1 COIN sqn with 10 MB-326KD/LD.
Tpts incl 2 C-130H, 1 L-100-30, 1 Boeing
   720-023B, 1 G-222, 4 C-212, 5 *Islander,* 9
   DHC-5D, 1 Cessna 182.
Hel incl 7 *Alouette* III with AS-11, 8 AB-205, 6
   AB-206, 3 AB-212, 9 *Puma,* 4 AS-332F *Super
   Puma,* 10 *Gazelle.*
Trg ac: some 2 *Hawk,* 6 SF-260TP.
AAM: R-550 *Magic.*
ASM: AS-11/-12.
(On order: 18 *Mirage* 2000 ftrs (3 recce, 3 trg), 3
   Alpha Jet FGA/trg, 1 G-222, 1 C-130H-30 tpt,
   4 MB-339, some 24 *Hawk* (8 Mk 61, 16 Mk
   63) trg ac; 4 AS-332F *Super Puma, Lynx* hel;
   Skyguard AD system with twin 35mm guns.)

Para-Military Forces: Coastguard: 47 coastal
   patrol boats/craft.

YEMEN ARAB REPUBLIC (NORTH)

Population: 7,500,000.
Military service: conscription, 3 years.
Total armed forces: 36,550.
Est GDP 1981: YR 13.120 bn ($2.875 bn). 1982:
   14.637 bn ($3.208 bn).
Est def exp 1981: YR 2.025 bn ($443.836 m).
   1982: 2.404 bn ($526.904 m).
GDP growth: 5.3% (1982), 4.2% (1983).
Inflation: 2.9% (1982), 5.0% (1983).
Debt: $1.3 bn (1982).
   $1 = rial 4.5625 (1981/2).

Army: 35,000.
1 armd bde.
1 mech, 5 inf bdes.
1 Special Forces bde.
1 para/cdo bde.
1 central guard force.
3 arty bdes.
3 AA arty, 2 AD bns (1 with SA-2 SAM).
AFV: 100 T-34, 500 T-54/-55, 64 M-60 MBT;
   50 *Saladin* armd, *Ferret* scout cars; BMP
   MICV; 90 M-113, 300 BTR-40/-60/-152 APC.
Arty: 200 M-1942 76mm, M-102 105mm, M-38
   122mm and M-115 155mm towed how; 30
   SU-100 SP guns; 200 82mm and 120mm mor;
   65 BM-21 122mm MRL.
ATK: 75mm, 82mm RCL; *LAW* RL; 20 *Vigilant,
   TOW,* 24 *Dragon* ATGW.
AD: ZU-23 23mm, 37mm, 57mm, 85mm
   towed, 40 ZSU-23-4, 72 M-163 *Vulcan* 20mm
   (20 SP) AA guns; SA-2/-7 SAM.

Navy: 550.
4 Sov P-4 FAC(T)⟨.
6 patrol craft⟨: 3 US *Broadsword*; 3 Sov (2 *Zhuk,*
   1 *Poluchat*).
2 T-4 LCM.

Base: Hodeida.

Air Force: 1,000; 76 combat ac.‡
5 ftr sqns: 2 with 40 MiG-21; 1 with 10
   MiG-17F; 1 with 11 F-5E; 1 with 15 Su-22.
Tpts: 2 C-130H, 2 C-47, 2 *Skyvan,* 1 Il-14, 1
   An-24, 3 An-26.
Trainers: 4 F-5B, 4 MiG-15UTI.

---

* The Union Defence Force and the armed forces of
the United Arab Emirates (Abu Dhabi, Dubai, Ras Al
Khaimah and Sharjah) were formally merged in 1976;
Abu Dhabi and Dubai still maintain a degree of
independence. Perhaps a third of the force is drawn
from non-nationals.
† Excl defence expenditure by Dubai.
‡ Some 15 ac in storage.

Hel: 20 Mi-8, 6 AB-206, 5 AB-212, 2 *Alouette*.
1 AD regt with 12 SA-2 SAM.
AAM: AA-2 *Atoll*, AIM-9 *Sidewinder*.

Para-Military Forces: Ministry of National Security Force 5,000; tribal levies at least 20,000.

YEMEN: PEOPLE'S DEMOCRATIC REPUBLIC (SOUTH)

Population: 2,200,000.
Military service: 2 years.
Total armed forces: 27,500 (18,000 conscripts).
GDP 1981: YD 364.4 m ($1.055 bn). 1982: 318.8 m ($923 m).
Def exp 1981: YD 56.044 m ($162.258 m). 1982: 55.06 m ($159.409 m).
GDP growth: 2% (1982), 1.0% (1983).
Inflation: 15% (1982), 10.0% (1983).
Debt: $762 m (1982).
　$1 = dinar 0.3454 (1981/3).

Army: 24,000.
1 armd bde.
1 mech bdes.
10 inf 'bdes' (regts) (some being mechanized).
1 arty bde.
10 arty bns.
1 SSM bde with *FROG* and *Scud* B.
450 T-54/-55/-62 MBT; BRDM-2 scout cars; some 100 BMP MICV; 300 BTR-40/-60/-152 APC; 350 M-1945 85mm, M-1955 100mm, M-46 and coastal 130mm guns; M-38 and D-30 122mm how; BM-21 122mm MRL; 120mm, 160mm mor; 12 *FROG*-7, 6 *Scud* B SSM; 200 ZU-23-2 23mm, 37mm, 57mm towed and ZSU-23-4 SP AA guns; 6 SA-2, 3 SA-3, SA-6/-7 SAM.*

Navy: 1,000.
1 Sov corvette (converted T-58 minesweeper).
8 Sov *Osa* FAC(G) with 4 *Styx* SSM.
2 Sov SO-1 large patrol craft.
2 Sov P-6 FAC(T)⟨.
2 Sov *Zhuk* FAC(P)⟨.
1 Sov *Ropucha* LST; 3 Sov *Polnocny* LCT; 3 Sov T-4 LCA.

Bases: Aden, Perim Island.

Air Force: 2,500; 103 combat ac, some 15 armed hel.*
4 FGA sqns: 2 with 30 MiG-17F; 1 with 12 MiG-21; 1 with 25 Su-20/-22.
3 interceptor sqns with 36 MiG-21F.
1 tpt sqn with 3 An-24.
1 hel sqn with 15 Mi-24, 30 Mi-8.
1 SAM regt with 48 SA-2.
Trainers: 3 MiG-15UTI.
AAM: AA-2 *Atoll*.
ASM: AT-2 *Sagger*.

Para-Military Forces: People's Militia 15,000. Public Security Force: 30,000 (increasing). 1 *Tracker* 2, 4 *Spear*, 1 *Interceptor* patrol craft.

---

* Some eqpt believed in storage; some ac believed flown by Soviet and Cuban crews.

Sub-Saharan Africa

Bilateral External Agreements

The US has had mutual defence and assistance agreements with Ethiopia (1975), Ghana (1972), Kenya (1980), Liberia (1972), Mali (1972), Niger (1962), Senegal (1962) and Zaire (1972); most may now be in abeyance. Agreements with Somalia and Kenya allow limited US access to naval and air facilities; Somalia has received some military aid.

The Soviet Union has Treaties of Friendship and Co-operation with Angola (October 1976), Mozambique (March 1977) and Ethiopia (November 1978, ratified April 1979). Relations with the Congo Republic are close but no such agreement is known to exist. Military aid has been given to Angola (under additional Military Co-operation Agreements, including one signed in May 1983), Ethiopia, Guinea, Guinea-Bissau, Mali, Mozambique, Nigeria, Somalia, Uganda and Zambia (1980). The Soviet Navy has facilities in the Dahlak Islands, Ethiopia. Reports of a Soviet facility in São Tomé and Príncipe have been received.

China has military assistance agreements with Cameroon, Equatorial Guinea, Guinea, Mali and Tanzania, and provided aid to Mozambique and Zaire (under a 1982 sales credit).

Britain maintains overflying, training and defence agreements with Kenya, helps Zimbabwe form and train her forces, and heads a Commonwealth Training Team (Australia, Britain, Canada, Guyana, Jamaica, Kenya, Sierra Leone and Tanzania) which is helping to rebuild the Ugandan defence forces.

France has signed defence and/or military co-operation agreements with Benin, Cameroon (February 1974), the Central African Republic, Congo, Djibouti (1977, including permission to deploy forces), Gabon (1974), Ivory Coast, Madagascar, Mali (since terminated), Mauritania, Niger, Senegal (March 1974), Togo, Upper Volta and Zaire. The agreement with Chad has led to a French military presence defending the government from Libyan-backed insurgents.

Belgium has a military co-operation agreement with Zaire.

Spain has a military agreement with Equatorial Guinea (1981) and is providing training and some equipment.

Cuba has some 19,000 men in Angola, training the Angolan armed forces and assisting with internal security, and 3,000 in Ethiopia. Cuban, Soviet and East German advisers are present in a number of other African countries.

Some military links exist between South Africa and Israel, between Zaire and Israel, and between both Mozambique and Angola on the one hand, and East Germany, Bulgaria, Romania (1982) and Yugoslavia (1982) on the other. Hungary signed a Friendship Treaty with Ethiopia and with Mozambique in September 1980. North Korea signed a Treaty of Friendship and Co-operation with Togo in October 1981; she also had a 100-man training team with Zimbabwe's elite armoured brigade and a smaller team in Uganda; Ethiopia signed a Treaty of Friendship with Libya and South Yemen in 1981.

Multilateral Regional Agreements

The Organization of African Unity (OAU), constituted in May 1963 to include all internationally recognized independent African states except South Africa, has a Defence Commission – responsible for defence and security co-operation and the defence of the sovereignty, territorial integrity and independence of its members. In 1979 this approved in principle an African Intervention Force and ordered planning for its formation, funding and equipping. Little progress has been reported. It did agree in 1981 on an Inter-African Force for Chad, with troops from Nigeria, Senegal and Zaire. OAU financing was inadequate; the Force was withdrawn in June 1982.

In 1961 the Central African Republic, Chad, the Congo and Gabon formed the Defence Council of Equatorial Africa, with French help. Chad's present position in relation to the Council is unclear.

In May 1981 the Economic Community of Western African States (ECOWAS) adopted a Protocol on Mutual Assistance on Defence Matters calling for a joint Defence Commission, comprising Defence Ministers and their Chiefs of Defence Staff, and a Defence Council of the Heads of State. It is intended to create a joint force, using assigned units of the national armies, which could serve as an intervention or peace-keeping force. Of the then 16 ECOWAS members (Benin, Cape Verde, The Gambia, Ghana, Guinea, Guinea-Bissau, Ivory Coast, Liberia, Mali, Mauritania, Niger, Nigeria, Senegal, Sierra Leone, Togo and Upper Volta), 12 have signed, Cape Verde, Guinea-Bissau and Mali declined, and Mauritania signed only after the Protocol was amended to call for the withdrawal of foreign troops once ECOWAS could guarantee mutual defence.

Bilateral Regional Arrangements

Kenya signed a defence agreement with Ethiopia in November 1963 and a Treaty of Friendship and Co-operation in January 1979; Kenya and Somalia agreed in 1981 to control border incursions. Sierra Leone and Guinea signed a Defence Agreement in 1971 and a Mutual Defence Pact in August 1981. In December 1981 Senegal and The Gambia signed a confederation pact which united the two countries as Senegambia. Although they stated their intent to integrate their armed forces, the Protocols still have not been signed. Djibouti signed a Friendship Treaty with Ethiopia and with the Somali Republic in early 1981. Nigeria and Benin signed a military co-operation agreement in January 1983 providing for joint exercises and unspecified 'other things'. Mozambique trains Tanzanian and Zimbabwe troops; the agreement providing this facility is unknown. Tanzania provides instructors for Uganda under a defence pact signed in August 1981. In March 1984 South Africa signed one agreement with Mozambique mutually to curb insurgency and another with Angola providing for disengagement by South African forces and neutral supervision of guerrilla activity.

The only country in the area with an indigenous arms industry is South Africa, which builds equipment both under licence and of her own design.

ANGOLA

Population: 7,800,000.
Military service: 2 years.
Total armed forces: 43,000* (perhaps 27,000 conscripts).
Est GDP 1981: K 100 bn ($4.0 bn).
Est def exp 1981: K 20.0 ($800 m).
Debt: $2.5 bn (1982).
$1 = kwanza 25.0 (1981).

Army: 40,000.
6 Military Regions.
5 div HQ.
2 mot inf bdes (each of 1 tk, 2 inf bns).
17 inf bdes.
4 AA arty bdes.
10 tk bns.
6 arty bns.
10 SAM btys.
175 T-34, 150 T-54, 120 T-62 MBT; some 50 PT-76 lt tks; 200 BRDM-1/-2, AML armd cars; 150 BTR-60/-152 APC; 200 guns/how, incl 76mm, 85mm, 100mm, SU-100 SP, 122mm, 130mm, 152mm; 460 82mm, 40 120mm mor; 50 BM-21 122mm MRL; 2,000 75mm, 82mm and 107mm RCL; *Sagger* ATGW; ZPU-4 14.5mm, ZU-23 23mm, 37mm towed,

ZSU-23-4, 40 ZSU-57-2 SP AA guns; 72 SA-6, SA-7, 48 SA-8 SAM.†

Navy: 1,500.
4 *Osa*-II FAC(G) with 4 SS-N-2 SSM.
4 Sov *Shershen* FAC(T).
5 Port *Argos* large patrol craft.‡
8 coastal patrol craft: 3 Sov (1 *Zhuk*, 2 *Poluchat*); 5 Port (1 *Jupiter*, 4 *Bellatrix*).‡
4 LCT: 3 Sov *Polnocny*, 1 Port *Alfange*.‡
5 Sov T-4 LCM.

Bases: Luanda, Lobito, Moçâmedes.

Air Force: 1,500; 64 combat ac, some 10 armed hel.†
2 FGA sqns with 38 MiG-21MF, 25 MiG-17F ftrs.
MR ac: 1 F-27MPA.
2 tpt sqns: 6 *Noratlas*, 2 L-100-20, 3 C-47, 6 An-2, 18 An-26, 4 *Turbo-Porter*, 8 *Islander*, 10 Do-27, 1 F-27-400M, 1 FH-227.

---

* Some 19,000 Cuban and 450 E. German military operate ac and hy eqpt. There are also Portuguese and some 700 Soviet advisers and technicians.
† Delivery data incomplete; eqpt totals uncertain.
‡ Serviceability uncertain.

2 hel sqns: some 10 Mi-24, 35 Mi-8, 27 *Alouette* III and IAR-316B, 27 SA-365N *Dauphin*.
Trainers incl 1 MiG-15UTI, 6 Yak-11, 6 PC-7.
AAM: AA-2 *Atoll*.
SAM: 20 SA-3 *Goa*.
(On order: some 6 PC-7 *Turbo-Trainer* ac.)

Para-Military Forces: Militia 10,000; 11+ inf bns; 'Organization of Popular Defence': 500,000.

Opposition: UNITA, some 15,000 'regulars', 20,000 spt militia; BM-21 122mm MRL, 82mm mor, 75mm RCL, 12.7mm hy machine guns.

CAMEROON

Est population: 9,400,000.
Total armed forces: 7,300.
GDP 1981/2: fr CFA 2,038 bn ($6.869 bn).
Def budget 1982/3: fr CFA 27.796 bn ($78.376 m). 1983/4: 34.912 bn ($84.934 m).
Debt: $2.5 bn (1982).
  $1 = francs CFA 296.68 (1981/2), 354.65 (1982/3), 411.05 (1983/4).

Army: 6,600.
1 armd car bn.
1 para/cdo bn.
4 inf bns.
1 engr bn.
5 fd, 6 AA arty btys.
HQ regt, spt units.
M-8 armd, *Ferret* scout cars; some 38 *Commando*, M-3 half-track APC; 6 75mm pack, 16 M-101 105mm how; 60mm, 20 81mm, 16 120mm mor; 13 57mm ATK guns; 89mm ACL-STRIM RL; 40 106mm RCL; *Milan* ATGW; 18 Type-58 14.5mm, 18 twin 35mm, 18 Type-63 37mm, 18 40mm AA guns.
(On order: some 17 V-150 *Commando* APC.)

Navy: 350.
3 FAC(G): 2 P-48S *Combattante* with 8 *Exocet* MM-40 SSM, 1 PR-48 with 8 SS-12.
2 Ch *Shanghai*-II FAC.
9 coastal patrol craft⟨.
2 LCM, 5 LCVP, 1 LCU, 6 lt assault craft.
(On order: 1 PR-48 large patrol craft.)

Bases: Douala, Port Gentil.

Air Force: 350; 12 combat ac, 2 armed hel.
1 mixed sqn.
1 Presidential flt.
6 *Alpha Jet* FGA; 4 *Magister* COIN; 2 Do-128D-6 (MR); 3 C-47, 1 DHC-4, 4 DHC-5D, 3 C-130, 2 HS-748, 7 *Broussard*, 1 Boeing 727-20 tpts; 1 *Puma*, 3 *Alouette* II/III, 4 *Gazelle* (2 with *HOT* ATGW), 1 SA-365 *Dauphin* II hel.

Para-Military Forces: 5,000. Gendarmerie: 7 Regional groups.

CONGO

Est population: 1,700,000.
Total armed forces: 8,700.
Est GDP 1982: fr CFA 590.0 bn ($1.796 bn).
Def budget1983: fr CFA 26.289 bn ($68.987 m). 1984: 21.597 ($51.117 m).
Debt: $1.7 bn (1981).
  $1 = francs CFA 328.62 (1982), 381.07 (1983), 422.50 (mid-1984).

Army: 8,000.
1 armd bn (5 sqns).
2 inf bns.
1 arty gp.
1 engr bn.
1 para/cdo bn.
35 T-54/-55, 15 T-59 MBT; 14 Ch T-62, 3 PT-76 lt tks; 25 BRDM-1/-2 scout cars; M-3, 20 BTR-50, 20 BTR-60, 44 BTR-152 APC; 6 M-116 75mm pack, 8 M-1942 76mm, 10 M-1944 100mm, 8 M-1938 122mm how; 8 BM-21 MRL; 82mm, 10 120mm mor; 5 57mm ATK guns; 57mm RCL; 28 37mm AA guns (some T-34 MBT in store).

Navy: 200.
1 Sov *Shershen* FAC(T).
3 Ch *Shanghai* FAC.
3 13-metre ARCO Type 43, 2 11.4-metre Type 38, 3 *Piraña* coastal, 4 Ch *Yulin* river patrol craft⟨.

Air Force: 500; 21 combat ac.
1 MiG-15, 20 MiG-17 FGA.
1 F-28, 5 An-24, 5 Il-14, 3 C-47, 1 *Frégate*, 2 *Broussard* tpts.
4 L-39 trg ac.
1 *Puma*, 4 *Alouette* II/III hel.

Para-Military Forces: 3,000

ETHIOPIA

Est population: 32,000,000–40,000,000.
Military service: conscription, 30 months, incl police, border guard.
Total armed forces: 306,000.*
GDP 1982/3: EB 9.794 bn ($4.731 bn).
Def budget 1981/2: EB 910 m ($439.61 m).†

---

* Some 1,400 Soviet, 3,000 Cuban and about 250 E. German technicians and advisers operate ac and hy eqpt. Some S. Yemeni troops may also serve.
† Incl public security budget.

GDP growth: 0% (1982).
Inflation: 15–20% (1982).
  $1 = birr 2.07 (official).

Army (incl People's Militia): 300,000.
1 armd div.
23 inf divs (3 mot, 2 mountain, 3 lt) with some
  20 tk bns.
4 para/cdo bdes.
30 arty bns.
30 AD bns.
40 M-47, 150 T-34, 800 T-54/-55, 30 T-62 MBT;
  40 M-41 lt tks; 100 BRDM-1/-2 scout cars, 40
  BMP-1 MICV; about 70 M-113, 600
  BTR-40/-60/-152, V-150 *Commando* APC;
  some 700 guns/how, incl M-116 75mm pack,
  52 M-101 105mm, 250 122mm (incl SP),
  M-1954 130mm, M-1955/D-20 152mm, 12
  towed, 12 M-109 SP 155mm; 60mm, 81mm,
  82mm, 100 M-38 120mm, 280 M-2/-30
  4.2-in. (107mm), 120mm mor; BM-21 122mm
  MRL; M-1955 100mm ATK guns; *Sagger*
  ATGW; ZU-23 23mm, 37mm towed, ZSU-23-4
  23mm, M-1950, ZSU-57-2 57mm SP AA guns;
  SA-2/-3/-6/-7 SAM.*

Navy: 2,500.*
2 Sov *Petya* frigates.
7 Sov *Osa*-II FAC(G) with 4 SS-N-2A.
9 large patrol craft: 1 Yug *Kraljevica*, 4 US
  PGM, 4 Swiftship 105-ft.
3 coastal patrol craft: 1 Sov *Poluchat*, 2 *Zhuk*.
1 Sov *Polnocny* LSM.

Bases: Massawa, Assab.

Air Force: 3,500; some 160 combat ac; 24 armed
  hel.*
10 FGA sqns: 1 with 10 MiG-17; 6 with 100
  MiG-21; 2 with 38 MiG-23; 1 with 12 Sukhoi.
1 tpt regt with 14 An-12, 4 An-22, 14 An-26, 1
  Il-14.
Trainers incl MiG-21U.
Hel incl 32 Mi-8, 24 Mi-24.

RESERVES: All citizens 18–50 do 6 months trg.
  Assigned to Army, Police and Border Guard).

Para-Military Forces: 169,000. Mobile emergency police force (9,000). Border Guard.

Opposition: Eritrean Liberation Front (ELF) some
  6,500; (14 'bdes'); Eritrean Liberation
  Front–People's Liberation Forces (ELF–PLF)
  some 10,000; People's Liberation Front
  Revolutionary Guard (PLFRG) some 5,000;
  Eritrean People's Liberation Front (EPLF) some
  12,000; Tigray People's Liberation Front
  (TPLF) 5,000; Western Somali Liberation
  Front. Captured eqpt incl T-54/55 MBT; APC;

76mm, 85mm, 120mm, 130mm arty; BM-21
MRL; 23mm, 37mm, 40mm AA guns.

GHANA

Population: 13,000,000.
Military service: voluntary.
Total armed forces: 12,600.
GDP 1981: C 76.655 bn.†
Def exp 1980: C 426.0 m.
GDP growth: –2.8% (1981).
Inflation: 220% (1981).
Debt: $1.8 bn (1982).
  $1 = cedi 2.7502 (1980/1 off.).

Army: 10,000.
2 bdes (6 inf bns and spt units).
1 recce bn.
1 para bn.
1 mor bn.
1 fd engr bn.
1 sigs bn.
1 AB coy.
25 *Saladin* armd cars; 100 MOWAG *Piranha*
  APC; 81mm, 28 Tampella 120mm mor; 50
  Carl Gustav 84mm RCL; SA-7 SAM.

Forces Abroad: Lebanon (UNIFIL): 1 bn (705).

Navy: 1,200.
2 *Kromantse* ASW corvettes.
4 FAC: 2 FPB-57, 2 FPB-45.
4 large patrol craft: 2 *Dela*, 2 Br *Ford*.
4 *Spear* II coastal patrol craft.

Bases: Sekondi, Tema.

Air Force: 1,400; 10 combat ac.
1 COIN sqn with 10 MB-326F/KB.
1 tpt sqn with 6 *Skyvan* 3M.
1 comms/liaison sqn with 5 F-27, 1 F-28.
Hel: 2 *Alouette* III, 2 Bell 212.
1 trg sqn with 11 *Bulldog*.
(On order: 8 SF-260TP COIN/trg ac.)

Para-Military Forces: Border Guard 5,000; 3
  bns. People's Militia.

GUINEA

Est population: 5,550,000.
Total armed forces: 9,900.
Est GDP 1981: Sy 34.987 bn ($ 1.635 bn).
Est def exp 1981: Sy 1.710 bn ($79.91 m).
  $1 = sylis 21.399 (1981).

---

* War situation makes equipment data suspect;
US equipment probably not now serviceable.
† Continuing economic crisis, hyper-inflation and the
introduction of multiple exchange rates make meaning-
ful dollar conversions impossible at present.

Army: 8,500.
1 armd bn.
5 inf bns.
1 arty bn.
1 engr bn.
1 cdo bn.
1 special force bn.
1 AD bn.
45 T-34/-54 MBT; 20 PT-76 lt tks; 25 BRDM-1/-2 armd cars; 40 BTR-40/-50/-60/-152 APC; 76mm, 85mm, 105mm, 122mm guns/how; 20 M-1938/43 120mm mor; 57mm ATK guns; 37mm, 57mm, 100mm AA guns; SA-7, SA-8, 24 SA-6 SAM.

Navy: 600.
6 Ch *Shanghai*-II FAC.
2 Sov *Shershen*, 6 P-6 FAC(P)⟨.
7 coastal patrol craft⟨, incl 5 Sov (3 *Poluchat*, 2 MO-6).
1 T-58 minesweeper; 2 LCU.

Bases: Conakry, Kakanda.

Air Force: 800; 6 combat ac.
6 MiG-17F FGA (serviceability questionable).
4 Il-14, 4 An-14, 2 Il-18, 2 C-119, 1 Yak-40 tpts.
1 Reims F-337 lt ac.
Trg ac: 2 MiG-15UTI, 5 Yak-18, 3 L-29.
Hel: 1 Bell 47G, 1 *Puma*, 1 *Gazelle*, 1 UH-12B.

Para-Military Forces: 9,000; People's Militia: 7,000; *Gendarmerie* (1,000); Republican Guard 1,000.

GUINEA-BISSAU

Est population: 610,000.
Total armed forces 6,050.
Est GDP 1981: pG 8.963 bn ($235 m).
Def exp 1981: pG 307.9 m ($8.073 m).
 $1 = Guinean pesos 38.14 (1981).

Army: 5,700.
4 inf bns.
1 engr unit.
1 tk sqn.
10 T-34 MBT; BTR-40/-50/-60/-152, 20 Ch Type-56 APC; 85mm, 105mm, 122mm guns; 8 120mm mor; 89mm RL; 75mm RCL; 23mm, 57mm AA guns; SA-7 SAM.

Navy: 275.
6 FAC(P): 2 Ch *Shantou*, 2 Sov (1 *Shershen*, 1 P-6⟨).
6 coastal patrol craft⟨, incl 1 Sov *Poluchat*.
2 T-4 LCVP, LCU.
(On order: 4 coastal patrol craft⟨.)

Base: Bissau.

Air Force: 75.
2 Do-27, 2 Yak-40 tpts, 1 Reims FTB-337 lt ac.
1 *Alouette* II, 2 *Alouette* III, 1 Mi-8 hel.

Para-Military Forces: 5,000.

KENYA

Population: 18,900,000.
Military service: voluntary.
Total armed forces: 13,650.
GDP 1983: K Sh 82.206 bn ($6.793 bn).
Est def exp 1981/2: K Sh 2.010 bn ($197.796 m).
 1982/3: 2.900 bn ($239.630 m).
GDP growth: 2.0% (1982), 3.5% (1983).
Inflation: 22.0% (1982), 25% (1983).
Est FMA: $40 m (1983).
 $1 = shillings 10.162 (1981/2), 12.102 (1982/3).

Army: 13,000.
2 bdes (1 with 2, 1 with 3 inf bns).
2 armd bns.
1 armd recce bn.
2 arty bns.
2 engr bns.
1 indep air cav bn.
6 inf bns (cadre).
1 para bn.
76 Vickers Mk 3 MBT; 30 AML-60, 38 -90, 8 *Shorland* armd cars; 50 UR-416, 12 Panhard M-3 APC; 40 lt, 16 pack 105mm guns; 12 M-109 155mm SP how; 20 81mm, 10 120mm mor; 50 *Carl Gustav* 84mm, *Wombat* 120mm RCL; *Milan*, 8 *Swingfire* ATGW; 32 Hughes hel (15 500 *Scout*, 15 500MD with *TOW* ATGW, 2 500D trg).

Navy: 650.
4 Brooke Marine FAC(G): (1 37.5-metre, 3 32.6-metre), 2 with *Gabriel* SSM.
3 Vosper 31-metre (*Simba*) large patrol craft.
(On order: 5 patrol boats; *Gabriel* SSM).

Base: Mombasa.

Air Force: disbanded 1982.
Inventory 28 combat ac: 9 F-5E, 2 F-5F FGA, 5 BAC-167 *Strikemaster*, 12 *Hawk* T-52 COIN, 5 DHC-4 *Caribou*, 6 DHC-5D *Buffalo*, 7 Do-28D, 1 Nord 262, 1 *Turbo Commander*, 1 *Navajo* lt tpt, 14 *Bulldog* 103 trg ac; 10 *Puma*, 2 Bell 47G hel; *Sidewinder* AAM; *Maverick* ASM.
Being re-formed under Army.

Para-Military Forces: Police (General Service Unit) 1,800: Police Air Wing, 7 Cessna lt ac, 3 Bell hel.

MADAGASCAR

Population: 9,700,000.
Military service: 18 months.
Total armed forces: 21,100.
GDP 1982: fr M 1,046 bn ($2.991 bn).
Def budget 1983: fr M 29.0 bn ($67.371 m).
  1984: 31.730 bn ($55.729 m).
Debt: $1.4 bn (1983).
  $1 = Malagasy francs 349.71 (1982), 430.45 (1983), 569.36 (mid-1984).

Army: 20,000.
2 bn gps.
1 engr regt.
1 sigs regt.
1 service regt.
7 construction regts.
12 PT-76 lt tks; 8 M-8 armd, M-3A1, 10 *Ferret*, BRDM-2 scout cars; M-3A1 half-track APC; 12 ZIS-3 76mm guns; 12 122mm how; 81mm mor; 106mm RCL; 50 ZPU-4 14.5mm AA guns.

Navy: 600 (incl 150 marines).
1 PR-48 large patrol craft.
1 *Batram* landing craft with 8 SS-12 SSM.
7 LCM: 4 N. Korean *Nampo*, 3 US.
1 marine coy.

Air Force: 500; 12 combat ac.
1 FGA sqn with 4 MiG-17, 8 MiG-21FL.
1 tpt sqn with 1 HS-748 (VIP); 4 An-26, 1 Yak-40, 1 C-53D, 5 C-47, 1 *Defender*, An-12, 1 *Aztec*, 3 *Super Skymaster*, 5 lt ac.
1 hel sqn with 1 Bell 47, 3 *Alouette* II/III, 2 Mi-8.

Para-Military Forces: *Gendarmerie* 8,000, incl maritime police with 5 patrol craft.

MAURITANIA

Est population: 1,800,000.
Total armed forces: 8,470.
GDP 1981: OM 34.504 bn ($716.79 m).
Est def exp 1982: OM 3.500 bn ($67.326 m).
GDP growth: 4.0% (1982), 2.0% (1983).
Inflation: 12.6% (1982), 1.0% (1983.
Debt: $1 bn (1982).
  $1 = Ouguiyas 48.137 (1981), 51.986 (1982).

Army: 8,000.
1 inf bn.
1 arty bn.
1 Camel Corps.
3 armd recce sqns.
1 AA bty.
1 engr coy.
1 para coy.
15 EBR-75 hy, 39 AML-60, 14 -90 armd cars; 40 M-3 half-track, 4 M-3 APC; 81mm, 120mm mor; 57mm, 75mm, 106mm RCL; 14.5mm, ZU-23-2, 6 37mm AA guns; SA-7 SAM.

Navy: 320.
8 patrol craft: 1 Fr *Rapière*, 3 *Barcelo*, 4 ⟨.

Bases: Port Etienne, Nouadhibou.

Air Force: 150; 9 combat ac.
5 *Defender*, 4 Cessna 337 COIN.
4 *Cheyenne* MR.
1 DHC-5D, 1 *Caravelle*, 2 *Skyvan*, 2 *Islander* tpts.

Para-Military Forces: 2,500.

MOZAMBIQUE

Est population: 12,000,000.
Military service: conscription (selective): 2 years (incl women).
Total armed forces: 15,650.*
Est GNP 1981: m 86.10 bn ($2.950 bn).
Est def exp 1982: m 6.0 bn ($196.721 m).
  $1 = metiça 29.19 (1981), 30.50 (1982).

Army: 14,000 (perhaps 75% conscripts).
1 tk bde (Presidential Guard).
7 inf bdes (each 1 tk, 3 inf, 2 mech, 2 arty, 1 AD bns, spt units).
195 T-34, some 90 T-54/-55 MBT; 35 BRDM-1/-2 scout cars; 200 BTR-60/-152 APC; 250 M-1942 76mm, M-1945 85mm, M-1955 100mm, M-1938-63 122mm and LM-1946/-1954 130mm guns; M-101 105mm how; BM-21 122mm MRL; 325 60mm, 82mm and 120mm mor; 75mm, B-10 82mm, B-11 107mm RCL; *Sagger* ATGW; 300 20mm, ZU-23 23mm, 37mm, 57mm towed and ZSU-23-4 SP AA guns; 30 SA-3, SA-7, 10 SA-8 SAM.

Navy: 650.
14 coastal patrol craft⟨: 4 Sov (3 *Zhuk*, 1 *Poluchat*), 6 Port (1 *Antares*, 3 *Jupiter*, 2 *Bellatrix*), 4 Neth.
1 Port *Albarda* LCT.

Bases: Maputo, Beira, Nacala, Pemba, Metangula.

Air Force: 1,000; 35 combat ac.
3 FGA sqns with 35 MiG-17.
1 hel sqn with 4 Mi-8.
1 tpt sqn with 1 Tu-134, 4 An-26, 6 *Noratlas*, 4 Cessna 182.
Trg ac: L-39, 7 Zlin, 3 MiG-15.

---

* Cuban, East German and Soviet advisers reported.

Para-Military Forces: Border Guard 6,000: 4 bdes. Provincial, People's Militias, Local Militias (village self-defence force).

Opposition: National Resistance Movement of Mozambique (MNR): perhaps 6,000 trained, 3,000 reserve.

NIGERIA

Population: 82,000,000.
Military service: voluntary.
Total armed forces: 133,000.
GDP 1982: N 44.884 bn ($66.673 bn).
Def exp 1983: N 1.050 bn ($1.451 bn). Revised def budget 1984: 928.2 m ($1.240 bn).
GDP growth: −2.2% (1982), −5% (1983).
Inflation: 25% (1982/3).
Debt: $14.8 bn (1983).
    $1 = naira 0.6732 (1982), 0.7234 (1983), 0.7486 (mid-1984).

Army: 120,000.
1 armd div (4 armd, 1 mech bdes).
1 composite div (incl 1 AB, 1 air portable, 1 amph bdes).
2 mech divs (each 3 mech bdes).
1 Guards bde (1 armd recce, 3 inf bns).
4 arty bdes ⎫
4 engr bdes ⎬ organic to divs (1 each).
4 recce bns ⎭
40 T-55, 25 Vickers Mk 3 MBT; 50 *Scorpion* lt tks; 20 *Saladin*, 90 AML-90 armd, 55 *Fox* scout cars; 10 *Saracen*, 6 M-3 VPC, 4 AMX VTT, 26 Steyr 4K-7FA APC; 76mm, 200 D-30/-74 122mm, M-46 130mm guns; 200 M-56 105mm pack how; 200 81mm mor; 20mm, 40mm towed, 30 ZSU-23-4 SP AA guns; *Blowpipe*, 16 *Roland* SAM.
(On order: 11 Vickers Mk 3 MBT; 70 4K-7FA APC; 25 Bofors FH-77B 155mm, 25 *Palmaria* 155mm SP how; *Swingfire* ATGW; *Blowpipe*, 16 *Roland* SAM

Navy: 4,000.
2 ASW frigates: 1 *Meko* 360 with 2 × 4 *Otomat* SSM, 1 × 8 *Aspide* SAM, 1 *Lynx* hel; 1 *Nigeria* (trg).
4 corvettes: 2 Vosper Thornycroft Mk 9 (*Hippo*) with 2 × 3 *Seacat* SAM; 2 Mk 3 (may not be operational).
6 FAC(G): 3 Lürssen Type-57 with 4 *Otomat* SSM; 3 *La Combattante* III with 2 × 2 *Exocet* MM-38.
8 large patrol craft: 4 Brook Marine, 4 Abeking & Rasmussen.
48 coastal patrol boats.
2 RoRo 1300 (*Crocodile*) LST.
Hel: 3 *Lynx* Mk 89 MR, SAR.

(On order: 1 MCM vessel, 9 coastal patrol launches, 2 LCT).

Bases: Apapa (Lagos; Western Command), Calabar (Eastern Command).

Air Force: 9,000; 42 combat ac.
3 FGA/interceptor sqns: 1 with 16 *Alpha Jet*; 2 with 18 MiG-21MF; 8 *Jaguar*.
1 SAR sqn with 2 F-27MPA MR ac; 20 BO-105C/D hel.
2 tpt sqns with 9 C-130H-30, 4 F-27, 1 F-28 (VIP), 1 *Gulfstream* III (VIP), 1 Beech *Super King Air*.
3 service sqns with 13 Do-28D, some 8 Do-128-6.
Hel incl 14 *Puma*.
Trg: 2 MiG-21U, P-149D, 25 *Bulldog* ac; 15 Hughes 300 hel.
AAM: AA-2 *Atoll*.
(On order: 10 *Jaguar*, 8 *Alpha Jet* FGA; 5 G-222 tpt; some 10 Do-128-6 utility; 12 MB-339 trg ac; 5 CH-47 *Chinook* hel.)

Para-Military Forces: Coastguard (forming); 3 landing craft, 27 launches. Police: 4 hel, 18 launches, 7 hovercraft (5 AV *Tiger*).

SENEGAMBIA

(Senegal and The Gambia signed and ratified a Confederation Pact in December 1981, and action to combine their forces continues. The pre-Confederation organizations and inventories are shown separately below; a Gambian Army has formed but Gambia's other Services are civilian-manned.

    (In December 1983 a defence confederal budget of fr CFA 3.451 bn was introduced.)

SENEGAL

Est population: 6,300,000.
Military service: conscription; selective.
Total armed forces: 9,700.
GDP 1981: fr CFA 689.4 bn ($2.324 bn).
Est def exp 1982/3 fr CFA: 18.0 bn ($50.754 m). 1983/4: 22.0 bn ($53.522 m).
GDP growth: −4.5% (1981).
Inflation: 12% (1982), 15% (1983).
Debt: $150 m (1983).
    $1 = francs CFA 296.68 (1981/2), 354.65 (1982/3), 411.045 (1983/4).

Army: 8,500.
4 Military Zone HQ.
5 inf bns.
1 engr bn.

1 trg bn.
1 Presidential Guard (horsed).
1 recce sqn.
1 arty bty.
1 AA arty bty.
2 para coys.
3 construction coys.
10 M-8, 4 M-20, 54 AML-60/-90 armd cars; 40 Panhard M-3, 12 VXB-170, M-3 half-track APC; 6 M-116 75mm pack, 6 M-101 105mm how; 8 81mm, 8 120mm mor; STRIM-89 RL; *Milan* ATGW; 21 M-693 20mm, 40mm AA guns.

Navy: 700.
9 patrol craft: 1 PR-72M, 3 P-48 large, 5 coastal⟨.
1 LCT, 2 LCM.

Base: Dakar.

Air Force: 500.
MR/SAR: 1 EMB-111, 1 DHC-6.
1 tpt sqn with 1 Boeing 727-200, 1 *Caravelle* (VIP); 5 C-47, 6 F-27-400M, 2 *Broussard*.
Trg ac incl 7 *Rallye* 235G, 1 Reims Cessna F-337 lt, 2 *Magister*.
Hel incl 1 *Gazelle*, 1 *Puma*, 2 *Alouette* II.

Forces Abroad: Lebanon (UNIFIL): 1 bn (559).

Para-Military Forces: 6,800; 12 VXB-170 APC.

THE GAMBIA

Est population: 670,000.
Military service: voluntary.
Total armed forces 475.
GDP 1981/2: D 491.40 m ($225.651 m).
    $1 = dalasi 2.1777 (1981/2).

Army (Field Force): 400.
1 coy.
8 *Ferret* scout cars; 4 M-20 3.5-in. (89mm) RL.

Navy: (50).
2 coastal patrol boats: 1 31-ton *Tracker*, 1 17-ton *Lance*.

Base: Banjul.

Air: (25).
1 *Skyvan* 3M, 1 *Defender* tpts.

SOMALI REPUBLIC

Est population: 6,000,000.
Military service: conscription (males 18–40) 2 years.
Total armed forces: 62,550.
Est GDP 1982: S Sh 15.0 bn ($1.395 bn). 1983: 20.0 bn ($1.267 bn).

Def budget 1983: S Sh 1.933 bn ($122.435 m). 1984: 2.602 bn ($148.211 m).
GDP growth: 9.0% (1982), 4.0% (1983).
Inflation: 24.0% (1982), 45.0% (1983).
Est FMA 1983: $40 m.
Debt: $1 bn (1982).
    $1 = Somali Shillings 10.750 (1982), 15.788 (1983), 17.556 (mid-1984).

Army: 60,000.
3 corps, 8 div HQ.
3 tk/mech bdes.
20 inf bdes.
1 cdo bde.
1 SAM bde.
13 fd, 10 AA arty bns.
55 T-34, 45 T-54/-55, 100 M-47, 40 *Centurion* MBT; 50 BRDM-2 recce, AML-90 armd cars, BTR-40/-50/-60, 100 BTR-152, V-150 *Commando*, 44 M-113 (24 -113A1 with *TOW*), 300 Fiat 6614/6616 APC/AFV; about 150 76mm, M-1945 85mm and M-1955 100mm, 60 122mm guns/how; 81mm, 250 120mm mor; 400 STRIM-89 RL; 106mm RCL; 60 *TOW*, 100 *Milan* ATGW; 250 14.5mm, ZU-23 23mm, 37mm, 57mm and 100mm towed, 12 *Vulcan* 20mm, 10 ZSU-23-4 SP AA guns; 6 SA-2, 6 SA-3, some SA-6 SAM.*
(On order: 100 M-47 MBT, 40 *Centaure* twin 20mm AA guns.)

Navy: 550.*
2 Sov *Osa*-II FAC(G) with *Styx* SSM.
8 Sov FAC(T): 4 *Mol*, 4 P-6⟨.
5 Sov *Poluchat* large patrol craft⟨.
1 Sov *Polnocny* LCT, 4 Sov T-4 LCM⟨.

Bases: Berbera, Mogadishu, Kismayu.

Air Force: 2,000; 64 combat ac.*
3 FGA sqns with 9 MiG-17, 10 *Hunter* FGA-76, 2 T-77.
3 ftr sqns with 7 MiG-21MF, 30 Ch F-6.
1 COIN sqn with 6 SF-260W.
1 tpt sqn with 5 *Islander*, 2 An-24/-26, 3 C-47, 4 G-222, 4 P-166-DL3 recce/tpt.
1 hel sqn with 4 Mi-4, 2 Mi-8, 1 AB-204, 4 AB-212 (2 VIP).
Trainers incl 6 P-148, 2 MiG-15UTI.
Other ac: 8 SF-260W.
AAM: AA-2 *Atoll*.
(On order: SIAI S-211 COIN, 6 C-212 tpt ac; 4 Augusta Bell hel.)

Para-Military Forces: 29,500. Police (8,000), 2 Do-28 ac; Border Guards (1,500); People's Militia (20,000).

---

* Spares are in short supply and much equipment is unserviceable.

SOUTH AFRICA

Population: 26,800,000 (excl 'homelands').
Military service: 24 months, 8 camps totalling up to 240 days, then reserve commitment to age 65.
Total armed forces: 83,400 (53,300 conscripts; total mobilizable strength 404,500).
GDP 1982: R 78.611 bn ($70.936 bn). 1983: 87.911 bn ($76.578 bn).
Est def exp 1983/4: R 3.100 bn ($2.700 bn).* Def budget 1984/5: 3.755 bn ($2.940 bn).*
GDP growth: –1.2% (1982), –2.9% (1983).
Inflation: 14% (1982), 11% (1983).
Debt: $15.5 bn (1982).
   $1 = rand 1.1082 (1982/3), 1.1480 (1983/4), 1.2770 (mid-1984).

Army: 67,400 (10,000 White, 5,400 Black and Coloured regulars, 2,000 women, 50,000 conscripts); 9 territorial commands.
2 div HQ (1 armd, 1 inf).
1 armd bde (2 tk, 2 MICV-borne inf bns).†
1 mech bde (1 tk, 3 MICV-borne inf bns).†
4 mot bdes (each 3 inf bns, 1 armd car bn).†
1 para bde (3 para bns).†
1 special recce regt.
9 fd, 4 med, 7 lt AA arty regts.†
1 AA missile regt (3 Crotale, 3 Tigercat btys).
15 fd engr sqns.†
3 sigs regts, 3 sigs sqns.
Some 250 Centurion/Olifant MBT; 1,400 Eland 90 armd cars; 1,200 Ratel MICV (20mm/60mm/90mm gun); 500 lt APC incl Buffalo, Hippo, Rhino; 65 25-pdr (88mm), 75 5.5-in. (140mm) towed, 50 Sexton 25-pdr SP, 40 G-5 towed, G-6 SP 155mm how; Valkiri 127mm SP MRL; 81mm, 200 120mm mor; 900 6-pdr (57mm) and 17-pdr (76mm), M-67 90mm ATK guns; 84mm, 106mm RCL; SS-11, 120 ENTAC ATGW; 20mm, 55 K-63 twin 35mm, 25 L/70 40mm, 15 3.7-in. (94mm) AA guns; 54 Cactus (Crotale), 54 Tigercat SAM.

RESERVES: Active Reservists serve in the Citizen Force for 12 years, in which they spend 720 days in uniform. They then serve 5 years in the Citizen Force Reserve and may be allocated to the Commando Force, where they serve 12 days a year up to age 55.

Navy: 6,000, incl 900 marines, 2,300 conscripts.
3 Daphne subs.
1 President (Br Type-12) ASW frigate with 1 Wasp hel (trg).
8 MOD (Minister of Defence) (Reshef-type) FAC(G) with 6 Skerpioen (Gabriel-type) SSM.
3 FAC(G) with 2 Skerpioen SSM.
4 Br Ford, 2 mod Ton large patrol craft.
6 Br Ton minesweepers, 2 Ton minehunters.
1 fleet replenishment ship.

30 Namacurra armed harbour patrol craft.
1 ocean, 1 inshore hydrographic ships.
(On order: 4 MOD, 3 Dvora-type FAC(G).)

MARINES: (900; 600 conscripts); 9 local harbour defence units.

Bases: Simonstown, Durban.

RESERVES: 2,000 Citizen Force.

Air Force: 10,000 (1,000 conscripts); 304 combat ac (incl 93 with Citizen Force), at least 10 armed hel.
Main Threat Area Command:
   2 lt bbr sqns: 1 with 5 Canberra B(I)12, 3 T-4; 1 with 6 Buccaneer S-50.
   4 FGA sqns: 1 with 32 Mirage F-1AZ; 3 with 82 MB-326M/K Impala I/II.
   2 FGA/interceptor/recce sqns: 1 with 21 Mirage IIICZ/EZ, 6 RZ/R2Z; 1 with 13 F-1CZ.
   4 hel sqns with 5 Super Frelon, 35 Puma, 40 Alouette II.
   3 tpt sqns: 1 with 7 C-130B, 9 Transall C-160Z; 1 with 7 DC-4, 12 C-47; 1 with 4 HS-125 Mercurius, 1 Viscount 781.
   3 liaison sqns with 15 AM-3C Bosbok, 25 C-4M Kudu.
Southern Air Command:
   2 MR sqns with 18 Piaggio P-166S-DL3MAR Albatross.
   2 attack sqns with 25 Impala I/II.
   1 ASW hel sqn with 10 Wasp HAS-1.
   2 utility hel sqns with 7 Super Frelon, 13 Puma, 27 Alouette III.
   1 tpt sqn with 12 C-47B.
Western Air Command:
   Namibia; no integral operational sqns.
Training Command:
   6 trg schools with 100 T-6G Harvard; 60 Impala I/II; 26 Mirage III (some 10 EZ, some R2Z, some 10 D2Z); 12 C-47 ac; 30 Alouette II/III hel.
AAM: R-530, R-550 Magic, Sidewinder, Kukri V-3 (Sidewinder-type).
ASM: AS-20/-30.

RESERVES: Citizen Force 25,000. 93 Impala COIN ac. 15 L-100 (Hercules) in civil airline service.

South West Africa Territory Force (SWATF):
14,000: Formed 1 Aug 1980. Separate force, South African control. Conscription: 24 months (all race groups), selective, with Citizen Force (Reserve) commitment. Four Area Commands. (Northern, Eastern, Central

---

* Excl internal intelligence and security force budgets.
† Cadre formations completing the 2 divs when brought to full strength on Citizen Force mobilization.

and Southern) comprising 26 *Area Force* units organized similarly to the Commandos in South Africa, 1 engr, 1 sigs bns. Air element (one sqn) with lt ac manned by Citizen Force. Northern sector has six Regular SWATF lt inf bns, one mounted Specialist unit.

Mobile Reserve: 1 mot inf bde (3 mot inf bns, 1 armd car regt, 1 arty regt, spt units). 1 mot inf bn regulars, rest Citizen Force.

Para-military: Industrial Defence units.

Para-Military Forces: Commandos 90,000: inf bn-type protective units in formations of 5+; 12 months initial, 19 days annual trg. 13 Air Commando sqns with private ac. South African Police 35,500 (19,500 White, 16,000 Non-white), Police Reserves 20,000. Coastguard to form; 7 MR ac planned.

Opposition: South West African People's Organization (SWAPO) (some 8,000): possibly 7 field bns: T-34/-54 MBT; BTR APC; RPG-7 ATGW; SA-7 SAM.

TANZANIA

Population: 20,500,000.
Military service: voluntary.
Total armed forces, 40,350.
GDP 1981/2: T Sh 47.853 bn ($5.503 bn).
Est def exp 1981/2: T Sh 2.745 bn ($315.662 m).
   1982/3: 3.0 bn ($307.314 m).
GDP growth: −4% (1982), −5% (1983).
Inflation: 35% (1982), 40% (1983).
Debt: $2.9 bn (1983).
   $1 = shillings 8.696 (1981/2), 9.762 (1982/3).

Army: 38,500.
2 div HQ.
8 inf bdes.
1 tk bn.
2 fd arty bns, 2 AA arty bns (6 btys).
2 mor bns.
1 SAM bn with SA-3, SA-6.
2 ATK bns.
2 sigs bns.
30 Ch Type-59 MBT; 30 Ch Type-62, 36 *Scorpion* lt tks; 20 BRDM-2 scout cars; 50 BTR-40/-152 APC; 40 ZIS-3 and Ch Type-54 76mm, 200 122mm, 50 130mm guns; 350 82mm and 120mm mor; 540 Ch Type-52 M-20 75mm RCL; 50 BM-21 122mm MRL; 280 ZPU-2/-4 14.5mm, 40 ZU-23, 120 Ch Type-55 37mm AA guns; 9 SA-3, 12 SA-6, 40 SA-7 SAM.

Navy: 850.
10 FAC(G): 6 Ch *Shanghai*-II, 4 GDR P-6⟨.
4 Ch *Huchwan* hydrofoil FAC(T).

12 coastal patrol craft⟨: 2 GDR *Schwalbe*, 2 GDR 50-ton, 4 Ch *Yulin*; 4 Vosper Thornycroft 75-ft in Zanzibar.
2 Ch LCM.

Bases: Dar es Salaam, Zanzibar.

Air Force: 1,000; 29 combat ac.
3 ftr sqns (Ch ac): 11 F-7, F-6, F-4.
1 tpt sqn: 1 HS-125-700, 1 An-2, 3 HS-748, 6 DHC-5D.
Trainers: 2 MiG-15UTI, 6 *Cherokee*, 6 Cessna 310, 2 404.
Hel: 2 Bell 47G, 5 AB-205, 6 AB-206.
(On order: An-26, An-32 tpt ac.)

Forces Abroad: Mozambique: trg team, 200; Seychelles: 120.

Para-Military Forces: Police Field Force; 1,400, Police Marine Unit; Citizen's Militia; 50,000.

UGANDA

Population: 14,500,000.
Total armed forces: 18,000.
Est GNP 1981: U Sh 177.980 bn ($3.556 bn).
Est def exp 1981: U Sh 5.600 bn ($111.884 m).
   $1 = shillings 50.052 (1981).

Army: 18,000 (20,000 planned).
3 bde HQ.
Some 18 inf bns.
10 T-34/-54/-55, 3 M-4 MBT; 150 BTR-40/-152, OT-64 and *Saracen* APC; 60 76mm, 20 122mm guns; 40 *Sagger* ATGW; 40 23mm, 40mm AA guns; SA-7 SAM.*

Air Force: (100; part of Army).
6 AS-202B trg ac.

Para-Military Forces: Armed Police Special Force: 3,000. People's Militia: perhaps 20,000.

ZAIRE

Population: 32,000,000.
Military service: voluntary.
Total armed forces: 26,000.
GDP 1981: Z 23.603 bn ($5.384 bn). 1982: 31.296 bn ($5.443 bn).
Def exp 1980: Zaires 419.0 m ($149.643 m).
GDP growth: −2% (1982), 1% (1983).
Inflation: 35% (1982), 50% (1983).
Est FMA: $20 m (1983).
Debt: $5.5 bn (1983).
   $1 = zaires 2.800 (1980), 4.384 (1981), 5.750 (1982).

---

* Serviceability doubtful.

Army: 22,000.
3 Military Regions.
1 inf div:
  1 armd bde.
  2 inf bdes (each 3 inf bns, 1 spt bn).
1 Special Forces div:
  1 para bde (3 para bns, 1 spt bn).
  1 special force (cdo) bde.
  1 Presidential Guard bde.
60 Ch Type-62 lt tks; 95 AML-60, 60 AML-90 armd cars; 12 M-113, K-63, 60 M-3, BTR-152, M-3 half-track APC; 120 75mm pack, 122mm, 130mm guns/how; 82mm, 4.2-in. (107mm), 120mm mor; *Blindicide* 83mm, 107mm RL; 57mm ATK guns; 57mm, 75mm, 106mm RCL; 37mm, 40mm AA guns.
(On order: 120mm mor.)

Navy: 1,500 incl marines.
4 Ch *Shanghai* II FAC.
51 patrol craft: 4 *Huchwan* hydrofoils, 6 Sewart, 3 N. Korean P-4, 8 US, 30 others.

MARINES: (600).

Bases: Banana, Matadi (coast), Kinshasa (river), Kalémié (lake).

Air Force: 2,500; 39 combat ac.
1 ftr sqn with 7 *Mirage* 5M/5DM.
3 COIN sqns with 20 Reims Cessna FTB-337; 6 MB-326K; 6 AT-6G.
1 tpt wing with 6 C-130H, 2 DC-6, 2 DHC-4A, 2 *Buffalo*, 8 C-47, 4 C-54, 2 MU-2, 1 *Falcon*-20.
1 hel sqn: 3 *Alouette* III, 4 *Puma*, 1 *Super Frelon* (VIP).
Trg ac incl 27 Cessna (15 310, 12 150), 13 MB-326GB, 9 SF-260MC.
(On order: S-211 COIN/trg, 4 F-27-500 tpt ac.)

Forces Abroad: Chad: 2,000, para units (inf), 6 combat ac.

Para-Military Forces: Gendarmerie 22,000; 40 bns.

ZAMBIA

Population: 6,600,000.
Military service: voluntary.
Total armed forces: 14,300.
GDP 1982: K 3.564 bn ($3.840 bn). 1983: 4.222 bn ($3.375 bn).
Est def exp 1981: K 283 m ($325.887 m).
GDP growth: 3.6% (1982), 1% (1983).
Inflation: 11% (1982), 20% (1983).
  $1 = kwacha 0.8684 (1981), 0.9282 (1982), 1.251 (1983).

Army: 12,500.
1 armd regt (incl 1 armd recce bn).
6 inf bns.
3 arty btys, 2 AA arty btys.
1 engr bn, 2 sigs sqns.
4 T-34, 30 T-54/55 and Type-59 MBT; 130 BRDM-1/-2 armd cars; 13 BTR-60 APC; 76mm, 35 130mm guns; 18 105mm pack, 25 122mm how; 50 BM-21 122mm MRL; M-18 57mm, *Carl Gustav* 84mm RCL; *Sagger* ATGW; 50 M-75 triple 20mm, 40 37mm, 55 57mm, 16 85mm AA guns; SA-7 SAM.

Air Force: 1,800; 44 combat ac.
2 FGA sqns: 1 with 12 Ch F-6; 1 with 14 Sov MiG-21.
1 COIN/trg sqn with 18 MB-326GB.
2 tpt sqns: 1 with 10 Do-28, 3 C-47; 1 with 6 DHC-2, 5 DHC-4, 5 DHC-5D.
1 VIP flt with 3 Yak-40, 1 HS-748.
Trainers incl 8 SF-260MZ, 20 *Safari*, 2 Ch BT-3, 5 *Jastreb/Galeb*.
1 hel sqn with 3 AB-205A, 3 AB-206, 2 AB-212, 2 Bell 47G, 11 Mi-8.
1 SAM bn; 3 btys with 12 *Rapier*; 3 *Tigercat*, SA-3 *Goa*.

Para-Military Forces: 1,200. Police Mobile Unit (PMU) 700; 1 bn of 4 coys. Police Para-Military Unit (PPMU) 500; 1 bn of 3 coys.

ZIMBABWE

Population: 8,300,000.
Military service: voluntary.
Total armed forces: 41,300.
GDP 1982: $Z 5.005 bn ($US 5.775 bn).
Def exp 1982/3: $Z 291.2 m ($US 336.026 m).
  Def budget 1983/4: 418.0 m ($US 458.585 m).
GDP growth: 2% (1982), −4% (1983).
Inflation: 15% (1982), 20% (1983).
Debt: $US 2.5 bn (1983).
  $US 1 = $Z 0.8666 (1982/3), 0.9115 (1983/4).

Army: 40,000.
6 bde HQ (incl 1 Presidential Guard).
1 armd regt.
35 inf bns.
1 arty regt.
1 cdo bn, 1 para bn.
7 engr, 6 sigs sqns.
10 T-34, 18 T-54, 20 Ch T-59 MBT; 90 EE-9 *Cascavel*, 28 AML-90 *Eland* armd, 15 *Ferret*, BRDM-2 scout cars; 20 BTR-152, UR-416, *Buffalo, Hippo, Hyena, Leopard, Crocodile* APC; 18 25-pdr (88mm), M-56 105mm pack, 8 122mm, 8 5.5-in. (140mm) guns/how; 81mm mor; 106mm RCL; 8 SA-7 SAM.

Air Force: 1,300; some 35 combat ac.
1 lt bbr sqn with 5 *Canberra* B-2, 2 T-4.
1 FGA sqn with 7 *Hunter* FGA-9/T-7.
1 ftr sqn with 7 *Hawk* T-54.
1 COIN/recce sqn: 9 Cessna 337 (O-2) *Lynx*.
2 trg/recce/liaison sqn with 17 SF-260W/C *Genet*.
1 tpt sqn with 6 C-212-200 (VIP), 12 C-47, 6 *Islander*.
2 hel sqns with 26 *Alouette* II/III, 10 Bell/AB 205A.

2 AA arty sqns: 14.5mm, 20mm, 23mm, 37mm.
2 security sqns.
(On order: 12 Ch F-6, 12 F-7, 5 *Hunter* ftrs; 10 SIAI S-211 COIN/trg, 5 SF-260TP trg ac; 2 AB-412 (VIP) hel).

Forces Abroad: Mozambique: 600.

Para-Military Forces: Zimbabwe Republic Police Force, incl Air Wing, 10,000. Police Support Unit 3,000. National Militia 20,000.

For the Armed Forces of other African states, see overleaf.

ARMED FORCES OF OTHER AFRICAN STATES

Country	Est population (000)	Est GDP 1982 ($m)	Est def exp 1982 ($m)	Total armed forces	Army Manpower and formations	Army Equipment	Navy Manpower and equipment	Air Force Manpower and equipment	Para-military forces
Benin	**3,800**	**1,061**	23.6 (1981)	**3,300**	**3,000** 3 inf bns 1 para/cdo bn 1 engr bn 1 service bn 1 armd sqn 1 arty bty	10 PT-76 lt tks; 7 M-8, M-20 armd cars; 8 BRDM-2 recce vehs; 4 M-101 105mm how; 60mm, 81mm mor	**200** 4 *Zhuk* patrol boats((2 P-6, 1 Fr, 1 more *Zhuk* inoperable)	**100** 2 C-47, 2 An-26, 1 F-27, 3 An-2, 1 *Falcon* 20, 1 *Aero Commander*, 1 *Corvette* 200, 2 *Broussard* tpts; 1 Reims 337 lt ac; 1 Bell 47, 1 *Alouette* II hel	**1,100**
Botswana	920	1,071 (1983)	26.6 (1981)	3,000*	2,850* 1 inf bn gp	*Shorland*, 20 Cadillac Gage armd cars; 30 BTR-60 APC; 81mm, 10 120mm mor; 84mm *Carl Gustav* RCL; SA-7 SAM	—	150* 5 *Defender* COIN; 2 *Skyvan* tpts; 2 Cessna 152, 6 *Bulldog* lt ac	1,260 (Police)
Burundi	4,680	1,110	40.0	5,200*	5,000* 2 inf bns 1 para bn 1 cdo bn 1 armd car coy	6 AML-60, 12 -90, *Shorland* armd cars; 9 M-3, 20 BTR-40, *Walid* APC; 15 75mm RCL; 83mm *Blindicide* RL; 18 82mm mor; 15 quad 14.5mm AA guns	50* 3 *Lambro* patrol boats((2 in reserve)	150* 3 SF-260W COIN; 3 DC-3, 2 Do-27 tpts; 2 *Gazelle*, 3 *Alouette* III hel	1,500
Cape Verde	360	150 (1980)	15.0 (1980)	1,100	1,000 4 inf coys Spt elms	8 BRDM-2 recce vehs; mor; 3.5-in (89mm) RL	75 2 *Shershen* FAC; 2 *Zhuk* coast patrol craft(	25 2 An-26 tpt ac	—
Central African Republic	2,500	650	35.0 (1981)	2,300	2,000 1 regt HQ 1 mech bn (forming) 1 inf bn 1 engr coy 1 sigs coy 1 tpt coy	4 T-55 MBT; 22 BRDM-2, 10 *Ferret* scout cars; 4 BTR-152 APC; 81mm, 4 120mm mor; 14 106mm RCL; 9 river patrol craft(	—	300 10 AL-60, 2 *Guerrier* lt ac; 1 DC-4, 4 DC-3/C-47, 1 *Caravelle*, 1 *Corvette*, 6 *Broussard*, 2 *Skymaster* tpts; 1 *Alouette* II, 4 H-34 hel	1,500

Chad†	**4,850**	**550** (1981)	**51.7** (1983)	**4,200**	**4,000** (incl 5 para coys) Pres Guard, 2 arty btys, 1 recce coy; 3 inf bns	10 AML-60, 16-90 armd cars; 90mm, 122mm guns; 81mm, 120mm mor; 68mm, 89mm RL; *APILAS* 112mm, *Milan*, 106mm RCL; 20mm, 30mm AA guns; *Redeye* SAM	—	**200** 10 AL-60, 1 C-54, 3 C-130 9 C-47, 1 *Noratlas*, 1 *Caravelle*, 1 C-212, 1 F-27, 1 F-28, 2 PC-6, 2 *Broussard* tpts; 4 Reims 337 lt ac, 11 *Alouette* II/III, 4 *Puma* hel	**6,000**
Djibouti	**370**	**355**	**25.0**	**2,700***	**2,600*** 1 inf regt, 1 armd sqn, 1 spt bn, 1 border cdo bn, 1 para coy	12 BRDM-2, 2 AML-60, 8 AML-90 armd cars; 12 BTR-60 APC; 105mm pack how; 81mm, 4 120mm mor; 89mm RL; 106mm RCL	**20*** 3 coast patrol boats‹	**80*** 1 *Rallye* 235; 1 *Mystère* 20, 2 *Noratlas* tpts; 1 *Cessna* 206G lt ac; 1 *Alouette* II hel	**2,100**
Equatorial Guinea	**400**	**140**	**6.0** (1981)	**1,550**	**1,400** 1 inf bn, Spt unit	10 BRDM-2 recce vehs; 10 BTR-152 APC; 81mm mor	**100** 1 P-6 FAC; 1 *Poluchat*, 4 other patrol craft	**50** 2 MiG-17, 1 Reims 337, 2 C-212, 1 Yak-40 ac; 2 *Alouette* III hel	**2,000** (Police)
Gabon	**580**	**3,603**	**88.8** (1981)	**4,880**	**3,900** Pres Guard bn gp (recce/armd coy, arty, AA btys), 8 inf coys, 1 engr coy, 1 para coy, 1 service coy	16 *Cascavel*, 24 AML-90, 12 EE-3 *Jararaca* armd cars; 12 EE-11 *Urutu*, 6 *Commando*, M-3, 12 VXB-170 APC; 4 M-101 105mm how; 140mm MRL; 81mm, 120mm mor; 106mm RCL; 10 37mm, 2 40mm AA	**180** 1 FAC(G) with 4 SS-12 SSM; 4 FAC; 2 patrol craft‹; 1 LST, 3 LCM	**800** 9 *Mirage* 5G/DG FGA; 1 EMB-111P1 MR ac; 5 *Hercules*, 3 C-47, 1 DC-8-63, 4 EMB-110, 1 *Gulfstream* III (VIP), 1 *Falcon*, 1 YS-11A, 3 Nord 262, 4 *Broussard* tpts; 2 Reims 337, 2 *Magister*, 4 T-34C lt ac; 4 *Puma*, 3 *Alouette* III hel	**5,300**
Ivory Coast	**9,160**	**7,586**	**92.5** (1982)	**6,000**	**4,500** 3 inf bns, 1 armd sqn, 1 arty bty, 1 AA arty bty, 1 engr coy, 1 HQ coy, 1 spt coy, 1 para coy	5 AMX-13 lt tks; 7 ERC-90, 10 AML-60 armd cars; 16 M-3 APC; 4 105mm how; 4 105mm mor; 89mm 120mm mor; 16 STRIM RL; 4 M-3 VDA 20mm SP, 10 20mm, 5 40mm towed AA guns	**700** 2 *Vigilant*, 4 *Patra* patrol boats (with 4 *Exocet* MM-40); 4 patrol craft‹; 1 *Bantral* lt tpt, 1 LCVP; 2 assault boats; 1 trg ship	**800** 5 *Alpha Jet* FGA; 3 F-27, 2 F-28, 6 F-33C, 1 *Merlin*, 2 Reims F-337, 1 *Cessna* 421, 1 *King Air*, 2 RC-150, 1 *Falcon*, 1 *Gulfstream* tpts; *Rallye* 160 and 235 lt ac; 3 *Puma*, 2 *Alouette* III, 4 *Dauphin* hel	**800**

Armed Forces of Other African States (cont.)

Country	Est population (000)	Est GDP 1982 ($m)	Est def exp 1982 ($m)	Total armed forces	Army Manpower and formations	Army Equipment	Navy Manpower and equipment	Air Force Manpower and equipment	Para-military forces
Liberia	2,300	841 (1981)	27.2‡	5,600	4,900 1 Guard bn 5 inf bns 1 arty bn 1 engr bn 1 service bn	12 M-3A1 scout cars; 75mm pack, 8 105mm how; 20 60mm, 10 81mm, 4.2-in. mor; 3.5-in. RL; 57mm, 106mm RCL	450 3 50-ton, 2 38-ton, 1 11-ton Swiftships coast patrol craft	250 2 C-47 tpts; 14 Cessna lt ac (2 172, 1 185, 1 207, 10 337)	1,750
Malawi	6,660	1,330	23.0 (1983)	4,650*	4,500* 3 inf bns 1 spt bn (incl 1 recce sqn)	10 Fox, 10 BRDM-2 scout cars; 9 105mm guns; 81mm mor; 3.5-in. RL; 57mm RCL; 14 Blowpipe SAM	100* 1 Spear, 3 lake patrol boats⟨	50* 6 Do-27, 8 Do-28, 1 BN-2T tpts; 3 Puma, 1 Alouette III hel	1,000
Mali	7,700	1,200	40.0 (1982)	4,950	4,600 1 tk bn 3 inf bns 1 arty bn 1 engr bn 1 para bn 1 special force bn 2 AA arty coys 1 SAM bty	21 T-34 MBT, 12 Type-62 lt tks; 20 BRDM-2 recce; 30 BTR-40, 10 BTR-152, BTR-60 APC; 6 85mm, 6 100mm, 8 D-30 122mm guns; 2 BM-21 122mm MRL; 81mm, 30 120mm mor; 37mm, 57mm AA guns; 6 SA-3 SAM	50 3 river patrol craft⟨	300 5 MiG-17 FGA; 2 C-47, 3 An-2, 2 An-24, 2 An-26, 1 Corvette 200 tpts; 1 MiG-15UTI, 6 Yak-11/-18 trg ac; 2 Mi-4, 1 Mi-8 hel	5,000
Niger	6,000	2,100	14.0	2,220	2,150 2 armd recce sqns 6 inf coys 1 engr coy 1 para coy 1 log/spt coy	10 M-8, 30 ERC-60-20 armd cars; 14 M-3 APC; 60mm, 81mm, 15 120mm mor; 57mm, 75mm RCL; 10 M-3 VDA 20mm SP AA guns	—	70 2 C-47, 2 C-130H, 1 Boeing 737 (VIP), 2 Noratlas, 3 Do-28D, 1 Aero Commander tpts; 1 Reims F-337 lt ac	2,550
Rwanda	5,500	1,280	30.0	5,150*	5,000* 1 cdo bn 1 recce sqn	12 AML-60/-90 armd cars; M-3 APC; 6	—	150* 2 Defender, 2 SF-260W COIN; 1 Caravelle (VIP),	1,200

Country	Population	GNP	Defence budget	Total armed forces	Army	Navy	Air Force	Para-Military
(continued)					8 inf coys, 1 engr coy; 57mm ATK guns; 8 81mm mor; 83mm *Blindicide* RL		2 C-27, 2 *Rallye* 235 G tpts; 3 AM-3C liaison, 1 *Magister* trg ac; 6 SA-342L, 2 *Alouette* III hel.	900
Seychelles	67	150 (1981)	8.3§	1,200*	1,000*; 1 inf bn, 2 arty tps, Spt coy; 6 BRDM-2, *Shorland* recce; 3 122mm guns; BM-21 MRL; 6 82mm mor; RPG-7 RL; SA-7 SAM	100*; 1 *Sirius*, 1 lt 42-metre, 2 *Zhuk* large, 1 coast patrol craft; 1 LCT	100*; 1 *Defender*, 1 *Merlin* MR, 1 *Islander*, 2 *Rallye* ac; 2 *Alouette* III hel	
Sierra Leone	3,840	1,278	22.0 (1982)	3,100	3,000; 2 inf bn, 2 arty btys, 1 engr sqn; 4 *Saladin* armd cars; 10 MOWAG *Piranha* APC; 10 25-pdr guns/how 60mm, 81mm mor; M-20 3.5-in. RL; *Carl Gustav* 84mm RCL; SA-7 SAM	100 (coastguard); 1 *Tracker* patrol boat	1 Bo-105 (VIP) hel	800
Togo	2,850	815	22.3 (1981)	5,080*	4,000*; 2 inf regts, 1 Pres Guard cdo regt, 1 para cdo regt, 1 fd, 2 AA arty btys, 1 log/tpt engr bn; 7 T-34, 2 T-54/-55 MBT; 6 M-8, 3 M-20, 3 AML-60/-90, 36 EE-9 *Cascavel* armd cars; 4 M-3A1, 30 UR-416 APC; 4 HM-2 105mm guns; 20 81/82mm mor; 5 ZIS-2 57mm, 12 Type-52/-56 75mm, Type-65 82mm RCL; 38 ZPU-4 14.5mm, 5 M-39 37mm AA guns	80*; 2 coastal patrol craft	250*; 6 EMB-326GB COIN; 5 *Alpha Jet* COIN/trg; 1 Boeing 727, 2 DHC-5D, 1 F-28 tpts; 5 *Magister* trg, 2 lt ac; 2 *Alouette* II, 1 *Puma*, 2 *Lama* hel	750*
Upper Volta	6,800	1,080	32.8	3,775*	3,700; 3 inf regts (bns), 1 recce sqn, 1 arty bty, 1 para coy; 15 AML-60/-90, 10 M-8, 4 M-20 armd cars, 30 *Ferret* scout cars; 13 M-3 APC; M-101, M-56 pack 105mm how; 60mm, 81mm mor; Type-63 107mm MRL; M-20 3.5-in. RL; Type-52 75mm RCL; RPG-7 RL; SA-7 SAM	—	75*; 2 C-47, 2 Nord 262, 2 HS-748, 1 Aero Commander, 3 *Broussard*, 2 *Super Skymaster*, 2 Cessna 172 tpts	900

* Including 'public order' budget.
† Politico-military conditions make data suspect. 50% of defence budget externally financed.

* All services form part of the Army.
‡ Including 'public order' budget.
§ Official budget title: 'Youth and Defence Ministry'.

Asia and Australasia

CHINA

Chinese defence policy has long maintained a balance, at times uneasy, between two concepts: nuclear force to deter strategic attack and People's War – mass mobilization of the population to deter or repel conventional invasion. Despite changes in the political leadership, there remain many supporters of the strategic concept that mass manpower is still the primary deterrent. The need to modernize the forces has been recognized. Programmes to re-equip, reorganize and enhance their military effectiveness are being implemented, but slowly.

The conventional arms inventory of the People's Liberation Army (PLA), technically much less advanced than that of wealthier nations, is being gradually updated by replacing Soviet and Soviet-type equipment with indigenous designs and some Western technology. The United States has agreed in principle to sell logistic and dual-purpose equipment and technology. China has obtained computers and radars and is negotiating the sale of a wide range of defensive and non-combat military equipment. Britain has sold aircraft engines, artillery and fire control equipment and radar. France has sold helicopters and radar. But the current phase of economic readjustment has meant a succession of cuts in the defence budget between 1980 and 1983, and the pace of modernization will be quite slow.

Nuclear Weapons

The research programme continues, but no nuclear test has been recorded since 1980. At least 26 tests have been made since 1964. A nuclear force capable of reaching large parts of the Soviet Union and Asia is operational.

A multi-stage ICBM with a limited range of 6,000–7,000 km was first tested in 1976. Two types of ICBM are now deployed, one with a range of some 13,000 km, the other some 10,000 km. No indication has been received of the deployment of multiple warheads, but a missile has been successfully used (and thus tested) as a launcher for three space research satellites. Deployment continues of an IRBM with an estimated 5,500 km range. Deployment of an MRBM with a range of some 1,800 km may be complete. China's first SSBN – the *Daqingyu* or *Xia* class – is reported still to be on trials; her SLBM is reported as the CSS-NX-3, a variant of the DF-3 IRBM. Four more of these boats are said to be under construction and as many as twelve may be planned. Two *Han*-class nuclear-powered submarines with six missile tubes are now in service; the cruise missile they are said to carry has been tested to a reported range of 1,600 km. So far all ballistic missiles have been liquid-fuelled. Solid propellants being developed are reported to have powered the 1980 ICBM test vehicle and may power the DF-5 ICBM. The missile forces are manned by the Second Artillery, which is directly controlled by the Ministry of Defence. There are no reports of tactical nuclear munitions (artillery, rockets, mines). If such munitions are available, fighter aircraft could be used for tactical delivery, and for longer ranges there are some 120 B-6 medium bombers, with a combat radius of up to 3,000 km.

Conventional Forces

The PLA embraces all arms and services, including naval and air elements. Essentially a defensive force, the PLA lacks facilities and logistic support for protracted large-scale operations at any significant distance outside Chinese borders. China is organized in 11 Military Regions (MR) with 28 Military Districts (MD). The field army's Main Force (MF) divisions are commanded by the Ministry of National Defence, although command is being transferred to the MR in which they are stationed and which are already responsible for their administration. They are available for operations in any region. Extensive reorganization of the Local Forces (LF), Border and Internal Defence forces and para-military units intended to defend their own Provinces is taking place. The field army strength is declining as transfers to the regional forces continue. Artillery, engineer and railway units are controlled by the Ministry of National Defence. Infantry units account for most of the ground-force manpower and 119 of the some 158 MF line divisions; there are only 12 armoured divisions.

The naval and air elements of the PLA have only about one-fifth of the total manpower, compared with about a quarter for their counterparts in the Soviet Union, but naval strength is increasing. The naval force is organized in three fleets, two of them controlled by the Northern Naval Region. The naval air arm is shore-based, and there is an independent Coast Defence Force. The air component is organized into 8 Regions and 3 minor geographic commands; combat organization is similar to the Soviet system, with air armies of divisions of three regiments each with some 45 aircraft.

Major weapons systems include Type-59 MBT, Type-60/-63 amphibious and Type-62 light tanks and Type-531 APC; modified R- and W-class medium-range diesel submarines, SSM destroyers, frigates, fast patrol boats, amphibious transports and landing craft; J-6/-7 and Q-5 fighters, SA-2-type SAM. Production rates for this equipment are, at best, broad estimates only. Actual rates may be considerably lower than many such estimates suggest.

Bilateral Agreements

There is a mutual defence agreement with North Korea, dating from 1961, and an agreement to provide free military aid. There are friendship and non-aggression pacts with Afghanistan, Burma, Nepal (1960) and Kampuchea (*Khmer Rouge*). Chinese military equipment and logistic support have been offered to a number of countries. Major recipients include Albania, Egypt, Iraq, Pakistan and Tanzania.

Gross National Product and Defence Expenditure

Official Chinese sources claim a GNP figure of 989.4 bn yuan for 1982 and 1,105.2 bn for 1983, an increase of 11.7%. National income is reported by the IMF to be 424.7 bn yuan for 1982 and 467.3 bn for 1983. (GNP figures include the service and other sectors.) Western estimates of GNP have varied greatly, from $260 bn to $600 bn in 1982, and it is difficult to choose from a range of figures, variously defined and calculated.

Since 1981 the Chinese government has released official defence budget figures. In 1983 the defence budget amounted to 17.713 bn yuan ($8.959 bn), while for 1984 the figure of 17.870 bn yuan ($8.189 bn) was reported. These figures are not comparable to Western defence estimates, since they exclude a number of items, notably pay and allowances for the troops. Chinese budgetary practices are not known in detail, but they are certainly different from those in the West. Because of the differences, the official budget figure must be considered as an indicator of proportion, rather than a clear measurement of actual costs.

Population: 1,039,000,000.
Military service: conscription; Army, 3 years; Navy/Air 4 years. Technical volunteers can serve 8–12 more years to maximum age 35.
Total regular forces: 4,000,000.*
GNP and defence expenditure: see note above.
Debt 1982: $4.7 bn.
  $1 = 1.887 yuan (1982), 1.9772 (1983), 2.1821 (mid-1984) (official rate).

Strategic Forces:
OFFENSIVE:
(a) *Missiles*:
  ICBM: 2 DF-5 (*Dong Feng*; = *East Wind*): range 13,000 km; 5 MT warhead. 4 DF-4: range 10,000 km; 3 MT.

IRBM: 60 DF-3: range 5,500 km; 2 MT.
MRBM: 50 DF-2: range 1,800 km; 20 KT.
(b) *Submarines*:
  1 *Daqingyu* (*Xia*) SSBN with 12 CSS-NX-3 (mod DF-3, range perhaps 2,800 km – possibly 1 × 2 MT warhead) in development.
  (On order: 4 *Daqingyu* SSBN reported).

DEFENSIVE:
(a) Tracking stations in Xinjiang (cover central Asia) and Shanxi (northern border) and a limited shipborne capability.

---

* The term 'People's Liberation Army' comprises all services; the Ground, Naval and Air components of the PLA are listed separately for purposes of comparison.

(b) Ballistic missile EW phased-array radar complex.

(c) Air Force AD system with over 4,000 naval and air force fighters, about 100 *Honggi-2* (*Red Flag*; SA-2-type) SAM units and over 16,000 AA guns; capable of limited defence of key urban and industrial areas, military installations and weapons complexes.

(d) A civil defence shelter/evacuation/local defence system in Beijing and other key cities.

Army*: 3,160,000.
Main Forces (Field Army):
   11 Military Regions, 27 Military Districts, 1 indep MD, 3 Garrison Commands.
   Some 35 Armies (46,300 men), each normally of 3 divs, 1 arty regt and spt tps (some have 1 indep tk regt, some have 1 arty, 1 AA regts), comprising:
   13 armd divs.
   118 inf divs.
   Some 17 field arty divs.
   16 AA arty divs.
   Some indep arty, AA regts.
   Some 21 sigs, CW regts; 20 indep recce, engr, sigs, chemical bns (Army tps).
   50 indep engr regts.
Local Forces (29 provinces; being reorganized).
   73 divs (70 LF (border/internal defence), 3 garrison).
   140 indep regts.
AFV: 11,450 Sov IS-2 hy (trg), T-34 (trg), T-54, Ch Type-59 and T-69 (mod Type-59) MBT; Type-62 lt and Type-60/-63 lt amph tks; 2,800 Type 531, Type-55/-56 (BTR-40/-152)/-63 APC.
Arty: 12,800 Type-56 85mm (fd/ATK), (Type-59?) 100mm, Type-60 122mm, Type-59 130mm towed, ISU-122/-152 SP (trg?) guns; Type-66 152mm towed gun/how; Type-54 122mm and Type-56 152mm towed, 122mm SP how (Type-531 chassis); 4,500 Type-63 12 ×107mm, 40 × 122mm, Type-63 19 × 130mm (incl SP), BM-13-16 16 × 132mm, BM-14-16 16 × 140mm, 10 × 180mm and 10 × 320mm MRL; 14,000 Type-53 82mm, Type-55 120mm and Type-56 160mm mor.
ATK: 40mm, 57mm, 90mm RL; 7,800 57mm, 175mm and 82mm RCL; Type-55 57mm, Type-54 76mm guns; *Sagger*-type ATGW.
AA: 15,000: Type-63 37mm (incl twin SP), Type-59 57mm, Type-56 85mm and Type-59 100mm guns.

DEPLOYMENT:
Excl arty and engrs, MF and LF divs may be:
North-East: Shenyang MR (Heilongjiang, Jilin, Liaoning MD): 4 armd, 19 inf; 13 LF.†
North: Beijing MR (Beijing, Tienjiang Garrison Commands; Hebei, Nei Monggol, Shanxi MD): 4 armd, 25 inf; 13 LF.

North-West: Lanzhou MR (Gansu, Ningxia, Qinghai, Shaanxi MD): 1 armd, 8 inf; 2 LF.†
West: Ürümqi MR (North and South Xinjiang MD): 5 inf; 7 LF.†
South-west: Chengdu MR (Sichuan, Xizang MD): 8 inf; 4 LF.†
South: Kunming MR (Guizhou, Yunnan MD): 7 inf. Guangzhou MR (Guangdong, Hunan, Guanxi MD, Hainan (an MD-equivalent)): 11 inf; 8 LF.†
Centre: Wuhan MR (Henan, Hubei MD): 2 armd, 10 inf, 3 AB (Air Force); 6 LF.
East: Jinan MR (Shandong MD): 1 armd, 9 inf; 6 LF. Nanjing MR (Shanghai Garrison Command; Anhui, Jiangsu, Zhejiang MD): 1 armd, 10 inf; 9 LF. Fuzhou MR (Fujian, Jiangxi MD): 6 inf; 5 LF.

Navy*: 350,000 incl Naval Air Force and Coast Defence Forces: 2 SSN, 100 diesel attack subs; 36 major surface combat ships.
2 *Han* SSN.
100 diesel subs (1 *Golf* missile (trials), 76 *R*-, 21 *W*-class, 2 *Ming* trg).
14 GW destroyers: 10 O-51 *Lüda* (Kotlin-type) with 2 × 3 HY-2 (*Hai Ying*; = *Sea Eagle*; *Styx*-type) SSM; 4 *Anshan* (ex-Sov *Gordy*) with 2 × 2 HY-2.
22 frigates: 17 GW (11 O-37 *Jianghu* with 2 × 2 HY-2, 2 *Jiangdong* with 2 × 2 SAM; 4 *Chengdu* (ex-Sov *Riga*) with 1 × 2 HY-2); 5 *Jiangnan* (*Riga*-type).
8 patrol escorts: 6 ex-Jap, 1 ex-Br, 1 ex-Aus.
216 FAC(G) with HY-2: 116 *Osa/Huangfen* (4 msls), *Hola* (2 msls), 98 *Hoku*⟨, 1 *Homa* hydrofoil (2 msls).
48 patrol craft: 28 *Hainan*, 20 *Kronshtadt*.
341 FAC: 10 *Shanghai* I, 295 *Shanghai* II/III/IV/V, 3 *Haikou*, 30 *Swatow*; 3 *Shandong* hydrofoils⟨.
290 FAC(T)⟨: 140 *Huchwan* I/II hydrofoils; 70 P-6, 80 P-4.
About 120 coastal and river patrol craft⟨.
23 T-43 ocean minesweepers.
18 LST incl ex-US 511-1152, 35 LSM, 6 inf landing ships, 320 LCU, 150 LCM; some 61-ton hovercraft.
7 sub, 6 other spt, 10 supply ships; 23 tankers.
(On order (reports tentative): 4 *Han* SSN; 4 *Lüda* DDG; 8 *Jianghu* (4 mod), 2 *Jiangdong* FFG; *Huangfen*, *Hoku* FAC(G); 3 LST.)

Coastal Defence Forces: (38,000): indep arty regts deployed near naval bases, offshore islands, and other vulnerable points; 85mm,

---

* The term 'People's Liberation Army' comprises all services; the Ground, Naval and Air components of the PLA are listed separately for purposes of comparison.
† There are 2–3 divs worth of border tps in these MR.

100mm, 130mm guns; HY-2 ('CSSC-2') land-based SSM.

DEPLOYMENT AND BASES:
North Sea Fleet: about 500 vessels (over half ⟨⟩, incl 2 sub sqns; from the Yalu River to south of Lianyungang. Qingdao (HQ), Lüda, Lüshun, Huludao, Weihai, Chengshan.
East Sea Fleet: about 750 vessels (about 400 ⟨⟩ with air, AD and coastal missile units; from south of Lianyungang to Dongshan. Ningbo (HQ), Zhoushan, Taohua Dao, Heimen, Wenzhou, Fuzhou.
South Sea Fleet: about 600 vessels (some half⟨⟩, incl 25 subs, 200 FAC, amph; from Dongshan to Vietnamese frontier. Zhanjiang (HQ), Shantou, Guangzhou, Haikou, Yulin, Beihai.
Some 800 ocean-going vessels and several thousand junks could augment the existing limited sealift capacity.

NAVAL AIR FORCE: (38,000); about 800 shore-based combat aircraft,‡ org in 3 bbr, 6 fighter divs, incl some H(Hong; = bomber)-6, about 100 H-5 torpedo-carrying and 50 Il-28 lt bbrs; some 600 fighters, incl J(Jian; = ftr)-5/-6/-7 interceptors; H-5 recce, 8 ex-Sov Be-6 MR/ASW ac; 40 Z(Zhi; = helicopter)-5, 12 *Super Frelon* ASW hel; some 60 lt tpt ac. Naval fighters are integrated into the national AD system.

Air Force*: 490,000, incl strategic forces and 220,000 AD personnel; some 5,300 combat ac.‡
8 Military Air Regions, 3 minor regional comds, HQ Beijing; combat elms org in Armies of varying numbers of air divs (each with 3 regts of 3 sqns of 3 flts of 4–5 ac, 1 maintenance unit, some tpt and trg ac). Tpt ac in regts only.
Med bbrs: 120 H-6.
Lt bbrs: some 500 H-5.
FGA: some 500 J-4 and Q(Qiang = attack)-5.
Ftrs: some 4,000, incl 400 J-5, some 60 regts with about 3,000 J-6/B/D/E, 200 J-7, 30 J-8.
Recce: Some 130 JZ-6, HZ-5 ac.
Tpts: Some 550 fixed-wing, incl some 300 Y(Yun = transport)-5/An-2, some 10 Y-7 (An-24), Y-8 (An-12), some 75 ex-Sov Li-2, Il-14, Il-18 (to be retired), 18 *Trident*. (These could be supplemented by some 400 ac, incl some 150 hy tpts, from Civil Aviation Administration).
Hel: 400: incl Z-5/-6; Z-9 (Fr SA-365N *Dauphin*), Alouette III, SA-321 *Super Frelon*.
Trainers: incl CJ-5/-6, MiG-15UTI, JJ-4/-5/-6, HJ-5.
AAM: PL-2 *Atoll*-type.
Airborne tps: 1 corps of 3 divs, 1 indep div: 82mm, 120mm mor; 82mm RCL; 37mm AA guns.
20 AA arty divs, 28 indep AD regts (100 SAM units) with CSA-1 SAM, 16,000 57mm, 85mm and 100mm guns.

RESERVES: ex-Service to age 45. Perhaps 5,000,000 with service in the past 5 years.

Para-Military Forces: Some 12,000,000.
Militia. *Basic Militia*: some 4.3 million; men and women aged 18–28 who have had, or will have, military service, grouped in the Armed Militia; serve with the Regulars for 30–40 days per year; organized into about 75 cadre divisions and 2,000 regts and a Naval (Maritime) Militia with armed trawlers. *Ordinary Militia*: up to 6 million (ages 18–35), including the Urban Militia, receive some basic training but are generally unarmed. Some play a local AD role; all support the security forces.
People's Armed Police Force (Ministry of Security): ex-soldiers and personnel transferred from some 4 LF divs; Internal Defence divs and 30 indep regts; border security, patrol and internal security duties; small arms only.

‡ Many Chinese aircraft designs stem from Soviet types. Using Chinese terms, H-5 = Il-28, H-6 = Tu-16, J-5 = MiG-17, J-6 = MiG-19, Q-5 = MiG-19, J-7 = MiG-21, J-8 = MiG-23, Y-5 = An-2, Y-7 = An-24, Y-8 = An-12 ac; Z-5 = Mi-4, Z-6 = Mi-8 hel. In export models the J is generally read as F.

OTHER ASIAN COUNTRIES AND AUSTRALASIA

Bilateral Agreements

The United States has mutual co-operation and security treaties with Japan (1960), the Republic of Korea (1954) and the Philippines (1951, 1983); military co-operation agreements with Australia (1951, 1963, 1974 and 1980); and a military aid agreement with Thailand. That with Taiwan lapsed on 1 January 1980; arms supply and production arrangements continue under the 1979 Taiwan Relations Act. Washington also provides continuing military aid to Indonesia, South Korea, Malaysia, Pakistan, the Philippines and Thailand. There are major US bases in Japan, South Korea and the Philippines (agreement renewed 1983), and air (B-52) and naval refuelling facilities in north and west Australia.

In 1965 Britain purchased the Chagos Archipelago, which included Diego Garcia and three other islands, from Mauritius for $3 m and established it as the British Indian Ocean Territory. A joint US/British base was constructed on Diego Garcia, and a small British naval contingent was deployed there. Agreements in 1966, 1972 and 1976 provided for the development of a major US naval and air support facility with a 50-year tenure. The three small islands have since been turned over to the Seychelles. Britain has a Defence Agreement with Sri Lanka (1974) and one with Brunei which provides Gurkha troops and a British Forces training area.

The Soviet Union has Treaties of Friendship, Co-operation and Mutual Assistance with Afghanistan (1978), India (1971), Mongolia (1966), North Korea (1961) and Vietnam (1978). She concluded a Stationing of Forces Agreement with Afghanistan in April 1980. An agreement with India in December 1982 provides for collaboration on design and manufacture of naval vessels; other co-production arrangements are reported. Bulgaria has Friendship Treaties with Cambodia (1960), Laos (1979), Mongolia (1967) and Vietnam (1979), as have Czechoslovakia with Laos and Vietnam (1980) and Afghanistan (1981), Hungary with Afghanistan (1982), and East Germany with Vietnam (1977), Kampuchea (1980) and Afghanistan (1982).

The People's Republic of China has Friendship and Non-Aggression Treaties with Afghanistan, Burma and Nepal.

Cuba and Vietnam signed a Treaty of Friendship and Co-operation on 5 October 1982. Libya and North Korea signed a Treaty of Alliance or Friendship and Co-operation in November 1982, which is to permit exchanges of military data, specialists and supplies. North Korea and Tanzania have an agreement covering aspects of defence and security.

Australia has an agreement and subsidiary arrangements for the development of and assistance to the Papua New Guinea Defence Force, and some 135 personnel are on loan to it. She has supplied defence equipment to the Philippines, Malaysia, Singapore, Thailand, Indonesia and most of the smaller Pacific island states under a number of arrangements.

In July 1977 Vietnam and Laos signed a series of agreements which contained military provisions and a border pact, and may have covered the stationing of Vietnamese troops in Laos. A similar series of agreements seems to have been negotiated between Vietnam and the Heng Samrin regime in Kampuchea in February 1979 and December 1982.

Multilateral Agreements

In 1951 Australia, New Zealand and the United States signed a tripartite treaty (ANZUS), which came into effect on 29 April 1952 and is of indefinite duration. Each agrees to 'act to meet the common danger' in the event of attack on either metropolitan or island territory of any one of them, or on armed forces, public vessels or aircraft in the Pacific.

The Manila Pact, signed on 8 September 1954 by Australia, Britain, France, New Zealand, Pakistan, the Philippines, Thailand and the United States, remains in force, though France and Pakistan subsequently withdrew, and the South East Asia Treaty Organization (SEATO), set up to implement it, was disbanded in 1977. The Pact calls for action by each

Party to meet the common danger posed by armed aggression, and for consultation if any other threat is posed to the territory, sovereignty or political independence of any Party. Since 1962 the US commitment to Thailand has been based on this Pact.

The Association of South East Asian Nations (ASEAN), set up in 1967 by Indonesia, Malaysia, Philippines, Singapore and Thailand and joined by Brunei in 1984, is intended to foster regional economic development, not military co-operation. Under the rubric of the promotion of regional peace and security it has become concerned with the Vietnamese presence in Kampuchea. It supports the Kampuchean resistance movements politically, but reported arms transfers to the rebels are believed to be national initiatives rather than multilateral.

Five-Power Defence Arrangements (Australia, Malaysia, New Zealand, Singapore and Britain), relating to the defence of Malaysia and Singapore, came into effect on 1 November 1971. In the event of any externally organized or supported armed attack or threat of attack against Malaysia or Singapore, the five governments would consult together for the purpose of deciding what measures should be taken, jointly or separately. Britain withdrew her forces in March 1976, but New Zealand troops remain in Singapore, as do Australian air units in Malaysia and Singapore, with a small army component attached. Australian and New Zealand naval units visit Malaysia and Singapore regularly.

Economic Factors

After showing exceptionally low growth rates in 1982, the Asian economies recovered well in 1983. Regional average growth in real GNP/GDP amounted to some 4%, compared with some 1–2% in 1982. Singapore, the two Koreas and Taiwan led the recovery, while Australia, New Zealand, Indonesia and the Philippines continued to stagnate. Unlike those of Latin America and Africa, all Asian countries were able to control their inflation rates, the highest rates being those of the Philippines and Sri Lanka (10% and 14% respectively). The same two countries, plus South Korea and New Zealand, also faced serious debt problems: the Philippines' debt-to-GNP ratio exceeded 70%, while those of the other three were in the 40–50% range.

AFGHANISTAN

Est population: 14–17,000,000 (including exiles).
Military service: conscription 15–55; 3 years+ (non-combatants, 4 years).
Total armed forces: 46,000.*
Est GDP 1981/2: Afs 121.44 bn ($2.40 bn).
Est def exp 1980: Afs 10.500 bn ($207.510 m).
  1981: 16.500 bn ($326.087 m).
Est FMA: $ 300 m (1980/1).
Debt: $1.0 bn (1981).
  $1 = afghanis 50.60 (1980/4).

Army: 40,000 (mostly conscripts).*
3 corps HQ.
11 inf divs ⎫
3 armd divs ⎬ (under strength bdes).
1 mech inf bde.
2 mountain inf regts.
1 arty bde with 3 arty regts.
3 cdo regts.
50 T-34, 300 T-54/-55, 100 T-62 MBT; 60 PT-76 lt tks; 40 BMP-1 MICV; 400 BTR-40/-50/-60/-152 APC; 900 76mm, M-1944 100mm guns and M-30 122mm, D-1 152mm how; 82mm, 100 120mm, 160mm mor; 50 BM-13-16

132mm MRL; SPG-9 73mm, 82mm RCL; 76mm, 100mm ATK guns; 350 23mm, 37mm, 57mm, 85mm and 100mm towed, 20 ZSU-23-4 SP AA guns.

RESERVES: No formal reserve force identified; call-up from ex-servicemen, Youth League and regional tribes from age 20 to age 40.

Air Force: 6,000 (incl Air Defence Comd); perhaps 150 combat ac, some 20 armed hel.*
1 lt bbr sqn with some 15 Il-28 (status unclear).
12 FGA sqns: 4 with some 40 MiG-17, 3 with 35 MiG-21 *Fishbed*, 4 with 48 Su-7B *Fitter* A, 1 with 12 Su-17 *Fitter* C.
1 OCU with MiG-15/-17/-19/-21/-23UTI/U, Il-18U.
2 attack hel sqns with some 20 Mi-24.

---

* Actual strength suspect. Divs reported to average 2,500 (i.e., about quarter strength). Desertion is common. The Soviet High Command in Afghanistan (see pp. 22 for Soviet forces deployed) effectively controls the Afghan forces; it is not possible to differentiate between Soviet and Afghan holdings of identical equipment.

4 tpt sqns: 1 VIP with 2 Il-18D, 4 An-24 *Coke*; 3 with some 10 An-2, 10–15 An-26.
1 tpt hel regt (4 sqns) with some 12 Mi-4, up to 40 Mi-8.
1 flying school with Yak-18, L-39C.
1 AD div: 2 SAM bdes (each 3 bns) with 120 SA-2, 115 SA-3; 1 AA bde (2 bns) with 37mm, 85mm, 100mm guns; 1 radar bde (3 bns).

Para-Military Forces: Gendarmerie 30,000. Border Force. Ministry of Interior: *Khad* (secret police); *Sarandoy* 'Defence of the Revolution' forces, largely ex-military to age 55 org in provincial regts. Regional militias incl, 'Revolution Defence Groups' (Civil Defence), Pioneers, Afghan Communist Party Guards, *Khalqi* Youth, tribal.

Opposition: Perhaps 90,000 guerrillas (possibly 20,000 intermittently active) supported by some 15 exile political groups (6 active). Eqpt: small arms, T-55 MBT; BMP MICV, BTR-60 APC; D-30 122mm how; AGS-17 30mm grenade launchers; 2-in. (51mm), 60mm, M-41 82mm mor; RPG-7 RL; SPG-9, 3 75mm, 82mm RCL; 12.7mm, 14.5mm AA machine guns, ATK mines; some SA-7 SAM.

AUSTRALIA
Population: 15,410,000.
Military service: voluntary.
Total armed forces: 72,345.
GDP 1981/2: $A 155.170 bn ($US 171.458 bn).
   1982/3: 169.880 bn ($US 159.422 bn).
Def exp 1982/3: $A 4.942 bn ($US 4.638 bn).
   1983/4: 5.446 bn ($US 4.945 bn).
GDP growth: −2% (1982), 1.8% (1983).
Inflation: 10% (1982), 11% (1983).
   $US 1 = $A 0.9050 (1981/2), 1.0656 (1982/3), 1.1014 (1983/4).

Army: 32,680.
1 inf div with 3 bdes of 2 inf bns.
1 armd regt.
2 cav regts.
4 arty regts (1 med, 2 fd, 1 AD); 1 locating bty.
1 fd engr, 1 construction, 1 fd survey regts.
5 sigs regts.
1 Special Air Service regt.
3 tpt regts (one air support).
Army Aviation:
   1 regt (2 recce, 1 comd spt, 1 utility sqns).
   1 avn school + base workshop bn.
103 *Leopard* 1A3 MBT; 790 M-113 APC, incl 63 MICV with 76mm gun (48 with *Scorpion*, 15 with *Saladin* turret); some 34 5.5-in. (140mm) guns (to late 1984); 227 105mm, some 6 M-198 155mm how; 51 M-40 106mm RCL; 12

Milan ATGW launchers; *Redeye*, 20 *Rapier* SAM launchers; 15 *Turbo-Porter*, 11 *Nomad* ac; 47 Bell 206B-1 *Kiowa* hel; 36 watercraft, 87 LARC-5 amph vehs.
(On order: some 30 M-198 155mm how.)

RESERVES: 30,300 (with trg obligations); 2 inf div HQ, 4 bde HQ, 188 fd, spt, log and trg units; 1 cdo bn, 1 regional surveillance force.

Navy: 16,988 (incl Fleet Air Arm).
6 *Oxley* (*Oberon*) submarines.
3 *Perth* (US *Adams*) ASW msl destroyers with *Standard* SAM, 2 *Ikara* ASW.
4 *Adelaide* (FFG-7) frigates with 1 *Harpoon* SSM, 1 *Standard* SAM, 2 hel (to get AS-350 hel, early 1985).
6 *River* frigates with 1 × 4 *Seacat* SAM/SSM, 1 *Ikara* ASW.
13 PCF-420 *Freemantle*, 8 *Attack* large patrol craft.
1 mod Br *Ton* coastal minehunter.
6 LCT (1 with Reserve).
1 hy amph tpt ship; 1 destroyer tender with 1 *Wessex* hel; 2 trg ships (1 *Daring* destroyer, 1 ex-ocean ferry); 1 fleet tanker.

FLEET AIR ARM: (1,310); 8 combat hel.
1 ASW hel sqn with 8 *Sea King* Mk 50.
1 utility/SAR hel sqn with 10 *Wessex* 31B, 4 UH-1B, 4 Bell 206B, 6 AS-350B *Squirrel*; 2 HS-748 EW ac (trg).
1 trg sqn with 2 *Wessex* 31B hel.
(On order: 3 FFG-7 frigates, 2 PCF-420 large patrol craft, 2 MCM catamarans; *Harpoon* SSM, 2 *Phalanx* 20mm AA systems.)

Bases: Sydney, Melbourne, Jervis Bay, Brisbane, Cairns, Darwin, Cockburn Sound.

RESERVES: 1,200 (with trg obligations); 5 patrol craft, 1 LCT.

Air Force: 22,677; 133 combat ac.
2 FGA/recce sqns with 16 F-111C, 4 F-111A, 4 RF-111C.
3 interceptor/FGA sqns with 58 *Mirage* IIIO/D.
2 MR sqns: 1 with 6 P-3B *Orion*; 1 with 10 P-3C.
1 OCU with 19 *Mirage* IIIO/D, 10 MB-326H.
1 forward air controller flt: 6 CA-25 *Winjeel*.
6 tpt sqns: 2 with 24 C-130E/H; 1 with 4 Boeing 707-338C (to be tanker ac); 1 with 4 CC-08 (C-7A *Caribou*) ac, 4 UH-1B hel; 1 with 17 CC-08; 1 with 2 BAC-111, 2 HS-748, 3 *Mystère* 20.
1 med tpt hel sqn with 8 CH-47 *Chinook*.
2 utility hel sqns with 31 UH-1B/H *Iroquois*.
Trainers incl 81 MB-326H (72 being uprated), 8 HS-748T2, 48 CT-4/4A *Airtrainer*.
AAM: *Sidewinder*, R-530.
(4 *Chinook* hel in reserve.)
(On order: 75 F/A-18 FGA/interceptor/trg, 10

P-3C MR, 69 A-10 *Wamira* trg ac; 18 AS-350 *Ecureuil* utility hel; R-550 *Magic* AAM; *Harpoon* ASM.)

RESERVES: 1,400 (with trg obligations) in 8 auxiliary sqns.

Forces Abroad: Egypt (Sinai MFO): 110; 8 UH-1H hel. Malaysia/Singapore: 1 sqn with 20 *Mirage* IIIO, 1 flt with CC-08 ac. Papua New Guinea: 135; 2 engr units, 106 advisers. Indian Ocean: 1 destroyer, 2 patrol boats. Trg gps in Indonesia, Malaysia, Philippines, Singapore.

Para-Military Forces: Bureau of Customs: 10 *Searchmaster* MR ac.

BANGLADESH

Population: 96,500,000.
Military service: voluntary.
Total armed forces: 81,300.
GDP 1981/2: Tk 264.990 bn ($13.223 bn). 1982/3: 285.070 bn ($11.999 bn).
Est def exp 1982/3: Tk 4.200 bn ($176.784 m). 1983/4: 4.600 bn ($184.0 m).
GDP growth: 1% (1982/3), 4% (1983/4)
Inflation: 10.0% (1982/3). 9.0% (1983/4).
Debt: 4.0 bn (1983).
  $1 = taka 20.040 (1981/2), 23.7578 (1982/3), 25.0 (1983/4).

Army: 73,000.
5 inf div HQ.
12 inf bdes (32 inf bns).
2 armd regts.
9 arty regts.
7 engr bns.
20 Ch Type-59, 30 T-54/-55 MBT; 6 M-24 *Chaffee* lt tks; 30 Model 56 pack, 50 M-101 105mm, 5 25-pdr (88mm), Type-54 122mm guns/how; 81mm, 50 Type-53 120mm mor; 6-pdr (57mm), Ch Type-54 76mm ATK guns; 30 106mm RCL.*

Navy: 5,300.*
3 Br frigates (1 Type 61, 2 Type 41).
4 Ch *Hoku* FAC(G) with 2 HY-2 SSM.
8 Ch *Shanghai* II FAC.
4 large patrol craft (2 Yug *Kraljevica*, 2 Ind *Akshay*).
1 Ch *Hainan* FAC(P).
4 P-4 FAC(T)⟨.
5 *Shamjala* FAC.
5 *Pabna* river patrol boats⟨.
1 trg ship.

Bases: Chittagong (HQ), Dacca, Khulna, Chalna.

Air Force: 3,000: 27 combat ac.*
2 FGA sqns with 17 Ch F-6.
1 interceptor sqn with 8 MiG-21MF, 2 -21U.
1 tpt sqn with 1 An-24, 3 An-26.
1 hel sqn with 11 Bell 212, 4 Mi-8, 1 Mi-4.
Trainers incl 8 *Magister*, 16 Ch CJ-6.
AAM: AA-2 *Atoll*.

Para-Military Forces: 80,000: Bangladesh Rifles 30,000, Armed Police Reserve 36,000, Bangladesh *Ansans* (Security guards) 14,000.

BRUNEI

Population: 210,000.
Military service: voluntary.
Total armed forces 3,950.†
Est GDP 1981: $B 9.720 bn ($US 4.629 bn). 1982: 9.100 bn ($US 4.136 bn).
Est def exp 1982: $B 429 m ($US 195 m). 1983: 350 m ($US 162.791 m).
GDP growth: −12% (1982).
Inflation: 6% (1982), 4% (1983).
  $US 1 = $B 2.10 (1981), 2.20 (1982), 2.15 (1983).

Army: 3,500.
2 inf bns (3rd forming).
1 armd recce sqn.
1 AD bty with *Rapier*.
1 engr sqn.
1 sigs sqn.
16 *Scorpion* lt tks; 2 *Sultan* armd cars; 24 Sankey AT-104 APC; 16 81mm mor; 12 *Rapier/Blindfire* SAM.

Navy: (350).
3 *Waspada* FAC(G) with 2 *Exocet* MM-38 SSM.
3 *Perwira* coastal, 3 Rotork river patrol craft⟨.
2 *Loadmaster* landing craft.
24 assault boats.
1 special boat sqn.

Base: Muara.

Air Force: (100); 6 combat ac.
1 COIN sqn with 6 Saab 105CB.
1 hel sqn with 10 Bell 212.
1 composite sqn with 2 SF-260 ac, 3 Bell 206A/B hel.
VIP flt: 1 BO-105, 1 Bell 212, 1 S-76 hel.
Misc hel: 2 Bell 212, 1 206A.
(On order: 1 AUH-76 (S-76) armed hel.)

Para-Military Forces: Royal Brunei Police elms (1,750); Gurkha Reserve Unit (900).

---

* Spares are short; some eqpt unserviceable.
† All services form part of the Army.

BURMA

Population: 38,800,000.
Military service: voluntary.
Total armed forces: 180,500.
GDP 1982/3: K 46.945 bn ($5.960 bn). 1983/4:
  50.600 bn ($6.30 bn).
Est def exp 1982/3: K 1.650 bn ($209.487 m).
  1983/4: 1.770 bn ($220.366 m).
GDP growth: 6.5% (1982), 7.0% (1983).
Inflation: 5.2% (1981), 5.0% (1982).
Debt: $1.6 bn (1981).
  $1 = kyat 7.8764 (1982/3), 8.0321 (1983/4).

Army: 163,000.
9 Regional commands, 1 garrison.
3 lt inf divs (under central control, each with 3
  Tactical Operational Comds = bdes; 10
  bns). (3 more div HQ reported forming.)
16 bdes (Tactical Operational Comds).
2 armd bns.
85 inf bns (incl in divs and bdes).
4 arty bns.
1 AA bty.
24 *Comet* MBT; 40 Humber armd, 45 *Ferret*
  scout cars; 50 25-pdr (88mm), 5.5-in. (140mm)
  guns/how; 120 76mm, 80 M-101 105mm how;
  80 120mm mor; 50 6-pdr (57mm) and 17-pdr
  (76.2mm) ATK guns; 84mm *Carl Gustav* RCL;
  10 40mm AA guns.*

Navy: 10,000.*
4 corvettes: 2 US (1 PCE-827, 1 *Admirable*), 2
  Nawarat.
36 gunboats (15⟨).
46 river patrol craft⟨.
1 US LCU, 8 US LCM, 1 spt vessel.

Bases: Bassein, Mergui, Moulmein, Seikyi,
  Sinmalaik, Sittwe.

Air Force: 7,500; 38 combat ac.*
2 COIN sqns with 16 PC-7 *Turbo-Trainer*, 16
  SF-260WB, 6 AT-33A.
3 tpt sqns: 1 F-27F, 5 FH-227, 7 Pilatus
  PC-6/-6A, 2 DHC-5D.
Liaison flt: 6 Cessna 180, 1 Cessna 550.
4 hel sqns: 10 KB-47G, 2 KV-107/II, 7 HH-43B,
  10 *Alouette* III, 14 UH-1.
Trainers incl 10 SF-260MB, 9 T-37C.

Para-Military Forces: 73,000. People's Police
  Force (38,000); People's Militia (35,000).
  Fishery Dept: 3 *Osprey*, 12 patrol boats(⟨.

Opposition:
  Burmese Communist Party: 12,000 regulars;
    8,000 militia.
  Kayan New Land Party: perhaps 100.
  Karen National Liberation Army: some 7,500;
    5 bdes, 3 indep bns.

Shan State Army: some 3,500.
Shan United Revolutionary Army: some
  900–1,200.
Shan United Army: 4,000.
Palaung State Liberation Army ⎤ a few
Pa-O National Army   ⎬ hundred
Wa National Army   ⎦ each
Kachin Independence Army: 8,000; 4 bdes.
Karenni Army: perhaps 600; 4 'bdes'.
Mon State Army: two groups: one some 500;
  other perhaps 200.
Kawthoolei Muslim Liberation Front (Karen
  linked) absorbed OMMAT Liberation and
  Rohingya Patriotic Fronts.

FIJI

Population: 680,000.
Military service: voluntary.
Total armed forces: 2,660.
Est GDP 1981: $F 1.088 bn ($US 1.275 bn).
  1982: 1.010 bn ($US 1.084 bn).
Est def exp 1982: $F 9.320 m ($US 10.0 m).
Debt: $US 300m (1983).
  $US 1 = $F 0.8532 (1981), 0.932 (1982).

Army: 2,500.
3 inf bns.
1 engr coy.
1 arty tp.
Spt units.
4 25-pdr (88mm) guns/how; 12 81mm mor.

Navy: 160.
3 US *Redwing* coastal minesweepers.
3 marine survey vessels.

Base: Suva.

Forces Abroad: 1,095; 2 inf bns. Lebanon
  (UNIFIL) (626); Egypt (Sinai MFO) (469).

INDIA

Population: 743,300,000.
Military service: voluntary.
Total armed forces: 1,120,000.
Est GDP 1982/3: Rs 1,665.0 bn ($172.924 bn).
  1983/4: 1,815.0 bn ($176.0 bn).
Est def exp 1983/4: Rs 58.620 bn ($5.684 bn).
  Def budget 1984/5: 68.0 bn ($6.326 bn).
GDP growth: 5.0% (1982), 2.0% (1983).
Inflation: 9.0% (1982), 7.0% (1983).
Debt: $23 bn (1982).
  $1 = rupees 9.6285 (1982/3), 10.3123
  (1983/4), 10.750 (1984).

---

* Spares are short; some equipment is unserviceable.

Army: 960,000.
5 Regional Commands.
8 corps HQ.
2 armd divs.
1 mech div.
18 inf divs.
10 mountain divs.
5 indep armd bdes.
7 indep inf bdes.
1 para bde.
17 indep arty bdes, incl about 20 AD regts.
AFV: 700 T-54/-55, 300 T-72, 1,900 *Vijayanta*
MBT, 250 BMP-1 MICV; 500 OT-62/-64,
BTR-60 APC.
Arty: Yug M-48 76mm, 25-pdr (88mm)
(retiring), 100 100mm, 200 105mm, 550 M-46
130mm (some SP), 5.5-in. (140mm) (retiring),
S-23 180mm guns; 75/24 75mm mountain,
105mm (incl M-56 pack, *Abbot* SP), D-20
152mm how; 81mm, 500 120mm, 20 160mm
mor.
ATK: M-18 57mm, *Carl Gustav* 84mm, M-40
106mm RCL; 6-pdr (57mm) ATK guns; SS-11-
B1, *Milan*, AT-3 *Sagger* ATGW.
AD: 20mm, 40mm, L/60mm, L/70mm, 500
3.7-in. (94mm) towed, ZSU-23-4 SP AA guns;
SA-6/-7/-9, 40 *Tigercat* SAM.
(On order: T-72M MBT, BRDM recce, BMP-1/-
2/BMD MICV, *Milan* ATGW launchers, 3,700
msls.)

RESERVES: 200,000. Territorial Army 50,000.

Navy: 47,000, incl naval air force.
8 Sov *F*-class submarines.
1 Br *Majestic* aircraft carrier (capacity 18 attack,
4 ASW ac, ASW hel).
1 Br *Fiji* cruiser (trg).
3 Sov *Kashin* II GW destroyers with 4 *Styx* SSM,
2×2 SA-N-1 SAM, 1 Ka-25 hel.
23 frigates: 2 *Godavari* with 2 *Styx* SSM, 1
SA-N-4 SAM, 2 *Sea King* hel; 6 *Leander* with
2×4 *Seacat* SAM, 1 hel; 2 Br *Whitby* with 3
Styx SSM; 10 Sov *Petya* II; 3 Br *Leopard* (trg).
3 Sov *Nanuchka* corvettes with 4 SS-N-2 SSM, 1
SA-N-4 SAM.
8 Sov *Osa*-I (6 FAC(G), 2 FAC), 8 *Osa*-II with 4
Styx SSM.
1 *Abhay*, 6 SDB-2 large patrol craft.
6 Sov *Natya* ocean, 4 Br *Ham* minesweepers; 6
Sov *Yevgenya* inshore minehunters.
6 Sov *Polnocny* LCT, 4 LCU.
(On order: Sov *T*-class, 4 Type 1500 subs, 2
Kashin GW destroyers, 4 *Godavari* (mod
Leander) FFG, 2 *Nanuchka* corvettes, 6
Polnocny LCT, *Exocet* SSM.)

Bases: Western Fleet: Bombay, Goa. Southern
Fleet: Cochin. Eastern Fleet: Vishakapatnam,
Port Blair.

NAVAL AIR FORCE: (2,000); some 37 combat ac,
23 combat hel.
1 attack sqn with 15 *Sea Hawk* FGA-6 (being
retired), 8 *Sea Harrier* FRS Mk-51 (2 T-60 trg)
(10 ac in carrier).
1 ASW sqn with 5 *Alizé* 1050 (4 in carrier).
2 MR sqns with 4 L-1049 *Super Constellation*, 3
Il-38 *May*.
1 comms sqn with 18 *Defender* (some MR).
4 ASW hel sqns with 10 *Sea King* (carrier,
frigates); 5 Ka-25 *Hormone* (in *Kashins*);
8 *Alouette* III (in frigates).
1 SAR/liaison hel sqn with 10 *Alouette* III.
2 trg sqns with 6 HJT-16 *Kiran*, 2 *Sea Hawk*
FB-5 ac; 3 *Alouette* III, 4 Hughes 269 hel.
(On order: 10 *Sea Harrier* Mk 51, 1 T-60; 3
Il-38 MR ac; 12 *Sea King* Mk 42B hel; *Sea
Eagle* SSM; *Exocet* AM-39 ASM.)

Air Force: 113,000; some 920 combat ac; some
60 armed hel.
4 Air Commands.
3 lt bbr sqns (1 maritime role): 35 *Canberra*
B(I)58/B(I)12 (to be replaced); 18 *Jaguar*.
15 FGA sqns: 1 with some 18 *Hunter* F-56A
(*Jaguar* to replace); 3 with 50 *Jaguar* GR-1, 6
T-2; 2 with 36 Su-7BM; 1 with 18 HF-24
Marut (MiG-23BN to replace); 4 with 72
MiG-23BN *Flogger* H; 4 with 72 *Ajeet*.
21 AD sqns: 19 with 400 MiG-21/FL/PFMA/
MF/bis; 2 with 45 MiG-23MF *Flogger* B.
2 recce sqns: 1 with 8 *Canberra* PR-57, 4
HS-748; 1 with 12 MiG-25R, 1 MiG-25U.
9 tpt sqns: 3 with 90 An-32; 2 with 30 An-12B; 2
with 20 DHC-3; 1 with 12 DHC-4; 1 with 9
HS-748M.
1 HQ comms sqn with 7 HS-748M, 2 Boeing
737-248 (leased).
Liaison flts and dets with 15 HS-748, C-47.
6 tpt hel sqns with 72 Mi-8.
8 liaison hel sqns with 100 SA-316B *Chetak*
(*Alouette* III), some 60 SA-315B *Cheetah*
(*Lama*); some with 4 AS-11B ATGW.
Trg Comd: 3 trg and conversion sqns with 12
Canberra T-4/-13/-67, 30 *Hunter* F-56/T-66,
40 MiG-21U, 16 Su-7U; MiG-21, Su-7, 13
MiG-23UM *Flogger* CL; 60 HT-2, 83 HJT-16
Kiran, 15 *Marut* Mk 1T, some HPT-32
(replacing HT-2), 44 TS-11 *Iskra*, 27 HS-748
ac; *Chetak* hel.
AAM: R-23R/T *Apex*, R-60 *Aphid*, R-550.
ASM: AS-30; AS-11B (ATGW).
30 SAM sqns with 180 *Divina* V 750VK, SA-2,
SA-3.
Air Defence Ground Environment System.
(On order: 36 *Mirage* 2000H, 4 TH, 115 *Jaguar*
(to be locally assembled), some 100 MiG-27M
Flogger D/J, MiG-21bis, 20 *Ajeet* ftrs; 6
An-32, Do-228, 20 Il-76, 10 HS-748 tpts; 90
Kiran Mk 2, 140 HPT-32, 171 *Hawk* trg ac;

Mi-8, Mi-24, 45 *Chetak* hel; R-23R *Apex*, R-60 *Aphid* AAM.)

Para-Military Forces: Border Security Force 85,000; 175,000 in other organizations. Coastguard 2,000: 2 Br Type 14 frigates, 2 FAC(P), 5 *Poluchat* large patrol craft, 2 air sqns with 2 F-27, 5 *Defender* ac, 4 *Chetak* hel.
(On order: 3 offshore, 9 inshore patrol vessels, 9 lt tpt ac, 6 hel.)

INDONESIA

Population: 158,300,000.
Military service: selective.
Total armed forces: 281,000.
GDP 1982: Rp 59,633 bn ($88.458 bn). 1983: 72,111 bn ($73.331 bn).
Est def exp 1982/3: Rp 1,935 bn ($2.870 bn). 1983/4: 2,485 bn ($2.527 bn).
GDP growth: 0% (1982), 4.5% (1983).
Inflation: 10% (1982), 12% (1983).
Debt: $23.6 bn (1982).
$1 = rupiahs 674.14 (1982/3), 983.36 (1983/4).

Army: 210,000.
4 Regional, 16 Military Area Commands.
4 inf divs (each 2 bdes).
1 armd cav bde (10 cav bns, spt units).
2 indep inf bdes, 11 indep inf regts (39 inf bns).
2 AB inf bdes (6 bns).
2 fd arty regts (6 bns).
1 AA arty regt (3 bns).
4 special warfare gps.
8 indep fd arty bns.
7 indep AA arty bns; 4 indep btys.
2 construction engr regts (4 bns); 4 indep bns.
1 fd engr regt (2 bns); 6 indep bns; 10 indep dets.
33 indep inf bns.
4 indep AB inf bns.
Marine transport.
Army Aviation:
  1 composite sqn; 1 hel sqn.
AFV: 93 AMX-13, 41 PT-76 lt tks; 75 *Saladin* armd, 60 *Ferret* scout cars; 200 AMX-VCI MICV, 60 *Saracen*, 60 V-150 *Commando*, BTR-40/-152 APC.
Arty: some 30 M-1938 76mm pack, 170 105mm guns/how; 480 81/82mm, M-43 120mm mor; 480 M-67 90mm, M-40 106mm RCL.
AA: 20 20mm, 90 M-1 40mm, 200 57mm AA guns.
Avn: 5 NC-212 *Aviocar*, 2 *Aero Commander* 680, 1 Beech 18 ac; 6 Bell 205, 2 *Alouette* III, 16 BO-105 hel.
Amph: 1 LST, 20 LCU, 14 small tpt ships.
(On order: 100 AMX-13 lt tks, 50 AMX L-30 105mm SP how; 2 NC-212-200 *Aviocar* ac; 6 Bell 212, 26 *Super Puma* hel.)

Navy: 42,000 incl naval air and marines.
3 subs: 2 Type 209, 1 Sov *W*-class (trg).
9 frigates: 3 *Fatahillah* with 4 *Exocet* MM-38 SSM (1 with 1 *Wasp* hel); 4 US *Jones*; 2 Sov *Riga*.
14 large patrol craft: 3 Sov *Kronshtadt*, 4 Yug *Kraljevica*, 2 *Kelabang*, 3 *Attack*, 1 US PGM-39, 1 *Komar*.
4 *Dagger* FAC(G) with 4 *Exocet* SSM.
2 Lürssen TNC-45 FAC(T).
6 Aus *Carpentaria* coastal patrol craft(.
2 Sov T-43 ocean minesweepers.
1 comd/spt ship; 1 trg ship with 4 *Exocet*, 1 hel.
12 LST, 4 LCU, 2 control craft.
Spt: 4 cargo ships, 4 tankers, 2 tpts.
(Plus non-operational incl: 1 *Pattimura* frigate; 1 *Kronshtadt*, 2 *Kelabang*, 2 PGM-39, 2 *Attack* patrol craft; 1 *R*-class coastal minesweeper; 1 comd/spt ship.)

Bases: Jakarta (Tanjung Priok), Surabaya.

NAVAL AIR: (1,000); 17 combat ac, 10 combat hel.
10 *Wasp* ASW hel.
11 *Nomad* N-22B, 6 N-22L MR ac.
Other ac incl 6 C-47, 3 *Aero Commander* ac; 1 *Alouette* II, 4 BO-105 hel.

MARINES: (12,000).
2 inf regts (6 bns); 1 combat spt, 1 admin spt, 1 trg regts.
30 PT-76 lt tks; 40 AMX-10 PAC-90 MICV; 57 APC incl 25 AMX-10P; 40 M-38 122mm how; 40mm AA guns.

(On order: 1 T-209 sub, 3 *Tribal* frigates, 2 PB-57 FAC,* 2 minehunters, 4 jetfoil patrol boats*; 2 *Nomad*, 4 NC-212, 18 NC-235 tpt ac; 26 AS-332F *Super Puma* hel.*)

Air Force: 29,000; 83 combat aircraft.
6 Air Regions:
2 FGA sqns with 30 A-4E, 4 TA-4H *Skyhawk*.
1 interceptor sqn with 11 F-5E, 4 F-5F.
1 COIN sqn with 15 OV-10F.
1 MR sqn with 1 C-130H-MP, 3 Boeing 737-200, 5 HU-16.
4 tpt sqns: 2 with 21 C-130B/H/HS, 1 L-100-30; 2 with 1 C-140 *Jetstar*, 7 C-47, 1 SC-7 *Skyvan*, 8 F-27, 13 NC-212A4, 1 Boeing 707, 12 Cessna 207/401/402.
3 hel sqns: 1 with 9 Sikorsky UH-34T; 2 with 5 Bell 204B, 12 47G, 9 SA-330L *Puma*, 6 SA-332 *Super Puma*, 1 SA-332L (VIP), 12 Hughes 500; 6 NBO-105 (with forestry).
3 trg sqns: 13 *Hawk* T-53, 15 T-34C1 (OCU), 7 Cessna T-41D, 20 AS-202 *Bravo*.
5 bns Quick Reaction Tps.
(On order: 8 NC-212-200, 32 NC-235 tpt, 9

---

* May be for Coastguard.

T-34C1, 3 *Hawk* trg ac; (N)BO-105, SA-332 *Super Puma* Bell U-412, BK-117 hel.)

Other HQ:

National Strategic Command: HQ only; to command Strategic Reserve forces in strategic operations. Incl army, KOSTRAD, naval forces incl marines, combat and tpt ac.

KOSTRAD = Strategic Reserve Command: army command (16,500–19,000 men) under direct control of the Commander of the Armed Forces: 3 inf, 2 AB bdes, spt arms and services.

KOPKAMTIB = Command for the Restoration of Order and Security: no forces assigned.

KOPPASSANDHA = Special Forces Command: 4,000; 4 special para/cdo gps.

Para-Military Forces: Police mobile bde* org in coys: 12,000; 2 BO-105 hel. Militia, about 70,000. Coastguard: many small patrol boats. Customs: 12 28-metre, 8 57-metre Lùrssen patrol boats. Civil Defence Force (millions registered).

JAPAN

Population: 120,800,000.
Military service: voluntary.
Total armed forces: 245,000 (ceiling 272,162).
Est GDP 1982: yen 264,707 bn ($1,060.5 bn).
  1983: 279.500 bn ($1,178.9 bn).
Def budget: 1983/4: yen 2,754.2 bn ($11.617 bn).
  1984/5: 2,934.600 ($12.488 bn).
GDP growth: 3.3% (1982), 3.0% (1983).
Inflation: 3% (1982), 3.5% (1983).
Debt: $114.1 bn (1982).
  $1 = yen 249.607 (1982/3), 237.085 (1983/4), 235.000 (mid-1984).

Army: 155,000.
5 Army HQ (Regional Commands).
1 armd div.
12 inf divs (5 at 7,000, 7 at 9,000 men each).
2 composite bdes.
1 AB bde.
1 arty bde, 2 arty gps; 8 SAM gps (each of 4 btys).
1 sigs bde.
5 engr bdes.
Army Aviation:
1 hel bde: 24 sqns.
AFV: some 550 Type 61 (retiring), some 470 Type 74 (increasing) MBT; 430 Type 60, 120 Type 73 APC.
Arty: 354 105mm (incl some 20 Type 74), some 370 155mm SP (incl 166 Type 75), 70 203mm (incl 10 SP) guns/how; 50 Type 30 SSM; 800 81mm, 560 107mm mor (some SP); 50 Type 75 130mm SP MRL.
ATK: 1,600 75mm, *Carl Gustav* 84mm, 106mm

(incl Type 60 SP) RCL; 228 Type 64, 25 Type 79 ATGW.
AD: 110 35mm twin, 37mm, 40mm (incl M-42 SP), 75mm AA guns; 10 Type 81 *Tan*, 100 *HAWK*, 100 *Improved HAWK* SAM.
Avn: 33 ac and 354 hel: 21 LR-1, 2 TL-1, 9 L-19 ac; 2 AH-1S, 58 KV-107, 80 UH-1H, 65 UH-1B, 20 TH-55, 147 OH-6J/D hel.
(On order: 72 Type 74 MBT; 9 Type 73 APC; 24 Type 75 155mm, 24 M-110A2 203mm SP how; 8 Type 75 130mm MRL; Type 79 hy ATGW; 224 84mm RCL; 70 *Stinger*, 7 Type 81 *Tan* launchers, 48 *Improved HAWK* SAM; 3 OH-6D, 7 HU-1H hel.)

RESERVES: 43,000.

Navy: 44,000 (including naval air).
14 submarines: 5 *Yushio*, 7 *Uzushio*, 2 *Asashio*.
32 destroyers: 2 *Shirane* with *Sea Sparrow* SAM, 1 × 8 *ASROC* ASW msl launcher, 3 ASW hel; 2 *Haruna* with 1 × 8 *ASROC*, 3 ASW hel; 5 *Hatsuyuki* with 2 × 4 *Harpoon* SSM, 1 *Sea Sparrow*, 1 × 8 *ASROC*, 1 ASW hel; 3 *Tachikaze* with *Tartar/Standard* SAM, 1 × 8 *ASROC*; 1 *Amatsukaze* with 1 *Standard* SAM, 1 × 8 *ASROC*; 4 *Takatsuki* with 1 × 8 *ASROC*; 6 *Yamagumo* with 1 × 8 *ASROC*; 3 *Minegumo* with 1 × 8 *ASROC*; 2 *Akizuki*; 1 *Murasame*; 3 *Ayanami*.
18 frigates: 3 with 2 × 4 *Harpoon* SSM (2 *Yubari*, 1 *Ishikari*), 11 *Chikugo* with 1 × 8 *ASROC*; 4 *Isuzu*.
4 large patrol craft: 2 *Mizutori*, 2 *Umitaka*.
5 FAC(T).
9 coastal patrol craft⟨.
3 MCM spt ships, 30 coastal minesweepers (11 *Hatsushima*, 19 *Takami*), 6 *Nanago* MCM boats.
1 *Katori*, 2 *Ayanami* trg, 8 trg/spt ships incl 1 *Azuma*, 2 *Harukaze*.
6 LST (3 *Miura*, 3 *Atsumi*); 2 LSU.

Bases: Yokosuka, Kure, Sasebo, Maizuru, Ominato.

NAVAL AIR ARM: (12,000); 81 combat ac, 63 combat hel.
6 Air Wings.
7 MR sqns with 9 P-3C, 58 P-2J, 14 PS-1.
6 ASW hel sqns with 56 HSS-2/2A.
1 MCM hel sqn with 7 KV-107.
1 tpt sqn with 4 YS-11M, 1 B-65.
1 utility sqn with 3 UP-2J.
1 test sqn with 4 P-3C, 2 P-2J ac; 2 HSS-2A hel.
7 SAR flts with 8 US-1 ac, 13 S-61A/2 hel.
5 trg sqns incl OCU with 19 P-2J, 6 YS-11T, 18 TC-90, 7 B-65, 32 KM-2 ac; 11 HSS-2, 3 OH-6J/D, 4 Bell 47G hel.

---

* Part of Department of Defence and Security.

(On order: 3 *Yushio* subs; 2 Type 171 DDG, 8 *Hatsuyuki* DDG; 4 *Hatsushima* MCM; 1 supply ship; 19 P-3C, 2 TC-90 ac; 13 HSS-2B, 1 SH-60B *Seahawk* ASW, 10 H-6D, 1 US-1A hel.)

RESERVES: 600.

Air Force: 46,000; some 270 combat ac.
6 combat air wings; 1 combat air gp; 1 recce sqn.
3 FGA sqns with 50 F-1.
10 interceptor sqns: 2 with some 40 F-15J/DJ (2 more forming); 6 with 110 F-4EJ; 2 with 50 F-104J.
1 recce sqn with 14 RF-4EJ: early warning gp with 4 E-2C.
1 aggressor trg sqn with 5 T-2, 6 T-33.
1 tactical tpt wing of 3 sqns with 25 C-1, 10 YS-11.
1 SAR wing (10 dets) with MU-2 ac, 29 V-107 hel.
1 air test wing with F-4EJ, F-15J, F-104J/DJ, 2 T-1, 6 T-2, 2 T-3, T-33A, C-1, 4 C-130H.
1 air traffic control and weather wing with YS-11, MU-2J, T-33A.
5 trg wings: 10 sqns with 40 T-1A/B, 59 T-2, 40 T-3, 50 T-33A.
AAM: *Sparrow, Falcon, Sidewinder.*
Air Defence:
   3 aircraft control and warning wings and 1 group with 28 radar sites.
   6 SAM gps: 19 sqns with 180 *Nike*-J.
(On order: 53 F-15J-/DJ, 6 F-1 fighters, 2 C-130H tpt, 8 T-2 trg, 42 E-2C AEW ac; 1 V-107 hel; 4 Type 81 *Tan* SAM launchers.)

Para-Military Forces: Coast Guard: 42 large patrol vessels, 5 with 1 hel; 47 med, 19 small, 220 coastal patrol vessels (204〈); 1 C-130HMP, 5 YS-11, 2 *Skyvan*, 2 *King Air* ac, 5 Bell 212 hel.
   (On order: 1 large, 2 med, 1 coastal patrol craft.)

KAMPUCHEA/CAMBODIA*

Est population: 6–7 million.
Military service: conscription, 18 months minimum.
Total armed forces: some 30,000.

Armed Forces: some 30,000.
4 inf divs.
3 indep inf bdes.
Some 50 indep units incl cav (recce), arty, AD, pioneer.
T-54/-55 MBT; PT-76 lt tks; V-100, M-113, BTR-40/-60/-152 APC; M-1942 76mm, M-1938 122mm how; Type-63 107mm, BM-13-16 132mm, BM-14-16 140mm MRL; 82mm, 120mm mor; B-10 82mm, B-11

107mm RCL; M-1938 37mm, M-1950 57mm AA guns.
(On order: tks, arty, ships, ac, Mi-8 hel reported; details unknown.)
Provincial Forces: HQ; bn, coy district and subdistrict units.

Para-Military Forces: Militia; Regional Armed Forces/Self Defence forces (org in coys); People's Police force.

Opposition: Coalition of Democratic Kampuchea: Democratic Kampuchea (*Khmer Rouge*), some 35,000 org in bdes and bns; Kampuchean People's National Liberation Front (KPNLF), some 13,000 (plus perhaps 7,000 unarmed reserves), small arms, incl mor, RCL; *Armée Nationale Sihanoukienne* (ANS), perhaps 5,000. Though formally merged, the three forces appear to operate independently.

KOREA: DEMOCRATIC PEOPLE'S REPUBLIC (NORTH)

Population: 19,600,000.
Military service: Army, Navy 5 years; Air Force 3–4 years.
Total armed forces: 784,500.
Est GNP 1983: won 36.0 bn ($19.149 bn).
Def budget 1983: won 3.602 bn ($1.916 bn). 1984: 3.831 bn ($2.038 bn).†
GNP growth: 9.6% (1982), 7.3% (1983).
Inflation: 5% (1982).
Est debt: $3.0 bn (1982).
   $1 = won 0.94 (1983/4 off.), 1.88 (adj.).

Army: 700,000.
9 corps HQ.
2 armd divs.
3 mot inf divs.
34 inf divs.
2 AA divs, 3 indep AA regts.
5 indep tk bdes.
9 indep inf bdes (5–8 bns; up to 8,500 men).
2 indep tk regts.
2 hy arty, 2 mor regts ⎫
120 arty bns   ⎬ org in divs,
82 MRL bns   ⎭ bdes and regts
6 SSM bns with 54 *FROG.*
5 river crossing regts (13 bns).
AFV: 300 T-34, 2,200 T-54/-55/-62, 175 Type-59 MBT; 100 PT-76, 50 Type-62 lt tks; 140 BA-64 armd cars; BMP-1 MICV; 1,000 BTR-40/-50/-60/-152, Type-531 APC.
Arty: 3,300 76mm, 85mm, 100mm, M-30

---

* No reliable data since April 1975 available.
† South Korean sources estimate that North Korea spent $3.250 bn on defence in 1982.

122mm, M-46 130mm and S-23 180mm towed guns; 800 SU-76 and SU-100 SP guns; 122mm, 152mm how; 11,000 82mm, 120mm, 160mm and 240mm mor; 2,000 107mm, 122mm, 140mm, 200mm and 240mm MRL; 54 *FROG*-5/-7 SSM.

ATK: 1,500 B-10 82mm and B-11 107mm RCL; 45mm, 57mm, Type-52 75mm ATK guns; AT-3 *Sagger* ATGW.

AD: 8,000 23mm, 37mm, 57mm, 85mm, 100mm towed, ZSU-23-4 and ZSU-57-2 SP AA guns; SA-7 SAM.

RESERVES: 260,000, 23 divs (cadre, no hy eqpt). Up to 3,000,000 have some Reserve commitment.

Navy: 33,500.
21 subs (4 Sov *W*-, 4 Ch *R*-class, 13 local-built).
4 *Najin* frigates (2 may be in reserve).
24 FAC(G): 4 *Soju*, 10 *Osa*-I (4 *Styx* SSM); 10 *Komar* (2 *Styx* SSM)(.
33 large patrol craft: 2 Sov *Tral*, 15 SO-1, 3 *Sariwan*, 6 Ch *Hainan*, 7 *Taechong*.
155 FAC: 20 Sov MO-IV(; 23 Ch (15 Shanghai II, 8 Shantou(), 4 *Chodo*, 4 K-48, 66 *Chaho*(, 38 *Chong-Jin*(.
182 FAC(T): 80 Sov (4 *Shershen*, 64 P-6(, 12 P-4(); 102((9 *Sinpo*, 15 *Iwon*, 6 *An Ju*, 72 *Ku Song/Sin Hung*).
30 coastal patrol craft((10 Sov KM-4, 20 misc gunboats).
3 *Nantze* LSM, 9 LCU, 15 LCM, 80 *Nampo* landing craft(.
2 coast defence msl regts with *Samlet* in 6 sites; M-1931/-37 122mm, SM-4-1 130mm, M-1937 152mm guns.

RESERVES: 40,000.

Bases: East Coast: Wonsan, Cha-ho, Chongjin, Kimchaek, Toejo. West Coast: Nampo, Haeju, Pipaqwan, Sagwan-ri.

Air Force: 51,000; some 740 combat ac.
3 lt bbr sqns with 70 Il-28.
13 FGA sqns: 1 with 20 Su-7; 9 with some 290 MiG-15/-17; 3 with some 100 MiG-19/Q-5.
12 interceptor sqns with 160 MiG-21, some 100 MiG-19.
Tpts incl 250 An-2, 10 An-24, 5 Il-14, 4 Il-18, 2 Tu-154B, 1 Il-62.
Hel incl 40 Mi-4, 20 Mi-8.
Trainers incl 20 Yak-11, 70 Yak-18, 100 MiG-15UTI/-19UTI/-21U, Il-28, 30 CJ-6.
AAM: AA-2 *Atoll*.
4 SAM bdes (12 bns, 40 btys) with 250 SA-2, in 45 sites.

Forces Abroad: Iran 300; Madagascar 100; Uganda 40.

Para-Military Forces: Bureau of Reconnaissance Special forces (100,000): 1 HQ: 22 regts; 4 recce, 3 cdo, 1 river crossing regts; 5 AB, 3 amph bns. Security forces and border guards: 38,000. Workers-Farmers Youth Red Guard (civilian militia) 4,000,000: HQ (corps equivalent) in each of 9 Provinces and 3 towns. Bde HQ in towns; bns, coy/pl at village, farm, factory etc., some with small arms, some AA arty.

KOREA: REPUBLIC OF (SOUTH)

Population: 41,600,000.
Military service: Army and Marines 30 months, Navy and Air Force 3 years.
Total armed forces: 622,000.
GDP 1982: won 52,878 bn ($72.324 bn). 1983: 59,455 bn ($76.642 bn).
Est def exp 1983: won 3,419 bn ($4,407 bn). 1984: 3,452 bn ($4,315 bn).*
GDP growth: 7% (1982), 9.3% (1983).
Inflation: 7.2% (1982), 3.4% (1983).
Debt: $37 bn (1982).
$1 = won 731.13 (1982), 775.75 (1983), 800 (mid-1984).

Army: 540,000.
3 Army, 6 Corps HQ.
2 mech inf divs (each 3 bdes: 3 mech inf, 3 mot, 3 tk, 1 recce bns; 1 fd arty bde).
20 inf divs (each 3 inf regts, 1 recce, 1 tk, 1 engr bn, arty gp).
11 indep bdes incl 3 AB (4 AB, 1 recce, 1 hel bns, arty gp), 2 special forces, cdo, inf, 'Capital Command'.
2 AA arty bdes.
2 SSM bns with *Honest John*.
2 SAM bdes: 3 *HAWK*, 2 *Nike Hercules* bns.
1 army aviation bde.
AFV: 1,200 M-47/-48 (incl 600 A5) MBT; 500 M-113/-577, 350 Fiat 6614 APC.
Arty: 2,500 M-53 155mm, M-107 175mm SP guns and M-101 105mm, M-114 towed, 100 M-109A2 SP 155mm, M-115 towed, 20 M-110 SP 203mm how; 130mm MRL; 5,300 81mm and 107mm mor; 12 *Honest John* SSM.
ATK: 8 M-18 76mm, 50 M-36 90mm ATK guns; *LAW* RL; 57mm, 75mm, 106mm RCL; *TOW* ATGW.
AD: 66 *Vulcan* 20mm, 40 40mm AA guns; 110 *HAWK*, 100 *Nike Hercules* SAM.
Avn: 14 O-2A ac; 100 UH-1B, Hughes 500MD *Defender* (50 with *TOW*), 100 OH-6A, 100 *Scout* hel.
(On order: *TOW* ATGW; *Stinger*, 56 OH-6A, 20 Hughes 500MD/*TOW* hel).

* Excl 1982–6 plans to purchase some $3.5 bn worth of new equipment from the US.

RESERVES: Regular Army Reserves 1,400,000: 23 inf divs (cadre). Homeland Reserve Defence Force 3,300,000.

Navy: 49,000 incl marines.
11 US destroyers: 7 *Gearing* with 8 *Harpoon* SSM (2 with 1 *Alouette* III hel), 2 *Sumner*, 2 *Fletcher*.
8 frigates: 1 *Ulsan* with 8 *Harpoon*; 7 US (1 *Rudderow*, 6 *Lawrence/Crosley*).
3 US *Auk* corvettes.
11 US large patrol craft with *Standard* SAM (8 PSMM-5 with 4, 1 *Asheville* with 2).
12 other large patrol craft incl 8 US *Cape*.
2 *Kist* FAC(G) with 2 *Exocet*.
6 CPIC FAC(P).
4 coastal patrol craft⟨ incl 2 *Schoolboy* I/II.
8 MSC-268/-294 coastal minesweepers, 1 minesweeping boat⟨.
33 US landing ships (8 LST, 9 LSM, 6 LCU, 10 LCM).
2 ASW sqns: 1 with 22 S-2A/F ac; 1 with 10 Hughes 500MD hel; 12 *Alouette* III hel flts.

Bases: Chinhae (HQ), Cheju, Inchon, Mokpo, Mukho, Pukpyong, Pohang, Pusan.

RESERVES: 25,000.

Marines: (20,000).
2 divs, 1 bde.
M-47 MBT; LVTP-7 APC.

(On order: 1 sub, 7 CKX corvettes, 20 FAC(G) (7 types), 75 *Harpoon* SSM; 40 LVTP-7).

RESERVES: 60,000.

Air Force: 33,000; some 440 combat ac.
7 combat, 2 tpt wings.
18 FGA sqns: 14 with 260 F-5A/B/E/F; 4 with 70 F-86F.
4 AD sqns with 72 F-4D/E.
1 COIN sqn with 24 OV-10G, some A-37.
1 recce sqn with 10 RF-5A.
1 SAR hel sqn with 6 UH-1H, 20 UH-1B/H.
5 tpt sqns with 10 C-54, 16 C-123J/K, 2 HS-748, 6 C-130H, *Aero Commander*.
Trainers incl: 20 T-28D, 33 T-33A, 39 T-37C, 20 T-41D, 35 F-5B, 63 F-5F.
AAM: *Sidewinder*, *Sparrow*.
(On order: 30 F-16A, 6 F-16B, 36 F-5E, 30 F-5F ftr; 25 T-27 *Tucano* trg ac; *Maverick* ASM.)

RESERVES: 55,000.

Para-Military Forces: Civilian Defence Corps (to age 50) 4,400,000; Student Homeland Defence Corps (Schools) 1,820,000. Coastguard: 25 small craft, 9 Hughes 500D hel.

LAOS

Est population: 4,000,000.
Military service: conscription, 18 months minimum.
Total armed forces: 53,700.
Est GNP 1980: k 4 bn ($400 m).
Est def exp 1981: k 260 m ($26 m).*
Est FMA: $ 100 m (1982).
$1= kip 10 (1980/81, off.).

Army: 50,000.
4 inf divs.
1 arty div.
7 indep inf regts.
1 engr regt.
2 construction regts, indep construction bns.
5 arty, 9 AA arty bns.
65 indep inf coys.
1 lt ac liaison flt.
30 T-34/-54/-55 MBT; 25 PT-76 lt tks; 8 BTR-40, 40 BTR-152, M-113 APC; 80 M-116 75mm, M-1942 76mm, M-101 105mm, D-30 122mm, M-114 155mm how; 81mm, 82mm, 107mm (4.2-in.) mor; M-18/A1 57mm, 107mm RCL; M-1939 37mm, M-1950 57mm AA guns.

Navy: 1,700.
6 river patrol craft, incl Sov *Shmel*.
(Perhaps 25 more vessels, incl 4 LCM, 7 tpts⟨ in reserve).

Air Force: 2,000; 20 combat ac.
3 FGA sqns with some 20 MiG-21.
1 tpt sqn with 2 Yak-40, 5 An-24, 2 An-26, 6 An-2.
1 hel sqn with 10 Mi-8, 2 Mi-6, Mi-4.
Trg: MiG-17/-21UTI.
AAM: AA-2 *Atoll*.

Para-Military Forces: Militia, Self-Defence forces.

MALAYSIA

Population: 15,850,000.
Military service: voluntary.
Total armed forces: 124,500.
GDP 1982: $R 61.196 bn ($US 26.204 bn). 1983: 67.480 bn ($US 29.070 bn).
Def exp 1982: $R 4.978 bn ($US 2.144 bn). 1983: 5.480 bn ($US 2.361 bn). Budget 1984: 5.0 bn ($US 2.170 bn).†
GDP growth: 4.2% (1982), 5.5% (1983).
Inflation: 5.8% (1982), 3.7% (1983).
Debt: $US 9.5 bn (1982).

---

* Data unreliable.
† All figures include internal security budget.

$1 = ringgits 2.3354 (1982), 2.3213 (1983), 2.3044 (mid-1984).

Army: 100,500.
1 corps, 4 div HQ.
12 inf bdes, consisting of 36 inf bns (1 APC), 4 cav, 4 fd arty, 1 AA arty, 5 sigs regts; administrative units.
1 Special Service bde gp.
25 *Scorpion* lt tks; some 46 SIBMAS, 140 AML armd, 93 *Ferret* scout cars; AT-105, 200 V-100/-150 *Commando*, some 10 *Stormer*, some 320 *Condor* APC; 12 5.5-in. (140mm) guns, 114 Model 56 105mm pack how; 81mm mor; M-20 89mm RL; 150 106mm, 5 120mm RCL; SS-11 ATGW; 70 12.7mm, 25 40mm AA guns.
(On order: some 25 *Scorpion* lt tks; some 138 SIBMAS AFV, some 10 *Stormer*, some 140 *Condor* APC (being delivered).)

RESERVES: Malaysian Territorial Army 45,000; Local Defence Corps, some 15,000.

Navy: 11,000 (being expanded).
2 frigates: 1 *Yarrow* (1 × 4 *Seacat* SAM); 1 Type 41.
8 FAC(G) with 4 or 2 *Exocet* MM-38 SSM: 4 *Handalan* (*Spica*-M), 4 *Perdana*.
6 *Jerong* FAC.
21 large patrol craft: 3 *Kedah*, 4 *Sabah*, 14 *Kris*.
2 Br *Ton* coastal minesweepers.
2 US 511-1152 LST, 29 small amph vessels.
1 spt, 1 fleet ammunition ship.
(On order: 2 FS-1500 frigates with *Exocet*, 2 1,300-ton patrol vessels, 4 *Spica*-M FAC(G) (*Exocet* MM-40), 4 *Lerici* minehunters, 2 LST.)

Bases: Woodlands (Singapore; trg base), Kuantan, Labuan, Lumut.

RESERVES: about 600.

Air Force: 13,000 (being expanded); 34 combat ac.
2 Air Regions, (5 bns), 1 Spt Command.
1 FGA sqn with 13 F-5E, 4 F-5F, 2 RF-5E.
2 COIN/trg sqns with 12 MB-339.
1 MR sqn with 3 PC-130H.
3 tpt, 1 liaison sqns: 1 with 6 C-130H; 2 with 14 DHC-4A; 1 with 2 HS-125, 2 F-28, 12 Cessna 402B.
2 tpt hel sqns with 36 S-61A-4; 2 liaison sqns with 24 SA-316B *Alouette* III.
3 trg schools: with 11 *Bulldog* 102, 40 PC-7 ac; 7 Bell 47, 2 *Alouette* hel.
AAM: *Sidewinder*.
(On order: 34 A-4S FGA, 6 TA-4 trg (plus 20 more for spares), 4 NC-212 *Aviocar* tpt ac; *Super Sidewinder* AAM.)

RESERVES: 600: 10 CL-41G6 *Tebuan* trg ac.

Para-Military Forces: Police Field Force 12,000; 21 bns (incl 2 Aboriginal), *Shorland* armd cars and SB-301 APC, 210 patrol boats(; 4 Cessna 206. Area Security Units (Home Guard): 3,100 men in 89 units; Border Scouts (in Sabah, Sarawak): 1,200. People's Volunteer Corps (RELA), over 350,000.

MONGOLIA

Population: 1,800,000.
Military service: 3 years.
Total armed forces: 36,500.
Est def exp 1983: tugriks 816.4 m ($247.394 m). Budget 1984: 763.8 m ($231.455 m).
Est FMA: $600 m (1982).
$1 = tugrik 3.30 (1983/4, off.).

Army: 33,000.
2 inf divs.
1 inf bde (may be forming a div).
T-54/-55/-62 MBT; BRDM-2 recce; BMP MICV; 70 BTR-60/-152 APC; ZIS-3 76mm, 100mm incl SU-100 SP, 122mm, 130mm guns; M-1937 152mm gun/how; 152mm how; *Snapper* ATGW; 37mm, 57mm AA guns.

RESERVES: 40,000.

Air Force: 3,500 (100 pilots); Soviet technicians; 12 combat ac. (Operates civil air line.)
1 ftr sqn with 12 MiG-21.
At least 2 tpt sqns with 20 An-2, 19 An-24, 1 An-26.
1 hel sqn with Mi-8, 10 Mi-4.
Trainers: Yak-11/-18, 3 PZL-104 *Wilga* utility.

Para-Military Forces: Ministry of Public Security (15,000): Militia (Police), internal security troops, frontier guards; BTR-40/-152.

NEPAL

Population: 16,100,000.
Military service: voluntary.
Total armed forces: 25,000.
GDP 1981/2: NR 30.539 bn ($2.361 bn). 1982/3: 33.929 bn ($2.459 bn).
Def budget 1983/4: NR 464 m ($30.386 m).
GDP growth: 4% (1982), −1.3% (1983).
Inflation: 13% (1982),14% (1983).
$1 = rupees 12.936 (1981/2), 13.796 (1982/3), 15.270 (1983/4).

Army: 25,000.
6 inf bdes (1 Palace Guard incl 1 cav sqn, 1 garrison bn).
1 arty bn.
1 engr bn.

1 sigs bn.
1 para bn.
1 tpt bn.
1 air sqn (1 comms flt, 1 Army flt).
6 75mm pack, 4 3.7-in. (94mm) mountain how;
   15 4.2-in. (107mm), 18 120mm mor; 2 40mm
   AA guns; 3 *Skyvan*, 1 HS-748 ac; 4 *Chetak*
   (*Alouette* III), 2 *Puma* hel.

Para-Military Forces: Police force 15,000.

NEW ZEALAND

Population: 3,300,000.
Military service: voluntary, supplemented by
   Territorial Army service: 7 weeks basic, 20
   days per year.
Total armed forces: 12,692.
GDP 1982/3: $NZ 31.235 bn ($US 22.783 bn).
   Est 1983/4: 33.0 bn ($US 21.682 bn).
Def exp 1982/3: $NZ 652.10 m ($US 475.638 m).
   Budget 1983/4: 715.32 m ($US 469.987 m).
GDP growth: 3.2% (1982), 0% (1983).
Inflation: 15.8% (1982), 12.6% (1983).
Debt: $US 10.2 bn (1982).
FMA: $US 0.51 m (1982/3), $US 0.55 m
   (1983/4).*
   $US 1 = $NZ 1.3710 (1982/3), 1.5221
   (1983/4).

Army: 5,548.
2 inf bns.
1 arty bty.
1 lt armd sqn.
26 *Scorpion* lt tks; 72 M-113 APC; 10 5.5-in.
   (140mm) guns; 41 105mm (incl pack) how; 71
   81mm mor; 22 106mm RCL.

RESERVES: 1,410 Regular, 6,288 Territorial. 6
   Territorial inf bns, 4 fd, 1 med arty btys, 1
   recce, 1 APC, 1 ATK sqns.

Navy: 2,827.
4 *Leander* frigates: with 1 *Wasp* hel, *Seacat* SAM:
   1 with 1 × 4 SAM; 2 with 2 × 4; 1 with 2 × 4,
   Ikara ASW.
4 *Lake* patrol craft.
2 inshore patrol craft.
7 *Wasp* hel.

Base: Auckland.

RESERVES: 708 Regular, 400 Territorial.

Air Force: 4,317; 33 combat ac.
1 FGA sqn with 9 A-4K, 3 TA-4K *Skyhawk*.
1 OCU with 16 BAC-167 *Strikemaster*.
1 MR sqn with 5 P-3B *Orion*.
2 med tpt sqns with 5 C-130H, 6 *Andover* (to
   retire), 2 Boeing 727-100C.
1 tpt hel sqn with 6 *Sioux*, 11 UH-1D/H.

1 comms sqn with 4 *Andover*, 3 Cessna 421C.
Trainers: 4 *Airtourer*, 15 CT-4 *Airtrainer*, 3 F-27
   Friendship ac; 3 *Sioux* hel.

RESERVES: 866 Regular, 201 Territorial.

Forces Abroad: Singapore: 1 inf bn with log spt;
   1 spt hel unit (3 UH-1). Egypt (Sinai MFO): 35;
   2 UH-1 hel.

PAKISTAN

Population: 92,450,000 (excl Afghan refugees).
Military service: voluntary.
Total armed forces: 478,600.
GDP 1982/3: Rs 366.15 bn ($28.831 bn). Est
   1983/4: 415.41 bn ($30.859 bn).
Def exp 1982/3: Rs 23.224 bn ($1.829 bn).
   Est 1983/4: 25.219 bn ($1.873 bn).
GDP growth: 6.6% (1982), 4.5% (1983).
Inflation: 12% (1982), 9.0% (1983).
FMA: $1.6 bn (1983).†
Debt: $10.4 bn (1983).
   $1 = rupees 12.6998 (1982/3), 13.4616
   (1983/4).

Army: 450,000.
7 Corps HQ; 1 Territorial Command.
2 armd divs.
16 inf divs.
4 indep armd bdes.
5 indep inf bdes.
7 arty bdes.
2 AA arty bdes.
6 armd recce regts.
6 SAM btys with 6 *Crotale* (each 4 msls).
1 special services group.
AFV: 370 M-47/-48 (incl A5), 51 T-54/-55,
   1,000 Type-59 MBT; 500 M-113, 50 UR-416
   APC.
Arty: some 1,000 25-pdr (88mm), Type-59
   100mm, 130mm, 5.5-in. (140mm) and 155mm
   guns and M-116 75mm pack, 105mm incl
   pack, 12 M-7 SP, 155mm towed, M-109 SP,
   M-115 203mm how; 122mm MRL; 107mm,
   120mm mor.
ATK: 75mm, 3.5-in. (89mm) RL; Type 52
   75mm, 106mm RCL; *Cobra*, 200 *TOW* ATGW.
AD: 14.5mm, 37mm, 40mm, 57mm AA guns;
   6 *Crotale* SAM.
Aviation:
   1 liaison sqn with 20 *Supporter* ac.
   4 hel sqns.
   Indep army observation flts.
      45 O-1E, Cessna 421, 50 *Mashshaq* (Saab
      Safari), *Turbo Commander*, *Queen Air* ac;
      some 15 Bell AH-1S, 16 Mi-8, 35 *Puma*, 23

---

* Defence Mutual Assistance Programme.
† FMA commitment 1983/7.

Alouette III, 13 Bell 47G hel.
(On order: M-113 APC; 75 M-198 towed, 100 M-109A2 SP 155mm, 40 M-110 SP 203mm how; *TOW* ATGW launchers (incl 24 M-901 *Improved TOW* SP, 1,000 msls); some 5 AH-1S hel; 144 RBS-70 SAM launchers, 400 msls.)

RESERVES: 500,000.

Navy: 11,000.
11 subs: 2 *Agosta*, 4 *Daphne*, 5 SX-404 midget.
8 destroyers: 1 Br *County*, 2 × 4 *Seacat* SAM, 1 *Alouette* hel; 6 US *Gearing* with 1 × 8 *ASROC* ASW; 1 Br *Battle*.
4 Ch *Hainan* FAC(P), 1 *Town* patrol craft.
4 Ch *Hoku* FAC(G) (2 msls).
12 Ch *Shanghai*-II FAC.
4 Ch *Huchwan* hydrofoil FAC(T)(.
19 coastal patrol craft: 1 *Spear*, 18 MC-55 Type.
3 US *Adjutant* and MSC-268 coastal MCM.
1 US *Mission* underway replenishment tanker.
1 Br *Dido* cruiser (cadet trg/AA ship; non-operational).

NAVAL AIR: 3 combat ac, 6 combat hel.
1 ASW/MR sqn with 3 *Atlantic* with *Exocet* ASM.
2 ASW/SAR hel sqns with 6 *Sea King* ASW with *Exocet* AM-39, 4 *Alouette* III.
ASM: AM-39 *Exocet*.

Base: Karachi.

RESERVES: 5,000.

Air Force: 17,600; 314 combat ac.
9 FGA sqns: 1 with 17 *Mirage* IIIEP; 4 with 50 *Mirage* 5PA3; 4 with 52 Ch Q-5.
9 interceptor/FGA sqns with 170 Ch F-6; (1 converting to F-16 (6)).
1 recce sqn with 13 *Mirage* IIIRP.
1 OCU with some 6 F-16.
2 tpt sqns: 1 with 13 C-130B/E, 1 L-100; 1 with 1 *Falcon* 20, 1 F-27-200 (with Navy), 1 *Super King Air*, 1 *Bonanza*.
1 SAR hel sqn with 6 HH-43B, 4 *Alouette* III.
1 utility hel sqn with 4 *Super Frelon*, 12 Bell 47G.
1 trg sqn with 20 T-33A, 4 MiG-15UTI.
Other trainers incl 2 *Mirage* 5DPA2, 3 *Mirage* IIIDP, 25 *Mashshaq* (Saab *Supporter*), 35 T-37C, 45 Ch FT-5 (MiG-17U), 12 CJ-6, 24 Reims FTB-337.
AAM: *Sidewinder*, R-530, R-550 *Magic*.
(On order: 28 F-16, 14 Ch Q-5 FGA.)

RESERVES: 8,000.

Forces Abroad: 30,000 contract personnel: Saudi Arabia (20,000); Jordan, Libya, Oman, UAE.

Para-Military Forces: 109,100: National Guard (22,000); Frontier Corps (65,000); Pakistan Rangers (15,000); Coast Guard (2,000); Frontier Constabulary (5,100).

PAPUA NEW GUINEA

Population: 3,400,000.
Military service: voluntary.
Total armed forces: 3,232 (all part of army).
GDP 1982: K 1.798 bn ($2.438 bn). 1983: 1.940 bn ($2.326 bn).
Est def exp 1983: K 26.9 m ($32.250 m). Budget 1984: 27.4 m ($30.444 m).
GDP growth: −1.5% (1982), 2.0% (1983).
FMA: $15.0 m (1982), 16.0 m (1983).
$1 = kina 0.7375 (1982), 0.8341 (1983), 0.9000 (mid-1984).

Army: 2,846.
2 inf bns.
1 engr bn.
1 sigs sqn.
Log units.

Navy: 300.
5 *Attack* large patrol craft.
2 310-ton landing craft.

Bases: Port Moresby, Lombrum.

Air Force: 86.
1 tpt sqn with 6 C-47, 4 *Nomad* MR ac.

Para-Military Forces: 4,600 Police.

PHILIPPINES

Population: 53,400,000.
Military service: voluntary.
Total armed forces: 104,800.
GDP 1982: P 340.360 bn ($39.855 bn). 1983: 380.820 bn ($34.268 bn).
Est def exp 1983: P 7.404 bn ($666.247 m). Budget 1984: 8.420 bn ($601.343 m).
GDP growth: 2.7% (1982), 1.0% (1983).
Inflation: 12.7% (1982), 10% (1983).
FMA: $1.75 bn (1981).
Debt: $24.5 bn (1982).
$1 = pesos 8.54 (1982), 11.113 (1983), 14.002 (mid-1984).

Army : 60,000.
5 inf divs.
1 special warfare bde.
1 special security bde (1 armd, 2 inf, 2 COIN bns, spt units).
(1 ranger regt (2 ranger, 1 mountain bns, 5 scout coys) being reactivated.)
2 engr bdes.

1 lt armd regt.
4 arty regts.
28 *Scorpion* lt tks; 45 MICV; 80 M-113, 20
   Chaimite APC; 200 105mm (incl pack), 12
   M-114 155mm how; 81mm, 107mm mor;
   M-20 75mm, M-67 90mm, M-40 106mm RCL.
(On order: 24 M-167A1 towed *Vulcan* AD
   systems.)

RESERVES: 20,000, 18 bns; some 70,000 more
   have Reserve commitments.

Navy: 28,000 (9,600 marines, 2,000 Coast
   Guard).
7 US frigates: 4 *Casco*, 1 *Savage*, 2 *Cannon*.
10 US corvettes: 2 *Auk*, 7 PCE-827, 1
   Admirable.
3 PSMM-5 FAC(G) with 4 *Exocet*.
16 large patrol craft, incl 1 command ship, 4
   Katapangan, 5 PGM-39/-71, 2 US PC-461.
62 coastal patrol craft.
31 US landing ships (3 spt, 24 LST, 4 LSM), 61
   LCM, 7 LCVP, 3 LCU.
1 SAR sqn with 9 *Islander* ac, 5 BO-105 hel.
3 marine bdes (9 bns) with 30 LVTP-5, 55
   LVTP-7 APC; 150 105mm how; 4.2-in.
   (107mm) mor.
(On order: 2 ex-US destroyers, 3 PSMM-5
   FAC(G), 50 patrol boats, 12 LST, 1 trg ship.)

Base: Sangley Point/Cavite, Zamboanga.

RESERVES: 12,000.

Air Force: 16,800; 82 combat ac.
1 FGA sqn with 24 F-8H.
1 AD sqn with 19 F-5A, 3 F-5B.
3 COIN sqns: 1 with 16 SF-260WP; 2 with 20
   T-28D.
1 hel wing with 50 UH-1H, some 7 H(S)-76,
   2 S-70AS (tpt).
1 Presidential tpt sqn with 1 Boeing 707, 1
   BAC-111, 1 YS-11 ac; 1 S-62A, 2 UH-1N, 1
   Puma hel.
5 tpt sqns: 1 with 4 C-130H; 1 with 5 C-47, 8
   F-27, 3 F-27MR; 1 with 12 *Nomad*; 1 with 12
   Islander ac; 1 with 12 BO-105 hel.
1 liaison sqn with O-1E, 1 Cessna U-17A/B, 8
   Beaver (being withdrawn).
4 trg sqns: 1 with 10 T/RT-33A; 1 with 12
   T-41D; 1 with 30 SF-260MP; 1 with 10
   T-34A.
1 weather sqn with 3 Cessna 210.
AAM: *Sidewinder*.
(On order: 16 Bell 412, 10 S-76, 12 UH-1H hel.)

RESERVES: 16,000.

Para-Military Forces: (Ministry of Defence):
   Philippine Constabulary 43,500 (1 bde, 13
   bns, 180 provincial coys); by law part of armed
   forces. Civil Home Defence Force 65,000.

Opposition: Moro National Liberation Army:
   1,000. New People's Army: 10,000

SINGAPORE

Population: 2,550,000.
Military service: 24 months; officers/NCOs 30
   months.
Total armed forces: 55,500 (34,800 conscripts).
Est GDP 1982/3: $S 32.300 bn ($US 15.125 bn).
Est def exp 1983/4: $S 2.294 bn ($US 1.081 bn).
   Budget 1984/5: 2.260 bn ($US 1.075 bn).*
GDP growth: 6.3% (1982), 7.9% (1983).
Inflation: 4.0% (1982), 1.1% (1983).
Debt: $US 2.0 bn (1982).
   $US 1 = $S 2.1355 (1982/3), 2.1226 (1983/4),
   2.1015 (mid-1984).

Army: 45,000 (30,000 conscripts).
1 div HQ.
1 armd bde (1 recce, 1 tk, 2 APC bns).
3 inf bdes (each 3 inf bns).
6 arty bns.
1 cdo bn.
6 engr, 3 sigs bns.
350 AMX-13 lt tks; 720 M-113, 280 V-100/
   -150/-200 *Commando* APC; 60 155mm how;
   60mm, 81mm, 50 120mm mor (some SP in
   M-113); 89mm RL; *Carl Gustav* 84mm, 90
   106mm RCL; 20mm, 35mm, L-70 40mm AA
   guns.

RESERVES: 150,000; 2 armd div, 6 inf bde HQ; 18
   inf, 1 cdo, 9 arty, 6 engr, 2 sigs bns. Annual trg
   to age 40 for men; 50 for officers.

Navy: 4,500 (1,800 conscripts).
6 TNC-45 FAC(G) each with 5 *Gabriel* II SSM.
6 Vosper A/B FAC.
2 large patrol craft (trg ships).
12 *Swift* coastal patrol craft.
2 US *Redwing* coastal minesweepers.
6 US 511-1152 LST (1 in reserve), 6 landing
   craft\.
(On order: 3 FPB-57 FAC.)

Base: Paulau Brani (Singapore).

Air Force: 6,000 (3,000 conscripts); 167 combat
   ac.
2 FGA sqns with 41 A-4S/SI, 6 TA-4S *Skyhawk*.
1 FGA sqn with 21 *Hunter* FGA-74.
1 recce sqn with 7 *Hunter* FR-74S, 4 T-75S.
1 AD sqn with 24 F-5E, 3 F-5F.
3 COIN/trg sqns: 1 with 18 BAC-167; 1 with 11
   SF-260W, 12 SF-260MS; 1 with 20 T-33A.
1 tpt/SAR sqn with 8 C-130B/H.
2 hel sqns with 36 UH-1B/H, 3 AB-212, 6
   AS-350B *Ecureuil*.

---

* Incl defence development budget.

4 SAM sqns: 1 with 28 *Bloodhound* 2; 1 with 10 *Rapier*; 1 with 6 *Improved HAWK*; 1 with Bofors RBS-70.

AAM: *Sidewinder*-9J/P.

(On order: 70 A-4SI (being rebuilt), 30 SIAI S-211 ac; 22 AS-332 *Super Puma* hel; *Rapier/Blindfire* SAM; 200 *Maverick* ASM.)

Forces Abroad: Brunei: (500); trg school.

Para-Military Forces: Police/marine police 7,500: 49 patrol craft; Gurkha guard units; People's Defence Force, some 30,000.

SRI LANKA

Population: 15,800,000.
Military service: voluntary.
Total armed forces: 16,560.
GDP 1982: Rs 100.140 bn ($4.812 bn). 1983: 122.322 bn ($5.199 bn).
Est def exp 1982: Rs 1.400 bn ($67.269 m). 1983: 1.80 bn ($76.501 m).
GDP growth: 4.1% (1982).
Inflation: 11% (1982), 14% (1983).
Debt: $ 2.6 bn (1982).
$1 = rupees 20.812 (1982), 23.529 (1983).

Army: 11,000.
5 inf bdes (each with 1 regular, 2 reserve bns).
1 recce regt (bn)   ⎫ (each with one
1 fd arty, 1 AA regts ⎬ regular and
1 engr regt   ⎭ one reserve unit
1 sigs bn.
Support services.
18 *Saladin* armd, 15 *Ferret* scout cars; 10 BTR-152 APC; 12 76mm, 12 85mm guns; 12 82mm, 12 4.2-in. (107mm) mor; M-60 82mm RCL; 24 40mm, 12 3.7-in. (94mm) AA guns.

RESERVES: 14,000; 10 bns, plus supporting services and a Pioneer Corps.

Navy: 2,960.
8 FAC: 7 *Sooraya* (Ch *Shanghai*-II), 1 Sov *Mol.*
26 coastal patrol craft⟨.
(On order: 2 large patrol craft.)

Bases: Trincomalee, Karainagar, Colombo, Tangalla, Kalpitiya.

RESERVES: Naval Volunteer Force 582.

Air Force: 2,600.
1 tpt sqn with 1 HS-748, 2 DC-3, 3 Riley, 1 *Heron*, 3 Cessna 337, 1 206, 1 421C.
1 hel sqn with 7 Bell 206, 2 SA-365.
Trainers incl 4 Cessna 150/152, 7 *Chipmunk*, 3 *Dove*.
(In storage: 5 MiG-17F, 1 MiG-15UTI, 2 *Jet Provost* Mk 51 ac; 4 Bell 206, 2 Ka-26 hel.)

RESERVES: 1,000; 3 sqns Air Force Regt, 1 sqn Airfield Construction Regt.

Para-Military Forces: Police Force 14,500. Volunteer Force 5,000. Home Guard.

TAIWAN

Population: 19,600,000.
Military service: 2 years.
Total armed forces: 484,000.
GDP 1982/3: $NT 1,829 bn ($US 45.385 bn). Est 1983/4: 1,993 bn ($US 49.825 bn).
Est def exp 1983/4: $NT 135.9 bn ($US 3.398 bn).* Budget 1984/5: 141.9 bn ($US 3.574 bn).*
GDP growth: 3.8% (1982), 6.0% (1983).
Inflation: 3.0% (1982), 2.0% (1983).
FMA: $US 830 m (1982–3).
Debt: $US 9.2 bn (1982).
$US 1 = $NT 40.3 (1982/3), 40.0 (1983/4), 39.7 (mid-1984).

Army: 330,000.
3 Army, 6 Corps HQ.
12 hy inf divs.
6 lt inf divs.
6 armd/inf bdes.
3 AB bdes.
4 tk gps.
20 fd arty bns.
5 SAM bns: 2 with *Nike Hercules*, 3 with *HAWK*.
6 army aviation sqns.
309 M-48 MBT; 325 M-24 (90mm gun), 795 M-41 lt tks; M-8 armd cars; M-3 half-track, 1,100 M-113, 150 V-150 *Commando* APC; 390 M-59 155mm guns/how; 350 M-116 75mm pack, 550 M-101 (T-64) 105mm, 90 M-114 (T-65) 155mm, 10 M-115 203mm towed, 225 M-108 105mm, 125 M-109 A-1 155mm, 75 M-110 203mm SP how; 81mm mor; *Kung Feng* (*Worker Bee*) towed and SP 127mm MRL; *Hsiung Feng* (*Drone Bee* = *Gabriel*-type) coastal defence SSM, *Ching Feng* (*Green Bee* = *Nike Hercules*-type) SSM/SAM; 150 M-18 76mm SP ATK guns; 500 106mm RCL; *Kun Wu* (*Fire God* = *TOW*-type), *TOW* (some SP) ATGW; 300 40mm AA guns (some M-42 SP); 400 *Nike Hercules*, 800 *HAWK*, 20 *Chaparral* SAM; 118 UH-1H, 2 KH-4, 7 CH-34 hel.
(On order: 164 M-113 APC (incl variants), 125 M-109 155mm, 75 M-110A 203mm SP how; 1,000 *TOW*, *Kun Wu* ATGW; 504 MIM-72F *Chaparral* msls; 370 *Improved HAWK* SAM.)

DEPLOYMENT: Quemoy: 60,000; Matsu: 20,000.

RESERVES: 1,500,000: 9 divs; an additional 1.3 million have some Reserve obligation.

---

* Estimates for each year run up to $NT 165.0 bn.

Navy: 38,000.
2 US *Guppy*-II submarines.
23 US destroyers: 10 *Gearing* with 1 hel (4 with
  3 *Hsiung Feng (HF)* SSM, 7 with 1 × 8
  ASROC); 1 *Gearing* radar picket with 3 *HF*; 8
  Sumner (1 with 1 × 3, 2 with 2 × 3 *HF*); 4
  Fletcher with 1 × 2 *Sea Chaparral* SAM.
9 US frigates: 8 *Lawrence*, 1 *Crosley*.
3 US *Auk* corvettes.
28 FAC(G) with *HF* SSM: 2 *Lung Chiang* with
  4 × 1, 26 *Tzu Chiang* (*Dvora*) with 2 × 1.
30 coastal patrol craft.
14 US *Adjutant* and MSC-268 coastal MCM.
2 LSD, 23 LST, 4 LSM, 22 LCU, some 400 small
  landing craft.
1 repair ship; 2 tpts; 7 tankers.
(On order: 2 *Lung Chiang*, 4 *Tzu Chiang* FAC(G);
  10 ASW hel; ASROC ASW; 170 *Standard* SM-1,
  284 *Improved Sea Chaparral* SAM.)

Bases: Tsoying, Makung (Pescadores), Keelung.

RESERVES: 45,000.

Marines: 39,000.
3 divs.
LVT-4/-5 APC; 105mm, 155mm how; 106mm
  RCL.

RESERVES: 35,000.

Air Force: 77,000; 547 combat ac, 12 armed hel.
5 combat wings.
13 ftr sqns with 226 F-5E, 30 F-5F, 42
  F-100A/D, 60 F-104G.
1 interceptor sqn with 19 F-104A.
1 recce sqn with 8 RF-104G.
1 MR sqn with 9 S-2A, 20 S-2E.
1 ASW hel sqn with 12 Hughes *Defender* 500MD.
1 SAR sqn with 8 UH-16B ac, 10 UH-1H hel.
6 tpt sqns with 20 C-47, 5 C-54, 1 C-118B, 40
  C-119, 10 C-123, 1 Boeing 720B, 4 727-100.
OCU: 82 F-5A/B, 30 F/TF-104G, 6 F-104D, 15
  F-100F.
Trainers incl 55 PL-1B *Chien Shou*, 50 T-CH-1,
  32 T-33/-38, 10 T-28, AT-3.
2 hel sqns with 7 UH-19, 10 Bell 47G.
AAM: *Sidewinder*, *Shafrir*.
ASM: *Bullpup*, AGM-65A *Maverick*.
(On order: 39 F-104G, 27 TF-104G, 60 F-5E/F
  ftr, 12 C-130 tpt, 50 XAT-3 trg ac; *Sparrow*
  AAM.)

RESERVES: 90,000.

Para-Military Forces: Taiwan Garrison Command, 25,000.

THAILAND

Population: 50,700,000.
Military service: 2 years.

Total armed forces: 235,300.
GDP 1982: baht 846.14 bn ($36.789 bn). 1983:
  928.55 bn ($40.372 bn).
Def exp 1982/3: baht 35.500 bn ($1.543 bn).*
  Budget 1983/4: 37.989 bn ($1.652 bn).*
GDP growth: 5.2% (1982), 3.8% (1983).
Inflation: 5.3% (1982), 4.0% (1983).
FMA: $142 m (1982), $70 m (1983).
Debt: $11.7 bn (1982).
  $1 = baht 23.0 (1982/4).

Army: 160,000.
4 Regions; 4 Army HQ.
1 cav div (2 cav, 1 arty regts).
1 armd div (1 tk, 1 cav, 1 mech regts).
7 inf divs (5 with 1 tk bn).
2 special forces divs.
1 arty div, 1 AA div (2 AA arty regts).
11 engr bns.
8 indep inf bns.
4 recce coys.
AFV: 150 M-48A5 MBT; 200 M-41 (most in
  reserve), 144 *Scorpion*, M-24 lt tks; 32 *Shorland* Mk 3 recce; 340 M-113, M-3A1 half-
  track, 120 V-150 *Commando*, 20 *Saracen* APC.
Arty: 300 M-116 75mm pack, M-101/-101 mod
  105mm, 80 M-114, some 24 M-198 155mm
  how; 81mm, 120mm mor.
ATK: M-72 *LAW* RL; 57mm, M-20 75mm, 215
  106mm RCL; *TOW*, *Dragon* ATGW.
AA: 24 20mm M-163 *Vulcan*, 80 M-1/L-70/
  M-42 SP 40mm AA guns, *Redeye* SAM.
Army Aviation:
  3 airmobile coys, some hel flts.
  4 C-47, 1 *King Air* tpt, 80 O-1, 13 U-17A, 1
    Beech 99 lt, 23 T-41A trg ac; 76 UH-1B/H,
    4 CH-47A, 15 OH-13H, 3 OH-58A, 11
    TH-55A hel.
(On order: 40 M-48A5, 16 M-60A3 MBT; 56
  Cascavel armd cars; 148 M-113 (incl variants),
  164 V-150 APC; 34 M-114, 38 M-198 155mm
  how; 105mm MRL; *Blowpipe* SAM; 2 Bell
  214ST, 4 UH-60A hel.)

RESERVES: 500,000. 4 div HQ.

Navy: 32,200, incl naval air and marines.
6 frigates: 1 *Yarrow*-type with 1 × 4 *Seacat* SAM;
  2 PF-103; 2 US *Tacoma*; 1 *Cannon*.
6 FAC(G): 3 Breda BMB-230 with 4 *Exocet* SSM; 3
  TNC-45 with 5 *Gabriel* SSM.
3 MV-400 FAC.
19 US large patrol craft: 6 PC-461, 10 PGM-71,
  3 *Cape*.
31 coastal, 40 river patrol craft〈.
4 US *Bluebird* coastal minesweepers, 5 minesweeping boats〈.
5 LST, 3 LSM, 2 LSIL-351, 1 LCG, 10 LCU, 26 LCM
  (all US), 4 LCA, 12 LCVP.

* Excl Internal Security Budget.

3 trg ships: 2 Br (1 *Algerine*, 1 *Flower*), 1 *Maeklong*.

NAVAL AIR: some 15 combat ac.
1 MR/ASW sqn with 10 S-2F.
1 MR/SAR sqn with 4 F-27MPA, 4 *Searchmaster*, 2 HU-16B, 2 CL-215, 5 C-47.
1 trg/SAR hel sqn with 11 UH-1H/N.
1 observation sqn with 13 U-17, 10 O-1A, 7 O-2, 2 LA-4 ac.

MARINES: (13,000).
1 bde: 2 inf, 1 arty regts; 1 amph assault bn; 40 LVTP-7 amph APC, 24 GC-45 155mm guns/how, support weapons.

(On order: 1 *Descubierta* frigate, 4 PSMM-5 FAC(G), 2 corvettes, 4 large, 3 coastal patrol craft; *Harpoon* SSM; 10 *Exocet* MM-39 coast defence msls; 2 F-27MPA MR ac.)

Bases: Bangkok, Sattahip, Songkla, Phangnga.

Air Force: 43,100; 188 combat ac.
1 FGA sqn with 13 F-5A/B.
2 AD sqns with 34 F-5E, 5 F-5F.
7 COIN sqns: 1 with 22 T-28D; 2 with 25 OV-10C; 1 with 15 A-37B; 1 with 25 AU-23A; 1 with 14 AC-47; 1 with 14 T-33A, 3 RT-33.
1 recce sqn with 4 RF-5A, 6 RC-47D, 3 *Arava* 201, 1 *Queen Air* 65, 1 Cessna 340.
3 tpt sqns, incl Royal flt: 1 with 10 C-47, 2 *Merlin* IVA; 2 with 16 C-123B, 3 C-130H; 8 HS-748; 1 737-200, some 15 N-22B *Nomad*, 5 NC-212 *Aviocar*.
3 liaison sqns with 4 U-10, 23 O-1.
2 hel sqns: 18 CH-34C, 27 UH-1H, 2 Bell 412.
Trainers incl 10 T-37B, 6 O-1A, 9 T-41A, 16 SF-260MT, 23 CT-4, some 7 *Fantrainer*.
AAM: AIM-9 *Sidewinder*.
Airfield defence troops: 4 bns; *Blowpipe* SAM.
(On order: 8 F-5E, 2 RF-2E, 6 RC-47; 2 *Merlin* IVA, some 5 *Nomad*, 6 HS-748, 1 C-130H-30 tpt; 47 *Fantrainer* trg ac; 4 UH-60 hel; AIM-9P AAM; *Blowpipe* SAM.)

Para-Military Forces: Volunteer Defence Corps 33,000. Marine Police 1,700. Police Aviation 500; 3 *Skyvan*, 8 PC-6, 2 DHC-4, 1 Do-28, 2 Cessna 310, 1 *Airtourer*, 1 CT-4 ac; 27 Bell 205, 13 206, 1 S-62, 6 HH-12, 1 KH-4 hel. Border Patrol Police 20,000. Special Action Force 3,800. Rangers 13,000. Village Scouts. National Defence Volunteers. 20 V-150 *Commando* APC, 1 Coastguard cutter.
(On order: 7 *Nomad*.)

VIETNAM

Population: 58,840,000.
Military service: 3 years; specialists 4 years; some ethnic minorities 2 years.

Total armed forces: 1,227,000 (excl para-military).
GNP 1982/3: estimates range from $6.0 bn to $16.0 bn.
Est FMA: $1 bn (1982).
Debt: $5.3 bn (1982).

Army: 1,000,000.
16 Corps HQ.
1 armd div.
56 inf divs.*
10 marine bdes.
7 engr, 15 economic construction divs.†
5 fd arty divs (some 10 regts).
4 indep engr bdes.
10 indep armd regts.
AFV: 1,500 T-34/-54/-55/-62, Type-59, 400 M-48 MBT; 450 PT-76 and Type-60/63, 150 M-41 lt tks; M-8, M-20 armd cars; BRDM-2 recce; 1,500 BTR-50/-60, Ch Type-55/-56, Type-531, 1,200 M-113, V-100 *Commando* APC.
Arty: 300 76mm, 85mm, 100mm, 122mm, 200 130mm, M-107 175mm guns; 75mm pack, M-101/-102 105mm, 122mm, 100 152mm, M-114 155mm how; 90 SU-76, SU-100, ISU-122, 200 M-109 155mm and M-110 203mm SP how; Type-63 107mm, BM-21 122mm, BM-14-16 140mm MRL; 60mm, 81mm, 82mm, 107mm, 120mm, 160mm mor.
ATK: Type-36 57mm, 75mm, 82mm, Type-51 88mm, 107mm RCL.
AD: 3,000 23mm, 30mm, 37mm, 40mm, 57mm, Type-63 37mm, M-42 40mm, ZSU-23-4, ZSU-57-2 SP AA guns; SA-6/-7/-9 SAM.‡

Navy: 12,000.‡
6 frigates: 4 Sov *Petya*, 2 US (1 *Barnegat*, 1 *Savage*).
10 FAC(G) with *Styx* SSM: 8 Sov *Osa*-II, 2 Komar.
17 Sov FAC(T): 8 Shershen, 3 P-4⟨, 6 P-6⟨.
22 Ch FAC: 8 Shanghai, 14 Swatow.
6 Sov SO-1, 19 US PGM-59/-71 large patrol craft.
9 Sov coastal patrol craft⟨: 6 Zhuk, 3 PO-2.
3 US 510-1152, 3 Sov *Polnocny* LST.
1 SAR hel sqn with 10 Mi-4.
Perhaps some 1,300 ex-US, South Vietnamese naval vessels, naval and civilian junks and coasters could augment this force.

Bases: Cam Ranh Bay, Da Nang, Haiphong,

---

* Incl Forces Abroad. Inf div strengths vary by geographic location, composition and role between 5,000 and 15,000, but 10,500 is 'average'.
† Men beyond normal military age; unit strength about 3,000 each, fully armed, with military and economic role; most in northern Vietnam.
‡ Much US eqpt is inoperable.

Hanoi, Ha Tou, Ho Chi Minh City. Kampuchea: Kompong Som.

Air Force: 15,000; 290 combat ac, 40 armed hel (plus many in store).
4 Air Divs.
3 FGA regts with 70 MiG-17, 40 Su-7/-20 (Su-22 reported).
4 interceptor regts with 180 MiG-21bis/F/PF, MiG-15.
3 tpt regts (350 ac) incl 20 An-2 and 20 Li-2, 9 An-24, 50 An-26, 2 An-30, 6 Tu-34, 11 Yak-40, 7 Il-14, 2 Il-18; 2 C-130, 1 DC-3, 4 DC-4, 2 DC-6, 2 Boeing 707, 7 U-17.
1 hel div (3 hel regts; 150 ac) 25 Mi-6, 40 Mi-8, 25 Mi-24, 15 Ka-25, 45 UH-1.
4 trg regts (60 ac) incl L-29, L-39, MiG-17, MiG-21.
AAM: AA-2 *Atoll*.
Air Defence Force: 60,000: 4 AA divs (30,000): 1,000 85mm, 100mm and 130mm towed; 20 SAM regts (20,000): some 60 sites with SA-2/3; 6 radar bdes (10,000): 100 sites.

RESERVES (all services):
'Tactical Rear Force' 500,000 semi-mobilized first-line quick reinforcement org.
'Strategic Rear Force': 2,500,000.

Forces Abroad (numbers fluctuate): Laos: 40,000 (3 inf divs and spt tps). Kampuchea/Cambodia: 160,000 (2 Front HQ, 12 army divs plus spt tps, naval base, fighter ac incl MiG-21).

Para-Military Forces:
Border Defence Forces 60,000.
Peoples Regional Force (militia; 500,000): 1 regt HQ at each provincial capital; local inf coys, small arms. Some Northern regts org in divs. Some AA eqpt.
People's Self Defence Force: (1,000,000): Two components: Urban; Rural (People's militia): local coy-sized units in towns, some mobile police function and support. Small arms.
Armed Youth Assault Force (South Vietnam) (1,500,000): Young People only. Training incl use of inf weapons, some field service.

Latin America

Continental Treaties and Agreements

The Act of Chapultepec. Signed by Argentina, Bolivia, Brazil, Chile, Colombia, Costa Rica, Cuba, the Dominican Republic, Ecuador, Guatemala, Haiti, Honduras, Mexico, Nicaragua, Panama, Paraguay, Peru, the US, Uruguay and Venezuela in March and April 1945, this Act declared that if any aggression across boundaries established by treaty occurs, or threatens, the signatories will consult to agree upon measures up to and including the use of armed force to prevent or repel it.

The Inter-American Treaty of Reciprocal Assistance (Treaty of Rio). Signed in September 1947 by all parties to the Act of Chapultepec plus El Salvador and Trinidad and Tobago but except Ecuador and Nicaragua, this Treaty expands the Act, constrains signatories to settle disputes among themselves peacefully and provides for collective self-defence should any member be subjected to external attack. It came into force on 3 December 1948 and has been invoked some twelve times since. Cuba withdrew in March 1960.

The Charter of the Organization of American States (OAS). Dated April 1948, the Charter embraces declarations based upon the Treaty of Rio. The members of the OAS – the signatories to the Act of Chapultepec plus Antigua and Barbuda, Barbados, Dominica, El Salvador, Grenada, Jamaica, St Kitts-Nevis (1984), St Lucia, St Vincent, Suriname, and Trinidad and Tobago – are bound to settle internal disputes peacefully and take collective action in the event of external attack upon any signatory. Amendments (Rio, 1965; Bogotá, 1966) reiterated the goal of peaceful settlement of disputes. In 1965/6 an Inter-American Peace Force was formed for service in the Dominican Republic. Subsequent attempts to create a permanent force failed, but an Inter-American Defence Board has been formed to co-ordinate planning. Declarations condemning Communism in the Western Hemisphere, signed in Bogotá in 1948 by 17 nations (Brazil, Chile, the Dominican Republic and the US abstaining), were reiterated at Caracas (1954, 1973), San José (1960), Punta del Este (1962) and Washington (1972).

The Treaty for the Prohibition of Nuclear Weapons in Latin America (Tlatelolco Treaty). This was signed in February 1967 by 25 Latin American countries, 24 of which have ratified it (Argentina has not). Brazil and Chile will not implement it until all other Latin American states have done so. Cuba and Guyana have not signed it. The Treaty therefore is not in force for those five countries. Britain and the Netherlands have ratified it for the territories within the Treaty area for which they are internationally responsible and, with France and the US, have signed Protocol I (which commits states outside the region to accept, for their territories within it, the Treaty restrictions regarding the emplacement or storage of nuclear weapons); Britain, China, France, the USSR and the US have signed Protocol II (an undertaking not to use or threaten to use nuclear weapons against the parties to the Treaty). An Agency was set up to monitor compliance.

Regional Agreements

The 1903 treaty with the Republic of Panama, granting the United States virtual sovereign rights over the Canal Zone in perpetuity, was renegotiated, and the resulting 1977 Treaties came into force in October 1979. About 40% of the former Canal Zone will remain under US control until 31 December 1999. Panama received 11 of 14 US bases. Defence of the Canal will be the joint responsibility of both nations, with Panama assuming an increasing role until the total accession of the Canal to her sovereignty. The US has guaranteed the area's neutrality after 2000.

Belize (British Honduras) became independent on 21 September 1981. Britain agreed to leave troops as protection and to train the Belizean defence forces 'for an appropriate time'.

The US is also providing aid and training. Under the 'Commonwealth Pact', if a threat to Belize's independence occurs, Britain, Barbados, Bahamas, Canada, Guyana, Jamaica and Trinidad and Tobago will meet and consult.

The Central American Defence Council (CONDECA; El Salvador, Honduras and Panama) formed in 1965 to contain Nicaraguan influence, is reported to have been revived and to be creating a common military training centre. In November 1981 El Salvador, Guatemala and Honduras agreed an informal alliance against Cuba, Nicaragua and domestic guerrilla movements in each member country. The US provides assistance to Honduran-based rebels against Nicaragua and to the Government against rebels in El Salvador. A similar regional grouping, the *Communidad Democrática Centroamericana* (Costa Rica, Honduras and El Salvador; observers, Colombia, the US and Venezuela) agreed in January 1982 to provide mutual aid in case of external aggression. Argentina and Peru reportedly entered into a Military Pact in late 1982. A Caribbean Defence Pact, signed in October 1982 between Antigua, Barbados, Dominica, St Lucia and St Vincent, was joined by St Kitts-Nevis on 8 February, 1984. Grenada reportedly will join after November 1984.

The US has had a bilateral agreement with Cuba for jurisdiction and control over Guantánamo Bay since 1934. In 1960 she stated that it could be modified or abrogated only by mutual agreement and that she had no intention of giving such an agreement. She has also leased 2.3 square miles from Bermuda for a naval and air base since 1941.

The US, which has bilateral military sales arrangements at varying levels with most countries of the region, concluded a status of forces agreement with Antigua in 1977/8. The USSR has no known formal defence agreements with any of the states in the area.

Cuba and Vietnam signed a 25-year Treaty of Friendship and Co-operation in October 1982. Cuba and the USSR supplied arms to Grenada before October 1983 and to Nicaragua. Most countries in the region, however, obtain their major equipments from Western, rather than Communist, countries.

Argentina and Brazil are designing and manufacturing for export their own military equipment. Brazil has sold hers to the Middle East (Algeria, Iraq, Libya, Tunisia), Africa (Zambia), and Belgium and Canada, as well as Latin America, and has a training agreement with Suriname. Chile is assembling *Mirage* 50 aircraft and light AFV under licence and reportedly has made some transfers to Paraguay.

Economic Factors

For the past three years Latin American countries generally have experienced a continuous decline in GDP. The Inter-American Development Bank (IDB) reports an overall drop of 3%, and a 6% decline in real per-capita income. Massive international debts have caused many countries (especially Mexico, Brazil, Venezuela and Argentina) serious problems in meeting demands for repayment of their international borrowings. (Brazil and Mexico alone account for 25% of the world debt total.) These factors, coupled with hyper-inflation (in some countries over 400%) and an over-valued dollar, have distorted the economic profile of most Latin American countries. The economic data in this section must therefore be viewed with great caution, since in most cases international comparison in dollar terms is not possible at present.

ARGENTINA

Population: 29,500,000.
Military service: Army and Air Force 1 year, Navy 14 months.
Total armed forces: 153,000 (108,000 conscripts).
GDP 1981: $123.0 bn.
Est def exp 1983: $2.80 bn. Budget 1984: $1.90 bn.*

GDP growth: −5.4% (1982), 2% (1983).
Inflation: 210% (1982), 435% (1983).
Debt: $44.0 bn (1983).

Army: 100,000 (80,000 conscripts).
5 army corps; 5 Military Regions; 1 Garrison HQ.

*High inflation and fluctuating exchange rates make these figures unreliable. The figures also apparently exclude foreign arms purchases (est $10 bn. 1978–82). Excl 1984 security budget ($652 m).

2 armd cav bdes (each 2 armd cav, 1 tk regts; 1 arty bn).

1 mech, 4 mot inf bdes (each 3 regts, plus armd cav sqn, engr, arty bns).

3 mountain inf bdes (each 3 regts; arty, engr bn; recce det).

1 jungle bde.

1 AB bde (3 AB regts, 1 arty gp).

(1 air cav bde to form 1984/5.)

16 arty bns (2 SP; 12 with brigades.)

1 Presidential Guard tk regt.

4 indep cav regts (3 horsed).

1 indep mech inf regt.

1 AB trg regt.

5 AD bns.

1 indep engr gp (regt), 5 indep engr bns.

5 log bns.

1 aviation bn (5 dets); 1 spt coy.

AFV: 125 M-4 *Sherman*, 130 *TAM* MBT; 50 M-41, 60 AMX-13 lt tks; VBC-90 armd cars; 300 AMX-VTP, some 150 *TAM* VCPT MICV; 85 M-3, 125 M-113, 80 MOWAG *Roland*, 5 BDX APC.

Arty: 18 M-59 155mm towed guns; 180 105mm incl M-56 pack, 70 M-114 155mm towed, 20 M-2A1/M-101 105mm, 24 Mk F3, 6 M-109 155mm SP how; SALM-Pampera 105mm; SAPBA-1 127mm MRL; 81mm, 200 120mm (some SP in VCTM MICV) mor; 227 *Kuerassier* 105mm SP ATK guns; 75mm, 90mm, 105mm RCL; Rh 202 twin HSS-669 20mm, HS-83/4 30mm, K-63 35mm, 40mm, 88mm, 50 M-1A1 90mm (trg) AA guns.

Msls: SS-11/-12, *Bantam*, *Cobra*, *Mathogo*, *Mamba* ATGW; *Tigercat*, *Blowpipe*, *Roland*, SAM-7 SAM.

Air: 3 G-222, 3 DHC-6, 5 *Turbo-Commander* 690A, 2 *Turbo-Porter*, 5 *Merlin* IIIA, 2 *Queen Air*, 1 *Sabreliner*; 49 Cessna (15 182, 20 U-17A/B, 7 207, 1 *Citation*, 5 T-4D) ac; 9 A-109, 31 Bell (7 206, 18 UH-1H, 2 47G, 4 212), 6 FH-1100, 1 CH-47C, 6 SA-315B *Lama*, 12 SA-330 *Puma*, some 6 AS-332B *Super Puma* hel.

(On order: 85 *TAM* MBT; 25 155mm SP how conversion kits; 198 *Kuerassier* SP ATK; some 18 AS-332B (being delivered), 9 A-109 hel.)

RESERVES: 250,000: National Guard, 200,000; Territorial Guard 50,000.

Navy: 36,000 (18,000 conscripts), incl naval air force and marines.

3 subs: 2 Type 209, 1 TR-1700.

1 Br *Colossus* aircraft carrier (up to 12 *Super Etendard*/A-4, 6 S-2 ac; 4 S-61 hel).

10 destroyers: 4 *Meko* 360H-2 with 2 × 4 *Exocet* MM-40 SSM, 1 × 8 *Aspide* multi-role msls, 2 *Lynx* hel; 2 Type 42 with 4 *Exocet* MM-38, 1 × 2 *Sea Dart* SAM, 1 *Lynx* hel; 4 US (3 *Sumner*, 1 *Gearing* with 4 *Exocet*).

6 corvettes with *Exocet* SSM: 3 *Espora* (*Meko* 140) with 4 MM-40, 1 hel; 3 Fr A-69 with 4 MM-38.

5 patrol ships: 2 US *Cherokee*, 2 *King* (1 trg), 1 US *Sotoyomo*.

1 large patrol vessel.

2 TNC-45 FAC(G).

4 *Dabur* FAC(P).

2 US *Higgins* FAC(T).

6 Br *Ton* coastal minesweepers/hunters.

1 LST, some LCVP, 4 LCM.

3 tankers: 1 14,000-, 1 6,000-, 1 1,600-ton.

Some 10 coast defence batteries: 12 M-1898 87mm, 16 M-3 155mm, 12 280mm guns.

(On order: 2 TR-1400, 3 TR-1700 subs, 6 *Espora* corvettes.)

Bases: Buenos Aires, Río Santiago, Puerto Belgrano, Mar del Plata, Ushuaia.

NAVAL AIR FORCE: (3,000); 54 combat ac, 8 combat hel.

3 attack sqns with 24 A-4Q, 14 *Super Etendard*.

2 MR sqns: 1 with 3 S-2A, 6 S-2E; 1 with 7 L-188E *Electra*.

2 tpt sqns with 8 *Super King Air*, 1 HS-125, 3 F-28.

1 liaison sqn with 5 *Queen Air*, 3 *Turbo-Porter*.

1 Antarctic flt with 3 PC-6, 1 C-45.

Hel incl 6 SH-3D/NR ASW, 8 *Alouette* A-103 (III), 2 WG-13 (*Sea Lynx*).

3 trg sqns with 4 EMB-326GB *Xavante*, 11 T-34C, 12 T-28, 10 MB-339A.

ASM: 20 *Exocet* AM-39.

(On order: 6 EMB-326 trg ac; 6 WG-13 hel.)

MARINES: (10,000).

2 Fleet Forces:

1 marine inf bde (2 bns, 1 amph recce gp, 1 fd arty bn, 1 hy mor, 1 ATK, 1 engr coys.)

1 marine inf bde (2 bns).

1 amph spt force:

2 special forces gps.

1 amph veh bn.

1 AA regt.

1 sigs bn.

1 service/log bn.

6 indep inf (security) coys.

12 Panhard ERC-90 *Lynx* recce; 15 LVT-3/-4, 19 LVTP-7, 15 LARC-5, 6 MOWAG *Roland* APC; 40 105mm how; 81mm, 106mm mor; 75mm, 90mm, 105mm RCL; 20 *Bantam* ATGW; 20mm, 35mm AA guns; 7 *Tigercat* SAM.

Air Force: 17,000 (10,000 conscripts); 170 combat ac, 18 armed hel; 6 more may be armed.

9 air bdes (1 more forming).

AD Command (4 bdes):

4 FGA/interceptor sqns: 2 (1 OCU) with 15 *Mirage* IIIEA, 22 IIICJ; 2 with 9 5P; 32 *Dagger* (*Nesher*).

Air Operations Command:
1 bbr sqn with 6 *Canberra* B-62, 2 T-64.
3 FGA sqns with 54 A-4P *Skyhawk*.
2 COIN sqns with 30 IA-58A *Pucará*.
1 COIN hel sqn with 12 Hughes 500M (369HM),
6 UH-1H.
1 SAR hel sqn with 5 *Lama*.
5 tpt sqns with 4 Boeing 707, 8 C-130E/H, 1
KC-130H, 3 *Learjet* 35A, 4 C-47, 13 F-27, 5
F-28, 5 DHC-6, 14 IA-50 *Guaraní* II, 2 *Merlin*
IVA ac; 2 S-58T (VIP) hel.
1 Antarctic sqn with 1 DHC-6, 1 LC-47 ac; 2
S-61R/NR, 4 UH-19, 2 CH-47C (SAR); 15 Bell
(3 UH-1D, 4 47G, 8 212) hel.
1 comms sqn with 13 *Shrike Commander*.
Air Training Command:
24 *Paris*, 12 EMB-326GB *Xavante*, 48 T-34C,
35 Cessna 182.
AAM: R-530.
ASM: AS-11/-12; *Pescador* ('*Kingfisher*').
(On order: 100 IA-58 *Pucará* COIN; 2 C-130, 16
Turbo-Commander tpt; 100 IA-63, 10
MB-339 trg ac, 3 AS-332B *Super Puma* hel.)

Para-Military Forces: (Ministry of Defence):
21,000. Gendarmerie 12,000: *Shorland* armd
cars, 40 M-113 APC, 22 lt ac, 3 hel, mainly for
frontier duties. Argentine Naval Prefecture
(coastguard) 9,000: 20 large (9 *Halcón* with 1
hel; 1 more on order), 19 coastal patrol
craft; 5 SC-7 *Skyvan* ac; 6 Hughes 500M
Defender; 3 *Puma* hel.

V-100 *Commando*, 22 MOWAG *Roland*, 24
EE-11 *Urutu* APC; 26 75mm guns; 6 M-116
75mm pack, 6 M-101 105mm how; 60mm, 45
81mm mor; 36 JPz-SK *Kuerassier* 105mm SP
ATK guns; 37mm AA guns.

Navy: 3,600 (incl 550 marines).
1 lt cargo ship.
40 lake and river patrol craft (35⟨).
1 Cessna U-206G, 2 AT-6G ac.
1 marine bn.

Bases: Tiquina, Puerto Busch, Riberalta, Trinidad, Guayaramerín.

Air Force: 4,000; 22 combat ac; 9 armed hel.
1 fighter/trg sqn with 12 T-33A/N, 5 F-86F.
2 COIN sqns with 5 AT-6G.
1 Special Operations Group with 9 Hughes 500
armed hel.
1 SAR hel sqn with 5 SA-315B *Gavião* (*Lama*).
1 tpt sqn: 1 *Electra*, 1 L-100-30, 1 C-130H, 1
Sabreliner, 2 *Learjet*, 2 *Arava*, 2 CV-440, 3
CV-580, 8 C-47, 3 *King Air*, 6 F-27, 2 U-3A.
Utility ac incl 1 *Turbo-Porter*, 27 Cessna (3
172K, 3 *Turbo-Centurion*, 8 185/U-17A, 9
U-206C/G, 2 414, 2 421); 5 UH-1H, 2 Bell
212 hel.
Trg ac incl: 4 T-6G, 3 T-41D, 18 T-23 *Uirapuru*, 4 SF-260M, 25 PC-7 *Turbo-Trainer*.
1 para bn.
1 airbase defence regt (Bofors L/40mm AA guns).

BOLIVIA

Population: 6,250,000.
Military service: 12 months, selective.
Total armed forces: 27,600.
Est GDP 1981: pB 162.81 bn ($6.643 bn). 1982:
398.458 bn ($6.214 bn).
Def budget 1981: pB 4.441 bn ($181.191 m).
1982: 6.006 bn ($93.668 m).
GDP growth: −9.2% (1982).
Inflation: 300% (1982), 330% (1983).
Debt: $3.6 bn (1983).
　$1 = pesos 24.510 (1981), 64.12 (1982).

Army: 20,000.
6 Military Regions: 4 corps (1 forming 1984), 10
div HQ.
6 cav regts (horsed).
2 mech inf regts (each 2 bns).
13 inf regts (incl 1 Presidential Guard, 2 mountain), each with 2 bns.
3 arty regts.
2 ranger regts.
1 para regt.
2 armd bns.
6 engr bns.
24 EE-9 *Cascavel* armd cars; 18 M-113, 15

BRAZIL

Population: 131,000,000.
Military service: 12 months.
Total armed forces: 274,000 (134,200 con-
scripts).
Est GDP 1982: Cr$ 45,000 bn ($250.682 bn).
1983: 131,000 bn ($227.021 bn).
Est def exp 1981: Cr$ 145.0 bn ($1.557 bn).
1982: 330.0 bn ($1.838 bn).
GDP growth: 1.4% (1982), −3.3% (1983).
Inflation: 100% (1982), 211% (1983).
Debt: $94 bn (1983).
　$1 = cruzeiros 93.12 (1981), 179.51 (1982),
577.04 (1983).

Army: 183,000 (132,000 conscripts) (to be
282,000).
4 army, 2 regional comd, 12 military region, 8
div HQ.
1 armd cav bde.
3 armd inf bdes.
4 mech cav bdes.
12 motor inf bdes.
1 AB bde.
1 AA arty bde.
10 fd arty regts (2 hy, 1 AB).

8 coast arty gps.

10 AA arty gps (5 hy).

2 special forces bdes (6 'jungle' inf bns).

2 engr gps.

AFV: 75 M-4 MBT; some 250 M-3A1, 24 X-1A2, 315 M-41B lt tks; 196 EE-9 *Cascavel*, 29 M-8 armd cars; 170 EE-11 *Urutu*, 22 M-59, some 600 M-113 APC.

Arty: 500 M-116 75mm pack, 413 105mm, 150 M-114 155mm towed, some 60 M-7/-108 105mm SP how; some 240 57mm to 12-in. (304.8mm) coast arty guns incl some 100 Mk 5 6-in. (152mm); 81mm, 4.2-in. (107mm), 120mm mor; SS-06 108mm,SS-40 180mm, SS-60 300mm incl SP MRL.

ATK: 240 M-18A1 57mm, M-20 75mm, 106mm RCL; 3.5-in. (89mm) RL; 300 *Cobra* ATGW.

AD: 30 35mm, 30 40mm, some 180 57mm, M-2A1 90mm AA guns; 4 *Roland* II SAM.

(On order: 50 X-1A2 lt tks; SS-60 (FGT-X40) 300mm MRL, *TOW* ATGW.)

RESERVES: Trained first-line 1,115,000: 400,000 subject to immediate recall. Second-line (limited trg) 225,000; state military police schools, centres.

Navy: 46,000 incl naval air force, marines (2,200 conscripts).

7 subs: 3 *Oberon*, 4 US *Guppy* II/III.

1 Br *Colossus* ASW carrier (converting to attack) (capacity 7–8 S-2E ASW ac; 12–13 SH-3D *Sea King* hel).

10 US destroyers: 5 *Sumner* (1 with 1 × 4 *Seacat* SAM, 4 with 1 *Wasp* hel); 2 *Gearing* with *ASROC* ASW, 1 *Wasp* hel; 3 *Fletcher*.

6 *Niteroi* frigates with 2 × 3 *Seacat* SAM, 1 *Lynx* hel: 2 GP with 2 × 2 *Exocet* SSM, 4 ASW with *Ikara*.

9 *Imperial Marinheiro* patrol vessels.

5 river patrol ships: 2 *Pedro Teixeira*, 3 *Roraima*.

1 river monitor with 1 × 3-in. (76mm), 2 × 40mm, 2 × 47mm, 6 × 20mm guns.

6 *Piratini* large patrol craft.

6 *Aratu* (*Schütze*-type) coastal minesweepers.

2 US LST, 3 LCM, 4 US 1610 LCU.

28 river tpts.

1 fleet spt tanker; 1 repair, 1 spt ships; 5 ocean, 18 harbour tugs; 1 riverine oiler, 18 tpts.

Bases: Rio de Janeiro, Aratu (Salvador, Bahía), Val-de-Caes (Belem), Natal, Ladario (Mato Grosso province), Rio Negro (Amazonas province).

NAVAL AIR FORCE: (700); 17 combat hel.

2 ASW hel sqns with 4 SH-3D, 4 ASH-3H *Sea King*, 9 WG-13 *Sea Lynx*.

1 utility hel sqn with 8 *Wasp* HAS-1, 9 AS-350B *Esquilo* (*Ecureuil*).

1 hel trg sqn with 13 Bell *Jetranger* II.

MARINES: (13,500).

Fleet Force: 1 amph div (1 comd, 3 inf, 1 service bns, 1 arty gp).

1 Reinforcement Comd: 5 bns incl 1 engr, 1 special operations, supply.

Internal Security Force: 6 Regional, 1 Special Operations Gps.

5 EE-9 *Cascavel* armd cars; 30 M-113, 5 EE-11 *Urutu* APC; 8 M-102 105mm how; SS-06 108mm MRL.

(On order: 2 Type 209 subs, 4 corvettes, 1 trg ship; 12 *Exocet* SSM; 60 *Tigerfish* torpedoes; 12 LVTP-7A1 APC).

Air Force: 45,000; 215 combat ac.

Air Defence Command: (14 combat ac)

1 interceptor gp (2 sqns) with 13 F-103E (*Mirage* IIIEBR), 1 F-103D (DBR).

Tactical Command: 8 gps (155 combat ac).

2 FGA sqns with 32 F-5E, 4 F-5B.

5 COIN sqns with 100 AT-26 *Xavante*.

2 recce sqns with 8 RC-95, 11 RT-26 *Xavante*.

4 liaison sqns: 27 Neiva C/U/L-42, 2 EMB-810C (U-7A) *Seneca* ac, 23 UH-1H hel.

1 hel sqn with 2 UH-1H, 6 SA-330 *Puma*.

Maritime Command: 4 gps (46 combat ac).

1 ASW sqn with 8 S-2E; 7 S-2A (trg).

3 MR/SAR sqns with 5 RC-130E, 14 EMB-110, 12 P-95 (EMB-111).

Transport Comd: 6 gps (12 sqns), 6 indep sqns:

2 sqns with 9 C-130E/H, 1 with 2 KC-130H, 4 with 19 C-115 (DHC-5); 2 Boeing 737, 23 EMB-810C, 9 HS-125, 12 C-91 (HS-748), 90 EMB-110 *Bandeirante* (50 C-95, 20 C-95A, 20 -B), 6 EMB-121 (VU-9) *Xingu*, 6 *Seneca* ac.

Training Command:

50 T-23 *Uirapuru* (being replaced by 100 YT-17), 80 T-25 *Universal* (being replaced), some 38 T-27, 90 AT-26, some EMB-110, 5 Neiva U-42 ac; 16 Bell 47 (H-13J), 8 UH-1D hel.

1 calibration unit: 2 HS-125 (EC-93, U-93), 2 C-95A, 4 EC-95.

AAM: R-530, *Piranha* (MAA-1).

(On order: 88 AM-X, 12 EMB-120 *Brasilia* tpt, 100 YT-17 (A-123) *Tangará*, some 80 T-27 *Tucano* (EMB-312) trg ac; *Piranha* AAM.)

Para-Military Forces: Some 185,000 Public Security Forces in state, military police orgs (State Militias) under Army control and considered an Army Reserve.

CHILE

Population: 12,000,000.

Military service: 2 years (Army and Navy only).

Total armed forces: 96,000 (33,000 conscripts).

GDP 1981: pC 1,288.9 bn ($33.049 bn). 1982: 1,228.7 bn ($24.135 bn).
Est def exp 1980: pC 80.0 bn ($2.051 bn). 1981: 82.0 bn ($2.103 bn).
GDP growth: −14% (1982), −1% (1983).
Inflation: 10% (1982), 27.0% (1983).
Debt: $11 bn (1982).
  $1 = pesos 39.00 (1980/1), 50.909 (1982).

Army: 53,000 (30,000 conscripts).
6 div HQ.
2 armd regts.
8 cav regts (3 mech, 5 horsed).
24 inf regts (14 with 2 bns, 10 mountain with 1 to 4 bns each).
10 arty bns (6 fd, 3 mountain, 1 AA).
7 engr bns.
1 hel-borne ranger unit.
Army Aviation:
  1 composite gp with 1 tac bn and spt unit.
150 M-4A3, 21 AMX-30 MBT; 15 M-3, 50 M-41 lt tks; 200 EE-9 *Cascavel* armd cars; 60 M-113, 150 Cardoen/MOWAG *Piranha*, 250 EE-11 *Urutu*, APC; 124 105mm how; 12 Mk F3 155mm SP how; M-1 81mm, 120mm mor; M-18 57mm, 106mm RCL; *Milan/Mamba* ATGW; HS-639/665 20mm, 35mm AA guns.
Avn: 6 C-212A 10 tpts, 1 *Citation*, 8 *Dakota* 236, 4 *Navajo*, 18 R-172 *Hawk* XP trg ac; 12 SA-330FL *Puma*, 1 AS-332 *Super Puma*, 10 SA-315B *Lama*, 2 AB-206B hel.
(On order: 50 *Piranha, Orca, Alacrán*, APC).

RESERVES: 240,000.

Navy: 28,000 (3,000 conscripts), incl naval air and marines.
1 Type 209, 2 *Oberon* subs.
2 cruisers: 1 Br *County* with 4 *Exocet* MM-38 SSM, 1 × 2 *Seaslug*, 2 × 2 *Seacat* SAM, 1 hel; 1 Swed *Gota Lejon*.
4 destroyers: 2 *Almirante* with 4 *Exocet* MM-38, 2 × 4 *Seacat*, 2 US *Sumner* with 1 hel.
2 *Leander* frigates with 4 *Exocet* MM-38 SSM, 1 × 4 *Seacat* SAM, 1 hel.
2 *Saar*-IV FAC(G) with 6 *Gabriel* SSM.
4 Lürssen-type FAC(T).
4 US large patrol craft: 2 *Sotoyomo*, 1 *Cherokee*, 1 PC-1638.
22 coastal patrol craft, 20(.
1 511-1152 LST, 2 *Batral* lt, 2 amph tpts, 3 LSM, 1 LCU.
3 tankers, 66 spt ships/tpts.
(On order: 1 Type 209 subs, 1 GW destroyer (1984), 1 *Reshef* FAC).

Bases: Talcahuano, Valparaiso, Puerto Montt, Punta Arenas, Puerto Williams, Iquique, Arica.

NAVAL AIR FORCE: (500); 5 combat ac.
1 MR sqn with 5 EMB-111N.

1 utility sqn with 3 EMB-110N *Bandeirante*, 3 C-212A.
1 hel sqn with 9 *Alouette* III, 4 SH-57 (Bell 206A).
1 trg sqn with 10 Pilatus PC-7.

MARINES: (5,000).
4 bn gps, each with 1 inf bn+, 1 coast, 1 AA arty btys.
MOWAG *Roland*, LVTP-5 APC; 16 105mm, 35 155mm how; 16 GPFM-3 155mm coast guns; 50 60mm, 50 81mm mor; 20 37mm AA guns; *Crotale* SAM.

Air Force: 15,000; 102 combat ac.
4 Air Bdes.
4 combat wings and 2 gps; each wing also has a comms flt with ac/hel.
2 FGA sqns with 31 *Hunter* F-71, 15 F-5E, 3 F-5F.
2 COIN sqns with 29 A-37B.
1 ftr/recce sqn with 11 *Mirage* 50FC, 9 C-101 *Aviojet*.
2 photo recce sqns with 2 *Canberra* PR-9, 2 *Learjet* 35-A.
1 tpt sqn with 1 Boeing 727-22C, 1 707-351C, 2 C-130H, 5 DC-6B, 9 Beech 99A, 1 *King Air* 90 ac; 2 SA-315B *Lama*, 1 Bell 47 hel.
Utility/liaison flts incl 17 DHC-6, 3 *Twin Bonanza* ac, 3 S-55T, 4 *Lama* hel.
1 trg wing, 3 flying schools: 4 *Hunter* T-72, 30 T-34A, 25 T-37B/C, 8 T-41A, 4 Piper T-35 *Pillan*, 10 Cessna 180, 10 Piper *Dakota* 236 ac; 6 UH-1H, 3 Bell 212 hel.
AAM: AIM-9L *Sidewinder, Shafrir*.
ASM: AGM-65B *Maverick*, AS-11/-12.
1 AA arty regt of 5 gps with GAI-CO1 twin 20mm, K-63 twin 35mm, 24 M-1A1 37mm AA guns; *Blowpipe*, 12 *Cactus* (*Crotale*) SAM, 4 radar sqns.
(On order: 3 *Mirage* 50 ftr, 13 C-101BB, 2 EMB-120 tpt, *Dakota, Pillan* ac; 3 *Super Puma* hel.)

Para-Military Forces: 27,000 *Carabineros*.

COLOMBIA

Population: 28,200,000.
Military service: 2 years.
Total armed forces: 69,700 (28,500 conscripts).
GDP 1981: pC 2,005 bn ($36.795 bn), 1982: 2,458.8 bn ($38.358 bn).
Def exp 1983: pC 35.940 bn ($455.762 m). Est budget 1984: pC 31.240 bn ($320.568 m).
GDP growth: −0.5 (1981), 1.3% (1982).
Inflation: 25% (1982), 17% (1983).
Debt: $10.6 bn (1982).
  $1 = pesos 54.491 (1981), 64.102 (1982), 78.857 (1983), 97.452 (mid-1984).

Army: 57,000 (28,500 conscripts).
10 inf bdes ('Regional Bdes'): 6 with 3 inf, 1 arty,
1 engr gp, 1 mech or horsed cav gp; 4 with 2
inf bns only.
1 trg bde, incl Presidential Guard (mech bn).
1 indep mech gp.
1 Ranger, 1 para, 1 AA bns.
12 M-3A1 lt tks; 41 M-8, 200 EE-9 *Cascavel*
armd cars; 15 EE-11 *Urutu*, 45 M-3A2 half-
track, M-113A1 APC; 48 M-101 105mm how;
125 81mm, 148 107mm mor; 30 M-1A1
40mm AA guns.

RESERVES: 70,000.

Navy: 8,500 (incl 2,500 marines).
2 Type 209 subs.
2 SX-506 midget subs (in reserve).
2 destroyers: 1 *Halland*, 1 US *Sumner*.
4 frigates: 3 FS-1500 with 8 *Exocet* MM-40 SSM,
1 US *Courtney*.
3 US *Cherokee* large patrol craft.
6 gunboats: 2 *Asheville*, 3 *Arauca*, 1 *Barran-
quilla*.
2 coastal, 8 river patrol craft.
2 marine bns; 3 indep coys, cdo units.
(On order: 1 FV-1500 corvette.)

NAVAL AIR: forming late 1984 with 1 ac sqn, 4
hel flts.

Bases: Cartagena, Buenaventura (2 more are
planned).

Air Force: 4,200; 46 combat ac, 17 armed hel.
Combat Command:
2 FGA sqns: 9 *Mirage* 5COA, 2 5COR, 2
5COD; 12 *Kfir* C-2.
1 COIN sqn with 12 AT-33A and 9 A-37D.
1 recce hel sqn: 10 Hughes 500C (OH-6A), 7
Hughes 300C.
Military Air Transport Command:
Tpt sqn: 1 C-130E, 4 C-54, 20 C-47, 3
HS-748, 3 *Arava*, 2 F-28, 10 DHC-2, 1 *Aero
Commander* 560A, 12 PC-6 *Turbo-Porter*.
Hel sqn: 19 UH-1B/H, 13 Bell 205A1, 20
SA-315B *Lama*.
Training and Support Command:
11 T-37C, 27 T-41D, 3 RT-33, 12 T-33A, 25
T-34A/B, 10 A-37B ac; 8 Bell 47 (OH-13), 2
Hughes 300C hel.
Skyguard/Sparrow AD system.
AAM: R-530.
(On order: 2 F-27 tpt, 14 EMB-326 *Xavante* trg
ac; 12 UH-1H, 9 Hughes 300C hel; AIM/
RIM-7F *Sparrow* AAM; ASM.)

Forces Abroad: Egypt (Sinai MFO) 500.

Para-Military Forces: National Police 50,000; 1
HS-748 ac, 30 hel; Coastguard: 9 craft⟨.

CUBA

Population: 10,000,000.
Military service: 3 years.
Total armed forces: 153,000 (some 94,500 con-
scripts).
Est GNP 1981: pC 12.085 bn ($16.525 bn).*
1982: 12.251 bn ($15.488 bn).*
Est def exp 1982: pC 990 m ($1.252 bn).†
GNP growth: 2.5% (1982), 5% (1983).
Est FMA: $300 m (1981), 300 m (1982).
Debt: $3.5 bn (1983).
$1 = pesos 0.7313 (1981), 0.7910 (1982).

Army: 125,000 (incl proportion of Ready
Reserve) (some 75,000 conscripts).
3 Regional Commands, 2 Army, 4 Corps HQ.
3 armd divs (2 cadre).
3 mech divs.
13 inf divs (8 cadre, others at about 60%).
1 AB assault bde; Special Force (1,000) 2 bns.
8 indep inf regts.
1 arty div (3 fd arty bdes).
AFV: 350 T-34, 350 T-54/-55, some 150 T-62
MBT; 40 PT-76 lt tks; some 150 BRDM-1/-2
armd cars; some 100 BMP MICV; 400
BTR-40/-60/-152 APC.
Arty: 1,200 guns/how incl: M-1942 76mm,
85mm, 100 SU-100 SP, 122mm, M-46
130mm, D-1, D-2, ML-20 152mm; BM-21
122mm, BM-14 140mm, BM-24 240mm MRL;
65 *FROG*-4/-7 SSM; M-43 120mm mor;
additionally, some 60 JS-2 hy, T-34/85 tks,
SU-100 SP guns may be static defence arty.
ATK: M-1943 57mm guns; 57mm RCL; *Sagger*,
Snapper ATGW.
AD: At least 26 regts: 1,500 AA guns incl: ZU-23,
37mm, 57mm, 85mm, 100mm towed,
ZSU-23-4 23mm, 30mm M-53 (twin)/BTR-
60P, ZSU-57 57mm SP; SA-7/-9 SAM.

RESERVES: Ready Reserves 190,000 (serve 45
days per year); to fill out Regular and 18
Reserve inf divs.

Navy: 12,000 (8,500 conscripts).
4 Sov subs: 3 *F*-class; 1 *W*-class (non-operational; trg).
2 Sov *Koni* frigates.
11 Sov large patrol craft: 9 SO-1, 2 *Kronshtadt*.
26 Sov FAC(G) with *Styx* SSM: 5 *Osa*-I, 13 *Osa*-II,
8 *Komar*⟨.
26 Sov FAC(T): 8 *Turya*, 6 P-6⟨, 12 P-4⟨.
22 Sov *Zhuk* FAC(P)⟨; 12 coastal patrol craft⟨.
12 Sov minesweepers: 2 *Sonya*, 10 *Yevgenya*⟨.
2 *Polnocny* LSM, 7 T-4 LCM.

NAVAL INFANTRY: (some 350); 1 amph assault bn.

---

* The Cuban economy is heavily subsidized through
Soviet aid (est. $3.0–4.5 p.a.). GNP in 1974 pesos.
† Official budget pC 228.40 m ($312.320 m).

COASTAL DEFENCE:
M-1931/37 122mm, M-1937 152mm, SM-4-1 130mm guns; 50 *Samlet* SSM.

Bases: Cienfuegos, Cabañas, Havana, Mariel, Punta Ballenatos, Banes.

Air Force: 16,000, incl air defence forces (11,000 conscripts); 250 combat ac, some 38 armed hel.
4 FGA sqns: 1 with 15 MiG-17; 3 with 36 MiG-23BN *Flogger* F.
16 interceptor sqns: 2 with 30 MiG-21F; 3 with 34 -21PFM; 2 with 20 -21PFMA; 8 with 100 -21bis; 1 with 15 MiG-23 *Flogger* E.
4 tpt sqns: 16 Il-14, 35 An-2, 3 An-24, 22 An-26, 4 Yak-40.
8 hel sqns: 60 Mi-4, 40 Mi-8 (perhaps 20 armd), 18 Mi-24 *Hind* D.
Trainers incl 2 MiG-23U, 10 MiG-21U, some An-2, 30 Zlin 326, some L-39.
AAM: AA-1 *Alkali*, AA-2 *Atoll*, AA-8 *Aphid*.
30 SAM bns: 28 with 60 SA-2, 140 SA-3; 2 with 12 SA-6.
The Civil Airline has 9 Il-62, some 4 Tu-154, which are used as tp tpts.

Forces Abroad: Angola 19,000; Congo 750; Ethiopia 3,000; Mozambique 750; Other Africa 500; Iraq 2,000; Libya 3,000; S. Yemen 300; Nicaragua 3,000; Afghanistan ?500.

Para-Military Forces: Ministry of Interior: State Security 15,000; Frontier Guards 3,500; some 22 craft. Ministry of Defence: Youth Labour Army 100,000; Civil Defence Force: 100,000; Territorial Militia 530,000.

DOMINICAN REPUBLIC

Population: 6,000,000.
Military service: voluntary.
Total armed forces: 23,000.
GDP 1982: $RD 7.877 bn ($US 7.877 bn). Est 1983: 8.735 bn ($US 8.735 bn).
Def exp 1982: $RD 127.9 m ($US 127.9 m). 1983: 129.3 m ($US 129.3 m).
GDP growth: 1.6% (1982).
Inflation: 7.6% (1982), 8% (1983).
Debt: $2.1 bn (1982).
   $1 = peso 1.00 (1982/3).

Army: 14,000.
3 Defence Zones.
3 inf bdes (10 bns).
1 fd arty regt (2 bns).
1 mixed armd bn.
1 Presidential Guard (mounted rifle) bn.
1 engr bn.
13 AMX lt tks; 20 AML armd cars; 8 V-150

Commando, 25 M-3A1 half-track APC; 20 M-101 105mm how; 24 120mm mor.

Navy: 4,500, incl naval inf.
1 Cdn *River* frigate (trg).
5 US corvettes: 2 *Admirable* (ex-minesweepers), 3 *Cohoes*.
5 large patrol craft (3 US *Argo*, in reserve).
11 coastal patrol craft (8⟨).
1 LSM, 2 LCU.
1 naval inf bn; 1 cdo unit.

Bases: Santo Domingo, Bani, Haina.

Air Force: 4,500; 19 combat ac.
1 ftr sqn with 8 F-51D *Mustang* (to retire), 11 T-34B *Mentor*.
1 tpt sqn with 5 C-47, 1 DHC-2, 1 *Aero Commander*.
1 hel sqn with 2 Bell 205A-1, 2 UH-12E, 6 OH-6A, 3 *Alouette* II/III, 2 H-19, 2 UH-1.
1 Presidential tpt flt with 1 SA-365 *Dauphin* 2.
Trg: 12 T-6G, 2 AT-11, 2 T-33A, 3 Cessna 170, 4 T-41D, T-34.
1 para gp.
1 AA arty bn: 20 40mm AA guns.

Para-Military Forces: Gendarmerie 10,000.

ECUADOR

Population: 9,700,000.
Military service: 2 years, selective.
Total armed forces: 39,300.
GDP 1982: ES 408.9 bn ($13.618 bn). Est 1983: 573.5 bn ($13.0 bn).
Est def exp 1982: ES 6.898 bn ($229.734 m). 1983: 7.898 bn ($179.032 m).
GNP growth: 1.4% (1982).
Inflation: 25% (1982), 50% (1983).
Debt: $8.0 bn (1983).
   $1 = sucres 30.026 (1982), 44.115 (1983).

Army: 30,000.
4 Military zones.
6 div HQ.
2 armd bdes   ⎫
9 inf bdes (3 'jungle') ⎬ 23 bns.
1 Presidential Guard regt.
1 special forces (AB) bde of 4 units.
3 arty gps.
3 AA bns (12 btys).
2 engr bns.
45 M-3, 150 AMX-13 lt tks; 27 AML-60, 18 AML-90 armd cars; 20 M-113, 55 AMX-VCI APC; M-56 pack, 18 M-101 105mm towed, 10 Mk F3 155mm SP how; 12 160mm mor; 28 M-167 20mm, 30 40mm AA guns; 240 *Blowpipe* SAM.
Avn: 3 DHC-5D, 3 *Turbo-Porter*, 1 *Learjet*,

2 *King Air*, 3 *Arava*, 6 Cessna (2 T-41D, 3 172G, 1 185D) tpt ac; 5 *Puma*, 3 *Super Puma*, 12 *Gazelle*, 1 *Lama*, 1 *Alouette* III hel.

Navy: 4,500 incl some 1,000 marines.
2 Type 209 submarines.
2 US destroyers: 1 *Gearing*, 1 *Lawrence*.
6 *Esmeraldas* corvettes with 4 *Exocet* MM-40 SSM, 1 × 4 *Albatros/Aspide* SAM, 1 AB-212 hel.
6 FAC(G): 3 *Quito* (Lürssen) with 4 *Otomat* SSM, 3 *Manta* with 4 *Gabriel* 2.
7 coastal patrol craft⟨.
4 US LSM.
1 *Super King Air*, 3 T-34C, 1 *Arava*, 1 Cessna 320E ac; 2 *Alouette* III hel.
3 marine bns, 2 on garrison duties; 1 cdo.

Bases: Guayaquil, San Lorenzo, Galápagos Islands.

Air Force: 4,800; 65 combat ac.
4 Wings.
1 lt bbr sqn with 3 *Canberra* B-6.
2 interceptor sqns: 1 with 15 *Mirage* F-1JE, 2 F-1JB; 1 with 10 F-5E, 2 -5F.
2 FGA sqns: 9 *Jaguar* (7 S, 2 B), 12 *Kfir* C-2.
1 COIN sqn with 6 A-37B.
1 COIN/trg sqn: 6 BAC-167 *Strikemaster* Mk 89.
Military Air Transport Gp (incl civil/military airline): 1 Boeing 727-2T3, 4 707, 3 720, 4 *Electra*, 1 C-130H, 1 L-100-30, 2 DC-6B, 2 HS-748, 5 *Arava*.
Liaison/SAR flts: 1 *Navajo* ac; 2 SA-330C *Puma*, 6 SA-316 *Alouette* III, 2 Bell UH-1D hel.
Training ac incl 20 T-34C, 10 T-41, Cessna A-150, T-33A.
AAM: R-550 *Magic*.
1 para sqn.

Para-Military Forces: coastguard (500): 2 PGM-71, 14 small patrol craft.

EL SALVADOR

Population: 5,300,000.
Military service: conscription, selective, 2 years.
Total armed forces: 41,650 (being increased).
GDP 1981: C 8.647 bn ($3.459 bn). 1982: 8.915 bn ($3.566 bn).
Est def exp* 1982: C 347.5 m ($139.0 m). 1983: 393.75 m ($157.50 m).
GDP growth: −9.5% (1981), −6.0% (1982).
Inflation: 12% (1981), 14% (1982).
Est FMA: $82 m (1982), $126 m (1983), $200 m (1984).
 $1 = colones 2.50 (1981/3).

Army: 39,000.
3 Military zones.

4 inf bdes (9 bns).
1 mech cav regt.
1 arty bde (2 bns).
14 indep inf bns.
1 engr bn.
1 AA arty bn ⎫
1 para bn ⎬ under Air Force control.
3 special forces bns.
12 AMX-13 lt tks; 18 AML-90 armd cars; 10 M-113, 20 UR-416 APC; 30 M-101, 6 Yug M-56 105mm, 6 M-114 155mm how; 81mm, 8 UB-M52 120mm mor; M-18 57mm, M-20 75mm RCL; *LAW* RL; 20mm, L/70 40mm AA guns.

RESERVES: 12 inf regts (48 bns).

Navy: 300.
6 patrol boats: 3 31-metre Camcraft, 1 20-metre Sewart, 2 US river⟨.

Air Force: 2,350 (incl AD and security gp); 59 combat ac, 9 armed hel.
2 FGA sqns with 11 *Ouragan*, 18 *Super Mystère* B-2.
1 lt COIN sqn with 7 *Magister*, 17 A-37.
1 recce unit with 6 O-2.
1 tpt sqn with 5 C-47, 2 DC-6B, 5 *Arava*, 2 C-123K.
2 hel sqns: 1 COIN with 9 UH-1H; 1 SAR/liaison with 3 SA-315B *Lama*, 2 *Alouette* III, 1 FH-1100.
Trg: 3 T-34, 8 T-6, 6 T-41, 9 Cessna (7 180, 1 182, 1 185), 3 CM-170 *Magister*.
1 para bn.
1 AA arty bn with Yug M-55 20mm (some SP) guns.
(On order: 9 UH-1H hel.)

Para-Military Forces: National Guard 2,500; National Police 4,500; Treasury Police 2,500; *Orden* (territorial civil defence force) perhaps 70,000 (2,000 effective).

Opposition: perhaps 10,000. *Dirección Revolucionaria Unificada* (DRU) – political wing *Frente Democrático Revolucionaria* (FDR), military wing *Frente Farabundo Marti para la Liberación Nacional* (FMLN): 8,000 plus 6,000 'reserves' claimed – plus 4 smaller gps.

GUATEMALA

Population: 8,200,000.
Military service: conscription; 24–30 months.
Total armed forces: 40,000 (being increased).
GDP 1982: q 8.607 bn ($8.607 bn). 1983: 8.724 bn ($8.724 bn).

---

* Including 'public security sector' budget.

Est def exp 1982: q 92.0 m ($92.0 m)*.
GDP growth: –0.5% (1982), –3.5% (1983).
Debt: $1.6 bn (1982).
  $1 = quetzal 1.00 (1982/3).

Army: 38,000.
4 Regional bde HQ:
  1 armd bn.
  17 inf bns.
  4 fd arty gps (12 btys).
  1 AA arty gp (2 btys).
  1 engr bn.
  4 recce sqns.
  1 Presidential Guard bde.
  1 Special Forces bde (2 bns).
8 AMX-13, 10 M-41A3, 7 M-3A1 lt tks; 8 M-8,
  10 RBY-1, 6 M-3A1 armd cars; 15 M-113, 7
  V-150 *Commando* APC; 12 M-116 75mm
  pack, 36 M-101 105mm how; M-1 81mm, 12
  M-30 4.2-in. (107mm), 12 EC1A 120mm mor;
  12 M-1A1 40mm AA guns.

Navy: 1,000 incl 650 marines (4 coys).†
15 coastal patrol craft.
1 LCM; 2 small tp carriers.
8 small craft; some armed.
12 *Zodiac*-type assault boats (marines).

Bases: Santo Tomás de Castillas, Sipacate.

Air Force: 1,00; 16 combat ac, 4 armed hel.†
1 COIN sqn with 10 A-37B, 6 PC-7 *Turbo-
Trainer*.
1 tpt sqn with 1 DC-6B, 10 C-47, 8 *Arava*.
1 comms sqn with 17 Cessna: 4 170A/B, 8 172K,
  2 180, 2 U-206C, 1 310.
1 hel sqn with 25 Bell (perhaps 6 operational): 9
  UH-1D (4 armed), 1 212, 6 412, 5 206B, 4
  206L-1.
1 Presidential flt with 1 *Super King Air* 200.
Trg: 5 PC-7 *Turbo-Trainer*, 5 T-33A, 3 T-37C,
  12 T-41.

Para-Military Forces: National Police 9,500;
  Treasury Police 2,100; Territorial Militia
  (500,000) formed; 70,000 may be armed. 10
  armed lt ac.

HONDURAS

Population: 4,250,000.
Military service: conscription; 18–24 months.
Total armed forces: 17,200 (12,250 conscripts).
GDP 1982: L 5.626 bn ($2.813 bn). 1983: 5.889
  bn ($2.944 bn)
Est def exp 1981: L 90.3 m ($45.15 m). 1982:
  120.0 m ($60.0 m).
Est FMA: $ 32.0 m (1982), $50.0 m (1983).
Debt: $1.9 bn (1982).
  $1 = lempiras 2.00 (1981/2).

Army: 15,500 (12,000 conscripts).
1 inf bde (1 tk, 3 inf bns).
1 Presidential Guard (2 inf bns).
3 inf bns (one mech).
3 arty bns.
1 engr bn.
1 special forces bn.
16 *Scorpion* lt tks; 12 RBY Mk 1 recce; M-116
  75mm pack, 24 M-102 105mm how; M-1
  81mm, 30 120mm mor; 106mm RCL.

Navy: 500 (50 conscripts).
9 Swiftships patrol craft: 1 106-ft, 3 105-ft fast, 5
  65-ft coastal(.

Bases: Puerto Cortés, Amapala.

Air Force: 1,200 (200 conscripts); 30 combat
  aircraft.
1 FGA sqn with 12 *Super Mystère* B2.
1 COIN sqn with 4 F-86E *Sabre*, 10 A-37B,
  4 *Tucano* (8 F-8E in reserve).
1 tpt sqn with 10 C-47, 2 *Arava*, 1 *Electra*, 1
  Westwind.
1 spt sqn with 1 Beech *Baron*, 4 Cessna (2 180, 2
  185), 1 PA-31 *Cheyenne* ac; 2 S-76 hel.
1 hel sqn with 10 UH-1H (on loan), 5 UH-1B.
Trg: 12 T-28A, 7 T-41A.
(On order: 4 *Tucano* COIN, 4 C-101BB *Aviojet* trg).

Para-Military Forces: Public Security Forces
  (FUSEP) (national police) 4,500.

MEXICO

Population: 78,000,000.
Military service: voluntary, with part-time con-
  script militia.
Total armed forces: 120,000 regular, 250,000
  part-time conscripts.
GDP 1981: pM 5,875 bn ($239.649 bn). 1982:
  9,256 bn ($164.108 bn).
Est def exp 1983: pM 72.0 bn ($ 599.530 m).
  Budget 1984: 94.243 bn ($581.747 m).
GDP growth: –0.2% (1982).
Inflation: 100% (1982), 104% (1983).
Debt: $90 bn (1983).
  $1 = pesos 24.515 (1981), 56.402 (1982),
  120.094 (1983), 162.0 (mid-1984).

Army: 94,500 regular, 250,000 conscripts.
1 inf div HQ.
1 mech bde gp (Presidential Guard) (3 bns).
2 inf bde gps (each of 2 inf, 1 armd recce, 1 arty
  bns).
1 AB bde (2 bns).

---

* Excl 'private-sector contributions' (some $60 m).
† National Armed Forces are combined; the Army
provides logistic support to the Navy and Air Force.

1 armd regt.
1 recce regt.
35 Zonal Garrisons incl: 28 indep cav (being mot), 3 arty regts, 64 indep inf bns.
AA, engr and support units.
40 M-3A1, 20 M-5A1 lt tks; 70 M-3A1, 15 M-8, 40 Panhard ERC-90, 15 MAC-1 armd cars; 50 HWK-11, 3 M-3 APC; 18 M-116 75mm pack, 50 M-101 105mm towed, some 40 M-8 75mm and M-7 105mm SP how; 1,600 60mm, 81mm, 4.2-in. (107mm) and 60 120mm mor; 35 M-3 37mm ATK guns; 40 12.7mm AA guns.
(On order: 27 Panhard recce veh.)

Navy: 20,000, incl naval air force and marines.
3 US destroyers: 2 *Gearing*, 1 *Fletcher*.
6 frigates: 4 US *Lawrence/Crosley*, 1 *Durango*, 1 US *Edsall* (trg ship).
6 *Halcón* (B-119) corvettes with 1 BO-105 hel.
34 US patrol ships: 18 *Auk*, 16 *Admirable* ex-minesweepers.
32 *Azteca* large patrol craft.
14 patrol craft: 5 *Polimar*, 2 *Azueta*, 1 *Guanajuato* coastal, 6 river.
2 US 511-1152, 1 *De Soto* LST; 1 repair ship.
Coastal defence: M-1902/1906 75mm, L/27 120mm guns.

Bases: Gulf: Vera Cruz, Tampico, Chetumal, Ciudad del Carmen, Yukalpetén. Pacific: Acapulco, Ensenada, La Paz, Puerto Cortés, Guaymas, Mazatlán, Manzanillo, Salina Cruz, Puerto Madero, Lázaro Cárdenas.

NAVAL AIR FORCE: (300); 8 combat ac.
1 MR sqn with 8 HU-16 *Albatross*.
1 liaison sqn with 1 *Learjet* 24D, 3 F-27, 6 *Bonanza*; 11 Cessna (3 150J, 3 180, 3 310, 2 337).
1 hel sqn with 4 *Alouette* II, 5 Bell 47G, 5 MBB BO-105.
Trg: 4 T-34B *Mentor*.

MARINES: (4,500).
3 bn HQ.
19 security coys.

(On order: 6 *Azteca* and *Olmeca*, 4 *Aguila* patrol boats.)

Air Force: 5,500 (2,000 para bde); 85 combat ac.
1 interceptor sqn with 10 F-5E, 2 F-5F.
6 COIN sqns with 55 PC-7, 10 T-33.
1 photo/recce sqn with 8 *Aero Commander* 500S.
2 SAR sqns: 1 with 8 *Arava* ac; 1 with 2 *Alouette* II/III, 1 Hiller 12E, 3 *Puma*, 17 Bell (1 47G, 5 206B, 1 212, 10 205A) hel.
1 Presidential (tpt) sqn with 9 Boeing 727, 2 737, 1 F-27, 1 *Jetstar*, 1 *Electra*, 1 HS-125-400, 5 *Sabreliner*, 1 Cessna 310R ac; 1 Bell 212, 2 *Puma* hel.

4 tpt sqns with 3 DC-6/-7, 2 C-118, 5 C-54, 12 C-47, 3 *Skyvan*, 1 *Islander*, 6 CF-27, 2 DHC-5D, 1 Cessna 182, 2 U-206E.
Trg: some 12 T-28D, 1 *Baron*, 20 Beech F-33-9, 2 *King Air*, 34 *Musketeer*, 5 PC-7 *Turbo-Trainer*, 20 CAP-10B ac.
1 para bn.

Para-Military Forces: Coastguard; 6 patrol craft. 17 ac and hel incl: 1 C-47, 2 *Baron*, 6 C-45, 2 Cessna 402, 4 *Alouette III*, 2 Bell UH-1H.

NICARAGUA

Population: 3,200,000.
Military service: conscription, 2 years.
Total armed forces: 61,800.
Est GDP 1981: $C 26.250 bn ($US 2.612 bn).
Est def exp range 1981: $C 0.945–1.7 bn ($US 94.03–169.154 m). 1982: 2.1–2.3 bn ($US 208.955–228.856 m).
GDP growth: –3% (1982), 3% (1983).
Inflation: 22% (1982).
Debt: $2.4 bn (1982).
$1 = córdobas 10.050 (1981/2).

Army: 60,000 (incl 12,000 Reserves).
7 Military Regions.
1 mot inf bde.
3 armd bns.
12 inf bns (being reorganized).
3 COIN (lt inf) bns.
1 fd arty gp (3 bns).
1 engr bn.
1 AA arty gp (9 btys; with Air Force).
3 M-4A3, 60 T-54/-55 MBT; 10 PT-76 lt tks; 20 BRDM-2, 20 *Staghound* armd cars; 80 BTR-40/-60/-152 APC; 30 M-1942 76mm guns; 12 105mm, 24 M-1938 122mm how; 12 D-30, some 12 D-20 152mm gun/how; perhaps 12 BM-21 122mm MRL; 24 120mm mor; SPG-9 73mm RCL; 48 ZIS-2 57mm AA.

Navy: 300.
1 Fr, 4 *Dabur*, 1 Sewart, 8 other coastal patrol craft; 1 LCM.

Air Force: 1,500, incl AD; 12 combat ac.
1 COIN sqn: 3 T-33A, 3 T-28D, 6 SF-260 *Warrior*.
1 tpt sqn: 1 C-212A, 1 *Arava*, 4 C-47, An-2, 1 *Falcon* 20.
1 hel sqn: 2 OH-6A, 2 *Alouette* III.
Trg: 6 L-39.
AD (Army/Air Force): 138 ZPU-4 14.5mm, ZU-23 23mm, 6 M-1939 37mm, some M-1950 57mm guns, SA-7 SAM.
(On order: MiG-21 ftrs; 100 Matra LRF-2 68mm ASM pods.)

RESERVES: (all services): 60,000, 12,000 on duty in army.

Para-Military Forces: Border Guard, some 4,000 (under Army); 6 bns. Civilian Militia, perhaps 40,000. Ministry of Interior Troops.

Opposition: some 15,000; perhaps 5,000 combat elms. Democratic Revolutionary Alliance, Nicaraguan Democratic Force.

PARAGUAY

Population: 3,600,000.
Military service: 18 months; Navy 2 years.
Total armed forces: 16,900 (10,900 conscripts).
GDP 1981: Pg 708.69 bn ($5.625 bn). 1982: 737.04 bn ($5.850 bn).
Est def exp 1981: Pg 11.04 bn ($87.619 m). 1982: 14 bn ($111.111 m).
GDP growth: −2.5% (1982).
Inflation: 7.7% (1982), 18% (1983).
    $1 = guaraníes 126.00 (1981/2).

Army: 12,500 (9,000 conscripts).
3 corps HQ.
1 cav div (bde) (2 mech cav regts, 1 mot inf bn, 1 arty bty).
6 inf divs (cadre; bn gps).
2 indep cav regts.
1 indep inf bn.
1 Presidential Escort regt.
1 spt comd with 1 arty regt, 5 engr bns, sigs; 1 log comd.
16 M-4A3 MBT; 15 M-3A1 lt tks; 12 M-8 recce, 12 M-3 APC; 25 Model 1935 75mm, 10 M-101 105mm how; 24 20mm, 12 M-1A1 40mm AA guns.

RESERVES: some 25,000; 12 inf regts on mobilization.

Navy: 2,500 (1,200 conscripts).
2 *Humaita* river defence vessels.
3 corvettes (Arg *Bouchard* minesweepers).
13 patrol craft: 1 large, 12 coastal.
1 US LSM (with hel deck: UH-12); 2 LCU.
6 spt/cargo ships.
1 marine 'regt' (bn) (400).

Coastal Defence: 8 M-1911 3-in. (76.2mm), 6 mobile 152mm guns.

NAVAL AIR FORCE (55):
Utility ac: 1 C-47, 9 Cessna (4 U-206, 4 150M, 1 210).
Trg ac: 2 T-6G.
Hel: 2 OH-13, 2 UH-12E.
(On order: 1 45-metre river patrol vessel).

Bases: Asunción/Puerto Sajonia, Bahía Negra, Puerto Presidente Stroessner.

Air Force: 1,900 (700 conscripts); 15 combat ac.
1 composite sqn:
    COIN flt: 8 EMB-326 *Xavante*, 7 AT-6G.
    Liaison flt: 7 Cessna (5 185, 1 337, 1 402) ac.
    Hel flt: 14 Bell 47G/OH-13A, 2 UH-12/SL-4.
1 tpt sqn with 2 C-54, 3 DC-6B, 1 C-131D, 23 C-47, 1 DHC-6 (VIP), 1 DHC-3, PBY-5A.
Trg: 10 Neiva T-25, 12 T-37C, 8 T-23 *Uirapuru*, 10 T-6, 5 T-41, 8 Fokker S-11, 1 MS-760A.
1 para regt (bn).
(On order: *Xavante* COIN, 4 C-212 *Aviocar*, 10 *Bandeirante* tpt, *Uirapuru* trg ac.)

Para-Military Forces: internal security forces (1,500).

PERU

Population: 19,800,000.
Military service: 2 years, selective.
Total armed forces: 135,500 (some 71,000 conscripts).
GDP 1981: S 8,416.0 bn ($19.903 bn). 1982: 13,813 bn ($19.802 bn).
Def exp 1982: S 1,134 bn ($1.626 bn).* Budget 1983: 1,345 bn ($828 m).
GDP growth: 0.7% (1982), −12% (1983).
Inflation: 80% (1982), 125% (1983).
FMA 1982: $700 m.
Debt: $11.6 bn (1982).
    $1 = soles 422.85 (1981), 697.57 (1982), 1,625 (1983).

Army: 75,000 (51,000 conscripts).
5 Military Regions.
2 armd divs (bdes).
1 cav div; 3 horsed regts.
7 inf divs (bdes, each of 4 bns, 1 arty gp).
1 para-cdo div (bde; 1 para, 2 cdo bns).
1 jungle div (bde).
2 indep fd arty gps.
1 AA gp, 1 SAM gp.
2 indep inf gps.
4 engr bns.
3 armd recce regts.
2 air sqns: 1 liaison, 1 hel.
270 T-54/-55, 25 M-4A3 MBT; 110 AMX-13 lt tks; 60 M-8/-20, 35 M-3A1, 20 Fiat 6616 scout cars; 150 M-113, 120 UR-416 APC; 10 M-56 pack, 170 M-101 105mm, 30 122mm incl SP, 30 M-1954 130mm, 36 M-114 155mm guns/how; 300 M-1951 120mm mor; 40 40mm, M-3 76mm towed, ZSU-23-4 SP AA guns; SA-3/-7 SAM.

---

* Original budget reportedly reduced by 50%. New aircraft purchase (some $700 m) financed by long-term credit. Arms purchase debt to USSR some $750 m.

Avn: 3 Helio H-391 ac; 29 Mi-8, 6 *Alouette* II hel.

(On order: 80 *TAM*, 100 SPz-12-3 MICV; 150 M-113 APC; 2 *Nomad* lt tpt ac.)

Navy: 20,500 (perhaps 7,000 conscripts) incl naval air, marines.
12 subs: 6 Type 209, 6 US (2 *Guppy* I, 4 *Abtao*).
2 Neth *De Ruyter* cruisers (1 with 3 SH-3D hel).
10 destroyers: 2 Br *Daring* with 8 *Exocet* MM-38 SSM; 8 Neth (1 *Holland*, 7 *Friesland*).
2 *Carvajal* frigates with 8 *Otomat* SSM, 1 × 8 *Albatros/Aspide* SAM, 1 AB-212 hel.
6 PR-72P FAC(G) with 4 *Exocet* MM-38 SSM.
5 river gunboats.
4 lake patrol craft⟨.
2 US LST, 2 US LSM.
2 tpts; 3 replenishment, 2 spt tankers.

NAVAL AIR FORCE: 9 combat ac; 10 combat hel.
1 ASW sqn with 7 S-2E *Tracker*.
1 ASW hel sqn with 4 SH-3D, 6 AB-212.
1 MR sqn with 2 F-27MPA.
1 utility hel sqn with 5 Bell 206B.
Tpts: 2 C-47, 1 *Aztec*.
Trg: 6 T-34A/C, 3 Beech B-200 ac; 4 Bell 47G hel.

MARINES: (2,200).
1 Marine bde (3 bns): amph veh, V-100 armd cars, 40 V-200 *Chaimite* APC, twin 20mm AA guns, 84mm RL.
3 coast defence btys: 18 155mm how.
(On order: 2 *Lupo* frigates, 2 *van Straelen* MCM, 3 EMB-111 MR ac).

Bases: Callao, San Lorenzo Island, Talara, Iquitos (river), Puno (lake), Madre de Dios (river).

Air Force: 40,000 (some 13,000 conscripts); 91 combat ac, some 16 armed hel.
2 lt bbr sqns with 15 *Canberra* B-2/B(I)-8.
6 FGA sqns: 2 with 16 *Mirage* 5P; 4 with 31 Su-22.
2 COIN sqns with 25 A-37B (MB-339 replacing).
1 COIN hel sqn with some 16 Mi-24.
1 photo recce sqn with 2 *Queen Air* A-80, 2 *Learjet* 25B.
4 tpt sqns: 7 L-100-20, 2 DC-8-62CF, 16 An-26, 8 DHC-6, 14 DHC-5, 6 *Turbo-Porter*, 5 C-47, 1 *Mystère* 20F.
2 hel sqns: 6 *Alouette* III, 6 Mi-6, 5 Mi-8, 3 BO-105, 37 Bell (9 206B, 16 212, 12 214ST).
Presidential Flt: 1 F-28 ac.
4 trg sqns: 19 T-41D, 23 T-37B/C, 10 *Queen Air* A-80, some 16 MB-339A.
ASM: AS-30, 30 *Exocet* AM-39.
(On order: 26 *Mirage* 2000P/DP (status uncertain), some 50 MB-339 COIN/trg ac; 8 UH-60A hel.)

Para-Military Forces: Guardia Civil, 26,500, with MOWAG *Roland* APC. Coastguard (700) with 23 patrol craft. Republican Guard 5,000.

URUGUAY

Population: 3,000,000.
Military service: voluntary.
Total armed forces: 29,800.
GDP 1981: $UR 120.704 bn ($US 11.155 bn). 1982: 128.403 bn ($US 9.232 bn).
Est def exp 1981: $UR 4.221 bn ($US 390.111 m). 1982: 5.445 bn ($US 391.473 m).
GDP growth: −1.3% (1981), −8.7% (1982)..
Inflation: 20% (1982), 50% (1983).
Debt: $4.3 bn (1982).
  $1 = new pesos 10.820 (1981), 13.909 (1982).

Army: 22,300.
4 div HQ (regional).
3 cav bdes (6 armd/mot, 5 horsed regts).
5 inf bdes, each with 3 bns (incl 1 armd inf, 1 AB, 1 tpt bns).
1 arty div: 5 fd, 1 AA gps.
1 horsed cav bde (2 regts + Presidential Guard).
1 engr bde: 4 combat engr, 1 road, 1 construction, 1 spt bns.
1 comms bde: 1 comms, 1 spt bns.
17 M-24, 29 M-3A1, 22 M-41A1 lt tks; 12 FN-4-RM-62, 16 EE-3 *Jararaca*, 15 EE-9 *Cascavel* scout cars; 15 M-113, 55 *Condor* APC; 12 Bofors M-1902 75mm, 40 M-101A1, 8 M-102 105mm, 8 M-114A2 155mm how; 6 M-167 *Vulcan* 20mm AA guns.
(On order: 15 *Scorpion* lt tks.)

Navy: 4,500 incl naval air, naval infantry.
3 US frigates: 1 *Dealey*, 2 *Cannon*.
1 US *Auk* corvette.
4 large (1 US *Adjutant*, 3 *Vigilante*), 4 coastal patrol craft⟨.
4 LCM.

NAVAL AIR FORCE (459): 7 combat ac.
1 ASW flt with 6 S-2A/G.
1 MR flt with 1 *Super King Air* 200T.
Tpts: 5 *Expeditor* (C-45J); 1 *Super Cub* utility.
Trg: 2 T-6G, 9 T-28, 1 T-34B, 2 T-34C ac.
Hel flt: 2 Bell 47G, 2 OH-13, 2 SH-34J, 1 Bell 222 SAR.

NAVAL INFANTRY: 1 bn (450).

Base: Montevideo.

Air Force: 3,000; some 24 combat ac.
2 COIN sqns: 1 with 5 AT-33A, 7 A-37B; 1 with 6 IA-58B *Pucará*.
1 recce/trg sqn with 6 T-6G.
1 SAR sqn: 8 U-17A ac; 2 Bell 212, 10 UH-1B/H hel.

3 tpt sqns with 5 C-212, 5 C-47, 6 *Queen Air* 80, 1 *Learjet* (VIP), 6 EMB-110B/C; 2 F-27, 2 FH-227.
Trg: 6 T-41D, 34 T-34B.
(On order: 6 *Pucará* COIN ac).

Forces Abroad: Egypt (Sinai MFO), 70.

Para-Military Forces: Metropolitan Guard: 650. Republican Guard: 520. Coastguard: 1,500; 6 coastal patrol craft⟨.

VENEZUELA

Population: 15,600,000.
Military service: 18 months, selective.
Total armed forces: 44,250 (some 10,000 conscripts).
GDP 1981: Bs 285.21 bn ($66.444 bn). 1982: 291.27 bn ($67.856 bn).
Def exp 1982: Bs 4.944 bn ($1.152 bn). Est 1983: 5.100 bn ($1.188 bn).
GNP growth: 0.6% (1982).
Inflation: 8.3% (1982), 6.0% (1983).
Debt: $32.6 bn (1982)
  $1 = bolívares 4.2925 (1981/3).

Army: 27,500.
5 div HQ (regional).
1 armd bde (3 med, 1 lt tk bns).
6 inf bdes (11 hy, 13 lt inf bns).
1 ranger bde (6 bns).
1 cav regt (horsed).
1 AB regt (2 bns).
2 indep mech bns.
6 arty gps, 1 AA arty gp.
5 engr bns.
75 AMX-30 MBT; 40 AMX-13 lt tks; 10 AML-245, 12 M-8, 60 M-706E1 armd cars; *Fuchs*/*Transportpanzer* 1, 25 AMX-VCI, 100 V-100 APC; 40 75mm pack, 50 M-56 105mm pack, 35 M-101 105mm towed, 20 Mk F3 155mm SP how; 25 160mm SP MRL; 81mm, 120mm mor; 35 M-18 76mm SP ATK guns; 106mm RCL; SS-11, AS-11 ATGW; 50 40mm towed; AML S530 twin 20mm SP AA guns.
Army Aviation:
  1 tpt sqn with 1 *Islander*, 4 IAI-202 *Arava*, 2 G-222, 1 *Queen Air*, 1 *Super King Air*, 9 Cessna (3 182, 6 206).
  1 hel sqn with 2 Bell 206, 4 UH-1H, 4 205A1.

Navy: 12,000 incl naval air and marines.
3 subs: 2 Type 209, 1 US *Guppy* II.
8 frigates: 6 *Sucre* (*Lupo*) with 8 *Otomat* SSM, 1 × 8 *Albatros*/*Aspide* SAM, 1 AB-212 hel (2 on refit); 2 *Almirante Clemente*.
6 Vosper Thornycroft FAC(G) with 2 *Otomat* SSM, 3 '121-ft'.
1 LST, 1 LSM, 12 LCVP (all US).
3 transports (one on refit).

NAVAL AIR FORCE: (3,500). 6 combat ac; 6 combat hel.
1 sqn with 6 S-E *Tracker* ac.
1 ASW hel sqn (afloat) with 6 AB-212AS.
1 SAR sqn with 3 C-212/200 MR.
1 tpt sqn: 1 DHC-7, 1 HS-748, 1 *King Air*, 2 Cessna 310/310R, 2 402 ac, 6 Bell 47J hel.

MARINES: (4,250).
3 bns.
1 arty bn.
1 AA coy.
1 amph coy.
11 LVTP-7 APC, 18 105mm how, 6 M-42 40mm twin SP AA guns.

(On order: 4 LST; 2 C-212 *Aviocar* tpts; 6 AB-212 ASW hel; 30 EE-11 *Urutu* APC).

Bases: Caracas, Puerto Cabello, La Guaira, Puerto de Hierro, Falcón.

Air Force: 4,750; 85 combat ac.
2 lt bbr/recce sqns: 20 *Canberra* (12 B-82, 5 B(I)-82, 1 PR-83, 2 T-84).
1 FGA sqn: 12 *Mirage* (5 IIIEV, 5 5V, 2 5DV).
3 interceptor/FGA sqns (1 forming): 2 with 14 (C)F-5A, 2 (C)F-5D; 1 with 16 *Mirage* (10 IIIEV, 4 5V, 2 5DV); 6 F-16 (3 -A, 3 -B).
1 COIN sqn with 15 OV-10E *Bronco*.
1 Presidential (tpt) sqn with 1 Boeing 737, 1 DC-9, 1 *Gulfstream* 2, 1 Cessna 500 ac; 2 Bell UH-1H hel.
2 tpt sqns with 5 C-130H, 5 C-47, 7 C-123A, 2 G-222.
2 utility/liaison/recce sqns with 3 *King Air*, 9 *Queen Air*, 8 Cessna 182N ac; 4 Bell 47G, 13 *Alouette* III hel.
1 hel sqn with 14 Bell (10 UH-1D/H; 2 214ST, 2 412).
Trg: 12 *Jet Provost*, 20 T-2D *Buckeye* (12 armed), 23 T-34 *Mentor*.
AAM: R-530 *Magic*.
1 para bn.
(On order: 15 F-16A, 15 (C)F-5A ftrs, 24 *Pucará* (6 trg), 6 G-222 tpt, 4 (C)F-5B, 3 F-16B/D trg).

Para-Military Forces: Fuerzas Armadas de Cooperación: 20,000: 25 UR-416 MICV; 15 *Shorland* APC; 120 60mm mor; 3 *Arava*, 1 *Islander*, 1 *King Air* ac; 3 Agusta 109A, 3 Bell (2 206B, 1 214ST) hel; (Coastguard) 40 coastal patrol craft.

ARMED FORCES OF OTHER LATIN AMERICAN STATES

Country	Est population (000)	Est GDP 1982 ($m)	Est def exp 1983 ($m)	Total armed forces	Army Manpower and formations	Army Equipment	Navy Manpower and equipment	Air Force Manpower and equipment	Para-military forces
Costa Rica*	2,450	1,661†	28.0	9,800§		1 V-100 armd car; M-113 APC	9 patrol craft, 1 armed tug	8 lt ac, 6 hel	(2,800)§
Grenada	113	108	2.3	Forces disbanded 1983. Eqpt incl 6 BTR-60P APC; 6 85mm guns; 24 81mm mor; 12 12.7mm, 6 ZU-23-2 AA guns.					
Guyana	955	485	60.0	6,500§	3 infbns 1 arty bty	EE-11 Urutu, 4 Shorland armd cars, 6 130mm guns; 12 81mm, 18 82mm, 20 Ch T-53 120mm mor; SA-7 SAM	300§ 1 large, 7 coastal patrol craft(	200§ 6 BN-2A, 2 DHC-6, 1 Super King Air 200, 1 Cessna U-206F tpts; 3 Bell 206B, 3 212 hel	5,000
Haiti	5,400	1,662	20.0	6,800	6,300 Pres Guard (1 infbn, 1 arty bty) 1 infbn 1 Special Forces bn Garrison det	5 M-5A1 lt tks; 6 M-113, 6 V-150 Commando APC; 4 M-1A1 75mm pack, 6 M-101 105mm how; 81 mm mor; M-18 57mm RCL; M-3 37mm, M-157mm ATK guns	300 (coastguard) 15 coastal patrol craft(	200 8 Cessna 337 COIN; 4 C-47, 2 DHC-2, 3 DHC-3, 1 Baron, 1 Cessna 310, 1 402 tpts; 6 SF-260TP, 3 Cessna 150, 1 172, 1 Bonanza trg ac; 6 S-58/CH-34C, 4 Hughes 269/369C hel	14,900 (Police)
Jamaica	2,310	3,184	n.a.	9,720§	3,500§ 2 infbns 1 Reserve bn 1 spt bn	10 V-150 Commando APC; 12 81mm mor	140§ 1 115-ft, 3 85-ft coastal patrol boats(	80§ 2 Islander, 1 King Air, 1 Cessna 337, 1 210 ac; 3 Bell 206, 3 212 hel	6,000§ (Police)
Panama*	2,160	4,287	n.a.	9,500§	1,500§ 7 lt inf coys	16 V-150 armd cars/APC	300 (coastguard)§ 6 patrol craft, 2 LSM, 3 LCM, 3 spt vessels	200§ 15 tpt, 12 lt ac, 20 hel	7,500§
Suriname	370	1,050 (1980)	n.a.	2,020§	1,800§ 1 infbn	5 YP-408 APC, 81 mm mor	160§ 3 large, 4 coastal, 3 river patrol craft	60§ 4 Defender ac	1,000
Trinidad and Tobago	1,200	6,900 (1981)	n.a.	1,500§	(1,200)§ 1 infbn 1 reserve bn 1 spt bn	6 81mm mor	(250) (coastguard)§ 6 large, 7 coastal patrol craft (4 armed)	(50)§ 1 Cessna 402 ac; 2 Gazelle, 2 S-76 (SAR) hel	n.a.§

Smaller states in the area: Bahamas, Barbados, St Vincent have small para-military marine components. Belize and Bermuda have small infantry forces.

* Costa Rica and Panama maintain para-military forces. † Incl Internal Security Forces and Police budget. § All services form part of the Army.

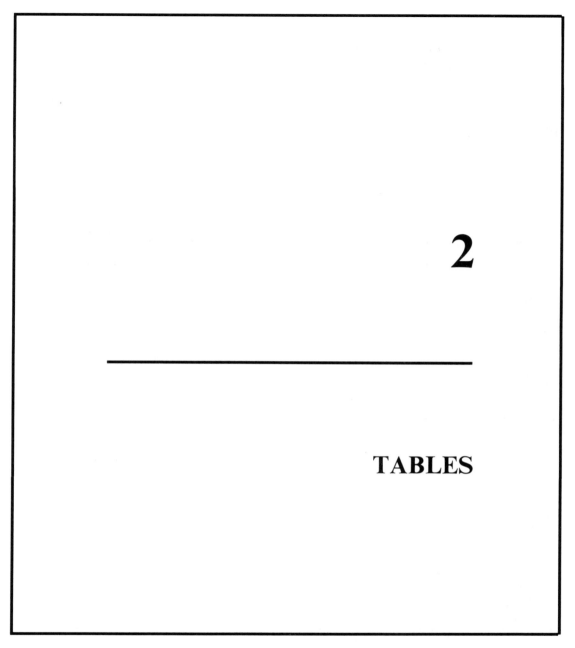

2

TABLES

NOTE

The tabular presentation of data on nuclear-capable weapon systems has been changed in this edition. Table 1, which includes systems in Chinese and South Korean hands, now gives world-wide coverage of nuclear-capable systems reported as deployed, with inventories and weapon and warhead characteristics, where known. Table 2 amplifies this by listing deployed launcher totals for categories of system (except some maritime systems) which directly affect the European Theatre.

No attempt has been made to compare totals directly, chiefly because weapon loading and the use to which dual-capable systems are put are so uncertain. Not every example of a nuclear-capable system necessarily has a nuclear role – indeed there may be no nuclear warheads available for it – nor are crews invariably trained in nuclear delivery.

1. NUCLEAR-CAPABLE DELIVERY VEHICLES: WORLD-WIDE

Category[a] and type	First year deployed	Range (km)[b]	Throw-weight (000 lb)[c]	CEP (m)[d]	Launcher total 7/84	Warhead details[e] and comments
UNITED STATES						
LAND-BASED						
Strategic						
ICBM						
LGM-25C *Titan* II	1962	15,000	8.3	1,300	37	1 × 9MT W-53/Mk 6. Being phased out
LGM-30F *Minuteman* II	1966	11,300	1.6	370	450	1 × 1.2MT W-56/Mk 11C. (442 launchers if 8 are comms vehs.)
LGM-30G *Minuteman* III	1970	14,800	1.5	280	250	3 × 170KT W-62/Mk 12 MIRV.
	1980	12,900	2.4	220	300	3 × 335KT W-78/Mk 12A MIRV.
Intermediate-/medium-range						
GLCM						
BGM-109A *Tomahawk*	1983	2,500	n.a.	n.a.	64	1 × 10–50KT W-84.
MRBM						
Pershing II	1983	1,800	n.a.	45	48	1 × 5–50KT W-85 (yield selectable).
Tactical						
SRBM						
MGM-31A/B *Pershing* IA	1967	160–720	(0.7)	400	90	1 × 60/400KT W-50.
MGM-52C *Lance*	1972	110	0.5	150–400	90	1 × 1/10/50KT W-70. Dual-capable
Artillery (dual-capable)						
M-110A1/A2 203mm SP how	1977/9	20	0.3	170	1,046	5–10KT W-33 (M-422) or 0.5–2KT W-79 (M-753).
M-109 155mm SP how	1963	18/24/30	0.128	n.a.	2,200	1 × 0.1KT W-48 (M-454).
M-198 155mm towed how	1979	1.6–14	0.128	n.a.	907	1 × 0.1KT W-48 (M-454).
Atomic Demolition Munitions (ADM = mines)						
Special ADM	1964	–	0.15	–	n.a.	Sub-KT.
Medium ADM	1965	–	0.4	–	n.a.	W-45. ?3 yields, 1–15KT.
SEA-BASED						
Strategic						
SLBM						
UGM-73A *Poseidon* C-3	1971	4,600	3.3	450	304	10 × 40–50KT W-68. Max 14 MIRV.
Trident C-4	1980	7,400	3.0+	450	288	8 × 100KT W-76 MIRV.
Tactical						
SLCM						
BGM-109A *Tomahawk*	1983	2,500	0.27	–	48	1 × 200–250KT (selectable) W-80. Dual-capable.
ASW						
UUM-44A *SUBROC*	1965	50	0.6	–	324	1 × 1–5KT W-55.
RUR-5A *ASROC*	1961	11	0.25	–	±800	1 × 1KT W-44. Dual-capable.
SAM (dual-capable)						
RIM-2D *Terrier* (BT-3A(N))	1956	37	0.35	–	±300	1 × 1KT W-45. (*Standard*-2 with W-81 to replace.)
MIM-14B *Nike Hercules*	1958	140	1.12	–		2/20/40KT W-31 mod 2. (Msl not in first-line service.)

For notes, see p. 136.

Category[a] and type	First year deployed	Range (km)[b]	Throw-weight (000 lb)[c]	CEP (m)[d]	Launcher total 7/84	Warhead details[e] and comments
AIR						
Strategic						
Long-range bombers						
B-52G	1959	12,000	0.95	45	151	12 ALCM, 4 SRAM, 4 × B-28/-43/-57/-61 bombs.
B-52H	1962	16,000	0.95	45	90	4 SRAM, 4 × B-28/-43/-57/-61 bombs.
Medium-range bombers						
FB-111A	1969	4,700	2.5	37.5	56	4 SRAM, 2 × B-43/-61 bombs.
Tactical[f]						
Land-based strike						
F-4E	1962	2,200	2.4	16	440	1 × B-28RG/-43/-57/-61 bombs.
F-111E/F	1967	4,700	2.2/2.5	25	230	3 × B-43/-57/-61 bombs.
F-16	1979	3,800	2+	12–15	456	1 × B-16 (also 1–2 × B-43) bombs.
Carrier-based strike						
A-6E	1963	3,200	0.9	15	170	3 × B-28/-43/-57/-61 bombs.
A-7	1966	2,800	0.9	15	288	4 × B-28/-43/-57/-61 bombs.
F/A-18	1982	1,000	2.2	17	63	2 × B-57/-61 bombs.
S-3	1974	?3,700	0.6	n.a.	110	1 × B-57 depth charge.
ASW						
P-3	1961	2,500	0.4	n.a.	213	2 × B-57 depth charges.
ALCM						
AGM-86B	1982	2,400	2.8	–	1,008	On 84 B-52G. Total excludes reloads.
Rockets (SRAM)						
AGM-69A	1972	55–60	2.2	–	924	200KT W-69. On B-52G/H, FB-111A.
Bombs						
B-28	1958	–	–	–	n.a.	Strategic: 1.45MT, ?28MT. Tactical: 70, 350KT, 1.1MT.
B-43	1960	–	–	–	n.a.	Strategic and tactical: 1MT.
B-57	n.a.	–	–	–	n.a.	Tactical: sub-KT to 10 (?20) KT.
B-61 mod 1	?1972	–	–	–	n.a.	Strategic: MT range.
mods 2/3/4/5	n.a.	–	–	–	n.a.	Tactical: 100–500KT.

NATO (excluding US)[g]

LAND-BASED[h]	First year deployed	Range (km)[b]	Throw-weight (000 lb)[c]	CEP (m)[d]	Launcher total 7/84	Warhead details[e] and comments
Intermediate-range						
IRBM						
SSBS S-3	1980	3,500	n.a.	n.a.	18	1 × 1MT. France.
Tactical						
SRBM						
MGR-1B *Honest John*	1953	40	n.a.	n.a.	54	1 × KT range. Greece, Turkey.
MGM-31A/B *Pershing* IA	1962	160–720	(0.7)	400	72	1 × KT range. FRG (Air Force).[i]
Pluton	1974	120	n.a.	n.a.	44	1 × 15KT or AN-51 25KT. France.
MGM-52C *Lance*	1976	110	0.5	150–400	56	1 × 50KT range. Belgium, Britain, FRG, Italy, Netherlands.

Category[a] and type	First year deployed	Range (km)[b]	Throw-weight (000 lb)[c]	CEP (m)[d]	Launcher total 7/84	Warhead details[e] and comments
Artillery (dual-capable)						
M-110 203mm SP how	1962	16.8	0.25	170	436	5–10KT W-33. Belgium, Britain, FRG, Greece, Italy, Netherlands, Turkey.
M-109 155mm SP how	1964	18	n.a.	n.a.	1,186	1 × 0.1KT W-48. Belgium, Britain, Canada, Denmark, FRG Greece, Italy, Netherlands, Norway, Portugal, Turkey.
SAM (dual-capable)						
MIM-14B *Nike Hercules*	1962	140	1.12	–	644	2/20/40KT W-31. Belgium, FRG, Italy, Netherlands.

SEA-BASED[h]

Strategic

SLBM

Polaris A-3	1967	4,600	n.a.	900	64	3 × 200KT MRV. Britain.
MSBS M-20	1977	3,000	n.a.	n.a.	80	1 × 1MT. M-4 (6 MIRV) to replace from 1985. France.

AIR

Tactical[h]

Land-based strike

Category and type	First year deployed	Range (km)	Max speed (Mach)	Weapon load (000 lb)	Launcher total 7/84	Comments
F-104	1958	2,400	2.2	4	281	FRG, Greece, Netherlands, Italy, Turkey.
F-4E/F	1967/73	2,200	2.4	16	131	FRG, Turkey.
F-16	1982	3,800	2+	12–15	178	Belgium, Denmark, Netherlands, Norway.
Buccaneer	1962	3,700	0.95	12	25	Britain, *Tornado* to replace.
Mirage IVA	1964	3,200	2.2	16	28	1 × AN-22 60KT bomb. France.
Mirage IIIE	1964	2,400	1.8	19	30	(2) × AN-52 15KT bombs. France.
Jaguar	1974	1,600	1.4	10	45	France. (British ac non-nuc.)
Tornado	1981	2,800	0.95	16	223	Britain, FRG, Italy.
Carrier-based strike						
Super Etendard	1980	1,500	1.0	2	36	(2) × AN-52 15KT bombs. France.
ASW						
P-3C	1961	2,500	0.4	n.a.	18	Netherlands, Norway.
Nimrod	1969	9,000	0.75	n.a.	28	Britain.
Atlantic	1965	n.a.	0.4	n.a.	55	France, FRG, Italy.

CHINA

LAND-BASED

Strategic

ICBM

	First year deployed	Range (km)	Throw-weight (000 lb)[c]	CEP (m)[d]	Launcher total	Warhead details
Dong Feng (DF)-5	1981	13,000	n.a.	n.a.	2	1 × 5MT.
DF-4	1978/9	10,000	n.a.	n.a.	4	1 × 3MT.
IRBM						
DF-3	1970	5,500	n.a.	n.a.	60	1 × 2MT.
MRBM						
DF-2	1970	1,800	n.a.	n.a.	50	1 × 20KT.

For notes, see p. 136.

Category[a] and type	First year deployed	Range (km)[b]	Throw-weight (000 lb)[c]	CEP (m)[d]	Launcher total 7/84	Warhead details[e] and comments
SEA-BASED						
Strategic						
SLBM						
CSS-NX-3	1983/4	2,800	n.a.	n.a.	12	1 × ?2MT

			Max speed (Mach)	Weapon load (000 lb)		
AIR						
Strategic						
Medium-range Bombers[f]						
H-6	1968/9	n.a.	n.a.	n.a.	120	

No Chinese *tactical* nuclear weapons have been identified.

SOUTH KOREA

			Throw-weight (000 lb)[c]	CEP (m)[d]		
LAND-BASED						
Tactical						
Artillery						
M-110 203mm SP how	n.a.	20.6	n.a.	n.a.	20 ⎱	
M-109 155mm SP how	n.a.	18/24/30	0.1	n.a.	100	No nuclear warheads are held for these weapons. As ex-US materiel, they have a *theoretical* nuclear capability only.
SSM						
MGR-1B *Honest John*	n.a.	40	n.a.	n.a.	12	
SAM						
MIM-14B *Nike Hercules*	n.a.	140	1.12	–	100 ⎰	

SOVIET UNION

			Throw-weight (000 lb)[c]	CEP (m)[d]		
LAND-BASED						
Strategic						
ICBM						
SS-11 *Sego* mods 1/2	1966/73	10/13,000	2	1,400 ⎱	520	1 × 1MT.[j] / 3 × 100–300KT.[j]
mod 3	1975	8,800	2.5	1,100 ⎰		
SS-13 *Savage*	1968	10,000	1	2,000	60	1 × 750KT.
SS-17 (RS-16) mod 1	1975	10,000	6	450		4 × 750KT MIRV.
(cold mod 2	1977	11,000	3.6	450 ⎱	150	1 × 6MT
launch) mod 3	1982	10,000	–	– ⎰		4 × 20KT MIRV.[j]
SS-18 (RS-20) mod 1	1975	12,000	16.5	450 ⎱		1 × 20MT.
(cold mod 2	1977	11,000	16.7	450	308	8 × 900KT MIRV.
launch) mod 3	1979	10,500	16	350		1 × 20MT.
mod 4	1982	11,000	16.7	300 ⎰		10 × 500KT MIRV.
(mod 5)	(1985)	(9,000)	(16)	(250)		(?10 × 750KT) MIRV.
SS-19 (RS-18) mod 2	1979	10,000	7.5	300 ⎱	360	1 × 5MT.
(hot launch) mod 3	1982	10,000	8	300 ⎰		6 × 550KT MIRV.[j]

Category[a] and type		First year deployed	Range (km)[b]	Throw-weight (000 lb)[c]	CEP (m)[d]	Launcher total 7/84	Warhead details[e] and comments
Intermediate-/medium-range							
I/MRBM							
SS-4 *Sandal*		1959	2,000	3	2,300	224	1 × 1MT. Retiring.
SS-20	mod 1	1977	5,000	n.a.	n.a.	378	1 × 1.5MT.
	mod 2	1977	5,000	n.a.	400		3 × 150KT.
Tactical							
SRBM							
SS-1b *Scud* A		1957	150	n.a.	n.a.	?540	1 × KT range. SS-23 replacing.
SS-1c *Scud* B		1965	300	n.a.	n.a.		
FROG-7		1965	70	n.a.	400	?530	1 × 200KT. SS-21 replacing.
SS-12 *Scaleboard*		1969	490–900	n.a.	900	?100	1 × 200KT. Multi-role. SS-22 replacing.
SS-21		1978	120	n.a.	300	?90	1 × 200KT.
SS-22		1979	900	n.a.	300	?40	1 × 500KT.
SS-23		1979/80	500	n.a.	n.a.	?100	1 × KT range.
GLCM							
SS-C-1b *Sepal*		1962	450	n.a.	n.a.	?100	1 × KT range. Coast defence.
Artillery							
M-1976 152mm towed gun		1981	n.a.	n.a.	n.a.	?3,000	?2–5KT. Front.
2-S5 152mm SP gun		1978	n.a.	n.a.	n.a.	n.a.	2–5KT. Army.
S-23 180mm towed gun		1959/55	30	0.2	n.a.	?180	2KT. Army. Retiring.
M-55/D-20 152mm towed gun/how		1955	n.a.	n.a.	n.a.	n.a.	2KT. Div.
M-1973/C2-S3 152mm SP gun/how		?1972	n.a.	n.a.	n.a.	n.a.	Sub-KT–5KT. Div.
M-1975 203mm SP how		1979	18+	n.a.	n.a.	n.a.	2–5KT. Front.
M-1975 240mm SP mor		1979	10	n.a.	n.a.	n.a.	n.a. Front.
SAM							
ABM-1B *Galosh*		1964	300	n.a.	–	32	1 × multi-MT. Moscow only.
Modified ABM-1		1983/84	n.a.	n.a.	–	?	1 warhead. Being deployed.
SA-10		1981	100	n.a.	–	?1,400	1 warhead.
SA-5 *Gammon*		1967	300	n.a.	–	?900	1 warhead.
SEA-BASED							
Strategic							
SLBM							
SS-N-5 *Serb*		1964	1,400	n.a.	2,800	45	1 × 1MT.
SS-N-6	mod 1	1968	2,400	1.5	900		1 × 1MT. Liquid-fuel.
Sawfly	mod 2	1973	3,000	n.a.	900	368	1 × 1MT. Liquid-fuel.
	mod 3	1974	3,000	1.5	1,400		2 warheads. Liquid-fuel.
SS-N-8	mod 1	1972	7,800	1.5	1,300	292	1 × 1MT.
	mod 2	n.a.	9,100	8	900		1 × 800MT.
SS-N-17		1977	3,900	2.5	1,500	12	1 × 1MT. Solid-fuel.
SS-N-18	mod 1	n.a.	6,500	5	1,400		3 × ?200KT. Solid-fuel.
	mod 2	1978	8,000	n.a.	600	224	1 × 450KT.
	mod 3	n.a.	6,500	n.a.	600		7 × 200KT MIRV.
SS-N-20		1981	8,300	n.a.	n.a.	40	9 × ?200KT MIRV.
Tactical							
SLCM							
SS-N-3 *Shaddock*		1962	450	2	n.a.	296	1 × 350KT (800KT, 1MT also reported).
SS-N-7 *Siren*		1968	45	1.2	n.a.	88	1 × 200KT.

For notes, see p. 136.

Category[a] and type	First year deployed	Range (km)[b]	Throw-weight (000 lb)[c]	CEP (m)[d]	Launcher total 7/84	Warhead details[e] and comments
SS-N-9	1968/9	280	n.a.	n.a.	200	1 × 200KT.
SS-N-12 *Sandbox*	1973	1,000	2.2	n.a.	96	1 × 350KT.
ASW						
SS-N-14 *Silex*	1974	55	n.a.	n.a.	216	KT range.
SS-N-15 torpedo	1982	45	n.a.	n.a.	?396	?KT range.
SS-N-16 torpedo	1962	n.a.	n.a.	n.a.	?306	?KT range.
SS-N-19	1980	500	n.a.	n.a.	88	1 warhead.
SS-NX-22	1982	n.a.	n.a.	n.a.	28	1 warhead. May be dual-capable.
FRAS-1 rockets (SUW-N-1)	1975	30	n.a.	n.a.	10	?5KT.
Mines	n.a.	–	–	–	n.a.	5–20KT.

			Max speed (Mach)	Weapon load (000 lb)		
AIR						
Strategic						
Long-range bombers						
Tu-95 *Bear* B/C	1956	12,800	0.78	40	100	1–2 AS-3/-4 ALCM, 2–3 bombs.
Mya-4 *Bison*	1956	11,200	0.87	20	43	4 bombs.
Medium-range bombers						
Tu-16 *Badger*	1955	4,800	0.8	20	410	1–2 AS-2/-3/-6 ALCM, 1 bomb. (*Badger* G carries (?6) AS-5.) Air Force (220), Navy (190).
Tu-22 *Blinder*	1962	4,000	1.5	12	160	1 AS-4 ALCM, 1 bomb. Air Force (125), Navy (35).
Tu-26 *Backfire*	1974	8,000	2.5	17.5	235	1 or 2 AS-4 ALCM, 2 bombs. Air Force (130), Navy (105).
Tactical[f]						
Land-based strike						
Su-7 *Fitter* A	1959	1,400	1.7	5.5	130	2 bombs.
MiG-21 *Fishbed* L	1970	1,100	2.2	2	160	2 bombs.
MiG-27 *Flogger* D/J	1971	1,400	1.7	7.5	730	2 bombs.
Su-17 *Fitter* D/H	1974	1,800	1.6	11	850	2 bombs.
Su-24 *Fencer*	1974	4,000	2.3	8	630	2 bombs.
ASW						
Tu-142 *Bear* F	1972	11,500	0.7	–	50	2 bombs.
Il-38 *May*	1970	7,200	0.5	–	50	(?2) bombs.
Be-12 *Mail*	1965	4,000	0.5	–	90	2 bombs.
ALCM (dual-capable)						
AS-2 *Kipper*	1961	200	2.2	–	90	1 × KT range.
AS-3 *Kangaroo*	1961	650	2	–	(100)	1 × ?800KT.
AS-4 *Kitchen*	1962	300–800	?2	–	up to 830	1 × 200KT.
AS-6 *Kingfish*	1977	250	3	–	up to 820	1 warhead. 350KT.
Bombs	n.a.	–	–	–	n.a.	Strategic: 5, 20, 50MT. Tactical: 250, 350KT.
Depth charges	n.a.	–	–	–	n.a.	Known to exist; no details.

WARSAW PACT (excluding USSR)[k]

			Throw-weight (000 lb)[c]	CEP (m)[d]		
LAND-BASED						
Tactical						
SRBM						
Scud B/C	1965	160–300	n.a.	n.a.	132	1 × KT range. All.
FROG-3/-5/-7	1957/65	40–70	n.a.	400	208	1 × 200KT range. All.

Category[a] and type	First year deployed	Range (km)[b]	Max speed (Mach)	Weapon load (000 lb)	Launcher total 7/84	Warhead details[c] and comments
Artillery M-55/-D-20 152mm towed gun/how	n.a.	n.a.	n.a.	n.a.	(100)	2KT. East Germany, Hungary, Romania.

AIR **Tactical**[f] *Land-based strike*			Weapon load (000 lb)	Launcher total 7/84		
Su-7 *Fitter* A	1959	1,400	1.7	5.5	95	2 bombs. Czechoslovakia, Poland.
Su-20 *Fitter* C	1974	1,800	1.6	4.0	35	2 bombs. Poland.
MiG-23 *Flogger* F/H	1975/6	?1,400	1.2	9.9	60	2 bombs. Bulgaria, Czechoslovakia, East Germany.

[a] ICBM = range of over 5,500 km; IRBM = 2,400–5,500 km; MRBM = 800–2,400 km; SRBM = 800 km or less.
Long range = over 9,000 km; medium-range = 5,600–9,000 km; bomber = aircraft primarily designed for bombing missions.
[b] Ranges given in km; for nautical miles, divide by 1.852. Use of maximum payload may reduce a missile's operational range by up to 25% of figures shown. Figures for aircraft are theoretical maximum unrefuelled range at optimum altitude and speed. Higher speeds, lower altitudes and full weapons loads reduce range, especially with strike ac; for instance an A-6, at operational height and speed and with typical weapons load, has a combat *radius* of some 1,500 km, compared with a maximum ferry *range* of 4,700 km.
[c] Throw-weight is the weight of post-boost vehicle (warheads, guidance systems, penetration aids) deliverable over a given range.
[d] CEP (circular error probable) = the radius of the circle around a target within which there is a 50% probability that a weapon aimed at that target will fall. For obvious reasons, this is a figure with a rather large degree of

uncertainty attached to it.
[e] Warhead yields vary greatly; figures given are estimated maxima. KT range = under 1 MT; MT range = over 1 MT. Yield figures for dual-capable weapons (which can deliver conventional or nuclear warheads) refer to nuclear warheads only.
[f] All the types listed are dual-capable. Total actually available as nuclear strike aircraft may be lower than the figure shown.
[g] Except in Britain and France, nuclear warheads are held in American custody. No nuclear warheads held on Canadian, Danish or Norwegian soil. In few cases is the M-109 likely to have a nuclear role.
[h] All NATO missiles of US origin, except SSBS, *Pluton* and MSBS (French).
[i] *Buccaneer*, *Nimrod* of British origin; A-7, F-4, F-16, F-104, P-3 American; *Mirage*, *Super Etendard*, *Atlantic* French; *Jaguar* Anglo-French; *Tornado* British-German-Italian.
[j] Variable range; some for peripheral targeting.
[k] Nuclear warheads held in Soviet custody. Ac all of Soviet origin. It is uncertain how many are nuclear capable.

2. NATO/WARSAW PACT POTENTIAL NUCLEAR WEAPON SYSTEMS, EUROPE

	NATO			WARSAW PACT	
Category and type	Countries deploying	Launcher total 7/84[a]	Launcher total 7/84	Countries deploying	Type
LAND-BASED					
ICBM			[b]	USSR	SS-11/-17/-19
IRBM SSBS S-3	France	18	224	USSR	SS-4
			243	USSR	SS-20
GLCM BGM-109A *Tomahawk*	USA	32			
MRBM *Pershing* II	USA	48			

	NATO		WARSAW PACT		
Category and type	Countries deploying	Launcher total 7/84[a]	Launcher total 7/84	Countries deploying	Type
SRBM					
Pershing IA	USA	60	(440)	USSR	SS-21/*FROG*
Pershing IA	FRG	72	(500)	USSR	SS-23/*Scud* A/B
Lance	USA	36	(90)	USSR	SS-12/-22
Lance	Allies[c]	56	208	Allies	*FROG*-/-3/-5/-7
Pluton	France	44	132	Allies	*Scud* B/C
Artillery[c]					
M-110	USA	500			M-1976, 2 S-5, S-23, M-55/D-20,
M-110	Allies	436	(3,500)	USSR	M-1973/C2-S3, M-1975
M-109	USA	500			how, M-1975 mor
M-109	Allies	1,186			
SAM (dual-capable)					
MIM-14B *Nike Hercules*	Allies[c]	644			
SEA-BASED					
SLBM					
UGM-73A *Poseidon* C-3	USA	40[a]	45	USSR	SS-N-5
Polaris A-3	Britain	64			
MSBS M-20	France	80			
SLCM					
			240[d]	USSR	SS-N-3[d]
			88[d]	USSR	SS-N-7[d]
			140[d]	USSR	SS-N-9[d]
			80[d]	USSR	SS-N-12[d]
AIR					
Land-based strike					
F-104	Allies[c]	281	(500)	USSR	Tu-95, Mya-4, Tu-16, Tu-22,
F-4E	USA	96		(Air Force)	Tu-26
F-4E/F	Allies[c]	131	(260)	USSR	Tu-16, Tu-22, Tu-26
F-111E/F	USA	150		(Navy)	
F-16	USA	72	(2,400)	USSR	Su-7, MiG-21, MiG-27, Su-17
F-16	Allies[c]	178		(Frontal)	Su-24
Buccaneer	Britain	25	95	Allies[c]	Su-7
Mirage IVA	France	28	0435	Poland	Su-20
Mirage IIIE	France	30	0460	Allies[c]	MiG-23
Jaguar	France[c]	45			
Tornado	Allies[c]	223			
Carrier-based strike					
A-7/F-18	USA	48[e]			
Super Etendard	France	36			
ASW					
S-3A	USA	20[e]	(130)	USSR	Tu-142, Il-38, Be-12
P-3	US	(12)			
P-3	Allies[c]	18			
Nimrod	Britain	28			
Atlantic	Allies[c]	55			

[a] Listings for US assume unreinforced deployments except in the case of *Poseidon* SLBM, 40 of which are assumed to be assigned to Supreme Allied Commander Europe from US central systems.

[b] A proportion of the launchers deployed (shown in Table 1) is assigned to peripheral targets.

[c] For detail, see Table 1.

[d] USSR types and totals based on estimated naval deployments and equipment.

[e] Figures assume 2 US carriers in European area.

3. WARSAW PACT AND NATO DEFENCE EXPENDITURE 1972–82 (millions of local currency units and US$)

		1972	1973	1974	1975	1976	1977	1978	1979	1980	1981	1982	1982 at 1975 prices	Change 1975–82
Warsaw Pact[a]														
Bulgaria	leva		422	483	548	645		518	649	790	859	901	757	38%
	$		410	488	596	725		617	791	878	1,011	1,287		
Czechoslovakia	koruny	15,920	16,700	17,300	19,280	20,400	18,240	19,450	20,290	22,400	23,100	24,156	22,788	18%
	$	1,951	2,085	2,246	2,835	3,096	3,097	3,430	3,743	4,392	4,812	3,774		
GDR[b]	ostmarks	7,800	8,328	8,900	9,564	10,223	11,020		13,060	13,100	14,116	14,954	13,594	42%
	$	3,197	3,544	4,083	4,665	5,163	5,770		7,637	8,137	9,338	7,312		
Hungary	forints	9,717		10,510	11,258	12,275	13,150	14,416	16,200	16,560	19,060	20,260	15,800	40%
	$	632		735	805	844	929	1,036	1,146	1,240	1,444	1,318		
Poland	zloty		39,210	45,200	47,300	52,928	57,280	58,800	65,300	70,400	76,900	174,000	70,388	49%
	$		2,483	2,850	3,270	3,367	3,672	3,886	4,466	4,996	5,696	6,234		
Romania	lei	7,710	7,900	8,640	9,710	10,570	11,300	12,000	11,835	12,500	10,490	10,755	8,808	–9%
	$	763	792	916	1,093	1,280	1,370	1,517	1,561	1,715	1,509	1,397		
USSR	roubles	17,900	17,854	17,650	17,430	17,430	17,230	17,200	17,200	17,100	17,054	17,050		
NATO[c]														
Belgium	francs	45,183	50,533	57,739	70,899	81,444	89,480	99,726	106,472	115,754	125,689	132,127	82,942	17.0%
	$	1,027	1,297	1,482	1,928	2,110	2,496	3,167	3,632	3,958	3,385	2,892		
Britain	£	2,815	3,512	4,160	5,165	6,132	6,810	7,616	9,029	11,510	12,688	14,534	6,114	18.4%
	$	8,151	8,612	9,731	11,478	11,077	11,887	14,621	19,158	23,356	23,944	24,296		
Canada	$C	2,238	2,405	2,862	3,127	3,589	4,124	4,662	4,825	5,499	6,289	7,655	4,040	29.2%
	$US	2,261	2,404	2,926	3,074	3,640	3,878	4,087	4,119	4,703	5,246	6,205		
Denmark	kroner	3,386	3,520	4,439	5,281	5,680	6,343	7,250	7,990	9,117	10,301	11,669	5,557	5.2%
	$	487	582	728	919	940	1,057	1,315	1,519	1,608	1,446	1,400		
France	francs	37,992	42,284	47,878	55,872	63,889	73,779	85,175	96,439	111,672	129,708	148,021	71,095	27.2%
	$	7,532	9,494	9,954	13,035	13,369	15,016	18,874	22,668	26,425	23,867	22,522		
FRG[d]	DM	28,720	31,908	35,644	37,589	38,922	40,184	43,019	45,415	48,518	52,193	54,234	39,878	6.1%
	$	9,007	11,939	13,773	15,278	15,458	17,304	21,417	24,778	40,850	23,094	22,350		
Greece	drachma	16,809	19,991	31,499	45,936	56,963	67,738	77,861	89,791	96,975	142,865	176,270	55,084	19.9%
	$	560	675	1,048	1,423	1,560	1,839	2,119	2,424	2,276	2,578	2,639		
Italy	lire (bn)	2,162	2,392	2,852	3,104	3,608	4,533	5,301	6,468	8,203	9,868	12,294	4,203	35.4%
	$ (m)	3,707	4,103	4,385	4,755	4,335	5,137	6,242	7,785	9,578	8,681	9,090		
Luxembourg	francs	517	601	710	836	983	1,029	1,154	1,242	1,534	1,715	1,893	1,193	42.7%
	$	12	15	18	23	26	29	37	42	53	46	41		

Country	Unit													%
Netherlands	guilders	4,886	5,360	6,144	7,119	7,662	9,092	9,146	10,106	10,476	11,296	11,921	7,879	10.7%
	$	1,522	1,917	2,285	2,815	2,898	3,707	4,227	5,038	5,269	4,527	4,464		
Norway	kroner	3,239	3,505	3,938	4,771	5,333	5,934	6,854	7,362	8,242	9,468	10,956	5,788	21.3%
	$	492	608	711	913	977	1,115	1,307	1,454	1,669	1,650	1,698		
Portugal	escudos	16,046	16,736	25,108	19,898	18,845	22,082	27,354	34,343	43,440	51,917	63,817	15,915	−20.0%
	$	594	678	988	779	624	577	623	702	868	844	803		
Turkey	liras	9,961	12,192	15,831	30,200	40,691	49,790	66,239	93,268	185,656	313,067	447,790	32,215	6.7%
	$	704	862	1,137	2,091	2,535	2,766	2,728	3,004	2,442	2,815	2,755		
USA	$	77,639	78,358	85,906	90,948	91,013	100,925	109,247	122,279	143,981	169,888	196,345	109,445	20.3%

a Warsaw Pact figures must be treated with great caution, since they only represent published statistics or (as in the case of Bulgaria) estimates. Imprecise data on inflation rates make constant-price time series unreliable also. 1975 prices have been calculated from a mix of consumer price indices (IMF, UN and commercial banks). The percentage change in defence expenditure between 1975 and 1982 should therefore be regarded as a general indication only, and not as a precise figure. Dollar conversions use implicit rates.
b Includes published budget for internal security forces.
c Based on official NATO figures for the NATO definition of defence expenditure and official consumer price deflators.
d Excluding aid to West Berlin, for which see Table 4.

4. COMPARISONS OF DEFENCE EXPENDITURE AND MILITARY MANPOWER 1979–84

Country	Defence Expenditure $ million[b]			$ per capita			% of government spending[c]			% of GDP/GNP[d]		Numbers in armed forces (000)			Est. reservists[e] (000)	Para-military[e] (000)
	1979	1981	1982	1979	1981	1982	1979	1981	1982	1979	1982	1979	1983	1984	1984	1984
Warsaw Pact[f]																
Bulgaria	791	1,011	1,287	90	114	141	n.a.	5.6	5.7	2.3–3.0	2.2–2.9	150.0	162.3	147.3	795.0	172.5
Czechoslovakia	3,743	4,812	3,774	246	314	246	7.3	7.4	7.7	3.4–4.0	2.8–5.2	194.0	204.5	207.3	525.0	131.0
GDR	7,637	9,338	7,312	456	558	434	9.3	8.4	8.4	5.0–8.0	3.7–6.5	159.0	167.0	172.0	635.0	82.5
Hungary	1,146	1,444	1,318	107	135	123	3.7	4.0	4.0	2.4	2.4	104.0	105.0	105.0	143.0	75.0
Poland	4,466	5,696	6,234	127	159	172	5.9	5.2	7.1	3.0	3.6–4.0	317.5	340.0	323.0	500.0	218.0
Romania	1,561	1,509	1,397	71	68	62	3.7	4.2	3.7	2.0	1.4	180.5	189.5	189.5	565.0	37.0
Soviet Union				*see pages 15–17*								3,658.0	5,050.0	5,115.0[g]	5,300.0[g]	80.67m
NATO[h]																
Belgium	3,632	3,385	2,892	369	343	294	9.3	8.8	8.3	3.3	3.4	86.8	94.7	93.6	178.5	16.2
Britain	19,697	24,226	24,296	352	434	436	10.6	10.9	11.4	4.6	5.3	322.9	320.6	325.9	284.5	–
Canada	4,119	5,229	6,182	174	215	251	8.6	9.4	9.8	1.8	2.1	80.0	82.9	82.9	17.5	7.8
Denmark	1,519	1,446	1,400	297	282	274	7.4	6.9	6.6	2.3	2.5	34.7	30.7	31.4	308.0	–
France	22,668	23,867	22,522	424	442	415	17.5	20.4	18.1	3.9	4.2	509.3	492.3	471.4	393.0	85.3
FRG[i]	30,995	29,047	28,453	504	471	462	27.9	28.2	28.2	4.1	4.1	495.0	495.0	495.0	750.0	20.0
Greece	2,424	2,578	2,639	257	265	270	30.4	31.2	25.7	6.3	7.0	184.6	185.0	178.0	350.0	29.0
Italy	7,784	8,681	9,090	137	152	162	7.0	6.4	5.9	2.4	2.6	365.0	373.1	375.1	799.0	116.1
Luxembourg	42	46	41	118	128	115	2.9	3.1	3.2	0.8	1.2	0.7	0.7	0.7	–	0.5
Netherlands	5,038	4,527	4,464	359	318	312	9.6	9.3	9.0	3.2	3.3	114.8	103.0	101.9	175.3	–
Norway	1,454	1,650	1,698	357	402	413	9.3	9.6	9.9	3.1	3.0	39.0	43.2	36.8	295.0	–
Portugal	702	844	803	71	85	80	10.4	10.6	11.3	3.5	3.4	60.5	63.5	63.5	169.0	37.3
Spain	4,546	4,577	4,529	122	122	119	17.4	15.4	14.3	2.3	2.5	321.0	347.0	330.0	1,085.0	110.5
Turkey	3,001	2,815	2,755	69	62	59	15.3	20.4	21.6	4.3	5.2	566.0	569.0	602.0	836.0	125.0
USA[g]	122,279	169,888	196,345	543	739	846	24.2	25.8	27.0	5.1	6.5	2,022.6	2,136.4	2,135.9	1,440.4	154.6
Other Europe																
Austria	876	818	844	117	109	112	4.1	3.8	3.9	1.3	1.3	38.0	50.0	50.0	1,128.0	–
Finland	616	765	862	129	159	179	5.5	5.8	6.1	1.5	1.8	39.9	40.4	56.5	700.0	4.1
Ireland	291	340	352	86	99	101	3.9	3.2	3.1	1.9	2.0	13.9	15.2	13.9	15.7	–
Sweden[g]	3,537	4,038	3,156	427	485	379	8.3	9.6	8.1	3.3	3.6	65.9	680.0	65.7	735.5	500.0
Switzerland	2,054	1,912	2,036	323	297	314	20.6	21.4	21.4	2.2	2.1	18.5	20.0	20.0	625.0	480.0
Yugoslavia	3,025	2,928	3,003	136	130	132	46.3	50.9	61.6	4.9[j]	5.2[j]	259.0	239.7	239.7	500.0	3–5m
Middle East																
Algeria	727	807	848	40	41	42	9.7	9.6	9.2	2.2	1.9	88.8	140.0	130.0	100.0	24.0
Egypt	1,715	2,100	2,495	42	48	56	13.1	15.0	14.9	9.5	8.6	395.0	447.0	460.0	335.0	139.0
Iran[g]	9,938	12,914	15,393	270	331	383	11.5	45.3	46.9	11.5	14.2	n.a.	n.a.	555.0	220–5	2,500

	1	2	3	4	5	6	7	8	9	10	11	12	13	14	15	16
Iraq[g]	2,673	4,572	8,127	213	338	580	n.a.	6.8	n.a.	10.0	n.a.	222.0	517.3	642.5	75.0	654.8
Israel[g]	4,517	5,661	6,879	1,192	1,433	1,711	33.0	38.9	44.6	29.8	35.7	165.6	172.0	141.0	328.0	4.5
Jordan	440	490	462	141	146	132	25.7	24.6	24.8	17.2	12.1	67.2	72.8	76.3	35.0	11.1
Kuwait	992	1,590	1,146	769	1,089	735	16.7	8.4	8.0	4.1	5.7	11.1	12.5	12.5	–	2.4
Lebanon	228	245	162	86	91	59	26.3	20.4	13.0	n.a.	n.a.	8.8	27.0	20.3	–	7.5
Libya	473	557	709	165	180	220	n.a.	n.a.	n.a.	1.8	n.a.	42.0	73.0	73.0	40.0	10.0
Morocco	923	986	1,328	47	48	61	16.6	16.4	20.3	5.8	9.0	98.0	144.0	144.0	–	30.0
Oman	779	1,685	1,714	906	1,832	1,804	40.6	47.5	43.4	22.9	23.8	19.2	23.6	21.5	n.a.	4.0
Qatar	482	896[k]	n.a.[k]	2,097	3,732[k]	n.a.[k]	n.a.	23.8[k]	n.a.[k]	n.a.	n.a.[k]	4.7	6.0	6.0	–	
Saudi Arabia	15,467	24,254	27,062	1,796	2,602	2,796	32.5	27.7	29.6	20.8	17.7	44.5	51.5	51.5	–	43.5[g]
Sudan	242	318	235	14	17	12	15.1	14.2	14.7	3.2	3.7	62.9	58.0	58.0	–	3.5
Syria	2,110	2,389	2,474	244	257	256	36.6	30.8	29.1	21.1	13.4	227.5	262.5	362.5	460.0	38.8
Tunisia	362	211	239	58	32	36	14.8	8.4	9.8	5.0	3.0	22.3	28.5	30.0	–	8.5
UAE	1,180	2,270	2,430	1,714	3,346	3,690	53.3	45.2	47.4	5.6	9.8	25.2	49.0	43.0	–	n.a.
North Yemen	351	444	527	62	75	87	36.5	23.9	27.6	15.7	16.4	36.6	21.6	36.6	–	25.0
South Yemen	116	162	159	61	80	76	52.5	48.3	n.a.	n.a.	n.a.	20.8	25.5	27.5	–	45.0
Africa																
Cameroon	83	93	97	10	11	11	9.2	7.4	7.7	1.0	1.7	8.5	7.3	7.3	–	5.0
Ethiopia	432	440	n.a.	14	14	n.a.	42.2	34.0	n.a.	11.2	n.a.	221.6	250.5	306.0	–	169.0
Ivory Coast	97	92	93	12	11	11	6.8	6.6	7.2	1.1	1.2	4.9	5.1	6.0	–	5.5
Kenya	299	198	240	20	11	13	14.3	10.2	13.5	4.9	4.2	12.4	16.0	13.7	–	1.8
Nigeria	1,858	1,858	1,671	25	23	20	7.9	10	8.8	2.8	2.5	193.0	133.0	133.0	–	
South Africa	2,458	2,863	2,676	86	95	86	16.7	16.2	15.4	4.3	3.8	61.3	82.4	83.4	157.0	139.0
Tanzania	505	316	307	28	17	16	30.5	19.1	16.4	11.2	6.3	51.7	40.4	40.4	–	51.4
Zaire	105	n.a.	n.a.	4	n.a.	n.a.	6.8	n.a.	n.a.	1.6	n.a.	20.5	26.0	26.0	–	22.0
Zambia	164	326	n.a.	29	55	n.a.	16.1	22.2	n.a.	4.9	n.a.	14.3	14.3	14.3	–	1.2
Zimbabwe	428	406	385	60	53	51	25.9	17.9	10.3	11.2	5.8	21.5	41.3	41.3	–	33.0
Asia																
Australia	3,373	4,901	5,028	232	328	331	8.9	10.3	10.1	2.8	3.2	70.3	72.4	72.3	32.9	–
Bangladesh	157	153	177	2	2	2	20.1	18.4	20.6	1.4	1.6	76.5	81.3	81.3	–	160.0
Burma	190	180	209	6	5	6	24.3	31.2	35.0	3.6	3.5	169.5	179.0	180.5	73.0	73.0
China	14,598	9,853	9,464	15	10	9	17.8	15.4	15.8	6.8	4.2	4,360.0	4,100.0	4,000.0	5,000.0	12,000.0
India	4,024	5,264	5,556	6	8	8	20.4	22.6	27.6	3.0	3.3	1,096.0	1,120.0	1,120.0	200.0	262.0
Indonesia	1,653	2,713	2,870	12	18	19	13.7	12.3	12.4	3.2	3.3	239.0	281.0	281.0	–	82.0
Japan	9,120	10,728	10,361	79	91	87	5.3	5.2	5.2	0.9	1.0	241.0	241.0	245.0	43.6	–
North Korea	1,363	1,601	1,724	78	87	92	16.0	14.8	14.6	9.8	10.2	672.0	784.5	784.5	3,300.0	4,138.0
South Korea	3,181	4,285	4,324	85	111	110	29.5	36.3	36.0	5.2	6.0	619.0	622.0	622.0	4,830.0	6,220.0
Malaysia	1,165	2,037	2,132	85	141	144	16.0	17.4	17.7	5.7	8.2	64.5	99.7	124.5	61.2	366.3
New Zealand	345	495	476	111	158	151	4.6	5.3	5.1	1.6	2.0	12.7	12.9	12.7	9.9	
Pakistan	1,278	1,857	1,829	16	22	21	34.9	51.4	45.6	6.4	7.1	429.0	478.6	478.6	513.0	109.1
Philippines	766	832	910	16	17	18	18.9	13.7	14.8	2.6	2.3	103.0	104.8	104.8	118.0	108.5
Singapore	529	789	922	222	323	373	23.4	20.0	22.9	5.7	n.a.	36.0	55.5	55.5	150.0	37.5
Taiwan	3,197	3,544	3,556	183	195	193	37.7	41.8	42.4	7.9	7.8	539.0	464.0	484.0	2,970.0	25.0
Thailand	1,554	1,669	1,822	34	35	38	29.9	25.8	25.3	5.7	5.0	216.0	235.3	235.3	500.0	72.0

	Defence Expenditure																
	$ million[b]			$ per capita			% of government spending[c]			% of GDP/GNP[d]		Numbers in armed forces (000)			Est. reservists[e] (000)	Para-military (000)
Country	1978	1981	1982	1978	1981	1982	1978	1981	1982	1978	1982	1978	1982	1983	1983	1983
Latin America																
Argentina[g]	2,819	8,557	10,099	102	305	354	16.8	23.1	n.a.	2.7	–	132.9	153.0	153.0	250.0	42.0
Bolivia	108	196	103	20	33	17	16.5	23.2	14.7	2.4	1.7	22.5	28.0	27.6	–	–
Brazil[g]	1,800	1,837	1,838	16	15	14	9.3	8.2	7.4	0.8	n.a.	281.0	277.1	274.0	1,115.0	185.0
Chile	1,031	2,103	n.a.	94	186	n.a.	25.2	31.4	n.a.	5.0	n.a.	85.0	96.0	96.0	24.0	27.0
Colombia	282	374	420	11	13	15	7.0	9.5	9.3	1.0	1.1	67.5	70.2	69.7	70.0	50.0
Cuba	1,168	1,272	1,252	120	131	128	5.6	5.4	7.2	10.6	9.7	189.0	153.0	153.0	190.0	748.5
Dominican Republic	108	118	128	20	21	22	10.7	10.8	12.4	2.0	1.6	18.5	23.0	23.0	–	10.0
Ecuador	186	266	208	23	31	23	15.8	10.6	9.5	2.0	1.7	32.8	36.8	39.3	–	0.5
El Salvador	65	117	139	15	24	28	10.3	15.6	16.9	1.9	3.9	6.9	24.7	41.7	n.a.	79.5
Guatemala	105	130	164	15	17	21	13.4	9.4	14.4	1.5	1.9	18.0	21.6	40.0	–	81.6
Mexico[g]	634	1,412	886	9	20	12	2.2	2.8	2.3	0.5	0.5	100.0	120.5	120.5	–	–
Paraguay	47	88	111	15	27	33	17.4	21.6	24.7	1.4	1.9	15.5	16.0	16.9	25.0	1.5
Peru[g]	535	887	1,626	31	49	87	20.6	19.3	28.1	3.9	8.2	92.0	135.5	135.5	–	32.5
Uruguay	186	390	391	64	133	133	17.6	19.7	17.7	2.5	4.2	27.5	30.5	29.8	–	0.7
Venezuela	700	815	1,152	52	57	78	5.6	3.5	5.0	1.4	1.7	41.5	40.5	44.3	–	20.0

[a] Statistical data is constantly under review. Differences between figures given in this issue of *The Military Balance* and those shown in previous issues may be due as much to re-evaluation as to new information.

[b] Current US dollars. These figures are subject to exchange rate fluctuations. Some military outlays include internal security expenses; in other cases research costs or paramilitary costs are borne by other ministries' budgets (e.g. Ministry of Interior).

[c] Based on local currency. This series is designed to show national trends only. International comparisons may be invalidated by differences in the scope of government sector and in budgetary definitions. Where possible, total government outlays (including development or capital expenditure) have been used.

[d] Based on local currency. See country entries. GDP figures are principally used (especially for NATO); or, in their absence, GNP figures. For Warsaw Pact countries GNP figures derived from NMP are given. Commercial bank estimates have been used where official GDP/GNP figures were not available.

[e] Countries' systems vary. The figures given vary. The figures given may include reservists with recent training, active territorial militia and forces available for later mobilization.

[f] The difficulty of calculating suitable exchange rates makes conversion to dollars and international comparisons imprecise. See also Table 3.

[g] See country entry.

[h] Defence expenditures are based on NATO definitions.

[i] Includes aid to West Berlin.

[j] Derived from Gross Material Product.

[k] 18-month budget 1982–3.

5. MAJOR IDENTIFIED ARMS AGREEMENTS JULY 1983 – JUNE 1984

Recipient	Primary supplier	Date of agreement	System	Quantity	Cost ($m)	Expected delivery
(a) USA	Britain	3/84	*Sherpa* tpt ac	18	54.6	1984/5
(b) NATO and Western Europe						
Britain	Netherlands	1/84	*Goalkeeper* naval fire control system	6	56.3	–
Cyprus	France	5/84	VAB APC	84	–	–
France	USA	8/83	Vought 227mm MLRS	55	–	–
Finland	Sweden	5/84	J-35 *Draken* ftr ac	10	38.8	–
Germany	Canada	5/84	CL-600 *Challenger* lt tpt ac	6	–	1985/6
Italy	USA	12/83	FIM-92A *Stinger* SAM	150	51	–
Netherlands	USA	2/84	*Patriot* SAM	20	33	1987/90
Portugal	USA	1/84	C-130 tpt ac	3	–	–
Spain	France	4/84	*Roland* AD system	18	180	–
	Italy	4/84	AB-412 hel	28	–	–
			CH-47D *Chinook* hel	12	–	–
Switzerland	FRG	8/83	*Leopard* 2 MBT	210	2,061.4	–
Turkey	USA	9/83	F-16 ftr ac (co-production)	160	4 bn	–
	Britain	9/83	*Rapier* SAM and *Blindfire* radars	36	220	–
	Netherlands	11/83	F-104G FGA ac	23	1.3	1983
	Belgium	11/83	F-104G FGA ac	18	–	1983
	Italy	6/84	G-222 tpt ac (50 local assembly)	52	533	–
(c) Middle East and North Africa						
Egypt	Brazil	12/83	EMB-312 *Tucano* trg ac	120	188	–
	USA	1/84	AN/TPS-59, AN/TPS-65 air search radars	4/8	210	–
Iran	Switzerland	12/83	PC-7 trg ac	6	5.5	–
Iraq	Egypt	11/83	M-77 MBT	140	–	–
	Egypt/Brazil	12/83	EMB-312 *Tucano* trg ac	80	–	–
	Italy	2/84	AB-212 ASW hel	–	164	–
			A-109 hel	–	–	–
	Brazil	6/84	*Astros II* MLRS	6	600	–
	USSR	83/84	*Scud* SSM, MBT	–	–	–
Kuwait	France	8/83	*Mirage* F-1C ftr ac	12	–	–
	Britain	10/83	*Hawk* COIN/trg ac	12	105	1985/6
	France	10/83	SA-365N hel	–	–	–
		11/83	AD system modernization	–	139	–
Lebanon	USA	9/83	M-48 MBT ⎫ delivery	68	–	1983
		10/83	M-113 APC ⎬ status	253	61	1983
		1/84	M-48A5 MBT ⎭ unclear	35	64	1984
Libya	Brazil	10/83	*Astros* II SS-40 MLRS	–	1	1983
	USSR	10/83	Mi-14 *Haze* ASW hel	6	–	–
Oman	FRG	2/84	Do-228-100 tpt ac	2	–	1984
Saudi Arabia	Spain	1/84	CN-235 tpt ac, tugs (may incl BMR-600 APC)	4/? (140)	150 (62)	– –
	France	1/84	*Shahine* SAM	100	4,000	–
	USA	6/84	FIM-92A *Stinger* SAM	200	40	–
Sudan	Britain	2/84	*Strikemaster* COIN/trg ac	7	–	–
	Spain	6/84	C-212 tpt ac	6	–	–
	USA	6/84	V-150 APC	36	10.7	–

Recipient	Primary supplier	Date of agreement	System	Quantity	Cost ($m)	Expected delivery
Syria	USSR	9/83	MiG-21 *Fishbed* ftr ac	–	–	1983
		10/83	SSM	–	–	1983
		10/83	T-72/-74 MBT, BMP MICV	200	–	1983
	France	6/84	*Gazelle* hel	12	–	–
Tunisia	USA	83/84	M-109 155mm SP how	19	–	–
UAE	Italy	3/84	MBB-339 COIN ac	4	–	–
(d) Sub-Saharan Africa						
Gabon	France	1984	*Mirage* 5 ftr ac	6	–	1984
Liberia	Israel	7/83	*Arava* STOL tpt ac	4	10	–
Mozambique	USSR	1983	SA-8 SAM	10	–	–
Nigeria	France	7/83	*Alpha Jet* COIN ac	12	–	–
	Italy	9/83	MCM vessel	1	100	–
	Britain	11/83	*Swingfire* ATGW	–	235	–
(e) Asia and Australasia						
Australia	France	8/83	*Milan* ATGW	–	5.3	–
	Britain	3/84	National comms system (incl military)	–	40.8	–
India	Britain	8/83	*Sea King* hel with *Sea Eagle* ASM	12	375.6	–
	FRG		Do-228-200 tpt ac	10	–	–
	USSR	1/84	MiG-27 *Flogger* ftr ac	–	–	–
		1/84	Il-76 tpt ac	–	–	–
	Britain	3/84	*Sea Harrier* attack ac	11	–	–
Indonesia	Britain	8/83	*Hawk* T-53 trg ac	3	–	–
	Australia	10/83	*Attack* patrol boats	1	–	delivered
	USA	11/83	Jet foil patrol boats	4	150	1984/6
	Britain	4/84	*Tribal* frigates	3	29.1	1986
	Netherlands	1984	AMX-13 lt tanks, AMX L-30 105mm SP how	100/50	–	–
S. Korea	Brazil	9/83	EMB-312 *Tucano* trg ac	25	–	–
Malaysia	S. Korea	1983	Patrol vessels	2	100	1985
			LST	2	–	–
Pakistan	USA	10/83	*Gearing* destroyer	1	–	1983
Philippines	USA	1983	Destroyers	2	160	–
		6/84	M-167A1 *Vulcan* AD system	24	30	–
Singapore	Italy	12/83	SIAI S-211 trg ac	30	60	–
	France	4/84	AS-332 *Super Puma* hel	22	–	–
Taiwan	USA	6/84	C-130 tpt ac	12	325	–
Thailand	Australia	11/83	*Searchmaster* MR ac	4	7.5	–
	Netherlands	4/84	F-27 MR ac	3	–	1984/5
	USA	1/84	F-5E ftr ac	8	–	–
			RF-5E recce ac	2	–	–
			Merlin IVA liaison ac	2	–	–
			RC-47 ECM ac	6	–	–
		6/84	Bell-214 ST hel	4	–	1984
(f) Latin America						
Argentina	France	9/83	AS-332B *Super Puma* hel	12	–	–
Brazil	USA	7/83	LVTP-7A1 APC	12	–	–
		2/84	*TOW* ATGW			

Recipient	Primary supplier	Date of agreement	System	Quantity	Cost ($m)	Expected delivery
Chile	Israel	3/84	*Reshef* FAC	1	–	–
	Britain	4/84	*County* DDG	1	–	1984
Colombia	Switzerland	8/83	PC-6 liaison ac	12	–	1983/84
	Netherlands	12/83	F-27 tpt ac	2	10	–
Cuba	USSR	1/84	F-class sub	1	–	1/84
		1/84	*Koni* frigate	1	–	1984
El Salvador	USA	2/84	UH-1H hel	10	–	–
Haiti	Italy	3/84	SIAI S-211 trg ac	4	–	–
Honduras	Spain	11/83	C-101B *Aviojet* COIN/trg ac	4	–	–
	Brazil	5/84	EMB-312 *Tucano* trg ac	8	10	1984
Mexico	France	5/84	VBL APC	27	–	–
Panama	Argentina	3/84	*TAM* MICV	60	–	–
	USA	4/84	V-300 AFV	12	–	–
Paraguay	Spain	6/84	C-212-200 tpt ac	4	–	–
Peru	USSR	9/83	Mi-24 hel	16	–	1983
	USA	10/83	UH-60A hel	8	110.5	–
	Italy	3/84	SH-3D ASW hel	4	–	3/84
	Netherlands	5/84	*Van Straelen* minesweepers	2	–	–
Uruguay	Argentina	2/84	IA-58 *Pucará* COIN ac	6	–	–
Venezuela	Argentina	4/84	IA-58 *Pucará* COIN ac	24	–	–

3

ANALYSIS

1. East West Conventional Balance in Europe

Assessing the conventional balance between NATO and the Warsaw Pact using comparisons of manpower, combat units or equipment contains quite a large margin of uncertainty. There are a number of characteristics which it is almost impossible to evaluate: the quality of units or equipment, geographical advantages, doctrine, military technology, deployment, training, logistic support, morale, leadership, tactical initiative, terrain, weather, political will and alliance cohesion. Such comparisons must in any case be set within the wider political and strategic contexts, including the nuclear balance, world-wide force deployments, the reinforcement potential of both sides and, most important, the relative strengths of the respective navies and long-range tactical and support air forces.

One cannot foretell the form and scope of any hostilities, their duration, their management or their results. Recent local conflicts have shown that the expenditure of materiel tends to run well above even the highest previous estimates. The impact of this factor on the ability to sustain combat, on the theatre logistics arrangements, or on the national infrastructures cannot be estimated. Yet all these factors have a bearing on the employment of the forces in Europe, on their reinforcement and on the resources needed to supply them.

Direct comparisons between items of military equipment are also difficult. It is possible to compare, for example, the numbers of tanks of each side, but the tanks in the respective Alliances are obviously not equivalent in terms of battle-worthiness. Some are old and un-modernized: others are modern and sophisticated. The former may not move as fast, take such advantage of the terrain, fire with the same chance of a first-round hit, resist fire so well or communicate with each other so well. Moreover, although the tank is still highly regarded as perhaps one of the best anti-tank weapons, other and very efficient tank-killers exist – such as armed helicopters, modern ground-attack aircraft, vehicle-mounted guided anti-tank weapons and mines. In short, there are many static and dynamic factors which must be considered if a true comparison of forces is to be made.

Bearing those considerations in mind, therefore, the question of numerical balance are reviewed in the table accompanying this essay using a number of different static indicators under the headings of Manpower, Divisions (including divisional equivalents), Ground Force Equipment, Naval Units, Naval and Maritime Aircraft, and Land Attack Aircraft and Fighters. Totals are given for NATO in Central and Northern Europe (taken together) and Southern

Europe, for US Forces in Europe or in sea areas adjacent to Europe and, by category, for NATO as a whole. Compared with these totals will be the equivalents for the Non-Soviet Warsaw Pact, for the Soviet Union's forces opposed to NATO and the totals for each category.

Defining the Combat Zone

One of the central problems for analysis is whether to compare forces at a very high level of aggregation (i.e. Alliance totals) or to attempt to define more realistic interactions (i.e. by fronts). It has to be acknowledged that quite large elements of the forces of both sides are not necessarily committed at the outset to specific combat zones. A substantial degree of flexibility exists, especially with Soviet reserve forces, to switch these at will. The Northern and Central European sectors are shown here as one entity, yet this is inevitably an incomplete notion. The Norwegian land forces, for example, have deployed a major element of their active field forces to protect the northern approaches to the country, against which the Soviet forces in the northern Leningrad Military District pose a substantial potential threat (and have plans to reinforce the far north in war). The Norwegian Navy must assign its larger vessels to support the Atlantic coastal flank of the forces in northern Norway, but the Soviet Baltic Fleet poses a threat to southern Norway, forcing the Navy to attend also to that area. The Norwegian Air Force has to be prepared to support both sectors. The West German province of Schleswig-Holstein, although also part of NATO's Northern Command, must anticipate attack both from the direction of East Germany and from the sea.

NATO's Southern Flank Commander has to be prepared to defend three widely separated fronts, each with its own peculiar tactical and supply requirements. Italy must contest any Pact threat from Central Europe. Greece and Turkey must between them defend Thrace and the Aegean Sea and its air space, while Turkey must also defend her eastern border in the Caucasus.

Manpower

The total number of men in uniform for all countries is given. Yet many of those in the armed forces of the super-powers may well be committed outside the NATO area. The totals for those forces available for combat and actually located in Europe include, for NATO, French and Canadian forces in Germany, but not Spanish forces. For the USSR, those in the Kola Peninsula opposite Norway are included, as are those in the Trans-Caucasus MD facing Turkey.

In the event of hostilities erupting, or threatening to erupt, the combat zones could be augmented. This could be done either by moving standing forces to Europe or by mobilizing the reserves, either for combat in place or to be moved to Europe by those outside powers. Again, not all of the total reserves in these states would be available for deployment in the European theatre or could necessarily be mobilized and moved in time to affect the outcome of hostilities.

Mobilization

The rate at which nations *can* mobilize will depend upon the system adopted, staff procedures and competence, distances and the transport facilities available. The rate at which nations *will* mobilize will depend on the warning received, on political will, on the ability to make decisions and put them into effect, and on how far enemy action obstructs mobilization. The Warsaw Pact countries have maintained reserves based upon conscripts who have completed their period of obligatory service. Those released less than five years previously would probably be available for immediate service; after more than five years the men would need refresher training. The Soviet Union, in particular, uses the Military District organization for recalling and placing reservists into skeleton formations ('Category 2' and 'Category 3' divisions) for war. The links between the central USSR and the borders are more than adequate for rapid movement towards potential battlefronts, so long as they stay free from attack. The limitations of Soviet internal communications might make it difficult to switch divisions from one part of the USSR to another.

Within Europe many countries can mobilize in place. In the case of Britain, movement to the mainland of Europe is less easy and is liable to interdiction. Those countries which must move reinforcements across the Atlantic clearly face the possibility of serious interruption. Finally, the United States, Britain and Canada do not have a pool of trained reserve manpower comparable to that available to other nations which have universal conscription.

Formations

The normal measure of force comparison is the division, defined as the smallest force capable of independent combat action – generally an all-arms force with its own logistics support. In all cases the term 'Tank' includes tank and armoured divisions; 'Mech' includes mechanized, motorized and motor rifle divisions; 'Other' includes airborne, air portable, air assault, mountain, amphibious and light infantry divisions. Not all national armies field divisional organizations in peacetime. To simplify the presentation, three brigades (nine battalions of armour, infantry or a mix) are considered to be a divisional equivalent – setting aside provision of support elements, including artillery, field engineers and logistics support units, etc. The first category in the Table shows divisions actually in place in Europe and manned in peacetime. For NATO they include, besides forces of the Continental states adjacent to the NATO fronts, Britain's BAOR, Canadian forces, France's Third Corps and the US Army in Europe. For the Soviet Union, this includes the formations in the Kola Peninsula and about half those in the Trans-Caucasus, in addition to those already in Eastern Europe.

The divisions earmarked for reinforcement prior to mobilization are listed separately. So also are those potential reinforcing divisions which would have to be mobilized from the reserves and earmarked for Europe as follow-on forces. In the case of the Soviet Union, formations for primary reinforcement include those divisions in the Western and Southern Theatres of the Soviet Union, two Category 1 divisions in Byelorussia and the Category 2 divisions in the Leningrad, Baltic, Byelorussian, Carpathian, and North Caucasus MD. Secondary reinforcement would include the Category 3 divisions and those cadre or 'shadow' formations in the above MD – equivalent to the existing organization plus the formations in the 'in depth' Military Districts, Kiev and Odessa, and, most probably, the cadre 'shadow' formations. Not included in these figures are territorial defence/Home Guard units, and no attempt has been made to calculate the force augmentation provided by support arms units under Corps/Army, Army or Army Group/Front control. There have been some significant changes in divisional readiness and deployment categories over earlier years, due partly to reorganization and partly to different assumptions about states of readiness. These assumptions, of necessity have had to be arbitrary.

Equipment

Equipment holdings can be broken down into categories. The complicating factors are that total holdings of equipment do not necessarily match the sum of what appears to be held on divisional establishments (there are equipment reserves, the holdings of non-divisional units and stockpiles to add), and not all equipment will be in theatre at the outbreak of hostilities. Soviet formations moving from the western USSR will be expected to take their full unit inventories. Some American reinforcing formations, on the other hand, plan to equip themselves from stockpiles in Europe. For these reasons, the Table includes for each side only the total holdings of equipment known or estimated to be in Europe and in the inventories of the reinforcing formations in the Warsaw Pact.

Naval Forces

In the case of NATO, we show the numbers of vessels presumed to be in the Eastern Atlantic, Channel, North Sea and Mediterranean. For the Warsaw Pact, we include the Soviet Northern, Baltic and Black Sea Fleets, together with non-Soviet Pact vessels in the Baltic and Black Seas. Soviet naval forces in the Mediterranean are drawn from the Black Sea Fleet or, in the case of submarines, from the Northern Fleet. As with ground force equipment, there are great disparities within categories, both with respect to capability and age. Classification by type of naval or maritime aircraft conforms to the nomenclature used in the country entries. The figures include both land- and sea-based aircraft with a clear maritime role in the above sea areas.

Air Force

Assessment of land attack aircraft, fighters and armed helicopters requires assumptions similar to those made for ground forces. The figures for US aircraft represent those based in Europe and do not take account of possible reinforcements from the continental US; the Soviet estimates show aircraft deployed in the territories of the Pact allies, together with a possible reinforcement of air units from the Western MD. The bomber figures given here are for all medium-range bombers, regardless of whether or not they might be reserved for nuclear delivery. The number of multi-role aircraft on both sides obviously complicates any listing by mission categories. Ground attack aircraft (FGA) often have at least a limited self-defence capability but function primarily in the former role. National terminologies generally separate the standard air-superiority fighter and the interceptor, usually making the distinction organizationally as well.

Commonality and Technology

The accompanying table shows that the Warsaw Pact enjoys numerical advantage in virtually all categories of weapons shown, the notable exceptions being most naval vessel types and naval aircraft. What these figures do not show, however, is a primary advantage enjoyed by the Warsaw Pact – namely that the weapons in service, and the tactical doctrines for their use, are common throughout the Pact. NATO suffers from doctrines by no means identical from country to country and from a wide variety of everything from weapon systems to support vehicles, with consequent duplication of supply systems and some considerable difficulties of interoperability.

The question of technological superiority is impossible to answer without the test of combat.

In general, however, Soviet equipment is thought to be rugged, relatively immune to mishandling and fairly reliable. Crew comfort and safety standards are significantly lower than those demanded in the West. While these factors may not be detrimental to efficiency in the short term, under the stress of combat the accident rate could rise and efficiency decline rather severely.

Logistics

NATO's logistic system is based almost entirely on national supply lines, and the difficulties are compounded by lack of standardization between nations and by lack of central co-ordination. In these respects it is markedly inferior to that of the Warsaw Pact. Certain NATO countries, too, still lack sufficient spares and ammunition, although there has recently been some attempt to remedy this situation. Some Pact nations may also suffer from shortages, but the fact that their equipment is standardized will enable them to restock more quickly. The Soviet logistic system, which uses a mix of rail, road and pipeline, has been greatly improved in recent years.

Air Power

Warsaw Pact doctrine has long envisaged the use of surface-to-surface missiles to deliver high-explosive, nuclear and chemical warheads against targets deep in enemy rear areas. In addition, the rising Soviet inventory of modern fighter-bombers poses an increasingly significant long-range threat. The Pact's defence against air attack combines a large number of interceptors with an impressive array of surface-to-air missiles and artillery. While advanced electronic counter-measures could probably go some way to nullify these defences, NATO air forces nevertheless face an increasingly formidable task in maintaining close air support for NATO ground forces on the European battlefield. Since NATO depends on its air forces to counter the apparent numerical superiority in Pact ground force numbers, their ability to penetrate Pact air defences could be a critical factor. Of particular concern is that NATO has yet to adopt a common IFF (Identification Friend or Foe) system and could lose aircraft to friendly air defence fire. However, it probably still enjoys a narrowing margin of overall electronic superiority, and may enjoy somewhat greater flexibility in command and control in combat conditions.

The Warsaw Pact continues to enjoy the benefits of standardized aircraft servicing and handling facilities. Although its aircraft generally cannot operate from unimproved runways, there are a very large number of modern airfields available to the Pact with hardened aircraft shelters. NATO, on the other hand, still suffers from too few airfields and too many types of aircraft, although considerable improvements have been made in interoperability, in preparing airfields to receive aircraft from outside the theatre (the co-located operating base (COB) concept) and in hardening its airfields.

Summary

The numerical balance – particularly in equipment – continues to move gradually in favour of the East. At the same time, the West has largely lost the technological edge in conventional equipment which allowed NATO to believe that quality could substitute for numbers. Because of the presence in the equation of so many unknown and unknowable factors, one cannot necessarily conclude that NATO would suffer defeat in war, nor that the Warsaw Pact would see its advantage as being sufficient to risk an attack, but one can conclude that there is still sufficient danger in the trend to require remedies in the Western Alliance, particularly as manpower shortage becomes a problem by the end of the 1980s.

Our conclusion remains that the conventional overall balance is still such as to make general military aggression a highly risky undertaking. Though tactical redeployments could certainly provide a local advantage in numbers sufficient to allow an attacker to believe that he might achieve limited tactical successes in some exposed areas, there would still appear to be insufficient overall strength on either side to guarantee victory. The consequences for an attacker would still be somewhat unpredictable, and the risks – particularly of nuclear escalation – incalculable.

For the table accompanying this essay, see overleaf.

Conventional Force Comparisons: NATO and Warsaw Pact

		NATO				*Ratios of NATO:Pact*	Warsaw Pact				
		Europe						Soviet		Non-Soviet	
		North[a]	South[b]	US	Total	*Totals*	Total	North[c]	South[d]	North[c]	South[d]
Manpower (000)											
Total uniformed manpower[e]		1,671	1,217	2,136	5,024	*1:1.23*	6,169	5,115		612	442
Reserves (all services)		2,076	1,908	1,440	5,424	*1:1.31*	7,119	5,300		1,115	704
Total ground forces		982	934	977	2,893	*1.09:1*	2,657	1,840		478	339
Total ground force reserves[f]		989	1,350	974	3,313	*1:1.50*	4,963	3,500		913	550
Total ground forces deployed in Europe		616	934	217	1,767	*1:1.11*	1,960	825	318	478	339
Divisions[g]											
Divs deployed in Europe, manned in peacetime	Tk[h]	12 1/3	2	2 1/3	16 2/3	*1:1.66*	27 2/3	15	2	8	2 2/3
	Mech	7 2/9	13	2 1/3	22 5/9	*1:1.51*	34	18	3	12	1
	Other	2 1/3	1	1 1/3	4 2/3	*1:3.14*	11 1/3	5 1/9	1 1/3	2 4/9	2 4/9
Divs manned and available for immediate frontal reinforcement[i]	Tk	5	1	2	8	*1:1.25*	10	4	2	2	2
	Mech	16 1/3	11	5 1/3	32 2/3	*1.56:1*	21	6	4	4	7
	Other	3 8/9	2 2/3	3	9 5/9	–	–	–	–	–	–
Extra divs available on mobilizing first-line reserves[fi]	Tk	1 1/3	3	3	7 1/3	*1:2.33*	17	14	3	–	–
	Mech	15	18 1/3	14	47 1/3	*1:1.25*	59	10	32	7	10
	Other	1	–	3	4	*3.60:1*	1/9	–	–	1/9	–
Total divs, war mobilized[fi]	Tk	18 2/3	6	7 1/3	32	*1:1.71*	54 2/3	33	7	10	4 2/3
	Mech	38 5/9	42 1/3	21 2/3	102 5/9	*1:1.11*	114	34	39	23	18
	Other	7 2/9	3 2/3	7 1/3	18 2/9	*1.60:1*	11 4/9	5 1/9	1 1/3	2 5/9	2 4/9
Ground Force Equipment											
Main battle tanks		8,716	7,026	5,000	20,742	*1:2.43*	50,500	22,000	14,000	10,100	4,400
Arty, MRL		4,855	4,940	670	10,465	*1:1.89*	19,800	7,000	6,500	3,500	2,800
SSM launchers		165	60	168	393	*1:5.25*	2,065	994	734	196	141
ATK guns		600	–	–	600	*1:7.80*	4,681	1,868	1,738	770	305
ATGW launchers (crew-served, see also armed hel.)		1,200*	148*	800*	2,148*	*1:2.01*	4,316	1,747	1,647	688	234
AA guns		3,630	1,680	100	5,410	*1:1.38*	7,487[j]	2,954	2,032	1,576	925
SAM launchers (crew-served, ground forces only)[k]		464	82	180	726	*1:4.76*	3,457[j]	1,138	874	720*	725

Naval Units

				NATO total	Ratio	WP total				
Submarines: cruise missile	–	–	–	–	–	42	41	1	–	–
attack	89	46	53	188	1.25:1	151	113	33	3	2
Carriers	4	3	7	14	4.67:1	3	1	2	–	–
Cruisers	–	3	11	14	1:1.79	25	14	11	–	–
Destroyers	44	39	38	121	2.37:1	51	27	23	1	–
Frigates	89	49	43	181	1.36:1	133	75	53	2	3
Corvettes/large patrol craft	78	43	–	121	3.67:1	33	10*	10*	10	3
FAC (G/T/P)	91	61	6	158	1:2.11	334	85	30	109	110
MCM [l]	179	82	3	264	1:1.55	408	190	95	77	46
Amphibious [m]	16	196	25	237	1.63:1	145	39	25	54	27

Naval and Maritime Aircraft

				NATO total	Ratio	WP total				
Bombers	–	–	–	–	–	254	174	80	–	–
Attack	77	20	336	433	4.16:1	104	40*	30*	34	–
Fighters	27	8	168	203	–	–	–	–	–	–
Asw	40	42	70	152	1.17:1	130*	80	50*	–	–
MR/ECM	60	37	77	174	1.39:1	125*	75*	40*	10	–
Asw hel	227	133	136	496	2.87:1	173*	110*	60*	–	3

Land Attack Aircraft and Fighters [n]

				NATO total	Ratio	WP total				
Bombers	28	–	–	28	1:16.8	470	470	–	–	–
FGA	1,142	626	522	2,290	1:1.05	2,430*	1,200*	670*	417	146
Fighters	42	–	–	42	1:2.98	125*	–	–	125	–
Interceptors	426	189	96	711	1:6.33	4,500*	1,800*	1,400*	855	455
Reconnaissance [o]	247	91	38	376	1:1.73	650*	300*	190	104	54
Armed hel	605	–	330*	935	1:3.37	3,150*	1,300*	1,750*	66	36

* Estimated figures.

a Comprises Norway, Denmark, W. Germany, Luxembourg, Netherlands and Belgium, and includes forces actually deployed from Britain, Canada, US (Second Fleet), France (Army; Navy: Atlantic-deployed elms incl Naval air).

b Comprises Turkey, Greece, Italy, Portugal, France (Navy), US Sixth Fleet and forces deployed in Southern Europe.

c Comprises Poland, E. Germany and Czechoslovakia, and includes Soviet forces in those countries and in the Leningrad, Baltic, Byelorussian and Kiev MD.

d Comprises Hungary, Romania and Bulgaria, and includes Soviet forces in Hungary and in the Carpathian, Odessa, Volga, North Caucasus and Trans-Caucasus MD.

e 'Uniformed manpower' refers to main forces only and does not include para-military forces.

f 'Reserves': Many countries have Reserve obligations into middle age; where not otherwise stated a five-year post conscript period has arbitrarily been selected in calculating the numbers. After five years, health and training standards begin to decline. In Pact countries a large proportion of these older reservists are probably assigned to 'shadow' formations and units with stored obsolete equipment, potentially doubling the mobilizable forces from those shown but necessarily at very low standards of efficiency. This table, however, shows equipment totals for listed Category 1, 2 and 3 divisions only.

g Divisions are not a standard formation between Armies; 3 brigades or regiments are considered to be a divisional equivalent.

h 'Tk' includes tank and armoured divs; 'Mech' includes mechanized, motorized and motor rifle; 'Other' includes airborne, air portable, mountain, amphibious, light infantry and naval infantry.

i Mobilization and reserve reinforcement systems vary considerably. A distinction between these two categories must of necessity be judgmental, especially for NATO. Readers may indeed wish to consider them as one.

j Figures in part on unit organization. Ratio between guns and SAM may vary.

k Field forces only; Soviet Air Force and *Voyska-PVO* equipment is considered primarily to be for airfield defence and not for use by field formations.

l Includes support craft and inshore boats.

m All types.

n OCU aircraft are included in these totals.

o Includes EW/ECM aircraft.

154

2. Deployment of Strategic Systems in the US and USSR

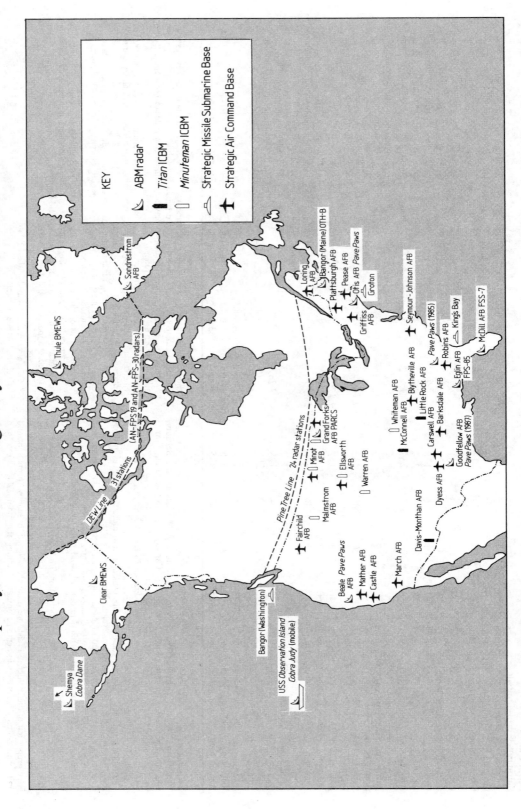

KEY

- ABM radar
- *Titan* ICBM
- *Minuteman* ICBM
- Strategic Missile Submarine Base
- Strategic Air Command Base

Shemya *Cobra Dane*

Thule BMEWS

Sondrestrom AFB

Clear BMEWS

Bangor (Washington)

USS Observation Island *Cobra Judy* (mobile)

DEW Line

31 stations

(AN-FPS-19 and AN-FPS-30 radars)

Pine Tree Line   24 radar stations

Fairchild AFB

Malmstrom AFB

Minot AFB

Grand Forks AFB PARCS

Ellsworth AFB

Warren AFB

Beale *Pave Paws* AFB

Mather AFB

Castle AFB

March AFB

Davis-Monthan AFB

Whiteman AFB

McConnell AFB

Little Rock AFB

Carswell AFB

Barksdale AFB

Dyess AFB

Goodfellow AFB *Pave Paws* (1987)

Griffiss AFB

Loring AFB

Bangor (Maine) OTH-B

Plattsburgh AFB

Pease AFB

Otis AFB *Pave Paws*

Groton

Seymour-Johnson AFB

Pave Paws (1985)

Robins AFB

King's Bay

Eglin AFB FPS-85

McDill AFB FSS-7

Blytheville AFB

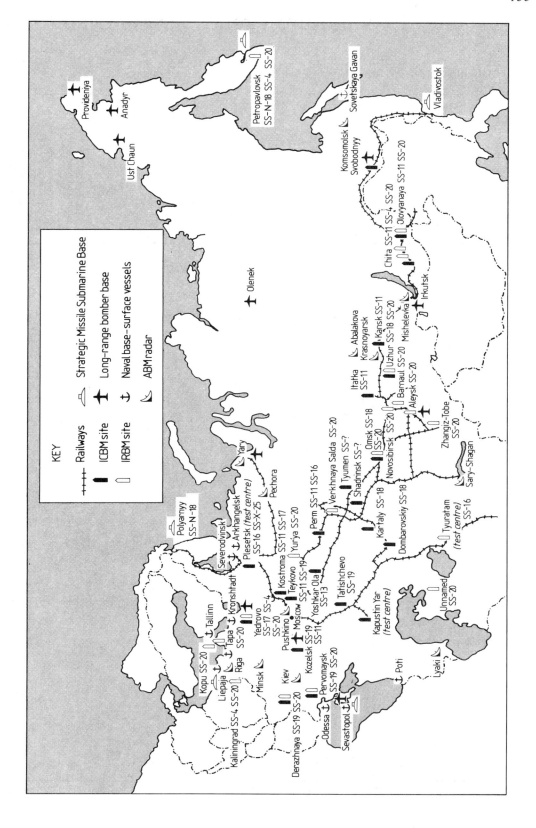

3. Defence Expenditure Trends – NATO and Japan

These charts are expressed in local currency, based on 1975 prices and using a 1975 deflator. The NATO definition of defence expenditure is used, except in the case of Japan.

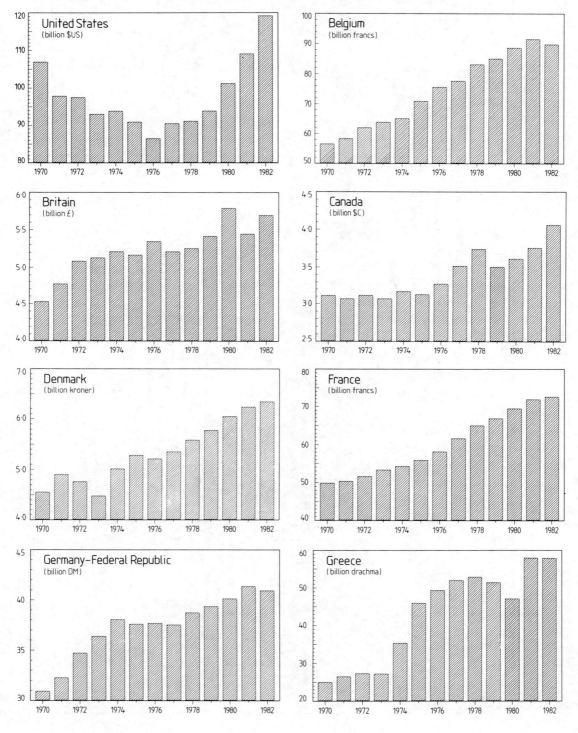

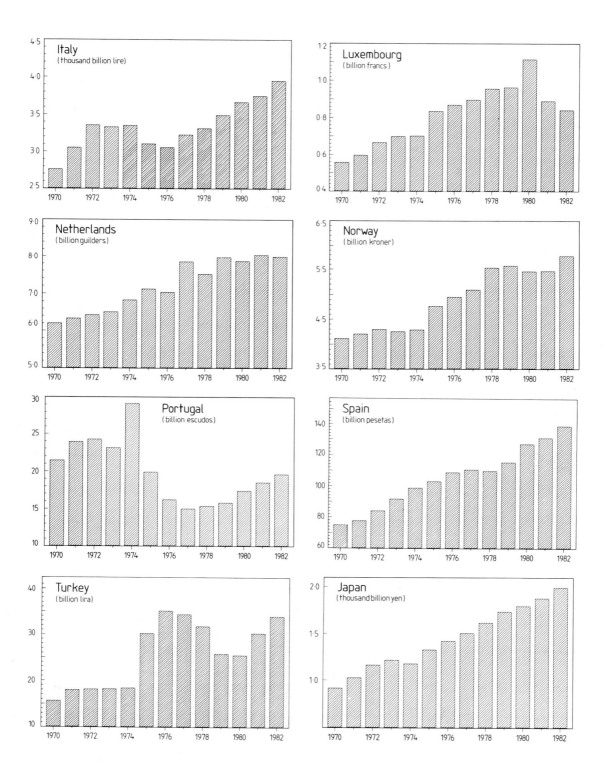

4. Economic Trends and Defence Expenditure

Compared to 1982, when the world's real GNP/GDP achieved virtually a zero growth rate, 1983 showed signs of quite strong recovery with the achievement of world-wide net growth of over 2.1%.[1] Even the non-oil-producing developing countries realized an overall 1.6% growth (0.1% in 1982). Nevertheless, many individual countries in Africa and Latin America continued to suffer and their economies to decline. The Arab oil-exporting countries, on the other hand, while still showing negative growth of 1.1% (led by Qatar with −16%) did considerably better than in 1982, when output fell by an average of 4.3%.

Despite these encouraging signs, and perhaps even better prospects for 1984, other and longer-term problems are present: high unemployment rates, fiscal deficits, high interest rates and high inflation rates – in some cases amounting to hyper-inflation. For many developing countries, debt servicing has become a financial nightmare, and between 1977 and 1983 (according to the OECD) developing country debt increased by 147% from $329 bn to $812 bn.[2] Latin American countries' debt increased by 184% (from $109 bn to $310 bn), that of African countries by 133% (from $30 bn to $70 bn), and Middle Eastern indebtedness by 154% (from $22 bn to $56 bn).[2] Debt as percentage of exports and services constituted 44% for Latin America in 1983, 25% for Africa (excluding South Africa), 21% for the Middle East, and 11% for Asia.

Eastern Europe, especially Poland and Hungary, also had serious debt problems; together they owed about $85.0 bn, equivalent to about 15% of their combined 1983 GDP. Poland's external debt/service ratio is the highest in Europe at 177% (followed by Portugal at 130%). Eastern Europe's NMP growth rates also did not meet the planned figures but, like those of Western Europe and the US, showed signs of recovery.

Despite the huge debt problems and budget deficits, military spending in real terms has not decreased significantly. Indeed, in many cases expenditure has gone up as a result of either regional security problems – e.g., in the cases of Central America and Iran–Iraq (and thus also of the adjacent Gulf states) – or the increase in tension in East–West relations. Another, and potentially significant factor is the high cost of new technology. This applies especially to sharply rising research and development costs, which must be met either by government or industry in the producing countries or by the export buyers.

The United States and NATO
After a decline in real defence spending in the post-Vietnam period, both the Carter Administration and subsequently (and especially) the Reagan Administration embarked on defence spending increases amounting to an average of about 9% per annum since 1980 (for FY 1985 an increase of 13% in real terms is planned). Whether the US Congress will continue to support the Administration in this may be doubted, and a levelling off of the rate of increase can be anticipated. However, the money committed forward (Total Obligational Authority, or TOA) for long-lead items is considerable, and it seems fairly certain that US budget will not decline in real terms.

European economic and social problems and rising public resistance to defence expenditure increases – in view of cutbacks in other sectors – will make it difficult for governments, whatever their political complexion, to persuade their legislatures to vote more funds. (Belgium, the Netherlands, Denmark and Portugal have particular problems here.) Even West Germany will not be able to meet the 3% annual increase in real terms which was agreed by NATO Ministers in 1978. She has commited herself only to a nominal 3.8% per annum increase over the next few years, and if inflation approaches that figure real growth will be close to zero. The British government, too, is committed to a 3% annual real increase 'in addition to the Falkland costs' on average until 1986, but thereafter little or no real growth is foreseen.[3] France has launched a five-year defence plan which totals fr 830,000m, but this will represent less than 2.1% real annual growth, and in any case almost a third of the funding is allocated to the nuclear programme. The rest of NATO Europe has fallen short of the 3% increase agreed in 1978, and will certainly fall short of the 1983–8 NATO force goals agreed in 1982.

Warsaw Pact
While it is difficult to calculate the real cost of non-Soviet Warsaw Pact defence expenditure, the availability of Romanian, Hungarian and Polish consumer price indices makes it possible broadly to estimate real defence expenditure trends. On the basis of this data it appears that between 1975 and 1982 Warsaw Pact defence expenditure increased by an average of 3.6% per annum in 1975 prices. Poland appears to have undertaken a major increase in military outlays over the two years from 1982 to 1984 (some 36%, based on 1979 prices), while East Germany has sustained an average increase of 6% per annum (1975 prices). Romania, who has frozen her defence budget at the 1982 level, showed a decrease of about 1.1%.

Middle East

Middle Eastern countries spent about $72 bn on the military sector in 1983, of which 39% was spent by the states comprising the Gulf Co-operation Council (GCC), 18% by Egypt, Israel, Lebanon and Syria, and 38% by Iran and Iraq. There is no indication that defence expenditures have decreased in 1984. The continuing Gulf War (the costs of which can only be estimated) and fear of its escalation have forced surrounding states to continue to buy arms in substantial quantities, despite reduced revenues and large current account deficts. The construction of a sophisticated air defence system by Saudi Arabia, at an estimated cost of $16 bn, and the development of similar systems in other Gulf states have forced these governments to maintain high defence outlays. Also, the GCC countries continue to provide financial support to Iraq, hitherto estimated at some $40 bn since 1980. It is only this aid, plus large credits from France (estimated at $5 bn) and the USSR (no estimate possible), that enables Iraq to continue the war.

The Palestinian conflict consumed at least $13 bn in 1983. Israel's hyper-inflation (400%+ in mid-1984) makes it impossible to calculate real defence costs, nor is it possible to estimate the real value of Soviet military aid to Syria. US military assistance to Egypt, Israel, Jordan and Lebanon in 1983 totalled over $3.2 bn.

Sub-Saharan Africa

There appears to have been no real increase in defence outlays in the continent since 1981, although reliable information is difficult to obtain for most countries. From the information available, however, it appears that in most smaller countries the largest amounts (possibly as high as 40%) are allocated to internal and border security forces. The greatest expenditures are those of South Africa and Nigeria – although in the latter case the most reliable statistics are available only up to 1980. South Africa increased her defence budget by almost 7% for 1984, but (as in many other countries) much of the cost is hidden in other departmental budgets (this applies especially to research and development). Nigeria's defence budget increased considerably in 1982, mostly due to the purchase of 18 *Jaguar* aircraft for the Air Force and to the provision of capital for infrastructure expansion. For Mozambique and Angola no reliable statistics are available.

Asia

Asia's GDP growth rate was better than that of any other area in the world, reaching about 3% in 1982 and 4.3% in 1983. Even two of the less wealthy countries, India and Pakistan, were able to attain growth rates of 4.5% and 6.5% respectively. Australia, Indonesia, New Zealand, and the Philippines had the lowest growth rates, and they also had very high debt service ratios (as did Thailand and South Korea). Nevertheless, Asian countries had significant increases in defence expenditure (above the GDP growth rate) reaching an average of about 7.1% in 1983. Regional security problems in the Indian subcontinent, in Thailand and on the Chinese–Vietnamese border continue unabated. Pakistan is to receive $1.6 bn in military aid from the US over the next few years; India has placed large aircraft orders with the USSR; and Indonesia, Malaysia and Singapore are modernizing their naval and air forces. For the region as a whole, however, defence expenditure growth has slowed during the past five years, from about 10% in the mid-1970s to some 5.6% in the early 1980s.

Japan (with a GDP growth rate of 3.0% in 1983) is under American pressure to raise her defence outlay above 1% of GNP (it is presently 0.99%). The opposition to the ruling Liberal Democratic Party will fight this strongly; a compromise may be reached by allocating additional funding to other ministries. In mid-1984, the Ministry of Defence was negotiating for a 7% increase in expenditure.

Latin America

Calculating military expenditures for many Latin American countries is again particularly difficult. Not only does hyper-inflation in some cases make it virtually impossible to determine the figures in local currency, but frequent devaluations also make dollar comparisons almost meaningless. Despite a very low regional GDP growth rate (0.5% from 1981 to 1982, and −1.6% in 1983) and some of the highest debts in the world relative to GNP/GDP, military spending in the region appears to have increased by over 10% since 1980. Argentina, whose losses during the Falklands war are estimated at over $2 bn, continues to perceive Britain as a threat in the South Atlantic and consequently has restored her losses and maintains a large military establishment. Brazil, with the highest debt in the world (over $90 bn and a debt/service ratio of 155% in 1982), is expanding her military manpower by almost 10%. Peru, with a debt/service ratio of 110% and a GDP reduction of 12% in 1983, continues to import weapons (including 26 *Mirage* 2000 aircraft) at an estimated cost of some $5 bn. The Central Bank of Colombia has also reported defence expenditure increases of 11% per annum since 1980.

---

[1] All information based on OECD, IMF and central bank reports.

[2] Excluding Iran, Iraq, Kuwait, Libya, Oman, Qatar, Saudi Arabia and the U.A.E.

[3] *Statement on Defence Estimates 1984(1)* (London: HMSO, Cmd 9227-I).